FORGOTTEN SOLDIERS

Bajram Angelo Koljenovic

Forgotten Soldiers

This book is semi-autobiographical creative non-fiction, that is, work
incorporating some historical facts and persons, and some which are
fictionalized. Some characters are historical persons, and are identified as
such. Other characters are entirely fictional. No character is intended to
represent any real person by some name other than that person's real name.

ISBN: 978-0-9791164-0-7

Bajram Angelo Koljenovic

Angelo was born and raised in the Montenegrin highland village of Gusinje in the valley of Plav. The grandson of an Ottoman officer, the son of a pioneer Communist, and one of the Muslim minority, he served in the Army of Yugoslavia before emmigrating to the United States in 1969.

Good luck and family connections led him to Las Vegas, Nevada, where he worked in many capacities in the great casino hotels, from teaching martial arts to the bodyguards of some of the celebrities who became his friends, looking out for the personal interests of some particularly important guests, to eventually owning his own restaurant.

"If I do nothing else," he says, "I just want to express my deep love of life, and of people everywhere, and my great appreciation for my adopted homeland in America. I will always thank America for giving me and everyone else who is willing to work to make a fresh start the chance to have a better life."

Over the years Angelo became deeply involved in the process of immigration, and worked to assist members of his family and many others in coming to America, and becoming citizens of the United States. His involvement in events surrounding the genocide of the Bosniak people led to some of the most turbulent and emotionally challenging years of his life, as described in this book.

Angelo now lives in Las Vegas with his wife Man Kiu and their children, still doing the work he loves meeting people in the grand resort hotels and welcoming them from all over the world to his town.

DEDICATION

Dedicated in memory to my parents:

> My mother Nurija,
> My father Halim,
> Who instilled in me love for life and humanity

Special thanks to my family:

> My wife, Mankiu
> My children,
>> son Neli.
>> daughter Nadira,
>> and the little one,
>> my son Halim Shaoyang

In Memory Of:

> Haljit S. Koljenovic
> Dr. General Dujnjic
> Dr. General Isidor Papa
> Pukovnik Haljilj Vukelj
> Hakija Nikocevic
> Jazo Hot & Braho Mrkuljic

Your selfless deeds have reaffirmed there is hope for the world and humanity.

Bajram A. Koljenovic

INTRODUCTION

This book is very different from previous work I was privileged to assist Angelo in writing. To a far greater extent, *Forgotten Soldiers* is a very personal book, and its outlook is far more subjective. Bajram Angelo Koljenovic is a deeply passionate man, motivated by the highest standards of personal, family, and national honor. He is also a man who cannot turn his back on suffering and injustice. His life has presented him with both heights of good fortune and accomplishment, and the terrible depths of disappointment and tragedy. This book is a reflection of both of those, the chronicle of a man struggling in his heart and mind to reconcile those contrasts, and to use his experience to accomplish something worthwhile for the people of his family's homeland, and for the America he so loves.

Angelo was one of the young men of Yugoslavia who rejected the yoke of communism, and also the rise of extreme Serbian nationalism, so he emigrated to the United States of America. He has been the friend of many influential people and celebrities, and he has enjoyed living the most spectacular and glamorous of lifestyles. In his ultimately hopeless attempt to prevent and oppose the tragedy of genocide against his people in Bosnia, he worked with high ranking officers of the US intelligence community, and also with men who had once been among Marshal Tito's cadre of expatriate enforcers and assassins, like a man juggling fire and ice.

This is the story of many such people who have fought heroically for righteousness sake, and whose stories have for the most part been swallowed up by history in anonymity. It is a narrative adventure, a declaration of faith, an indictment, a confession, and an exhortation. It has been my honor to have had a small part in bringing it to print.

James Nathan Post

FORGOTTEN SOLDIERS

As I reflect on how fortunate, lucky, and blessed I am in my life, I cannot help but to remind myself to think of and be grateful to those who have fought to defend the weak and down trodden, and to preserve freedom for me and for the rest of humanity. Without the selflessness and daring of these brave men and women, I doubt that the good fortune we enjoy today would ever have been possible to achieve. I look at my children and I am grateful for what those heroes did. It takes a gentle and deeply loving human soul to assume the terrible burden of living and dying as a warrior. May all their souls rest in peace until they are brought home to rest.

In the latest of many bloody wars that have raged throughout the world in Europe, and in Bosnia and Herzegovina, the American and allied soldiers rose to the occasion once again and found themselves fighting shoulder to shoulder alongside the courageous Bosnian freedom fighters. Many of them lost their lives. May God rest their souls. We brought them home to rest in peace. But for the many warriors who selflessly sacrificed their lives for the dreams of freedom they so thirsted for, for their Bosnia, they remain in unmarked graves, unnamed.

As a boy growing up in Yugoslavia, the land of my birth, I never knew what freedom and good life meant in contrast to any other way of life. Although many of my fellow Bosnian Bosnjak countrymen were dreaming of having that freedom and at the same time a free Yugoslavia, that was never to be. My father never stopped dreaming or fighting for it. The unfinished fight to freedom was passed on from his to my generation. My ancestral people are still suffering terribly at the hands of the bloody government in that region today. It may sadly seem the deaths of my ancestors were in vain and their selflessness forgotten. Their sacrifices were not in vain however, as those who were inspired by them are now fighting the battle for freedom which is still raging on in Bosnia, Kosovo, Croatia and the once Yugoslavia, that is no more.

This war took a course unlike any other. Five years of gun battle through the hills, ravines, prairies, cities and towns suddenly changed course in the drama of real blood spilling. The killers stored their bayonets, guns, and AK-47's away in their closets and donned three piece suits. They armed themselves with sharp pencils and notepads. Who will eventually triumph is yet to be seen, but the ultimate victory can only be freedom for the Bosnian people.

The highlands of the Balkans are truly astonishing in their natural beauty. For millennia men have been farming and living off this rugged yet fertile land. The people have become hard and proud like the land. In the dawn of early springs the mountains, prairies and meadows do their natural ritual of renewal from the dormant, frigid, punishing beast of winter, slowly transpiring into the most gentle yet powerful life giving forces. This is nature that has helped shape the people of this land to be what they are.

We have been ruled by kings, conquerors, fascists, and communists. Each of them created their own kind of oppression and their own kind of hell. Sacrifices by ones who have gone before me gave me the chance to be able to walk away from that tragically cursed and forsaken place. I left the mountains of the southern Balkans overlooking beautiful Lake Skudar, the mountains of Greben and Trojan, the beautiful Lake Plasko Jezero, and the shores of the Dalmatian coast which are harmoniously entwined with the majestic Adriatic Ocean. My journey has taken me across the Atlantic ocean to where I now call home in the magical city of Las Vegas, Nevada.

I have learned to love this great city that I wake up in every morning. Some people refer to it as "sin city," but I can truly call it my home. Every time I have left and returned from any trip away, as I have had to do many times, no matter how long I have been gone, as I drive or fly on my return trip, the closer I get to the outskirts of Las Vegas I am filled again with love for my city. When I observe the city at night with it's glittering lights glowing from inside that beautiful valley surrounded by majestic mountains, it is like an oasis in the desert and it makes me feel as if I am crossing into the gates of Heaven.

The experience of an early sunrise with the sun blazing on the glorious strip is a picture that cannot be drawn. It's a magic display of nature and art. There is a beauty like no other on that famous strip with all of the fabulous resorts. You can feel exhilaration when taking in the natural as well as the man-made beauty of places such as the Hoover Dam, Lake Mead, the Grand Canyon, the Colorado River, Sunrise Mountain, and the most majestic Red Rock Canyon — and as well of course that man made mosaic, the one of a kind glittering fabulous Las Vegas strip which is without doubt one of the greatest resort destinations in the world.

The hotels and resorts were built by pioneers and contributors such as Ed Torres, Benny Binion, Kirk Korkorian, Steve Wynn, William Bennett, owner of the Mandalay Resort and Casinos and the Sahara Hotel Resort and Casino, Mr. Bobby Stela and Gene Samarelli of the old Stardust and his boys, my good friends Art Doreli and Tony Fabria of the old Tropicana, and Mr. Adleson, owner of the Venetian Resort, (who I had the pleasure of meeting when a guest in his home), and undeniably the legendary architect and major contributor during the seventies and mid eighties in Las Vegas, the charismatic Howard Hughes. Sadly during the last days of his life he found himself a pitiful recluse alone and hiding in Las Vegas in one of his famous resorts, the Desert Inn, and later dying alone in some tiny hotel room in Cancun, Mexico. I had the pleasure of meeting many of his personal executives such as the late Walter Kane who became a close friend and was the director of entertainment for all of Mr. Hughes' hotels and resorts, including The Landmark, Desert Inn, the legendary Sands, the Silver Slipper and the Castaways, and the old Frontier Resort and casino. All of these resorts will always be legendary and remembered just like all the pioneers that built Las Vegas.

These people are true pioneers and leaders along with all the rest of the entrepreneurs who believed in this great city enough to create this beautiful place as it once was and has become today.

The combination of the all the different awesome architectural sights as well as the desert, mountains and the Las Vegas strip along with it's natural beauty create a visually exciting panorama that are a compliment to each other. It's a truly exciting place to live. No wonder the native people named it Las Vegas, meaning "the meadows," an appropriate name to describe the original natural beauty of the valley.

On any hot summer day as you walk along the valley you can see and feel the blazing vapors emanating under your feet, from the earth rising up to meet and kiss the torturing blaze of heat from the sun. Together they mix to create colorless flames emitting an energy of power coming from the sun and the earth that are truly magical to see and feel.

When I wake at sunrise my usual habit and ritual is to make an espresso coffee and by the time I start brewing it, I have a moment to reflect and thank God for everything I have been blessed with, my health, family, and my country that I love.

Where I grew up in the land of my ancestors, the Balkans, it is a contrast to the luxury I now enjoy in this high dry desert of the Sierras and Death Valley where the heat is sometimes known to exceed 125 degrees. You could fry an egg on top of a rock, but life still flourishes uninterrupted even under the harshest of conditions. In contrast to the hard and dry desert the land in the Balkans is a rich and fertile one and has sustained countless generations with a mosaic of beautiful people. The land sustained these beautiful people and they worked the land throughout the centuries. Both climates are unique in their own individual ways just as we are and both the Balkans and the desert of the high Sierras sustain life as nature has meant it to be. Only the Mojave and Sierra deserts have been spared from being interrupted by men's conflict, and their bayonets. That couldn't be said for the Balkans.

In the beginning of time and with evolution, nature has slowly evolved and life has flourished. Finally human life had come to play a role in it. During the time span of evolution much has changed. One could call it progress of men. Along with the people's traditions, cultures, ethnicities, and religions have evolved which created their own unique identities and allowed them to separate themselves and see themselves as individuals different from one another. Perhaps that started the downfall of man. The Balkans are one of many such places in our world that have innocently evolved with such a culture to clearly separate and identify themselves, and to see themselves as different and unique, but unknowingly making a large contribution to the world by becoming just one of many colorful cultures to make this world into one beautiful mosaic.

In the Balkans unfortunately, that unique natural kind of growth that separated them over time from their northern and western neighbors led to a clash and misunderstandings of one another over the differences in their ethnicity and culture, and brought about conflicts. The kings and rulers saw this as the perfect tool to enhance their grip of power for control of the masses of their people, and an opportunity for oppressing others who might have thought differently than they. This phenomena has not disappeared through the millenniums, but on the contrary has grown even stronger, especially with the introduction of more new religions and ideologies. Since man has become aware of the differences, the kings and rulers saw it as a perfect tool to fuel the power of their own dynasties. It spread like wildfire through tribes, villages, towns, cities, and kingdoms, and the flames are continuing to be fanned. The world hasn't had a single day of peace since in history. The planet has been burning, with blood spilled each and every day at some place or other on the planet. What is the wish of man? It seems like the wish of man is to be uprooted, but is denying that is what he has been doing. The very same people who were spawned from that mother tree are trying to uproot that very tree that gave them life.

The people found themselves being manipulated and forgetting, or choosing to ignore that all of this wonderful and beautiful progress that has developed over the millennia evolved from the same tree. Somehow over time we chose not to remember that, and instead we try to uproot that very tree that bore the fruit of goodness that we are enjoying today and that is life itself as we know it. We should never walk away from that if we are ever to understand the life giving of that very tree.

One should not be prosecuted for having a different faith or ethnicity, and it should not be a reason for rulers like these to wage destruction with wars, to exterminate and prosecute those who do not surrender or conform to their ideology. At best it should not happen as it has been happening in these civilized times when we should be capable to come to grips with all our differences and accept that we are different yet we are all unique and special together in our own ways. That is the beauty of that tree when you look back on it. Even with our unique cultural or ethnic differences we are all human. The most courageous of those who are oppressed have always struggled to resist the terrible things some people do in denying other people their freedom to live their lives in peace that is rightfully theirs by birth and God.

The people in this story are not all engraved in the pages of history although they are surely contributors to it. They were the ones who felt an empty space that was missing and needed filled and that space was the in their mind for freedom in their hearts and souls. They have in their own ways taken up the cause for righteousness as well as taken up swords and fought for what is right in the world. They may be forgotten but they have contributed something with their convictions and beliefs and love for a free life. Without their sacrifices we would not be able to enjoy what is ours today in this great nation.

Was it by the will of God or just fate and bad luck in leadership that brought such pain to that old ancient land called the Balkans? The leadership that ruled the land for centuries and since the beginning of time was always self serving and blind to the needs of the people. The rulers style of governing throughout the centuries and even now is unforgivably oppressive to their subjects and citizens.

Sometimes when my friends ask about my nationality and my birthplace, I try to be humorous by jokingly commenting that it was hell on the southeastern tip of the earth. Then and even today the people, all my forefathers, father, and also myself as a child came to be victims of an inescapable dark cloud that covered the land with oppression from the brutal selfish reigns of kings and bloody dictators. They poisoned the land with their thirst for killing. That heavy black cloud has yet to be lifted in the land of southern Slavs, the former Yugoslavia, what is now Bosnia, Herzegovina, Province of Sandjak, and Montenegro. It has just about uprooted all of my ancestors' people and there are places there that anything in nature with wings, even as freely as a bald eagle soars would not fly over. The eagles would take u-turns to avoid it because of all the blood and the sheer hopelessness.

When I think about it pictures flash back in my mind of that little valley with beautiful streams and mountains and the people working the beautiful fertile land, children running through the fields of freshly mown hay and mothers and fathers calling their children for lunch looking to rest from their back breaking work. Yet those are still some of my beautiful memories of childhood. I can remember the most beautiful people and nature that God has ever created.

There are three majestic rivers that originate from the high peaks of the Trojan Mountain and the Yellow Plateau, the Rivers Grncar, Dolja, and Vruja. They run through the meadows and the beautiful lush green valley until they reach a meeting place in the middle of the valley. The river banks are covered by thousands of ancient weeping willow trees.

The three majestic rivers merge just below the town of Gusinje, my own home town. Where the rivers merge as one they continue as the Ljuca River. The curves in the Ljuca are a picturesque blue green color, slow moving and quiet yet full of life. It seems a fisherman's heaven although no one fished there for some reason whether for cultural reasons or otherwise. Beef, lamb and dairy were the preferred diet no matter what season and for the mountainous people fish has never been on their preferred choice of menus at any time. The rainbow trout's lives are not and haven't ever been in danger from those farmers.

The rivers are like seeing a reflection of a crystal clear blue sky at night under a full moon with beautiful weeping willows that truly compliment the banks . The mountains and trees, homes and farms are all very much alive and the river is a major source of that life.

Each summer morning and day is a repeat of the one before and you can see and hear the sounds from men directing their horses and wagons, and tending their ranches and farms. The ancient familiar sounds echo throughout the valley from the barking of man's best friend to protect his masters property as he works hard in the fields cutting hay with ancient tools that require much physical strength and has always been back breaking labor but rewarding for him at the day's end.

I remember at my own family's ranch and farm, the labor and the days were hard but by sunset we felt rewarded by the land. No matter how much the reward or big or small, the proud faces never reflected emotions on the outside only from inside themselves. It was the father's responsibility to shape the character of the child and the mother's was to share that bond of earthly love from their hearts with their sons and daughters at times by singing songs that told the lore of days of old and opening their hearts to their children and telling them how proud they are of them and how much they really love them. Those were some of the moments that I shared with my mother and father and they had also shared with theirs. This is what has made us strong and proud as people and taught us to have love for life and humanity. Yet all of the happy moments and laughter never took the weight of responsibility off their faces. Moments like those I could see the portrait of Mona Lisa or an unknown face of a statue made of stone and clay. They seemed lost in a space and time, unable to show joy or pain.

Perhaps the hard life mixed in their culture and traditions that has evolved over the centuries has made them proud but emotionless. Perhaps that was the reason I never witnessed them displaying emotions in their expressions. One felt they should always present himself or herself no matter what the circumstances in a proud sober manner as if it was the law of the land, but it was not the law of the land, it was the culture that had evolved and grown in them for millenniums. If there are wounds inside their souls that have bled throughout time, it is only theirs to know. Culture does not allow them to share that. Their facades are invisible to outsiders, ones who have not been born or grown up with them. One cannot understand the spirit of the Balkan man's pride and honor. That's the way I see my people. I who was born from the same roots as they can see and feel their pain as my own.

Their faces were always tired. They are tired but not beaten and being a man meant they would not dare shed a tear for any pain or loss. All of their ingrained tradition and culture made them resilient to all the political and physical pressures that never conquered their hidden yet free spirits and pride that resides in the souls of those who know nothing but a hard life. I will never know if they knew or know what they missed or are missing by not knowing or experiencing what it means to be free.

When I look at the majestic eagle soaring in the sky, cutting through the wind, I can truly see how free and limitless his freedom is. Maybe the descendants of my ancestors and their children will walk the road to freedom and the soaring eagle will show them what it really means to be free. No man deserves anything less than that.

The people I have met in the current times and during the tragic crisis of this war in my ancestor's homeland, and with the tragedies that have occurred and been repeated numerous times in past history, I thought I knew. Looking back over it all I have come to the conclusion that the land and all the people in it are cursed.

Why is it that each of us that has left the homeland, that is a forsaken but at the same time a beautiful place, my ancestors homeland, now the country of Bosnia and Montenegro, that each individual that has left has become prosperous and successful after leaving there?

One fundamental answer with no need to go any further is the Bill of Rights and the Constitution of the relatively new country of The United States of America that makes it possible. A perfect mirror for my ancestors land and the rest of the world to look into is in America, to learn about the Bill of Rights and the American Constitution. These are the wheels to get the engine rolling, and if they would be adopted by the rest of the world, the future would and should look bright for all of humanity. It's only a mindless suggestion.

FORGOTTEN SOLDIERS

The west in the new frontier and the gold rush in the early 17th and 18th centuries to the golden state of California and the silver state of Nevada drew flocks of fortune diggers and aspiring entrepreneurs, as well as scammers seeking a quick fortune from around the world.. All of these people combined were trying to settle and conquer this new frontier for their own individual reasons. The greed for the limited riches of gold blinded prospectors to see the true and real riches of the fertile land in California and Nevada's new frontiers.

Soon when the riches of silver and gold were depleted by these people, the former farmers and now fortune seekers still did not see the land as a fertile place that could sustain and provide for them by farming the land without having to dig for the gold. The riches were already in the land all around them without having to pan for the gold. The land was silently crying for the people to stay and if they would only work the land then the land would reward them with riches beyond their dreams and imaginations.

Since there was no more gold to dig they packed up and left leaving huge craters in the mountains and hills looking like wounds as the ones soldiers have after a battle. Most of the forty-niners fortune hunters failed to see what the land and nature had to offer in the new frontier. The ones who did were rewarded beyond their comprehensions. Cities and towns were named after them.

When the new miners and pioneers settled and were living in the new land of California a result from the actions of some who didn't understand the richness of the land left it with the feeling of being raped, leaving craters as reminders of their greed for the riches and those nuggets which most of them never found. That became a ritual throughout the western frontier, especially in the southern Mohave Desert in the area of Death Valley. Each time the gold or silver was depleted they would pack up and leave the town and land in ruins. This was repeated many times during the settling of the west. The scars on the land can even be seen clearly today.

From the window in my own office I can look to the southwest at the Black Mountain where there are old mining caves and shafts by the hundreds. They remind me of fox holes, not a very pretty picture when looking out your window.

It wasn't pleasant for the miners either to dig those fox holes looking for their fortunes far away from any water. The nearest water source was the Colorado River, twenty five to thirty miles away. The ones who stayed to settle the west can be truly appreciated for their strength, determination and resilience. They are truly the founders of the western frontier and America's west. It took another century for people to hear the call from the land and come back to join the few who stayed and discover for themselves the really true riches hiding just under their feet. There were far more riches in this fertile dirt than the little specks of gold.

In the ancient lands across the Atlantic, at the shores of the Mediterranean, and Adriatic Oceans, and in Montenegro, Bosnia, and Sandjak there wasn't ever a gold rush but there was always a rush in the early spring after the harsh winter for the farmers to plow their land and harvest the crops to store for the next coming winter. The simple reason for the rush is that the winters are very long and the other seasons very short. The farmers and ranchers must work in harmony with nature to succeed during the short seasons the for the rush to sow the seeds and reap the harvest if there were to be another spring. Each year the process was repeated just as it was in the previous spring in order to prepare again for the hibernation of that long true winter that man was not intended to do but must because of the long, cold, frosty winters that are like the harsh winters in Alaska or Siberia.

These are the ranchers, farmers, and the people who had grown up with deep roots in the land for over many thousands of years. They came to know and love the land and the land came to know and love them, and through time they bonded in a harmonious way to equally respect and reward one another. That is the picture of the beneficiaries between that fertile land in the Balkans that has nursed and helped shape this special breed of people.

So then with tradition, the strings that bonded them were never broken year after year right after the harvest. It was, as one could call it, a cursed tradition during the month of December. This heartbreaking separation of loved ones has come to be like a tradition that has occurred in a fashion such as a firefly flashing during the night without being able to stop. This same heartbreaking month of truth has been repeated year after year throughout the centuries and it is for young boys and girls to leave their families to go seek a better future, traveling far and wide into the unknown world in much the same way as those miners did, to seek their dreams of fortune. The new world

16

came to be called home to some of the new wave of the younger generation. My family and clan of Koljenovic are examples of some of the ones who kept the tradition alive and immigrated after the harvest during that harsh month in December, the beginning of winter.

Some of the young and strong men and women even reached the Northern Sierra Nevada's during the time of the gold rush in northern California and Nevada. One of the young men from Montenegro and Sandjak was executed for murdering his distant cousin who apparently cheated him of his silver mining fortune in the town of Tonopah. The young man didn't respect the law of his new homeland and instead he used the ancient law of Montenegro and killed his distant cousin for the silver nuggets he was allegedly cheated out of. The man who was shot was rich, influential and a law officer in the town of Tonopah. All of that influence helped apply the law of the west and the newcomer from Montenegro and Sandjak was hanged even though he was a true victim in a sense. Others today through the descendants of those earlier immigrants are now senators, businessmen, politicians, and productive citizens.

The cycle of families being rendered apart has yet to cease to exist. Those children, young boys and girls, were supposed to be the future generation to carry on for their families and safeguard the tree that is the mother of their existence. Their intentions in leaving were not to uproot themselves but they soon found that their old ways of life did not apply in this new world although to prosper they accepted a new way of life without abandoning their ingrained beauty of their old mosaic. The old and new mosaics of beauty helped enrich and broaden their lives, not ever forgetting their old world but adapting easily to the new culture and new traditions but not without internal struggles in their hearts and souls. They were not reluctant to have to adjust in a new land but would not forget their heritage and everything that they had grown to love just as the generations before them had.

The tragic vicious cycle of the families being constantly broken and uprooted hasn't ever ended. This is still an unbroken, continuing narrative journey and still going on although now in even much greater numbers in the times of this turbulent world. Those heart broken mothers have never been able to stop their weeping and those fathers faces have never got to have the smile as God intended them to have. Instead they have to carry those images of their children in their memories, those children that they had to let go of and that they knew would not be coming back. Just as the that one boy whose fate was different than most of the others. He would never return because he was executed on that tragic day in Tonopah for the murder of a man over a nugget of silver he claimed he got cheated out of.

There is true pain etched in the faces of these people. Their wrinkled faces reveal a true picture of their lives and the voided space in their souls that only they can know how it feels. Perhaps it was a blessing that the some of the parents never found out the fates of their children.

Would it be an overstatement to quote something that brings to mind the famous words of a man who succeeded in life beyond his wildest dreams and was suddenly struck down with a deadly illness that was unheard of at the time? That man was Lou Gehrig. He found himself fighting a losing battle for his life yet he never lost his love for life and his passion for entertaining his fans and most importantly, he hadn't lost the love for his country and people since they had given to him as much or more than he had given them.

In contrast it was so unlike the children from the Province of Sandjak and the valley of Gusinje who had love from their families but were never fortunate enough to have the love of their country of Montenegro. There were obviously not enough reasons for the young and able to stay there then and now. The rights of full citizenship were never acknowledged or granted to Sandjak by King Nicola of the state of Montenegro and after he was dethroned by the Serbian King Alexander and his new Yugoslavia. Sandjak and it's children were in even more of a losing position.

Lou Gehrig was a much luckier man. He knew he belonged with a people in a nation he loved. On the day of his retirement at New York's Yankee Stadium he gave a passionate speech and declared that he was the luckiest man on earth even knowing himself that he was a dying man from a disease that is now named after him.

He knew what he had and how he had got to where he was through both his luck and his misfortunes. His luck surely outweighed his misfortune. Every Sunday people looked forward to seeing him at the baseball field performing his magic and entertaining the fans and the citizens he so loved. On the day of the last game he would ever play he stood in front of perhaps a hundred thousand of his fans who loved and respected him dearly, knowing deep in his heart that he loved his fans as well as his country. He had always entertained his fans by his passion and his love for baseball.

Such a great man may not be quite an appropriate comparison to my own circumstances and that of my ancestors but does have something to teach us. Why couldn't the children of the valley of Gusinje and the Province of Sandjak have such an example that they could look up to? The message is clearly there. Simply to state I think we all somehow learn to be thankful and reflect each day on our lives and surroundings as individuals. My blessing is that I have never forgotten where I came from and my journey to where I am here and now.

Even though I have a clear appreciation of my good life, forgive me, but I admit I have been spoiled and find myself sometimes complaining about how hard I have been working without enough time to play and forgetting how lucky I've been and am. My number one rule is to never forget what I have accomplished and the determination it took to get where I am.

Now here I was in one of the most beautiful cities in the world, Las Vegas, in my home, a successful businessman in real estate and in the bar and restaurant business surrounded by ordinary people like myself as well as the elite. I was fortunate enough that I received the friendship and respect of the people who respected and looked up to me and I readily accepted their true and honest friendship.

I have always been passionate about world and local politics. When watching the world news one evening something really caught my attention. It was a news broadcast on the senate floor debate concerning what to do about the ten million illegal immigrants, one who happened to be my little brother Jusuf, who was only six years old when I had left home many years ago, and was now a young man. I closely followed that debate and the issues being debated by the senate on immigration. Finally the bill was voted in by the senate, and President Reagan signed the bill. I saw the opportunity to make a difference and to help others and wasn't about to let it pass me by. I thought jokingly that I could even a make a name for myself, which in a way did happen.

There was clearly an opportunity to make a lot of money but that was the least of my worries and not my main motivation. It was more for the challenge to myself to see if I could actually do it. As I look back now I did it my way, just as Frank Sinatra sang, "I did it my way." I knew for a fact that the immigration lawyers were taking people to the cleaners and charging dearly without providing them the documentation for a legal status and the way to a green card and finally citizenship. Many people were misrepresented by the immoral and ignorant lawyers on immigration laws with no clue about immigration and the needs of these people. It is a legal racket that has continued to go on for hundreds of years. Many of the immigrants dreams for a better life were shattered just for the reason that many of the lawyers simply didn't care. I knew for sure I could fill the gap and make sure their dreams came true just I was able to do for many and all of my clientele.

I also had some contacts in INS so I called my friend Sprat who was then in charge of the immigration office. I asked him to explain what the bill meant exactly for a potential business. I then tried to investigate more on what Sprat had told me and talked to my our mutual friend Joey Valdez, then president of the League of United Latin American Citizens, and already deeply involved in the process of illegal immigrants. Joey asked during our conversation if we could get together with Luis Tapia at one of our favorite places and I agreed to meet them the next day at noon at the well known restaurant Chateau Vegas, owned by the younger brother of one of the richest and most flamboyant men on the planet today, Kirk Korkorian. I was excited and looking forward to meeting with Joey and hearing all about the program that looked so promising. It was almost like the phrases friends use frequently, "It sounds too good to be true," and if it truly is then, "It's a license to make a difference."

We met and had an in depth conversation on what it all meant. He said he had an interesting talk with Cardinal Mahoney in Los Angeles, who oversaw Catholic social services, and the Cardinal had been ecstatic about the bill the Senate had passed which would help millions. Hearing such a holy mean as he had such excitement for the program no doubt inspired me and I wanted to be a part of it. Joey Valdez confirmed the need for people like us to get together and represent the communities. I knew I was with the right group of people and that we thought alike.

We agreed to meet again the next day for lunch. Joey stressed there were some people whom I needed to meet who were going to be in charge of the new INS office. When we got together the next day at new immigration office, there were new officers who would be in charge. This new office was to be used to serve only the amnesty programs recently passed by the Senate.

During lunch I asked Sprat who was also there about the prospects of the success of the program. In one word and with a big smile he just said, "Bonanza!" Two ladies who were there sitting across the table from us, Barbara the wife of one of the prominent judges in the city and her associate Marlene, were going to be in charge of the new office repeated his sentiment like parrots.

I asked with a lot of curiosity, "Bonanza for whom? Myself or the immigrants I would be doing business with?"

He answered, "Both of you, if you want to you can charge for the service and you will be rewarded by being paid and the people will get permanent residency, their dream."

I replied that if I were to take on this responsibility, I would need a professional office and a full staff with at least some knowledge of filling out the applications and had some cultural and political knowledge of the countries the people are coming from. Therefore we could bring the cases and have them processed easier. They looked like my response was music to their ears. I added that the possible benefits to both ourselves and the immigrants could be very rewarding although I stressed again that I wasn't in it for the money. There was one more question I needed to ask and did, "Is everything within the boundaries of the law, legal and following the bills the senate has passed?"

Marlene and Barbara preened like peacocks and Barbara said, "Don't worry about anything, just make sure our day's labor is worth our efforts." Of course I knew exactly what she meant. We were not going to be sending anyone away without their temporary residency and work permits.

Sprat cut in to reaffirm Barbara's assurances, "Don't worry, you will be under the umbrella of LULAC, where your good friend is president and I'll also being watching everything. Barbara and Marlene will be there to assist and guide you in everything that you would need." That was music to my ears.

That was it. I thought it sounded pretty easy, and it was. My conviction to proceed on was sealed. I had my office and professional staff the next day. With my friends Joey, Sprat, and Barbara, I was into the immigration business. They worked on the inside and I was on the outside. It was a good team and I was still able to do it my way.

My new immigration legalization consulting firm became very successful and rewarding for myself and my clients. I was rewarded with the satisfaction I received and felt by helping each immigrant rather than the financial monetary gain but I was pleased with that as well. I was pleased just to break even and pay the staff. For others it was being able to realize their dream and come to America for a new life. I realized there were people who needed to be reached outside of the country instead of only the ones who were already in the country. I realized that I wanted to expand this adventure since for me it was just as I had said and needed to make it more challenging and I did. If I couldn't have then I probably would have walked away because it would have been too easy and boring for me. I came to the realization that there were those with professional skills and talents that this country needed, and who needed my help to help make their dream come true. I could get the personal satisfaction that I dreamed of to come true as well. Some I legalized like families with children without charging a cent. Once I traveled to Connecticut to legalize a Croatian family with a handicapped child. That was a most beautiful and gratifying feeling to me. Here I am, doing something meaningful and right. With no doubt it was rewarding to my soul.

Nothing was more gratifying than seeing the faces of all the people who received temporary or permanent residency and to see their happy tears and hear the thanks that came truly and deeply from their hearts just like a family I helped in Fort Lauderdale who were from Pakistan. The immigration officer who had interviewed them reached his hand across the desk to shake the man hand and told him, "Welcome to America." The man was trembling and so happy he cried and then fainted. The immigration officer Hector jumped over the desk to see if the man was OK. I smiled and gently put my hand on Hector's shoulder and told him, "Don't worry, he is just overwhelmed with the beginning of his new life and he'll be fine. You helped make it possible Hector, thank you. I doubt that this man will ever forget you." Hector went back to his desk clearly overjoyed knowing that he helped this man begin a new life.

For all these reasons I became addicted to my new venture. I began reaching outside of the country to bring the brightest and youngest from around the world to the U.S. and give them the chance they were looking for to be able to participate and create in the advancement of our great nation.

Without realizing it my routine became the same each day, and my life had done a complete three-sixty. It was twenty-four seven, only without chasing any of the beautiful girls like I was used to doing. This business became a serious responsibility. I woke up every morning with no girl around the house. I had to make my own coffee and drink it by myself. It was hard giving up my play time but duty called and I there I was checking my many messages and calls that came in throughout the previous night, not only local but statewide and international from people I'd never known or heard of. I sure missed the girls though and hated only just meeting with one I really liked when I had time, although I enjoyed them all, and then having to leave on business. I missed the tender care.

The nature of my business brought me to a place and time where my private personal life went out the window and life had become hectic and crazed and I didn't realize why or that I was starting to become a workaholic. I didn't forget the girls and I couldn't have, God forbid. If there were no girls on this planet there would be no point for me to be here either.

Nature did her part creating them and I had to do my part trying to keep them happy. My perks of the job gave me incentive and rewarded me after working hard.
I innocently purchased one thing that really added to my hectic schedule and gave me no privacy, the newest advancement in communication, the cellular telephone.

I just had to have one and didn't realize what I was buying and that my private time would vanish like a puff of smoke answering the phone at any and all times. I was the third person to have it in Las Vegas and got addicted to it right away. My brother introduced it to me and was the very first one in town to have one. I never did get used to the monthly bill that was so high I think anyone would scratch their head in disbelief when it came due. Initially the cost of my cell phone could have been put to making payments on a Ferrari instead. I thought I had made a good decision anyway.

I nevertheless found it convenient and figured, "Hey, I can afford it and everyone else has to use public phones." I lived with it, slept with it, and drove with it. It was my new very expensive toy for at least a couple of years. Then everyone else started to have one and it was just another tool to quickly communicate and conduct business which could be done over the phone. It seems the traditional person to person meetings and shaking of hands was disappearing. New technology has allowed people to have telephone conferences together on different sides of the world. They could even be having it at home in bed like I have done many times from my own bed with the phone.

This new form of telecommunication was a Motorola, heavy and ugly looking like a two-way military radio from World War II and not very comfortable to use. Still it was sort of an ego trip being the latest invention and at a cost of twelve hundred dollars to purchase the phone and then a charge of fifty cents per minute for each call from each party, the caller and receiver. It was a dollar a minute for each call and could get very expensive. A man would have to be a fool or out of his mind to have a phone like that. Unfortunately I was one of the fools.

Looking back on it I think I was out of my mind but I had it anyway. I always wanted to have things that not everyone had and be different than anyone else. I was different anyway for sure, but mostly in a good and kind sense. No matter how things go whether good or bad, winning or losing, I always remember to be thankful and look forward to a new day. Like I said I could have been driving a Ferrari for the kind of payment I was making but I already had the car I wanted and my favorite car, a Porsche.

Whatever I do I always want to do it right and show my character as if I am leaving my signature behind. I was taught that is the only way to do anything right from my father. I am determined to make sure of a successful outcome and see things through. I especially felt this way about the worthy and noble cause that I had become involved in.

I was always different and wanted to be that way. I took great satisfaction in my friends and myself seeing me that way and calling me unique and different. Even though I always seem to draw the attention of others and seem to project a presence that commands respect, at times I didn't enjoy it really and it and seemed I couldn't get away from it.

Some people said it was because I was such a pretty boy. At times it crossed my mind I should soak up the ego trip and compliments but I reminded myself of where I came from and how I'd gotten to where I am. That was with a strong will and the determination to do better, and I always double checked myself to remain thankful and humble.

I took my new business endeavor in immigration very seriously. At times it was dangerous because of the fact that I was dealing with different people from different cultures. In order to succeed, particularly in this complex business that plays with the lives of people and to win their trust, I had to be well aware of the reasons they were there and respect them, their traditions and culture, as well as understand all of the combination of their need for my help.

Understanding the complex combination of all these things taught me how to walk a thin line within the boundaries of the law and to get what I needed to obtain my goals of getting permanent status in the U.S. for my clients.

Each part of the process had to be carefully understood and balanced so I would not offend the potential immigrant or break the law. I was successful in walking that sharp thin line without offending either party and then to make it possible for the long life dreams of many of the families from around the globe to come true.

I am lucky that I have grown up with a culture in very deep rooted traditions and had no problems in finding common ground with any of the cultures or traditions I encountered. The experience that I had with the thousands of future new citizens who entrusted their faith in me to guide them in the long and complicated process which sometimes took years at a time, enriched me as a man, father, and husband, and has profoundly made me an unshakable patriot of this great nation that I feel very grateful and thank God for.

To balance my professional character and have respect for the job I took so seriously, I took satisfaction in knowing that I was providing hope to these potential new citizens of people from around the globe, not just to anyone but qualified people with the knowledge, skill, capability and the determination it takes to get what they hungered for, becoming legal residents of this country and experiencing the life of the American dream. Thus they were easily able to integrate without obstacles into our society in many different professional occupations with their higher education and skills into the work force of America. That was something I could be proud of.

Through my many old contacts and friends from around the globe a very old friend of mine, Zagar, referred to me a couple of young characters who seemed to be employed by him and communicated a need for my help. For a moment I thought he had finally gone straight but I guess he hadn't. He was still living a fast and dangerous life that was always on the edge. I shouldn't have expected any different because people such as he don't know any other way to live. The two boys were from Sydney, Australia, and would soon be traveling to Los Angeles, sent on a mission by Zagar, I assumed.

They were Nenad and his brother Branco, who I later found out were originally from my home state of Montenegro. I had never met them before. They were a couple of young, very determined, ambitious men, yet they were also dangerous and somewhat notorious in Australia.

After meeting them I could see they were carrying burning torches in their hands on paths to destruction, with no good in them. These are the kind of people you have to face head on. They were all body and no brains which is the kind of employees Zagar wanted to have. They obey and don't ask questions.

It seemed like they were trying to live the American image of the hard ass tough guy world of sex, drugs and rock and roll. Two of those I wouldn't have minded that much about them, the sex and rock and roll, but their main objective was the third one, drugs. They were into selling drugs. They wanted to be just like their role model, Pablo Escobar, who was a big drug lord in Columbia and had a goal of being the biggest drug pushers in Australia.

I was never fond of drugs nor had any respect for the ones who sold them. These boys were definitely on the road to their own funerals at Bunker Hill cemetery. All bodies with no brains and they were clearly a danger to themselves as well as anyone who associated with them. They seemed to love living on the edge of danger or they just did not understand any of the consequences from the business they were diving into. These boys had a lot of learning to do if they were to live very long. They had a lack of experience in life and dealing with people. I looked forward at first to meeting them since they came from where I had and expected to meet smart and capable young men. That wasn't what I saw in them. They were just two wanderers without a clear direction.

They were doing something I didn't like but I never bothered to let them know that and doubted they would listen to any of my advice if I had had any to give. I could see that they already thought themselves to be ten feet tall and bullet proof. That was their first of their misconceptions. The bigger you are the harder you will fall. Being young and I assume not too educated and not having had enough experience in life, they had the goal of becoming tough guys and making a lot of money by being drug lords as their road to glory. As dishonorable a goal as it was they definitely weren't cut out for it and were taking the wrong paths. It seemed like they saw it as the only way to glorify themselves and become rich and famous. This was the one and only way they saw to get what they wanted. Their motto was, "Do it or die trying." During my lifetime I have seen a few of those type of ambitious young men who found themselves behind bars or six feet under if they were lucky and got a proper burial, with no glory in sight. I wished I could have told them what I knew to be true and they would listen to me and believe me but there was no getting through to guys like them.

They didn't even look the part of the tough guys they wanted to be. They looked more like mama's milk boys who hardly had any fuzz growing on their faces. Just being around boys like Branco and Nenad you could end up being hurt if you were not being careful. You always see that these kind don't have friends, just others using one another until there is nothing left to use and they all become disposable eventually.

Whoever taught them about how to dress surely had no taste. Their fashion of dressing was nothing like what they should have portrayed in the line of business they wanted to succeed in. I told them, "If you want to impress anyone as being a tough guy then dress tough. You guys look pretty shaggy. I'm sure you can afford to go and get a nice suit." He thought I was joking at first but then said, "I think your probably right." I recommended a few stores they should go to when they returned to L.A. He never mentioned that he did have a personal tailor in L.A. who specialized in suits for drug smuggling with secret pockets and not much else going for them. I was surprised when Nenad mentioned it to me later. I thought maybe they are not as stupid as they pretend to be and just look that way. I asked about how the tailor created these wonder suits. He readily told me all about the suits. He said, "Listen Angie, we go and buy a nice double breasted but not expensive like yours are. They are only a couple hundred bucks. Then we have the tailor alter them for us."

"How does he make his alterations for your stash pockets?" I asked.

"Well in the shoulder and chest padding he takes the original material out then makes a new lining and fills in the white stuff and sews a new silk lining just like the original was. Then he inserts plastic more white stuff in plastic tubes that run up the lining of the suit closed of the hem of the jacket.. We can carry close to a kilo. No one has ever detected it."

"How often to you make a trip?" I asked.

"At least once a month or more often if we can. I find other people to do the carrying or do it myself now and then," he answered.

I thought to myself, "Man, I though you were stupid, but not that dumb. You are a couple dangerous fools." They were two healthy good looking guys who would pay dearly sooner or later for what they were doing. I'm sure the temptation is very hard to pass up when you buy a kilo somewhere here in Long Beach, or through his friend Bruno from Alaska for from four to six thousand dollars depending on it's purity, then can go and sell it in Australia for sixty thousand dollars. If they could make a hundred trips to make that kind of money and anyone stood in their way including their own mothers they would be ready to kill them.

The Montenegrin boys from Sydney arrived in Los Angeles and called the moment they got in. They delivered greetings from Zagar first and said they'd like to come see me. I told them I would make time in my schedule for them and to call me when they got to Las Vegas and they could meet me at my office in the Paseo Del Prado complex.

The next morning at eight thirty sharp they were waiting for me at the front door of my office. We hugged and kissed on both cheeks, as the people in Montenegro do when greeting each other, even though we had never met in person before. I invited them in and asked how they knew my friend Zagar.

Branco said, "Everyone knows Zagar, he's a legend."

I looked at Branco and laughed and laughed. "I love Zagar. He's a good friend but I am surprised that he is still alive. Every time someone comes to see me mentioning his name I always think they are delivering the bad news and his last message so I could send some flowers. To tell you the truth, I always hoped I wouldn't be having to be spending that kind of money on flowers. If it came down to the final draw I hope he will spend money on me instead of me on him."

The brothers were laughing heartedly thinking that was very funny. I had to calm them down some. "O.K, it's not all that funny but true."

Branco cut in, "You guys must be really close friends."

"I wouldn't exactly say that but we have always respected and truthful with each other. He never told me what I should do in my life and I never told him what he should do. If I ever need anything from him or him from me, we were always there for one another and knew it be taken care of, but I have never took him up on anything or has he from me. That is where Zaga and I stand."

"Your good friend Zagar from Split told us that you would take care of us for sure, and we wanted to just surprise you."

I was surprised and at the same time laughing to myself and I asked, "How is that old fox?"

Nenad replied happily, "He's been running a night club in Melbourne."

It occurred to me right away that my old friend must have gotten into the drug business in Melbourne and on the Gold Coast which were some distance apart and that these two boys were his runners. I said in a loud voice, "Well, Zagar must have fallen on hard times to be running a nightclub. That never was his cup of tea."

They looked almost embarrassed by my comment, and Branco the older one replied, "The night club is doing very well and Mr. Zagar needs a little excitement."

I said, "Yes, I know he always did like excitement but he always used to like it by observing from the sidelines and preferring to avoid being too much directly involved in anything. He always called himself the silent partner in any kind of business he's been in. That's why I'm surprised he's running a couple nightclubs and you would announce it. Usually if he owned a business no one knew about it, although he would show up every night as a guest with no one knowing he was the owner. That's the Zagar I know. So are you boys working for him or on your own? What do you do for a living?"

Branco replied, "Mr. Zagar said all we had to do was to mention his name and you would help us out and we really do need this favor from you."

"Yes," I agreed. "That is all you need to say, my old friend's name."

I walked them inside to my office and they wasted no time telling what they needed was the documents for new identifications. They wanted birth certificates under different names. I really didn't have a problem in being able to get that for them. I told them, "That's easy, but why do you want to change your identities when you can get permanent legal residence in your own real names?" Then it dawned on me exactly why they would want that. If they get caught in what they're doing they could have someone post bail for them and when they were out they could disappear as someone else.

They didn't want to hear me ask them that question and the look on their faces was very unfriendly. Nenad said, "It's not your business to ask why we need the identification, all we need is for you to provide it for us."

I replied, "Well, Mister, you're right, it's not my business to ask you why but it's going to cost you a lot. Show me you have the money then I will make some calls. I'll have a friend of mine come pick you up here. In about six hours time you will have the identities you want and can do whatever it is with them."

Branco stood and said, "O.K. Angie. We have money although I don't think I should really have to pay."

I said, "There are no free rides, mister. I won't be doing anything for you personally and don't care for the way you assume I will set it up for you for nothing. It all depends on how bad you need what I can get for you. If you want to insist that you shouldn't have pay for the services you want then the only thing you'll leave here with is a feeling that you're sorry you came to see me."

"Look, I'm sorry pal, I was only testing you," he said. "You passed." Then he looked over at his brother who pulled and envelope from his jacket stuffed with hundreds in American and Australian bills. "Which would you prefer Angie, Australian or U.S. currency?"

I said, "U.S. will be fine but you won't be giving it to me. You are going to deal with a guy named Louis who will be coming to pick you up soon."

"OK, I apologize, Angie," he said.

"No kidding. I thought that you didn't have those words in your vocabulary."

"Of course I do," Branco replied. "I'm a smart guy."

"I hope so, for your sake. Branco, like I was just telling you, I'm glad you understand. I was ready to send you to a one way trip to hell."

He said, "Man it's just we've had a long trip from Australia and everything's been going wrong since. We're starting to get on edge with everything."

I walked from behind my desk and extended my hand towards the door as a gesture they could leave. Nenad turned and left with

Branco and I followed behind him.

To my surprise Branco suddenly put his arm around my waist where my hand gun was tucked in the belt of my waist. I put my left arm over the hand he had on my back and said to him, "Branco, I don't need the gun because I can kick your ass anytime. Don't try and be a wise guy. You're not going to make any new friends with that kind of attitude. This advice is from a true friend and only because of Zagar. You'll live a longer and healthier life if you don't try biting the hand that could always be there when you need it."

He jumped back and removed his hand and apologized and said he wasn't meaning to check me out like that. It was just a habit he had with people he liked of putting his arm around their waist to hug them. I answered, "Around me you should get rid of that habit."

In the front of my offices I asked for my secretary to place a call to Louis who was going to be joining me as my partner in the next few days. He had just been an acquaintance before now. I thought we could work well together. He was someone you still had to look over your shoulder at because you couldn't be sure where he was coming from. Louis was a barracuda. He would make a deal with the devil and sell his soul if there was a dollar in it to be made and try to redeem his soul later.

When my secretary had him on the line I said, "Hey Louis, Angie here."

He replied, "Hey, what's up?"

I said, "Look here, Louis, I have a couple of friends here at the office that need a favor and they're going to need to see you. Could you please come by and pick them up? They don't have much time. There is something they would like you to do for them. I already told them it was going to cost ten thousand dollars a piece and the rest would be all up to you."

Louis lowered his voice almost whispering like he knew they were probably standing right next to me and said, "Is that a fifty-fifty deal Angie or would it be all mine?"

I replied, "Louis, I will just take one of your boxes of Cuban cigars that I saw on your desk a couple of days ago but I want a whole box."

He said, "You son of a bitch, you. You just think a Mexican Chilean doesn't look good enough to play mobster and smoke cigars."

I said, "I never called you a mobster Louis. You have a long

31

way to go for that kind of reputation. However if you can find me a Mexican Chilean who looks like a mobster bring him to me and I'll buy him a cigar and a three piece suit to make sure he looks like a mobster."

Louis said, "Screw you, Angie."

He knew I was just teasing and that I did love him as my friend but I would never forgot he was still a barracuda. I said "Come here and pick these boys up because they are going to be leaving tonight for L.A."

He was there almost immediately. By six that evening and before the INS office on Valley View had closed both of the boys had their identification cards and temporary green cards that they paid for and they thanked Louis. I told them there was no need in thanking me because all I had done was to introduce them to Louis.

Whatever the deal was that they made or that he gave them it was something I didn't even want to know about. Branco believed that I was still behind it all. He said, "That's all fine Angie. But I know this guy is working for you and he's your carrier."

I wanted to change the subject about the business in their being here and offered that they and Louis join me and come across the street to the Palace Station and I'd buy dinner. We went to the Fisherman's Wharf, a fine seafood restaurant that was inside the hotel.

A friend of mine, Joe Tempura, worked at the Palace Station Casino. Years ago when he was only eighteen years old he had worked under me at the Aladdin Hotel Casino as a laborer in the warehouse. He was attending night classes studying hotel management as well at the University of Las Vegas. Joe had the habit of falling asleep on the job soon after he came in to work and one of the assistant managers, Mickey, was always wanting to fire him. I made sure he would not do that and of course Joey was grateful to me for that and he would always tell me every time I saved his ass that one of these days he was going to be running one of the casinos and be the president of it. I would reply with laughter assuring him I believed that he would and he should not dream any other way.

Now here I was years later having dinner at one of the major and favorite local resorts without knowing that my favorite boy who was then eighteen and always sleeping on the job was the operating president and CEO now of a multi-million dollar resort casino property where I happened to be dining at that very moment.

32

After diner I called the waiter over to bring the check. The waiter said, "Mr. Angelo, your check has already been taken care of." I asked who took care of it. "Joe Tempura, the president of this hotel," he said. "He also asked if you could please wait around for a few minutes because he'd like to come by to see you and say hello."

A few moments later he was there and looked handsome, healthy and well dressed like a true executive. I noticed first thing the silver name badge identifying him as an executive of the property. I was proud of my boy Joey. In fact I think it was one of the proudest moments I've had in my life. I hadn't been given many chances myself when I was a boy growing up by anyone until I came here to the states. For me it was a proud moment to know I had had a hand in helping Joey to reach his dreams. To see a boy I gave a chance to once to now be running a multi-million dollar casino with thousands of employees under him was a true success story.

Why couldn't those two boys from Montenegro have the same kind of dreams? Instead they were taking roads that would bring nothing but destruction to them.

I am not proud of helping them by introducing them to Louis who provided them with the legal documents they needed in order to become temporary residents of the United States. I could have easily turned them away. That was the only time during my work in immigration that I wasn't proud of being able to help someone.

After dinner we walked through the casino and played a few hands of blackjack. By nine that evening it was time to go to an appointment I had. The two brothers left for Los Angeles with intentions of returning to Australia and we said that we would meet up again sometime. I told them, "Maybe the next time we see each other you guys can entertain me with some of your stories." Louis and I said goodbye and wished them the best of luck.

Some months later at way past midnight I received a call that awakened me from my sleep. The man who called introduced himself as Sharif from a place I least expected a call from, Prague in the Czech Republic. He was pretty straight forward and asked in a heavy Albanian accent if I would be able to do him a favor and help him out. He said he was a friend of my friends Branco and Nenad from Melbourne, and they assured him that if he mentioned them to me then I was the man who could do doing anything that he needed done. He was vague and didn't get specific. I thought since it was late at night I wanted him to get straight down to the point. "Sharif, what is it exactly you need and what is it I can do to help you?"

There was silence on the line for a moment. He coughed then and said what he needed was a connection in order to ship his cocaine from out of Europe and Los Angeles and into Australia. "Why are you calling me? They are the professionals. Why didn't you ask them?"

He answered, "Branco told me you could get people to do some traveling for me."

"Listen Sharif, I don't work for anybody and I don't deal in the type of merchandise you, Branco, and his brother are in. I help people in the immigration business and spend more money on it than I make. You may think I'm a sucker but I like to help lift up people. You on the other hand are into something very different and very illegal. It's bold of you to tell me your business or you are just very desperate and I don't deal with desperate people. They are too dangerous. I hope you don't mind hearing me out."

He replied, "Please."

I tried not to waste any of his or my time telling him that I was only in business to help people establish new residence in the United States, and what I do is legitimate. I am not in the business of selling or buying what you are referring to. I have known people who were, but I have never used, bought, or sold any of it, and don't endorse or approve of anyone who does. I added that if there was anything he needed other than that then I would be happy to help him free of charge. I told him to please tell Branco and Nenad hello for me and tell them the next time they come to L.A. from Sydney to give me a call.

A few days later during my morning shave my phone rang several times. There were a few brief messages from Branco who was calling from Australia and Bruno calling from Anchorage, Alaska, and one from Sharif who was calling from Prague, Czechoslovakia. All these guys were in cahoots and buddy buddies.

I decided not to respond to any of their calls. I knew they'd be calling back. I drove in to my office at Paseo del Prado. My office suite was on the third floor that I shared with Louis. By this time we employed three secretaries to handle the immigration paperwork because business was growing rapidly.

Occasionally when I drive down Sahara Boulevard and see the Palace Station always there to greet me, I reflect over the past thirty five years and how much that resort has grown just as Joey and I have grown. I can't help thinking about my boy Joey and the great success he has had and his sudden fall from the good high life. I had heard that there was a casino in Kansas City that he took over running for nearly a decade in Missouri. It had formerly belonged to him and his family and had been sold and renamed Sam's Town, because my boy Joey had lost his gaming license which is something that is a privilege to have, and one could have it taken at anytime by the gaming commission because of it's strict regulations. In our society one is innocent until proven guilty, but in Joey's case it looked like he was out of a job at least for a while. The last I hear he was waiting on his hearing with the gaming industry hoping to prove his innocence and have his license reinstated. As I know how Joey is I am sure he will able to bounce back and be successful once again.

CHAPTER TWO: A FRIEND OF THE IMMIGRANT

It was important for me to understand every angle of this Immigration business and have full control over every aspect of it to keep my business growing as my reputation was growing through word of mouth. I vowed not to fail myself in it. The only end of the road I could see was success. There were some financial rewards and all the expenses were covered. I needed professionals to work with me, especially a licensed lawyer that I could trust and was hungry to work but under my terms. I wanted to be covered on all points of the law. I wouldn't or couldn't have it any other way. I don't mind walking a thin line or being on that sharp edge of the boundary of the law, but I don't wish to break the law. It can be challenging living on the edge, keeping that balance without tipping over on one side. I was good at keeping the scales of justice balanced. The only way I could feel just and confident of doing the right thing was to have that umbrella of a lawyer and I made sure I found it. I discussed it with Louie and he agreed it would be very smart to have a lawyer.

It was a challenge for me to find a lawyer hungry enough to let me use his diploma to hang on the wall in my office and keep the doors open in a perfectly legal way and also be able to complete the process of immigration for each client. I wanted to be a law abiding citizen without depending entirely on my friends in immigration and LULAC for any help with the legalities. It was the proper and only smart way to do it so as not to have any unwanted consequences. It was going to be difficult but I knew I had to get it done.

I made some calls that same day. Some friends of mine had recommended a man from Chicago named Elliot, so I contacted him and introduced myself. I told him that he came highly recommended to me and was known for his trustworthiness and that was exactly what I was looking for in the business I was in. I needed someone with his professional skills. I didn't hesitate then to explain to the gentleman exactly what it was I needed from him.

After patiently hearing me out Elliot responded without a second thought that he thought my offer sounded both exciting and challenging. He advised me I should hire him and not be in a sense of a partnership in the business but a hired lawyer. In reality he became a partner but technically because of the law he was classified as a hired employee who represented the company in the legal matters concerning immigration. That way we covered all the bases.

I explained in detail to him about the business which he knew little about as well as explaining the financial potential for himself personally. After he patiently heard me out he said he didn't have any reservations about being on my team and joining me.

During our conversation he told me he had been practicing law for over thirty years and was tired of the divorce and traffic ticket cases. To him this not only sounded exciting and challenging but also presented an opportunity to learn in the field of immigration, which was not yet very familiar to him.

I assured him not to not worry because I would guide him and he would be learning much in the new trade of immigration and meeting many influential people in INS. I told him he could learn how to accomplish really good deeds being a lawyer and doing something that is worthwhile, maybe making more money than he ever dreamed of, and getting to travel at the same time, all for the reason to help people.

I asked him if he could also recommend one or two more lawyers who would be willing to join our crew. He wasn't anxious to add anyone else to part of the pie but he suggested that we work for a month or two and see how we did, and after that if I felt we still needed someone else he knew of a nice Jewish boy in Boca Raton, Florida. I asked the boy's name and he said it was Alex Grief.

"I hope he is not always causing grief," I said jokingly.

"No he is a red headed boy that is sharp," Elliot said, "a good listener and I think would be very loyal Angie. He's a good boy who will listen and is hungry because he doesn't get too much work in Florida."

I said, "All right, my brother Elliott, when shall we meet?"

"Anytime you want Angie, anytime is fine. I am an old man but I think this might keep me running for a few more years."

I replied, "Elliot, I promise I can keep you on your toes and so busy you probably won't like it. So, why don't you meet me in San Jose tomorrow night? Your ticket will be ready. I'll ask my secretary Mary to call you with a flight number and departure time on America West airlines. I'll meet you tomorrow in San Jose because I have about ten immigration cases there I need to process at the Salinas office."

Without hesitation Elliot asked, "Where will I be staying?"

"When you arrive in San Jose," I directed him, "ask the taxi driver to take you to the Le Baron Hotel. It's very exclusive and a comfortable Victorian style place that has a beautiful bar and restaurant. Just ask for the food and beverage director, a man named Steve. He will have a key to the suite ready for you. I'll give him a call as soon as we hang up. There won't be a need for you to check in. Then if we succeed in Salinas on Tuesday we will need to fly to the far east to meet some people in the land of Alexander, in Pakistan. Hopefully you are all up for this trip and feel well."

Elliot said with excitement in his voice, "Angie, all of my life I've wanted to travel and now here you are like a magic charm making it possible for me. I hope I am not dreaming in my old age. How do I recognize you when we meet?"

"Just ask Steve to seat you at the table reserved for me," I answered. "I'll meet you there at nine twenty sharp. It will probably be hard for me to miss you, Elliot. I feel like I've already known you for a long time and am very comfortable talking with you. I hope the two of us on our new endeavor and the adventures that we will have will be successful, and that I will earn your trust and you will earn mine, so I have someone to depend on or lean on if I need it. I don't need just a partner but also a friend that I'm able to lean on now and then."

Elliot replied, "Angelo, my mother and father came from Poland and settled in Chicago after running away from the prosecution there and the concentration camps. The job you are doing I have wanted to do all my life and have always wanted to help people to be able to experience the freedom that we know. You can have no doubt you'll have my shoulder to lean on."

These were the magic words that I wanted to hear from him. I said, "I am glad to hear that, Elliot. Believe me there will be a day when I need to use that shoulder and rest assured you can also use mine. The only thing left now is to arrange our trip to Pakistan. I'll call my executive secretary Mary and ask her to take care of the arrangements for us to stay for a couple weeks."

The next evening in San Jose at nine twenty I was wearing one of my best suits. As always I was greeted by my friend Steve in the lobby of the Le Baron Hotel with warm bear hugs, handshakes and a couple of kisses on both checks in respect and acknowledgement of our true friendship as men.

We walked to the steak house and Steve pointed out that we shouldn't keep Elliot waiting. I said, "By all means Steve, I'm looking forward to meeting Elliot, I think he will be everything I expect him to be."

The maitre'd name was Maury Cline, a professional and kind human being that I always looked forward to seeing. He walked us to the table where Elliot already was seated and looking comfortable and feeling at home enjoying a glass of Château La Fleur red wine.

Elliot saw us coming and stood up and said loud enough to be heard across the room, "Angelo, you are just as I imagined you to be when we talked on the phone, I swear, you don't need to introduce yourself." Everyone in the room was looking at us and smiling at Elliot's comment. Those were the kind of moments that brought out the shyness in me, when I caught the attention of everyone. It makes you feel like checking yourself inside and out to make sure you feel and look good inside and out.

We shook hands and hugged like we had known each other for a long time. Trust and good feelings grew in a short time. We had so much in common. Before I met him I had pictured what I thought he might look like by his voice and by our conversation. My imagining was right and he looked and acted very much as a fatherly figure.

Elliot showed his experience of life being an older man. He was in his late sixties and I could see in him a mind and heart with goodness that I could learn a lot from. I already felt I could trust him.

During our initial meeting we struck up a conversation and touched base on just about everything including our successes, politics, family and even of our failures. I felt all throughout our conversation that there was no hesitation from either of us to hold back on any subject.

There was one quality of Elliot's that I wanted to check and that was if he had the habit of looking you in the eye when he spoke to you or if he looked away. He never took his eyes from mine whether we were being serious or just joking around. I liked that very much. We found ourselves to be compatible wanting the same things professionally and personally and to have success and only success. We bonded with and with no doubt I bonded with him like no other person before with all of my experiences of dealing with people.

In the field of immigration I am with no doubt an expert because I have studied it in detail. Elliot showed surprise and was amazed that I hadn't been to law school with as much as I knew regarding the law. That was one thing he didn't quite believe about me. He said jokingly without trying to offend me, "Angelo, perhaps you were disbarred and now you need me." I found it very funny and I laughed. "May I ask a personal question?" Elliot asked.

Purposefully I didn't answer him. I wanted him to wonder about me and come to the right conclusions on his own of my knowledge of the law. I told him "Elliott, we have talked about so much tonight there is hardly anything left that you don't know about me that is personal, so go ahead and ask," I replied.

He said "In this journey in the new endeavor for myself and for us in the immigration business, will we find ourselves breaking any laws?"

"I don't break the law," I told him. "I only walk a fine line rubbing on the shoulder of the law but never breaking it, as only a fool would do that. You can rest assured that I am no fool. Everything we will do will be absolutely legal."

He laughed heartedly and with pleasure said, "Well, I guess we can travel to Pakistan and India, so when do we leave?"

"You see, I knew you would take me up on this Elliot. I have already arranged it. Tomorrow my friend," I said. "We will pick up the tickets tomorrow in Monterey Park at my friend Tono's office and then be on our way to the exotic capitol city of Islamabad in Pakistan."

Elliot seemed very emotional as we were boarding the plane to travel internationally. It was his first time to travel out of the country and he looked almost like a little boy almost about to cry for his mother. I put my hand on his shoulder and kissed his left temple and whispered to him, "Don't worry, I know how you feel. This is an experience you never could know what was like unless you took it yourself."

Then two days later, there we were. It was early in the morning and we were in an exotic country in the far east in the capitol city of Islamabad in Pakistan. We had settled comfortably in our suite at the hotel Ishtafar, a family owned establishment decorated in a Mongolian Arabian style. It was definitely a culture shock for Elliot in every way.

My friend Elliot and I already had a busy day scheduled but that didn't stop the phone from ringing and making our plans even more hectic than they already were. We had meetings scheduled with many intellectuals who held degrees in many fields and were anxious to move to the United States and make it home. During our meetings and as I had expected it seemed everyone had some kind of computer science degree and wanted to go to Silicon Valley in California, or to Phoenix, Arizona, to work for Motorola.

With all that we had to tried to and did accomplish I regretted not being able to fit in something I always wanted to do if I ever made it to this part of the world. That was to visit the Pakistani part of Cashmere. It is one of three places that any visitor would want to see. There is Mecca, the most holy place in Islam, Bethlehem, the birthplace of Christ, and I truly believe Cashmere is the third just because of it's sheer beauty.

The local people in the cafés where I had spent a few days had once called the beautiful land of Cashmere a paradise. Since Pakistan has become an independent country it has turned into one more neighborhood of hell on earth.

Elliot and I were curious to see the former paradise. Our wishes for that visit did not come true during our stay. I didn't feel so bad when he told me about someone else who he knew personally, surprisingly from a pretty high place, the White House, that had a similar experience of not getting to visit Cashmere.

Out of curiosity I asked, "Who was that?"

He laughingly replied, "Madeline Albright, the Secretary of State to President Clinton. She was here and because of security reasons she was not allowed to visit beautiful Cashmere although she very much wanted to."

I replied, "Of course not, the position she held put her personal freedom out the window so there was good reason she didn't get to see it. Here she was, one of the most powerful ladies on the planet and because of the position she held she was not free to go anywhere and everywhere she would like. That is the sacrifices one has to sometimes make and choose to give up their own personal freedom in order to reach their goals to serve their country and people. We should be able to do whatever we want on the other hand, just being ordinary Joe's and not so famous."

Elliott said that Madeline had promised when she was no longer in office she would come back and visit Cashmere. It must be even more special than I ever thought.

I said, "I hope her dream will come true, but since I'm not Secretary of State and just an ordinary citizen, either I will get to visit

Cashmere now or I will have to just keep my dream in the works and come back later."

The following Friday morning I was up before sunrise. Our suite at the hotel faced one of the most popular local hang outs, the Café Bengal which was right across the street and I could see it as I looked out the window and all of the hustle and bustle of the crowds, some were dressed traditionally and some in the western fashion. Right away one could see the mixture and the mosaic of cultures and the people which I was about to discover. This is the spot as I looked out the window that was a famous place where I was about to meet some new friends, and it was the Café Bengal that I was looking at. It's a place that has been there for no less than a hundred years.

I found the cafe, just like I was told by my friend Amir, who was born there and now resides in the United States, to have a magical and warm atmosphere and uniquely designed architecture of a Hindu, Oriental, and Persian blend. It has an ambience like none other I have ever seen. On each of the wooden pillars that hold all the massive arches are the imprints of fingers and hands of people who have passed through. In ancient times before the industrial revolution and the arrival of the automobile to this part of the world this place was a meeting spot for the caravan traders complete with their trains of camels and horses.

Just by being at the café you can sit and relax and touch a piece of furniture or gaze at one of the pieces of art, or appreciate the craftsmanship of one wall or pillar inside and feel all around you the good energy and aura of the noble men who have walked through this place before you.

Stories are repeated often even today about the good hearted men who once passed through here. One is about on a special day that Jews, Christians, and Muslims alike celebrate. It is the day when Abraham went to sacrifice his son to God as a test of his faith, and instead at the last moment God replaced his son with a ram. It is celebrated as a day for giving to the poor. Café Bengal still practices that tradition even today. It is the biggest Muslim celebration after all to reflect on all the blessings in your life and give to the less fortunate. People come from all over bringing food, clothing and things the poor need to be distributed to them. Once the story has it that a merchant left half of his goods from his caravan for the poor without leaving his name. He said that just that by being at the Café Bengal inspired him to be so generous.

Throughout the last century the café has developed a reputation as a place where the influential and elite once did, and still do, make and break deals that perhaps have affected the outcome of history all over the globe at some time.

Everything that is surrounding you even from outside at its entrance creates a therapeutic, relaxing feeling. They say that even the Cashmere prince and English governor during their occupations of India, before the independence of Pakistan, visited this café as well as many ordinary people like myself and my buddy Elliot.

Someone once told me that Prime Minister Butta started his campaign at this very cafe. Unfortunately he was hanged after winning the ministerial position to lead Pakistan shortly after taking office as the prime minister. His daughter, however, was elected years later to lead Pakistan as prime minister, a woman who helped to make her father's dream come true. She made Pakistan a nation to be respected, but was impeached during the last year of her second term, not because of any wrong doing by her but by her husband who abused the power that his wife's office gave him. It was better than her father's fate and least she did not end up hanged like her father twenty years before. It showed how far Pakistan had come as a civilized and democratic nation. At least there was an appearance of law and order, and a more civilized outlook replaced hanging and lynching.

I wondered if the legend told about the Café Bengal either being a curse or a blessing to some was a myth or just coincidental. They said some of the people who visited would either become infamous or be jinxed after being at this strange yet beautiful place.

I decided I would try something that I hadn't heard of anyone trying before, and that customs and tradition in Pakistan allowed. That was to be an even more generous customer than I usually am. I thought maybe if I earned favor from the sources of whoever or whatever was in charge of the fates and souls of those that had already passed through as well as present patrons, that they would grant me favor and the good luck charms from the place.

Each morning I looked forward with excitement to go to the Café Bengal and have my coffee. I would buy breakfast and coffee for anyone. I'd tell the waiter to hold the tab for me and treat for coffee and breakfast for people whom I'd never met before, yet felt that I had known all my life. The people knew that it was taken care of and felt I did it out of the warmth of my heart and not because they needed me to. I did that for the three days I was there. Ironically no one found it strange even though I hoped that no one had done this for them before. The same thing happened there every day, except it wasn't by a stranger like me but one of their own who came there every day and felt like blowing some of their money away and feeling like a big shot. Then everyone would look at him and joke that he must have had a good business day and wonder where he got all the dough. Everyone would laugh and have a good breakfast. They were not that surprised by my generosity but were very appreciative after all it was tradition for ones who were able to afford it or the newcomers who wanted to get know people. This was a way to do it and get your name known very quickly.

They would greet me with a deep bow, moving their bodies, hands, and eyes at the same time, looking respectful, strong, and proud. They reminded me of a strong tree bending in a powerful wind, being powerful and strong yet submitting to another powerful and strong source of nature. That meant to me an acknowledgement of mutual respect. As they bowed down they would say that wonderful phrase of Islam, "As salaam Alaikum," which means, "Peace be with you." This greeting of respect is not familiar in the west, unfortunately. As a westerner myself I found it to be very beautiful and sincere.

It seemed I became an instant celebrity and was feeling that the good spirits were on my side. I think if I had stayed one more day they would have been expecting me every day to take care of the tab and I had better not be late. Generally I felt very comfortable there and being with the people there. My friend Elliot thought I was crazy. Maybe I just wanted to show off that I could afford to buy now, once being called a poor little Muslim boy in my birthplace of Montenegro, who now felt like he had made it.

As I was drinking coffee with Elliot my cellular started right away to make its alarming sounds, so I answered it. It was a call from Las Vegas, and no ordinary phone call. At first I thought it was just my boys from home wanting to say hello. The call came from my restaurant, the Prima Café in Summerlin, an upscale development on the outskirts of Las Vegas. On the other end of the line was my manager Eddie, who sounded very serious and worried. He said, "Angelo, there is a man here who is looking for you."

I thought I would play a little joke with Eddie since I already knew who it was, and he seemed so nervous about the man he just met who was trying to reach me. "Can you describe for me what the man looks like?"

He said, "He looks well built and strong with white hair. He looks like a military man, or maybe the police. He says his name is Pace."

I responded in feigned surprise. "Never met the man. Ask him what he wants, and Eddie, do me a favor please and ask him to open up the left side of his jacket to see if he's wearing a piece."

I could hear Eddie's voice shaking as he said, "Ok, boss, ok." I heard him say, "Sir, my boss asked that you would pull back the left side of your jacket." Eddie hesitated and in gasped to me in surprise, "Hey, boss, he does have a piece!"

"Eddie, hand him the phone," I said sternly. "Maybe I can strike a deal with him so he won't rob the place and shoot you."

He was handing over the phone before I had even finished talking. I was glad to hear the voice of my friend and colleague Giles Pace. I had missed hearing from him because he had been gone for quite a while on a dangerous mission in Bosnia. In a way we were both on a dangerous missions.

During my visit to Pakistan on immigration business I also had related plans that Pace and I had discussed before concerning his visit to Bosnia and my visit to Pakistan. I wanted to discuss how we could create one path together that could enable us to provide weapons to the Bosnians. I told him that when I went to the Bosnian Embassy I received a cold welcome from all the staff there, and right from the start it seemed doomed.

Pace told me, "I warned you about that. I got the same treatment when I went there last year." His experience had also been disappointing in Tuzla.

I told him how when I was at the embassy compound I observed someone that I assumed was the ambassador's young son driving around in an electric toy car.

"Yes, I remember that boy." Pace said. It crossed my mind that meanwhile the children in Bosnia that I was hoping we could try to save were dying. From the start it was already a sinking mission with no hopes to hold onto, just like a tiny bubble in the ocean with no hope of being saved. The people I had known since I was young during the sixties, the people I had called my own people, looked like strangers to me, and I to them. We hardly thought alike or looked alike. Pace said, "Angelo, I told you so. These people are now only out for themselves. No one believes that Bosnia will survive and everyone is just trying to save their own lives. Don't be too hard on yourself."

His words comforted me but the hope I was looking for was diminishing. I told him, "Please spare me from my internal bleeding."

The first thing officials at the embassy told me was that I looked American, talked American, and thought American. I didn't get right to the issue I wanted to touch base on, the crisis in our homeland. I said to the ambassador and a couple of staff members outside in the courtyard where the child who was never even introduced to me was still driving the car around and around us and making noise, "This is the second time that I have received the best compliment of my life, one I've waited the last thirty years for." Unfortunately, it came from people I didn't care to hear it from. I am always asked where I am from because of my accent. In the States I am reminded almost every day that I am not a citizen by birth, and so the compliment did and did not matter to me.

The first time I got that compliment was in similar fashion but more profoundly expressed and was from Ambassador Sven Alkali at the Bosnian Embassy in Washington D.C. when he said, "Angelo, I have traveled the United States and Canada and have met many Bosnian Americans, and you are the only one I have met who thinks, looks, and always does things truly as an American ought to." His expertise on that I think was not that great since he had only been in the country a few months and knew very little about the American way of life. I still took the compliment in stride.

I told the ambassador I was sorry to hear that I was the only one he thought that of. I think when we choose a new homeland as our adopted new land we should accept and adapt to the land's culture and way of life while still holding on to a tight grip of the roots where we came from. "So thank you from the bottom of my heart," I told him. I had finally passed the exam of a true citizen in my adopted homeland. I am so proud of it.

Pace and I both looked forward to hearing from each other about any progress from our respective trips that may have been accomplished. After hearing his laughter and joy Eddie realized that Pace was my good friend and he wasn't going to be robbed anytime soon, at least not by Pace.

"Angie, my buddy, you son of bitch you, why did you have to scare that boy so much?" Pace asked, laughing.

"I wouldn't worry too much, he is a tough boy," I told him. "I thought you were going to meet me in Pakistan. What happened to you?"

He replied, "As you told me Angie, it was tough going entering Bosnia, and even tougher getting out. It seemed like we were surrounded with an invisible wall of the enemy on every side who were thirsty for the blood of your people. I can even call them my people now. Everything has become personal. Their war is my war and you and your people's war is my war."

I told him, "I am thrilled and honored to have you on my side and there is no place in my heart for doubts now. I know we will prevail and win because our cause is a just cause. I even made a bet with some Serbs here at the athletic club behind the Stardust. I was working out and kicking the bag when this Serbian guy, Dushan wanted to talk about the war in Bosnia. I told him that whatever he thinks or sees now they were going to lose and I was going to kick his fucking ass too. I told him to get the hell away from me, I didn't need to talk to Nazis. Let's make sure we walk the same road Pace, with the same determination to win. I hope someone who lives through this goes on to tell the story. If I can and I make it, I promise I will."

Now I am telling it just like it happened. I would give everything not to tell this horror story. In one sense I hope this story will prevent such horrifying events ever happening again and another example of history repeating itself. There has to be a way to close the door to another occurrence of these horrific and tragic events that should not have ever happened in the first place

I was anxious to hear the outcome of Pace's travel in the Balkans. "Did you go the mosque in Zagreb as I directed to you?" I asked him.

He said, "I did and was received well. They connected me there with a caravan that was going to Herzegovina. The caravan was so large and to my surprise there were lots of guns, food, medicine, blankets, and ammunition loaded inside. No one had any idea how to cross and avoid the Croatian militias and enter Bosnia."

Pace continued to elaborate, "I looked through the group of people and noticed two young boys who spoke English. I asked them if they had maps of the Bosnian area. To my surprise they showed me military maps like the ones you and I looked at when we were visited by Naval Intelligence at the Howard Hughes Plaza. Where they got them I don't know, but it was even better than I had hoped. They had exactly what I needed, detailed directions of every possible route including mountain roads and dirt roads. Their military didn't even know about these routes and probably wouldn't have noticed even if they had the maps.

"I found the drivers on that caravan the craziest people I ever met," Pace said.

I laughed and said, "Pace, they're not crazy, they just know they have no other options, succeed or die."

"Man, they drove those trucks through such narrow dirt roads which you could properly call donkey trails. No one else in a semi truck would ever even dare. I was really impressed by one guy named Meho. When he was sitting behind the wheel, I swear he must have felt as if he was part of that truck's body," he said. "It was flawless driving, I mean flawless, inspiring the other drivers to do it too."

I was thrilled just listening to him.

"We were ambushed by some Chetniks after crossing into Bosnia from Croatia," he said, referring to the notorious bands of guerrillas serving the leaders of Serbia for many decades. "I'll tell you I was the one who fired the first shots for your people."

In his telling me he was so exited and jubilant like he couldn't wait to tell me about it. I was overcome with emotion and called him my brother. "Thank you, for what you are doing for our people."

"We were sitting ducks, Angie," he told me. "The Chetniks were just over a hill looking straight at us. From the very first shot we received from them, I tell you it was just like Vietnam with the Special Forces."

I said, "It looks like you had all the fun."

Pace said, "I did, and I emptied two clips of AK-47 rounds all into the right places."

"Don't tell me they didn't throw you pineapples?" I asked.

He said, "No, they never had the chance."

"Not even a couple of rocket pears from RPG's?" I asked.

"Nope," he answered. "They didn't have time to fire back, they were too busy dodging away from what we were shooting at them."

"You probably sent them to their mamas, or maybe they just went to Hell where they belong."

"I think they went directly to Hell, Angelo, and they missed the road to Heaven," he said. "From there it was a free ride all the way to Tuzla. Three days later we finally arrived. When we got to the city after that gruesome and seemingly impossible drive, I reported to the commander and president in charge of the Tuzla area of civil defense."

I said, "That would be President Alija Islabogovic."

I corrected Pace and told him he hadn't met the president of Bosnia.

Pace said, "I know Angelo, I met the president of Tuzla county, Beslagic. He is a great man, Angelo, a good leader, strong in character and heart, but their defenses were so weak that when they took me to inspect their bunkers on the defensive lines, I could immediately see that anyone could have overrun it. They had no idea how to fortify their defenses. I asked the president if he would allow me to reorganize the defense lines since we had the tools and people to do it. He told me the command was mine, and I should do whatever needed to be done, and the men would obey my orders. I reinforced each bunker by digging them in twice as deep as they were, and I put three layers of heavy dirt and wood in a crisscross form. Pretty soon I had each one looking like a strong intimidating fortress and that's what was needed.

"The enemy was unbelievably close," he went on. "In some places we were only fifty to a hundred feet apart. Everyone knew each other by name from both sides of the line, as they had all been neighbors only days before this tragic war. That was the most astonishing thing, that they were now mortal enemies. At times they hurled insults by name to each other, cursing each other's mothers and sisters by their names. It seemed like sometimes they were doing it just out of boredom, while waiting for something to happen. Maybe they just needed to hear that the other side was still there to keep their sanity but at the same time fearing the enemies voices were still there."

Pace told me they were shouting the worst Bosnian curse, "Jebmti Krvavo Dijete," which means, "I will fuck your bloody little baby." Any Bosnian man would be enraged and insulted enough to kill when hearing that.

"By the time we finished our defense plans it was early morning of the third day," Pace went on. "I told one of our commanders to tell one of the Serbian commanders to stand up and look at our reinforcements, and maybe then they would consider quietly surrendering. Angie, do you know what? To our surprise, that

49

is exactly what they did. Then they sent over a liaison to ask us for a pack of cigarettes. We are shooting at each other and they call a truce to mooch cigarettes! I gave a pack of Marlboro's to our commander to hand to him. The truth is they didn't care about checking out the bunkers, but I made sure they knew about the reinforcements we made. They were checking out me, who they had already heard about. I was that American and Mormon Christian who was coming to help the Bosnians.

"About thirty minutes later they released a barrage of cannon shells on us for almost an hour. During their barrage of cannon shells and their machine guns, we were relaxing and sitting in the newly fortified bunkers talking about how we were going to give it back to them and more. When all the shooting was over on their part there was a particular cannon I wanted to quiet. I asked one of the soldiers how I could curse the Serbs in the Bosnian language. He told me, 'It's very easy, I know that guy with the cannon, he's my neighbor, his name is Mile.' Then he told me just how to curse him, saying, 'Jabot it mater, Mile,' which means, 'Fuck your mother, Mile.' He also told me how to let him know the message was from the American, because they already knew that I was there. A second later they opened fire on us again.

"I stood up Angie, and with my AK-47 told him, 'You sucker, I'll show you how to shoot!' I unloaded and gave him my experience in the Delta in Viet Nam and shot straight to where the flame from their machine gun fire was coming from about fifty yards away. After I unloaded there was total silence."

I asked, "You mean to tell me you didn't give them a twenty-one gun salute at the funeral? Man, I'm disappointed in you, but right now the only thing I can say is I love you and can't wait to see you."

"Angelo," he said, "when I arrived in Zagreb and reported to the mosque during the couple of days of preparation with the caravan, I met some interesting characters who were gun runners. They claimed to be brothers."

I asked, "What are their names, if you know?"

Pace answered, "The oldest brother's name is Alija Delamustafic, and it seemed like he was in charge. He owned several brand new Volvo semi trucks. It looked like about nine of them. He claimed he was making a killing running guns."

I said, "I have heard of him. Sadly, you have confirmed my

suspicions. He is a low life and traitor, a greedy hyena who preys on the corpses of the dead. This bastard shouldn't be selling the guns, he should be donating them to our people so they can protect themselves from being slaughtered by Serbs."

"Well, he is not doing that, Angie," Pace replied. "He is getting very rich bringing guns from Austria and Slovenia. I was told by the people who work at the mosque at Zagreb that Alija knew someone in the presidency or maybe the president himself in Sarajevo, and that he could do what he wanted. Everyone was afraid of him."

"I promise you this bastard needs to pay for getting rich on the blood of our people, even if I am the only one to make him pay," I replied. "I'll join you, I swear. He's a cocky little son of a bitch. It would be a good idea, Pace, if you would make a phone call before I get back to the States. Call Ambassador Alkali at the Bosnian embassy in Washington and ask him if we can get together to discuss this and find out what's going on. Hopefully he will be open to this issue about gun running and selling guns to the enemy. This seems like profiteering on our people's blood. This can not be happening. It has to be some kind of a bad dream."

Pace answered, "Angie, dream or not, I'm telling you this is what's happening. He and his brothers, along with a Croatian pal whose name they said was Ramljak, some kind of former soccer player or something, are big time gun runners."

I told him, "Just arrange this meeting with the ambassador and I think we can settle this issue. Goodbye for now and I'll see you soon."

To leave Pakistan, Elliot and I needed to make a stop in India but we could not fly directly into India. India and Pakistan have been at war for the last fifty years and there were no direct flights to their respective countries. Elliot and I had to fly all the way to Riyadh, Saudi Arabia. I was looking forward very much for a chance to visit and I tried before we landed to convince Elliot that it would be great if we could spend a couple of days in the capitol of Riyadh.

My Jewish friend had second thoughts but did finally agree to spend a couple of days there. I was excited about it without realizing the deep differences between Judaism and Islam that have existed over the last five decades since the creation of Israel and there was a deep mistrust between the two first cousins and the children of Abraham. I missed the boat in not seeing the reason for his reluctance in this case.

FORGOTTEN SOLDIERS

The moment we stepped off the plane officers from customs services asked my friend to follow them to their office. I insisted on accompanying him since we were business partners and I introduced myself to them showing them our business card which clearly identified him as owner and partner in a law firm specializing in crime and immigration laws.

At first they refused to allow me to come with him. They argued I had no business to go along as they only needed to talk to him. I protested and told them I would file a complaint at the American Embassy and the State Department right away. After a couple minutes of arguing in the hallway a door opened slowly and a gray-headed man with a beard stepped out with a smile on his face and motioned with his hand for me to come on in. I had spoken with him once earlier pleading our case of being allowed to walk around their city before our next flight. By then, however, I was already enraged and there was no smile on my face.

Elliot said, "Come on, Angie, go on in. They're ok."

I replied, "What do you mean they're ok? They're only ok when they open that gate for us so we can check into the hotel and relax for a couple days and see the town."

As we entered the office the door closed behind us with a loud metal clang. From the first office we saw through a clear glass window to the second office where a tall dark complexioned man with shining black hair well built and over six feet tall sat behind a desk. He spoke with a New England American accent I guessed came from Boston but he greeted me with an Islamic gesture, saying, "As salaam Alaikum, brother," as he reached with both hands to shake mine and big not very honest looking smile on his face.

I responded with, "Good afternoon, sir," which I think is as good as his greeting was and proper and good enough for me. He was surprised I didn't return his Islamic gesture since he knew I was Muslim from my name.

I said, "Sir, we are here in your respected country on our way to India. As you know India and Pakistan air spaces are closed to each others air flights, so we decided to come to your great country to spend a couple of days. I was very much looking forward to it but it looks like the good feelings and expectations I had has been ruined by the officers outside."

He was not hesitant to speak strongly. He said, "My brother,

52

you can go right now and spend as much time as you like in Riyadh but we need to ask your friend a few questions."

I told him, "I could tell you anything about him better than he can. He is not a Mossad Israeli agent for sure. He is honest and a people-loving human being and a very good friend of mine and also my business partner. If I go he goes and if he doesn't go I don't go either."

The officer was crushed and embarrassed by my forceful manner. He said, "I'm sorry brother but this is not my decision. It is a decision of higher authority. Any Jewish person who doesn't already have an approved Visa before coming to the country needs to be asked some questions."

I didn't want to waste any more time and neither did Elliot. We asked if we could just go back to a waiting area until the departure of our plane to India.

He said, "By all means, no problem and again we are very sorry if you want to stay and go anywhere in Arabia you are free to do so. You are a brother Muslim."

I laughed sarcastically and it crossed my mind that the higher authorities who order little people like us around only bring animosity and hatred and it ends up taken out on the battle fields with people dying.

I left Saudi Arabia with a feeling of regret that I even went there. I could go to any other country in the area but had chosen to go there and I doubt if I will ever go back. I want to see all men through God as equals regardless of their religion and political ideology. Man has created political and religious ideology but God has created the universe and the universe is God for me and we are all a part of it and we are all equal in creation.

Forty five minutes later we were on a 747 Pan Am jumbo jet on a flight back to New Delhi, where we spent a couple of days in the city that I would say never slept. It seemed like the whole world had come to New Delhi and lived there. The visit to India for me was a cultural shock and something I had heard about but never experienced. Animals and cows were everywhere in the streets and were treated respectfully as holy. I didn't have a problem believing that and believe in a way they are holy because they provide so much of themselves for human lives, milk, hides and fertilizer that the local people make natural gas from and nothing of the holy cow is wasted.

I personally enjoyed our trip but Elliot didn't. He just wanted to be done with our immigration appointments and get the hell out of India. I think he preferred Saudi Arabia. I told him maybe if there was no other way out of India that we definitely could always organize an old fashioned elephant caravan, and if that didn't work then maybe Aladdin could come by on his magic carpet — which I actually think is a 747 — but not to worry, we would be out of there soon, God willing.

We were finally out of India. Elliot was so happy because there was nothing to him like his Chicago, the windy city. New Delhi was a world apart in every aspect, misfortunate people forgotten by God were everywhere.

Elliot said, "Angie, if these guys ever want to do any business with us they have to come to L.A. or Chicago. I'm never going to that crazy place again. Did you see all those people? They're all wanderers. It seemed like I saw the same people in front of us and in back of us all the time, all day."

I said, "That's because they all look alike, you dumb old man. You're just losing it, you can't remember what you've seen anymore. I think you're getting senile, like Ronald Reagan, starting to forget things, but no offense O.K, I love my president."

It happened that Elliott liked him too but I told him, "I always thought you were a Democrat."

Elliot said, "No, Angie, I am a Democrat. I just think Reagan is a good president just like you do and that's why I and the rest of Chicago voted for him."

I replied, "I met Reagan once when he was visiting Las Vegas at Wayne Newton's ranch. He visited briefly during the last elections. He was charismatic and easy going but too busy to shake my hand. I thought by the way Reagan talked with Wayne that they seemed to be very close friends."

The immigration business we did in India was again successful for us. We had met quite a few individuals and intellectuals who were highly educated with degrees in many different fields like science, technology, programming and engineering.

I thought that between the trips to Pakistan and India if I succeeded in bringing all of these educated people to America I will have brought a gold mine and bonanza of educational wealth we can use right away and that we can never get enough of in the states. Our country in fact is short of qualified and educated people to fill the slots that are available. I was proud to be able to deliver this to the country.

On reflection we had legalized from San Pedro, California, more than one hundred Croatian intellectuals from every field to become productive citizens and hopefully we could do the same here.

We finally boarded our next flight straight to Honolulu where we had to stop over and landed and waited for one hour. It was beautiful and reassuring to be home in familiar land. Some passengers were boarding and the flight was packed once again. It was a smooth flight and the next thing I remembered was the stewardess telling everyone to fasten their seatbelts and we would be landing in fifteen minutes at LAX international airport.

My car was in the long term parking. We went down and picked up our luggage and an hour later were outside of customs feeling like locals. We went straight into the garage and hopped in my Porsche where it had been for the last few weeks covered with LA smog and dust. Still, boy did it feel good to be home, but I didn't let Elliot know. The first thing I did was pop in my favorite CD by Andrea Bocelli.

We headed down Interstate 405 to 10 West into the popular beach resort town of Santa Monica where we settled down at one of my favorite places I have been to many times, the Holiday Inn on Lincoln Boulevard. It overlooks the beach and the Santa Monica pier with fine restaurants and sidewalk entertainment. We checked in and showered and freshened up after our long trip. I was looking forward to visiting one of my favorite places, the Athenian Gardens and belly dance club just east of Santa Monica on Olympic Blvd.

I told Elliott during our flight to L.A. that I wanted to pay a visit to the Athenian Gardens and see one of my favorite beautiful belly dancers and also the owners and people I knew there. It was early in the evening when we arrived at the restaurant and of course we were expected and our reservations were ready. We were led to a private secluded booth that I had sat in many times before over the eight years of my patronizing this fine establishment. Every time I went there it seemed just as exciting and new as the first time. I think part of it's allure was the very beautiful girls who brought a lot of electricity and life and came from the Middle Eastern and Greek cultures with their traditions in the arts, music, and dancing.

I felt as if I had a role in the movie Casablanca with Humphrey Bogart only I'm sure my experience was even better. With all the attention I received from the beautiful ladies, well let's say I think Humphrey Bogart would be very jealous.

One thing that was different about this visit was that even though I wanted to go there very much and see the beautiful ladies, my heart was somewhere else. That was in Palm Desert, California, near the Salton Sea where a petite beautiful lady lived with her family and I would soon be visiting on our way into Las Vegas. We were at the club and our cocktails were served without the waiter coming to take our order.

Every time I went there they knew what to bring to eat and drink, my regular same favorite on the menu. I had learned when I first came to this country from the Italian boys that whatever the boss eats and drinks the rest of the boys also eat and drink. I figured the same would work for me and that whatever I would eat and drink my boys would also and it would bring our souls closer to each other.

There was wine, Turkish coffees, lamb chops, roast lamb, and not to be forgotten, a fabulously prepared Greek salad that the dinner wouldn't have been complete without.
The lamb chops and mint jelly were cooked to perfection. We were soon joined by my belly dancer friends before their show began at midnight. The owner and maitre'd shared the table with us for a few minutes at a time here and there while greeting other guests and taking care not to noticeably neglect or disrespect any of the rest of the guests.

It was obvious each and every time I arrived at the place I was always treated with respect as a guest and personal friend. Though I enjoyed the attention at times I wished I wasn't noticed as much. Sometimes too much attention spoils the good time you were wanting to have because you get too busy acknowledging everyone and returning their compliments and time seems to fly.

People become intimidated sometimes when someone else is getting all the attention and they are not getting any. Wherever I went it seemed like I always got all the attention even though that's not what I really wanted. I enjoyed commanding respect but I wanted to blend in with the crowd. It feels good not to check your shirt collar every second and to feel comfortable with everyone else.

By the end of the night I wasn't sure if I had come across as being a smart gentlemen or a dumb boor, but when I was with my friends it seemed I could do no wrong. What that did is make me check myself and reflect over the evening to make sure I had been a perfect gentleman and hadn't offended anyone in any way.

It would have been unforgivable of me not to acknowledge everyone in the place after all the attention and respect that they gave me. I had to make sure and shake every single hand and even go into the kitchen and thank the chef and give him a tip for his great dinner once again. The chef would not leave the kitchen until my visit at the end of night or it would be a night of failure for him if one of his favorite customers didn't acknowledge him for the artist he was. At the shake of my hand and embrace there was always a good tip greasing his palm to show my appreciation and tell him how wonderful his dishes looked and tasted. It is truly a compliment that every chef loves to hear.

In this way I could leave my presence to remember even after I was not there. It did not matter how long it was until I came back again. During the whole week and every week I would be a topic of conversation at least for a few minutes a night. It's a great feeling knowing that there are people who look forward to seeing you. I have to admit it can make you get a big head and grow with an ego big as a tall Sequoia tree. Thankfully I never got carried away and lost myself in the ego trip and remained a humble man but I sure did enjoy my ego at the time.

All throughout the night at the club we drank wine and danced a favorite Greek dance called the Hopa and threw money at the belly dancers, that is those who could afford to. There were one dollar bills, fives, twenties and money covering the whole dance floor. A fascinating thing that always happened and that I thought was extraordinary, was that with all that money on the floor, and not just a hundred or two but thousands, even the drunkest man would never pick up even a dollar bill to steal it. I cannot recall many games or places that are like that except in golf where one naturally keeps honest even if he is otherwise the biggest thief and crook. Somehow a golfer always feels guilty cheating in a game, like customers would if they took the belly dancers' money off the dance floor.

Why did I make this morally profound observation? I don't know but maybe because I'm a pretty decent golf player who would and could never cheat in a game, even if I lost money by being honest. I have tried to beat some of my good friends at golf for years playing the golf course at the Tropicana hotel in Las Vegas, friends like Mike

Collela, John Friendly, George Maxon and Tony Fabria Jr. from Phoenix, who are former professional golf players.

I could only beat these guys if I cheated. I wanted to beat them just once but the only chance I had was by cheating and I couldn't. I would not break the rules of honesty for the game.

I respect the art of belly dancing. I know how much and how hard the work they put into it is and is pleasing to the audience with their grace as professionals. Many times the audience is blind to that effort and exerting energy the art requires and the grace in the art to give a few minutes of enjoyment to them. That is what my friend and her partners did for us that night being so professional and artistic with grace. As I have always believed goods things like that never fade away.

In the early morning hours as the crowd dissipated and everything got quiet I was sitting with my dancer friend, Jennifer. I was complimenting the gracefulness of her dancing while at the same time taking in her beautiful body. I wished and wanted to hold her in my arms and make love to her. She would have responded to me as she has before. She would have had no objections there is no doubt and she was hoping we could spend time together after we left the club.

My plans were full already and I was running on a tight schedule. I told her I wanted to hold her and make love to her like we had in the past and promised I would see her again and cover her with roses before making love to her. I knew in my heart I would not see her again though because I was drawn to Palm Desert and my beautiful petite lady. I must admit, she was really the one I wanted to cover with roses and make love to.

Elliot and I drove from the club on to Santa Monica. We drove to the corner of Ocean and Lincoln Boulevard to the Holiday Inn. We picked up our luggage and drove back onto Highway 10 east heading to Palm Desert California to visit my favorite girl who had so taken my whole heart and mind. That was Mankiu.

Elliott assumed we were heading straight to Las Vegas. When he realized we didn't get off on the exit for I-15 North heading into Las Vegas, he asked, "Angie, where the hell you going? You missed the exit."

I replied, "I'm sorry Elliott, I should have mentioned it to you, I want to stop and see my girl, Mankiu, in Palm Desert. You will enjoy seeing where she lives. Her parents are in Hong Kong right now and she is there alone. We can relax there for a day and have some fun."

Elliott responded, "Angie, you have talked about a lot of girls you've known, but I've never heard you talk of her. How come?"

"There is something mystic about this girl and special like no other, and I think I will marry this girl," I told him. "Anything more I tell you about this girl wouldn't be fair, neither do I care to, but if it does comes true that I marry this girl you will play the role of best man, and of Godfather, grandfather, whatever you like."

Elliott laughed and said, "I accept the responsibility to be a godfather or grandfather anytime. I've never had the pleasure to play that role before, regretfully having no children of my own." I could feel the empty space in his heart.

I tried to lighten up the conversation and told him, "I think you will make a great Godfather."

He rubbed his salt and pepper full beard smiling proudly and we both laughed.

An hour later we entered the city of Palm Springs which passed through Palm Desert. Elliott was thrilled by the nature and relaxing atmosphere of the desert beauty with palm and date trees. The surrounding architecture blended with the nature. The thousands of giant electric windmills uniquely positioned throughout the hills and valleys to catch the natural wind and create electric currents for the surrounding areas and towns only added to it's beauty.

"What kind of place does she live in?" Elliott asked.

"Well let me see if I can paint a picture for you before we arrive," I said. "Every celebrity from Hollywood has owned a house in this town. Bob Hope, Liberace, Sinatra, Dean Martin, Elvis Presley, Bing Crosby, and even the charming beautiful Dinah Shore as well as many others. The home Mankiu and her family live in is a palace out of the Orient. It sits in the middle of six hundred acres of ranch and farmland. They have a couple of Arabian horses and a fish hatchery also."

Elliott looked at me as I was driving wanting me to look back at him as he asked, "Hey, your not trying to cash in on that palace are you? And what is a fish hatchery anyway?"

"No, but I'm cashing in on a real live flesh and blood beautiful girl and that will be my jackpot," I answered. "A fish hatchery is like an incubator where you grow baby fish from the eggs."

We laughed hysterically as I caught my breath and told him,

"No seriously, it is a fascinating and a very humbling experience watching hundreds of thousands of baby fish born from eggs. They float in a big container of water that constantly flows out and overflows and yet none of the babies will swim out through the drain. It made me appreciate the beauty and true magic of nature and the instinct for survival of all of the species a little bit more."

Elliott didn't seem to understand all of this and it seemed as if it was all very complicated to him. "OK Angelo, enough about the fish hatchery. How did you meet this girl?"

I said, "A couple of years ago I met a gentleman from Jakarta, Indonesia, through a friend of mine who had been killed in China. He was a true underground boss in Chinatown in L.A. and unfortunately lost his life in China while visiting there. His name was Phillip Louv. He was close friends with Eddie Nalapraya, the son of the former governor of Jakarta. I handled his legalization papers and his influence reached far beyond the Indonesian border. I had worked in Alhambra and Monterey Park around the Los Angeles area where I met Eddie and got his green card for him. It's an area that is a strong one hundred percent Asian community. Immigration is a strange business. If you are successful in doing it you become an underground instant celebrity. Your name is never spoken aloud but whispered by thousands of people, perhaps even millions. Eddie Nalapraya and I were invited to visit Hong Kong and Taiwan to meet with some Chinese businessmen who were interested in immigrating to the United States. As you already know, Elliott, England and the royal crown of the U.K. is leaving Hong Kong, and the rich business people from Hong Kong are thinking they are going to be raped by the Chinese Communist government."

Elliott asked, "What do you mean by raped, Angelo?"

"Well there are two ways to rape a person. One is raping them physically and the other is by taking away all their financial wealth and draining their moral and spiritual beliefs by kicking them out of their own countries empty handed with nothing but the shirts on their back as the Spaniards did to the Jews and Muslims during the Spanish exodus."

"I think maybe my grandma and grandpa were in Spain then," Elliott said. "I don't know, Angelo, but I know that they were not Polish descendants for sure."

"Elliott, the way you look is more Spanish than Polish so they were probably from Spain," I replied with laughter.

Elliott asked, "So why did you go to Hong Kong?"

I answered, "As I said, England was leaving and the future for many of the wealthy people there was suddenly uncertain and that's where I came in. That relates to a little saga that links my visit to Hong Kong to try to play the role of a savior and hopefully get very rich at the same time. It started at the Aladdin Hotel, a major resort that was recognized around the world as one of the godfathers headquarters with three thousand rooms in the heart of the Las Vegas strip and with more than two hundred black jack tables, six hundred slot machines, eight restaurants, and a domed theatre with eight thousand seats. It was closed down at that time because the owners had died twice in the last seven years, One of them was my dear friend Mr. Webby from St. Louis, a man who was of Lebanese and Italian descent, at least he claimed to be, as that was the only way to be able to claim the title as head of the family.

"The gaming commission had closed the hotel because of the accusations of having mafia connections. Of course they whole heartedly denied it but Mr. Webby was booted out anyway by the current senate and minority leader and the senator from Nevada who was elected because of the particular issue he took of closing the Aladdin and getting rid of mobsters. He became an instant celebrity with a new title, Senator Reid. One man got glory and a lifetime political career and the other I think died from a broken heart and couldn't live with the defeat. The second owner was from Japan, a man named Yashuda. He took the profits from the Aladdin which was his anyway to Caesars Palace or the legendary former Dunes hotel and casino to the baccarat tables where my good friend Paul Herb was supervisor and made sure he left his money there. He just couldn't keep his hands off the tables, which I thought was very unusual for the owner of a gaming establishment, to gamble with no control. I understand he didn't have to work very hard for his money. He bought the Aladdin after my friend died for almost a song considering the value of the place, for less than eighty million dollars. It also left me without my job and I promised one day I would buy the hotel back."

Elliott laughed. I told him it wasn't funny that the man bought the hotel for almost nothing and it was my understanding that he got his money selling a couple of pitiful condominiums in Tokyo where real estate at that time was priceless. It was easy for him to do whatever he was doing and put the place under by his management and blowing the profits. The local executives he hired privately resented him because he was an outsider and the fact that he was Asian and Japanese. Memories were still fresh from Pearl Harbor and he was not white American. It was a culture shock period for us locals. That helped grease his way to fail.

His purchase of the Aladdin was the topic of town and it did close when he passed away. His wife or no one else was interested in keeping the light of the Aladdin marquee on or buying it except me and I didn't have the money. I was thinking of how I could do it and in a few years time realize my dream that I hadn't shared with anyone yet. Since the Jap was dead his wife took over and didn't like what she saw because the place was in financial chaos and she made sure that Aladdin marquee light would never light again at least through her. Aladdin's three wishes from the genie had been used up and all unfortunately had ended in disaster, starting with my friend Webby. She closed the place down putting three thousand five hundred people out of jobs. I was one of the thousands of people complaining about and wanting to know what had happened to the Aladdin Hotel, and why what happened wasn't being reported on or explained or even investigated by the gaming commission. In the meantime the place was silent and dark.

I had some ideas on how to bring the Aladdin back to life but my friends in the gaming industry wouldn't listen to me. During this time real estate prices were falling in this town and the country was in a recession. The Jap's wife finally decided to put the place up for sale. Still fifty million was too much money to the local people in town and it had a reputation of being jinxed. I sure thought differently.

Harry Reid was the gaming commissioner then and now he is a senator. He became a celebrity by kicking out Mr. Webby at the Aladdin and he cashed in on the political opportunity to become a senator. As it happens, he became and a darn good one too.

The hotel was up for sale. I was ready to begin my quest to raise the money to buy the Aladdin. My friend Eddie and I went to Taiwan and Hong Kong to meet with three very wealthy investors who were willing to pay anything to get out of Hong Kong and Taiwan. I had a proposal for them to buy the Aladdin which was up for sale for fifty million dollars and told them they should look into it although I knew they could not get licensed because they were not U.S. citizens. I came up with the idea that if they were to buy the place and make myself fifty one percent owner I would guarantee to them in twelve months time they would all have legal and permanent residency."

Elliott said, "And how would you manage to do that Angelo?"

I answered, "Very easy, the INS law states as such that anyone who employs more than ten people and pays taxes on those people, the owner or owners of that company automatically become permanent residents of the U.S. In this case the odds were in my favor and I knew I would have thirty eight hundred people employed at the Aladdin Hotel and the taxes paid on those employees would be much more than I needed to legalize the four families of the businessmen."

Elliott replied, "Smart, very smart Angelo."

I replied, "My mamma didn't raise no fool but a smart boy."

Anyway in the end we didn't end up cutting the deal even though we brought them to Las Vegas to look at the purchase of the Aladdin and we had some serious discussions the deal still didn't go through.

I did meet a girl I wanted in Hong Kong however, and even though I didn't get the Aladdin, I found the girl of my dreams that I hadn't even been looking for. She was visiting Hong Kong at the time from Palm Desert, California. Her home birth place was in Hong Kong and I met her there at a restaurant where she was sitting at the table next to ours.

I noticed that she was wearing a t-shirt with Palm Desert written on it and a picture of a rose. I struck up a conversation with her by asking her to please forgive me and I didn't mean to intrude on her and her friends during their lunch, but I just had to ask, "How do I make sure that rose on your shirt can be delivered to my room after lunch?"

"The girls looked at each other and laughed and found it unusually funny. Then it was silent and she asked in her soft voice smiling what my name was." I replied by barking twice like a little dog.

She laughingly said, "Ok little doggie, what's your real name?"

I introduced myself and kissed her hand told her my name was Bajram Angelo and asked hers and then asked her to please not bark back her name because I'm afraid of dogs, especially the pretty female ones. We both burst out laughing. She said her name was Mankiu. Her girlfriend interrupted to say, "Hey I thought we were having lunch together, remember us?" She turned around to apologize and introduce me to her friends. To this day I can't remember their names.

We sat by a window overlooking the Hong Kong harbor that's view was really breathtaking. I laughed and told her that I hoped I didn't have to walk barefoot all the way up to the Buddhist monastery at the top of the mountain and seek advice from Buddha on how to get her to deliver her rose to me.

All the girls laughed again and covered their faces with their hands thinking it was very funny. She told me I was very nice but that she didn't think it was very appropriate for her being a nice girl to deliver her rose to my room as she was touching the rose on her chest. She said nice girls didn't do that and she was a nice girl but that if I didn't live too far from Palm Desert, like within four or five thousand miles, then I could call her and maybe we could have lunch sometime and then she would cut the rose off her t-shirt and give it to me.

I asked her if she was just buying time or inviting me. She answered that I didn't look like a guy who would make himself seem ungentlemanly with a girl and she asked if I that's what I was.

I told her of course not swearing holding both fingers up to take an oath. I told her what I really wanted to do was walk her over to the harbor and kiss her so passionately that one of her shoes fell off into the harbor.

"Mister, you're dreaming," she said.

I told her that I may be dreaming but I was for real and we made a date in the states and I promised I would be there. She gave me her business card with her telephone number and then turned without looking back at me. I was hoping she would, but it was still OK though, as it gave me a chance to size up her backside and check out who I had been flirting with for real. I thought, pretty nice, pretty nice, and a month later I did call her and I knew I was right, and it had been love at first sight. "Do you believe in that, Elliott, in love at first sight?" I asked him.

He replied laughing, "It's been so long ago Angelo, I can't even remember."

Now here we were just at the entrance to the gates of the ranch and I paged the call box to announce my arrival which she had been expecting. She drove a fancy little convertible toy car out to meet us at the front gate. The entrance looked rich and very oriental with two giant dragon heads that met at the top of the gates. It was intimidating to anyone seeing it for the first time. When the gates opened you were immediately introduced to a canopy of weeping willow trees that shielded every square inch of the driveway from the hot desert sun. The whole quarter of a mile long path to the house was really great to take a walk on any time of the day or night. On each side of the driveway there were two giant fish ponds filled with Koi fish, a special Japanese species of fish that are popular around the world and that people use to beautify their water ponds and gardens.

She waved and opened the gate but didn't get out of her car. I always knew she was a little shy. She motioned with her arm for us to follow her. A few minutes later we in the front of one of the beautiful water fountains which were full of the Koi fish and complimented the front entrance to the house. I walked toward her and we hugged, at the same time I introduced her to my friend Elliott. She shyly shook Elliott's hand and asked us to please come inside. She walked us through the hallway to the dining area and the dinner she was in the process of preparing for us was starting to fill the house with a delicious aroma.

I told Elliott whispering to him, "I think we're in for a real treat tonight, I think she's been working on a pretty fancy dinner for us."

Elliott replied, "I can't wait, it does smell good." Elliott was hooked right away on the artwork, statues, and vases around the house and especially the Shaolin Temple which was made from pure jade stone and at least four feet tall and three feet wide and very valuable.

It was a extraordinary piece of art even for one who such as myself is not exactly a connoisseur of fine art and sculpture. I could see and appreciate it's beauty with ease.
Elliott had forgotten for a moment about Mankiu and me. He was checking out every piece of art on the lower level of the house which was designed purposely to incorporate all of the paintings and sculptures throughout the house. It almost reminded me of the Metropolitan Museum.

I thought I'd take the opportunity to visit alone with my girl in the kitchen. I was kicked out in a second of course so I went to join Elliott wandering around the house.
I told Elliott, "I will be your tour guide now. I just got kicked out of the kitchen."

Elliott said, "You really think the world of this girl, don't you Angie?"

I said, "Well she may not the prettiest girl in the world's eyes but to me she is although I think beauty is in the eyes of the beholder and I am definitely in love with her. I think she has never been kissed by anyone except by her mother and father."

Elliott said, "What does her name, Mankiu, mean?"

I answered, "It means a pretty little one, and that she is. By the way, I think she is going to line up a job at UCLA and I think she will make a good professor too."

A few minutes later she called that dinner was ready and it sure was. She served three different kinds of fish all raised on their farm, tilapia, rainbow trout, and giant shrimps, all cooked to perfection. We also had good California red and white wines and a Chinese plum wine which I requested to her we should have. I knew Elliott hated that kind but would drink it so as not to insult Mankiu.

Dinner was absolutely great and I asked Mankiu if she would show us her laboratories where the baby fish eggs hatched. She was glad to show us her scientific knowledge and her laboratories. She took us on a tour around the grounds and showed us her new giant water pond with beautiful newly planted date and palm trees including some Japanese pines.

Jokingly Elliott asked me when I would be moving in. I said, "We're lucky to be spending the night here since mom and dad are away in Hong Kong, otherwise we'd both be in a hotel room, so don't push your luck."

Laughingly Mankiu replied, "Don't worry, even my dad would allow you to spend the night here. He trusts me." She turned around and pointed to two windows down at the other end of the house and said, "That one will be Elliott's and the one farthest away on the other side of the house will be yours, Angelo." We all busted out laughing and I told Elliott he was going to pay for shooting off his big mouth.

I asked her if we could saddle up the Arabian horses and take a ride before sunset. She called to one of the ranch hands who lived at the ranch, an elderly man named Carlos, a very gentle man of Mexican decent who was glad to get the horses ready for us to ride.

Mankiu had her own favorite, an American Indian pony with many spots on his body and we were on two of the other beautiful Arabian horses. After an enjoyable ride we were then back at the house a couple of hours later.

I had a chance during our horseback ride to talk to my friend

Pace in Las Vegas on my cell phone about what our next move regarding the Bosnian war was going to be.

We arranged to meet the next morning in Las Vegas at my Summerland restaurant, the Prima Café, so that we could discuss everything.

Early the next morning we thanked Mankiu for her hospitality and headed down I-15 North towards Las Vegas.

I asked Elliott where he would like to stay, at my house, or if he would rather go and watch my former girlfriends' legs and stay at the Rio.

Elliott answered, "Don't be a smart guy, you know what I like, I've been a guest at the Rio many times and the girls treat me good there and I already told you they don't act like they mind sharing themselves with someone as experienced and old as me."

I said, "You mean the cocktail waitresses? They want your money, you old fool." I laughed and said, "You're lucky I never caught with one, I would have arranged for you to have a cast on one of your legs."

"Hey, hey, hey!" Elliot responded, "Is that the way you treat good customers in Las Vegas?"

I said, "Of course, haven't you seen the desert in Las Vegas? The whole thing is a cemetery, for the men there are no markers, only for pets. Well maybe some have the men have markers."

"Who would they be?" Elliot asked.

I replied, "They are a very special breed, they gamble, lie, cheat, drink and use hookers six days out of the week, twenty-four six. The seventh day they all go to the Catholic church on Las Vegas Blvd. to confess all their sins."

"Did you ever go there to confess Angie?"

"Hell yes, and I was thrown out. The priest said since I was only half Roman Catholic he couldn't give me the communion. I was honest, telling the truth, I was Roman Catholic from my ancestors of two hundred years ago. I think I really pissed him off because he thought I was joking, so he shut me out of the Sunday mass. That was it for me."

Elliot said, "You were lucky Angie. The burden was lifted from your shoulders. Now you can you be as bad as you like without anyone to answer to, not even His Almighty." We laughed while Bocelli singing played on and I tried to compete with his singing.

As soon as we got to Vegas and got Elliott settled at the Rio

Hotel, I phoned Pace and said we would meet him soon at the restaurant and talk more where we had left off.

When we did met up it was really good to see Pace again. We both very anxious to discuss all the events that had been happening. We discussed the daily debates from the U.N., the quarrel between the French, Germans, and English about who would play Goliath and who would play David in saving or destroying Bosnia such as that illiterate English Prime Minister, John Major, who through his actions helped put Bosnia to a spin into Hell, Mitterand of France, or the U.N. secretary whose name I don't even wish to mention, but will anyway, Butros-Galli.

How could it have happened that these people held the key and more power than God for the life line to my ancestral land of Bosnia? If they wanted to play God, which in this situation they were, then the appropriate phrase from Shakespeare, "to be or not to be," applied to them, not for lending aid but instead for opening the doors of genocide, which is exactly what they did. However it is worth it to note that the U.K. tried to redeem themselves and finally tried to come to the aid and at least try to prevent more of the genocide that had already been done, although it was many days too late and many pounds too short. Like we say in America, "A day late and a dollar short." It was a failed mission to save the innocent.

CHAPTER THREE: AN HISTORICAL CONTEXT

I was glad to hear from Pace although his news was not good or what I was hoping to hear. I looked forward to getting to Las Vegas the first thing that morning. I noticed he looked clearly stressed and during our conversation I reminded my friend Pace, "the lone warrior" as I called him, that there have been many wars before the one that was going on now and there would be many wars after this, but no nation has ever conquered and won over all. The land masses are easy to conquer but hearts and minds of people have never been easily conquered. That takes a natural gift and talent with a lot of planning and understanding of ones culture, traditions, and faith. All of that must be conquered before anyone could claim to have conquered a nation or the nations. Only by reaching out with hands of goodwill and truth has anyone succeeded in conquering the land and people at the same time. In history there have only been a few leaders who have conquered the land and the hearts and minds of the people and sustained their leadership. One was Cyrus the Great of Persia whose empire stretched all the way from the Indian Ocean to the mouth of the Danube River on the shores of the Black Sea and throughout the land of Alexander, which is today Macedonia.

It seems that in over six millennia of history it has taught us nothing of the treachery and destruction of war. Every war has had a destructive leader and they all have failed to dominate the people by being bad kings or generals making bad and not thought out decisions, either dominating the people or the land, and never the two together. They never had the common sense to incorporate both and win both the land mass and the people, so as to then be able to call himself a true conqueror as Darius of Persia did do. I cannot recall any other leader who lived out a full life as a true conqueror. If both of the bodies, land and people are not conquered at the same time as one in the battlefields then there cannot be a true empire. It is only oppressive because the people are still resisting whoever is trying to conquer them. The resistance that arises shows the weakness and the inexperience of the new conqueror revealing that there is something in him that has broken the society he thinks he will conquer, most of the time it is the laws of the land that he breaks and its structure is not repairable, and leaves the door open for another destructive leader to walk in.

History has shown us in one example of Phillip of Macedonia, the father of Alexander the Great, who failed time and again to conquer with brutal force his southern cousins, the Athenians. He had fought all his life with his neighbors to expand his empire and failed in every attempt, winning over either just the land or just the people but never both. Each time that he lost in the battlefields he lost not only the battle but more and more of his own self respect. Finally he was give a new title, "Barbarian," with no doubt one could say he deserved. His son Alexander I think was just as disillusioned as his father was only smarter by watching the mistakes his father had made and becoming bitter and vengeful about the failures of his father at the same time. He did get his vengeance on a scale he perhaps never imagined. After the death of his father Philip, he built formidable forces of armies and in a very short time conquered every province of southern Greece.

In the western frontier at the boundaries of his new empire of Macedonia there was already a power broker empire of one of western Europe, the Roman Empire, already an old and stable empire, yet not strong enough to go any further than they already had and not really looking or dreaming of expansion at that time. Regardless of this complacency and the Romans' contentment as they were, Alexander's legacy was a prophecy that neither himself nor Rome could foresee for the future glory in Rome, and what it would become with his treacherous wars over his thirty year rule. Those wars opened and reawakened ambitions in Rome to become as glorious and powerful as it eventually did. There was no credit or glory for Alexander in opening that road. In the short period of thirty years he looted and burned everything that had been built throughout the centuries in the Persian empire covering large masses of lands from the Indian Ocean, across Mesopotamia, Armenia, Anatolia (today's Turkey), and bordering to the mouth of the Bosphorus, and the Black and Aegean Seas. For three decades Rome stood patiently watching. A short time after Alexander's death the Roman empire came to pick up the pieces of the failing empire that Alexander had left in ruins and without wasting a single arrow or spear.

So the ancient world of Rome became even more prosperous in every way. These events created an industrial revolution for Rome in fishing, farming, mining and some primitive textile as well as wealth in advancement in literature and the libraries and in the wealth and beauty in Athenian architecture . The Romans took every advantage of bringing this wealth of knowledge to Rome, and it become richer overnight just from picking up Alexander's mess. A vast mass of land stretched from the Mediterranean to the Indian Oceans and the Caspian and Black Sea all the way to the north Atlantic to the island of Brittany, and it suddenly became one nation under Rome's rule. It was a golden time for the next thousand years.

It was a world that lived in peace before Alexander and he had ravished and plundered it. One could call him a radical and power hungry, or just a plain mad young man determined to leave his mark on history and how he did it or what outcome didn't matter to him, only that there would be victorious and glorified returns for himself. Ironically, he ended up stateless and never wanting to return to his homeland, the impoverished Macedonia. He and his father originally only wanted for Macedonia to be a state of paradise. As any man throughout history has come to find, another human's bloodshed will never pay off and make them rich. Alexander as well as his father paid the ultimate price. As it has been done before him he ultimately failed just like all of the others.

Rome saw an opening after Alexander's unexpected sudden death. The empire he had just conquered and called his own was once strong and powerful, and was now just a nation with broken wings and was unable to defend or protect itself after his death. Rome moved in to fill the gap by invading the North African continent like vultures circling a dead corpse. As I see it by studying Alexander the Great and his thoughts, after he conquered the Persian empire he wasn't on his way back to Macedonia. He planned to come back and head west from the east with his army and conquer the Roman empire, but his sudden death changed all that, and Rome was spared the agony of Alexander's dream of conquering the west. That was not the only time almost unexplainable events spared Rome and the Roman Empire from bloodshed from outside forces. One could only wonder what kind of world it might be like today without Rome and if Alexander had lived to fulfill his dreams.

Alexander's destiny was not to be. The Romans conquered his homeland of Macedonia, his new adopted homeland of Egypt, and the capitol city of Alexandria as well as the rest of his empire. The rest is history.

Alexander "The Great" as some historians call him, I call "The Spoiler" and justly so. The reason being that he put the world in a backspin with his invasions on the Persian empire and did not contribute anything to the world then or ever on his short span of terror in his short life. It perhaps very good that a man such he had a very short life. Many of the kingdoms that he had conquered wished it had been even shorter. Only Rome benefitted in the end. He used only butchery for his betterment and his own well being and status. The countries he conquered were in every way, economically, scientifically, and agriculturally advanced beyond what Alexander himself could ever imagine.

His father's empire was one of the poorest in the region. He witnessed his father fighting the Greeks and losing every battle. It engraved in him a quest and thirst to invade and seek vengeance on the southern Greeks and to do what his father was unable to do.

He envisioned as a young man of conquering southern Greece and uniting it with Macedonia thus making him a dominant player in military as well as economic power and increasing the mass of land and population under his rule. He could also capitalize by incorporating along with his own army the vast Greek forces that were already there and well trained but had no leader. Alexander had learned from the ancient warriors of Sparta. He become a symbol of that to the southern Greek world of being like the Spartan patriot warrior who refused to retreat in the heat of battle.

Prior to his attack on the Persian empire he knew he needed a weapon to give him an advantage on the battlefield and not require the use of a charriot since the Persians already had that and he needed something more deadly and it would also require men who believed in him and his leadership and the weapon he would introduce to his soldiers. And he did have one. Through his genius and creativity he invented and introduced a long sharp deadly spear with a cast bronze point. It was an advantage that compares in today's battlefields to that of an F-16 jet fighter or even more profoundly an M1 American tank. Alexander's new weapon, the long spear, brought Alexander on the cutting edge of his times just as we as Americans feel today to be on the cutting edge of our times. One can only imagine the feeling of superiority of the well fit men having that long spear with a sharp and deadly point cast in bronze that could pierce the body of a horse as easily as a loaf of warm bread.

On the other hand today, the M-1 tank is capable of traveling hundreds of miles and delivering deadly blows to anything with no place to hide from it. Imagine the feeling of superiority of having such sophisticated weapons. Those weapons helped deliver the dreams of the leaders and nations and help them to become triumphant on the battlefields.

Alexander also had the loyalty of his men and won the loyalty of the vast Greek army that he had just defeated with his charasmatic leadership. On the front lines of the battlefield the Greeks hearts and minds were easily won over even though he was the enemy, although one to be feared and respected. It was just as it had happened in the land of Anatolia and the Babylons. A half-million strong army ceded and betrayed their own king of Pursia to join Alexander and that was the breaking point when the most elite of that Persian army joined Alexander and his long spear and brought with them the weapon that Alexander had also dreamed of having, charriots with two Arabian horses commanded by well trained soldiers. The four units of horses, men and the charriots along with the spear fuctioned as one powerful body. Alexander along with this new force paved the road to his invasion of Babylon and the capitol of the Babylons, Baghdad, and then finally the nations of Persia and India.

Baghdad always was the historical center for learning in literature, art and science. In a new era at the beginning of the twenty first century we find ourselves once again with volunteer armies marching to Baghdad to overthrow a tyrant, but not with the same ideas as Alexander had had. These armies in this new American empire are truly liberating the people of Babylon. History has repeated herself. The tyrant ruler was captured hiding in a fox hole in the ground just as his predessor was during the Persian invasion. A million men from Baghdad's army walked away from the battlefield knowing they had no chance to win and with again an awesome difference in military might. One could say the genie was favoring the American soldiers freedom fighters and Aladdin and his carpet could well be the F-16s and stealth fighters that were watching over these young men defeating the ancient nation and defeating the evil ruler, stripping him of his power.

In contrast of then and today, the long wooden bronzed headed spears and the Arabian warrior horses were replaced by the heavy artillary tanks and stealth fighters. My own home country, the United States of America has helped make that possible. Who's to say that history does not repeat itself? Baghdad has been conquered once again under the leadership not of a king or prince but of my President George

Bush.

The southern cousins of Alexander, the Greek generals and
their armies had slowly and surely been becoming to be leaderless.
Their fate was no doubt already written that an invasion was coming
and it happened to be their cousin Alexander from the north. I don't
think the loss to Alexander on the battlefield was a loss in their pride
but what they wanted and needed without admitting it and that was a
strong leader and that is what they got. The Greek army needed a
general and a leader who was like Alexander in battle and they got him
through being conquored by him. Alexandar took advantage of the
opportunity and mastered a half million able men willing and eager to
fight for him. Now he could not lose because he had conquered the
southern Greek territories. He won over the Greek army and they
pledged their alligence to him. After conquering the Greeks with
hardly any resistance there is no doubt Alexander saw himself as being
invincible. Some loyal generals from the Greek army even proclaimed
Alexander to be some kind of son of God. His mother affirmed it and
wasn't denying it. One more good shot of power in the arm for the
young warrior and a statue of respect for his mother.

It was the right move for him to go against Persia. His life had
changed instantly beyond his wildest dreams but he had handled it the
right way. I think he was aware of the possibilites and to be anything
less than he was becoming would mean he might not live to see
another day. He was surrounded he knew with others with ambitions
that were as strong as his own and wanted to be one step ahead of
everyone else and maintain that edge and the respect of his group of
advisors surrounding him. He may have learned over time but at the
time he didn't or couldn't as young and ambitious as he was appreciate
just what he had. He had proven to be very charismatic and creative
and willing to take chances more than his predecessors or opponents
had which perhaps gave him that edge over his generals and advisors.
The qualities of leaders like this are the true characteristics separating
men from the boys.

He himself had nothing to lose of his father's poverished
empire in Macedonia simply because his father had left him with
nothing, and he never looked back because he understood all of that
and knew there was nothing of Macedonia in a structured kind of state
that he could go back to except for some barbarian farmers, called so
by his cousins he invaded, the southern Greeks and the only name they

called them just as the Romans had in the northern territories. He had everything to gain by pressing forward. That is the true distinction and separation of the men and boys. The men will win and the boys will lose in those situations. It makes no difference if he comes from the side of the barbarians or the so called civilized side. It is important to know what one wants and how to go about getting it and then being smart enough to keep it and stay alive to enjoy it. It is a tough task, is it not?

It's very tragic when a man like Alexander who plundered and destroyed everything in his path with his mighty army all the way to the Hindu River on the edges of the Indian Ocean only gained fame after his death and who was not allowed by fate to reflect and possibly enjoy and rebuild what he had plundered and looted. You could say his conquering was wasted on himself. It was obvious that he didn't get to see what he thought was going to be a great outcome. The riches he had seen made him forget even his own birthplace in Macedonia, perhaps he was now ashamed of it.

In these circumstances I would call him a man who had ruled for a brief period of time a vast mass of land and yet in his heart felt stateless, wishing not even to be returned to his homeland in Macedonia that he wished not to claim and to be buried.

One can see why. The world he left in Macedonia was backward and undeveloped in every way. Even today there is nothing that shows anything of any wealth or riches they ever had, no monuments of any kind to show that Macedonia was ever a prosperous and thriving society. It was a land of barbarians with sticks and stones just as the Romans and the Greeks had always called it.

With Alexander's invasion of Greece he had only everything to gain and nothing to lose. His army was from every walk of life and one could call them hungry barbarians with a mission of a chance for a better life for themselves by being on the battlefields rather than being in even the peace time of Macedonia. This was the way to move forward and get a better life, to stay idle where they were was to go nowhere and life would be the hell they didn't want to return to. Perhaps this understanding of what they were leaving behind and possibly be gaining made them into invinciable warriors. Each step forward might give them the promise to win and be rewarded with some gold and land of their own for a home that they could call and feel they belonged. It is something in mankind that we feel and crave even today, the feeling inside of the human heart to be at home and belong and that yearning hasn't changed much. The moment the invasion of southern Greece was final Alexander was accepted as a Greek. An advanced society such as theirs had no choice but to accept him or lose much of what they had accomplished since Greece was a modern and civilized society, whether in Athens, Spartan or Peloponnesus.

Alexander's destiny was to conquer Asia-Minor, today's Turkey. First up was the city of Troy, in which he had to cross the Aegean Sea, and he did with remarkable success. One may call that luck, which many of us may have some of now and then in life on a small or large scale, however in military terms it is called smart planning without the knowledge of when it would be their be their very last battle. I think he was a great strategist and very sure of himself. I cannot see nor can I agree that Alexander's contribution to the world today or then is anything more than zero. His invasions only destroyed what was built and everything that should have been saved in the country and even for his own new empire. He ruined the empire of Persia which was a society that was once extraordinarily prosperous, except for their weakness in protecting the people and the kingdom from invaders, perhaps it was their very arrogance and assurance in their individual wealth that allowed Alexander to walk in and invade them. The society was so spoiled that no one wanted to risk anthing to fight back for what was theirs and thought maybe to allow the invader to come with hopes of not destroying anything and disturbing their good life. That was not going to happen. For each life lost of one of Alexander's soldiers a city or town was burned to the ground.

The name of "Alexander the Great," is hardly accurate in describing him. Maybe the "Great Destroyer" but not what many historians portrayed him to be. In thirty five years of Alexander's life what did he produce that was so great? In his short life and the trail that he blazed, it clearly shows there was nothing great about him expect to bring nothing but destruction without one benefit to civilization during his thirty year rampage but for the moral lessons of not doing as he did.

Then so be it, God forbid, to call other men great leaders who brought nothing of benefit and only suffering and humiliation to mankind during their reigns also. Hitler, Stalin, Mussolini, Milosevic, Hirohito the Emporor of Japan, and Saddam Hussein, who named

76

himself "The Great," preceding over the plummeting of his people and nation into a fire of Hell over more than thirty years that he had reigned, he became to be known as the worst general leading an army of 1 million men to war who were clearly not loyal to him. To call him a president should not even be would be a disservice and an insult to the position that many men have held respectablely throughout history. His only proper name to remember him by would be the worst general in history. Likewise there was Phillip of France, a crusader who along with Richard the Lion of England burned and looted everything from the mountains of the Alps to the Black Sea, to the Byzantium Canal city of Constantinople crossing into Anatolia and continuing to plunder the land in blood and fire all the way to Jerusalem and Palestine.

The men like Sadaam and others in history who were bad examples of kings without common sense and never cease to amaze the human man by their brutality. These are the men calling themselves leaders of respected states who instead of taking care of the needs of their nations, their priorities are their need for their adventures. How could one lead a country for years and call themselves representatives and protectors of their nations.

We can give no more credit to these leaders than we give Alexander who was filled with those same destructive intentions. Their deeds speak for themselves. I would not call these leaders "the Great" for the simplest of reasons that they were not builders but destroyers.

In the beginning of their wars and dominations they looted, burned and committed atrocities. Their Satanic ways have given reason for many who fought and will continue to fight to liberate man for a new way of life and freedom. Many of the freedom fighters names will never be known like the ones who fought and believed the world would be better off without these kind of dictators. Now for once in history there is a man who rose to the occasion as president of the nation and went across the globe to try to help free the nation of Iraq from oppression.

A long period of domination has made some leaders realize that conquering is not the same as destroying. Conquering is about bringing a new world of ideas for building and creating so people can see the benefits from their conqueror.

Some of them were great leaders who left their imprint on our personal lives even today and continue to be remembered in history. They were the ones such as Cyrus the "Truly Great," Pajazit of

Anatolia, from the Mangos Empire, Genghis Khan and his decendants, Attila the Hun and Timor and his empire, who continued on with the tradition of conquering in order to expand the Huns empire. With the sudden deaths of all of these leaders it changed the course of history again to one of uncertainity just as it did with their predessors. Their fates took a road similar to or the same as that of of Alexendar's which led to the break up of their empires.

For these reasons men have learned from history what it means to be free and have refused to be conquered, especially when the armies of invaders are as destructive as they have been, plundering their land in a fire of hell and blood..

Man has come a long way since the time of the Persian charriot and Alexander's spear and much has changed with man's advancement and our human mind has taken us for a ride even up to the far distance of the stars. Perhaps to understand it all requires the creativity and imagination that is beyond even our own comprehension. We have created much that we maybe don't even understand of what the consequenses and gains they have brought us may be. Today's technology and advanced methods of communicating have brought the world a way to have some hope of commonality and understanding of one another. It has enhanced people's knowledge that perhaps can save us from the self destruction that we are clearly heading into almost like a trap. Perhaps education will help us to keep from walking into that trap.

In today's world the sophistication and knowledge of man gives us the understanding of what we have and what we can lose. We are more willing to bear arms to protect the things sacred to us which is life and freedom from the aggressor. People can become more united in solidarity for that freedom that is precious to everyone.

History has repeated itself many times and it seems in more destructive ways each time such as during the wars of Hitler, with Italy, Russia and Japan as his allies on their rampages to plunder the world into fires of hell and now it is my Bosnia.

When and where will all this end? Could this be just a beginning for another great war, or will this be the final tears the mothers will shed for their children and loved ones, or will the world be saved from those few mindless men who hold power?

As I was sharing my thoughts with my friend Pace, I asked him, "Don't you agree with that Mr. Pace?"

"Whole heartedly, Mr. Angelo," he answered, "whole heartedly. My Mormon people were prosecuted by the rest of the citizens in this country a century ago. We were blessed to be able to preservere and to believe that men could show human kindness towards one another and now here we are in this great nation that every man dreams to be in and to enjoy such freedoms. We experienced hardships and the burning of our peoples homes. Our religion was rejected and misunderstood at that time. We preservered and showed to the rest of the country that they could be proud of us and our religion and that we had much in common in every aspect of life with our fellow man. We integrated ourselves on every level of American life and our love for this nation is unshakable and unquestionable."

"I envy you, Mr. Pace, I envy you," I told him. "The day will come that my religion will be accepted and the people of my faith will feel the same as yours. We will all be proud of each other and the success and the contributions we could make to this great nation and none of us will feel like outcasts as citizens. None of the bad experiences will shake the wills of our people who love freedom, as I'm sure we all do."

Pace replied, "We didn't earn respect standing by on the sidelines Angelo, we worked hard for it. We traveled thousands of miles with our women and children in primitive wagons and yet we are proud of every success we had. Yes we lost many material things, and yes we were run out of our homes but we built new ones as well as cities and towns and we settled on the most rugged terrain on the most rugged piece of land that we thought no one else wanted.

"To be honest my people thought it was probably the most forsaken piece of land my forefathers ever saw before in that valley of the salty lake. With no doubt in their minds it was forgotten by God. Somehow they thought they could be safe there. Although it wasn't as bad as we thought it was. We settled down with our families in that valley of the salty lake and started building from the first day that we arrived. Our hearts and minds were not conquered, they were only hardened and made more resilent to oppression and discrimination from our fellow man."

"My friend you have built a country," I said, "and you rightfully deserve to keep it. Utah and the Mormon people are testament to and proof for the people who believe they rightfully are part of the land and to never lose their will for living and never can be conquered. Their hearts and minds and spirits will always remain free no matter what the circumstances. I think our two peoples could relate to each other's gains and losses over the centuries. Now I understand why you are the only one from the Christian and respectfully Mormon world that fight on the side of the Bosnian people. Your fight is just and noble. I wonder Pace, if you will tell me what the instructions from Commander Beslagic were that you recieved before you left Tuzla?"

Pace answered "We need to raise money to buy guns and we need to bring everything to the eyes of every family around the world and enlighten them on what is going on. We need to convince the Croatians to keep the corridors open to the sea and land so we can bring the weapons to our fighters. We Bosnians are surrounded by enemies on all four sides. Enemies who are blinded by so much hatred no logic applies even to themselves. So as you can imagine what a danger they are even to themselves and how dangerous they are to us in that light." As I listened to Pace talk I couldn't help but notice him referring to himself as "we Bosnians," and I was touched by it and I felt as much a Mormon at that moment as he. My feelings haven't changed but become more than ever ingrained in my heart.

Pace enthusiasticly continued as I listened raptly. "I traveled from Tuzla with a few other fellow soldiers all the way to Dubronik on foot. We settled down for the night at one of the hotels in the city. I was standing right there in the hotel lobby as the Croatian military police were asking about me and asking the people and hotel clerks if they had seen or knew me. I thought things might get a little hairy for a moment. It seemed like they were so single minded and unexperienced that they didn't even notice I was right there across the room. Whatever knowledge of police work or rationality they had possessed it seems they just threw out the window period. I thought it would be best anyway if I got the hell out of Dodge, sooner rather than later.

"I walked casually to the elevator and up to the fourth floor to my room and decided if I was going to be getting cut by these Croatian militia, I better put up a fight because I wasn't going to go down without a fight or I would end up a dead man."

I told him, "These men were free to do as they wanted without anyone to answer to, so your life was defintely on the line and your observations were correct."

Pace said, "I thought if I didn't fight I'd find myself lying in the first ravine or ditch along the road face down in the dirt."

I replied, "That would be for sure, like many others did."

Pace said, "I thought it would be best and the odds would be better if I fought them if I had to. I don't believe in surrendering especially if it means dying. I loaded my Belgian semi-automatic and decided that if anyone was going to be dead it would be them before me.

"Lucky for me they were such inexperienced military police that I think even if I had been riding by on a white horse with the most beautiful saddle from the English Knights they would have missed seeing me. I picked up my clothes as fast as I could and threw everything in my bag zipping it so quickly it sounded like it was going to catch fire. I threw my bag over my shoulder and took a deep breath telling myself to try to calm down and not leave a trail of smoke behind myself for them to follow. I calmed down and thought it would be a good idea to alter my apperance a little and turned my jacket inside out so I that I looked a little different from when I came in. I also put a French beret on my head and lit up a cigarette from a package of Drina. As you know I hate to smoke but I kept it in my mouth constantly trying to blend in with the crowd. I thought I looked pretty good too and for some reason I felt pretty confident and secure."

I interrupted, "I should hope so. After all the years you ran through the jungles and hills in Vietnam, you had better be sure of yourself or you better be just damned good."

We laughed loudly, pounding each other on the shoulder in reassurance in knowing we both were pretty damn good at what we had accomplished on the roads we had walked through our lives so far. Pace continued, "I went down through the lobby and out the front doors and rubbed the shoulder of a military policeman who was looking for me. I said to him in Croatian,'izvini vojniche' which means 'excuse me, soldier.' I walked outside to the parking area where a bus happened to be going on his regular route to the city of Pula on the northern coast. The ticket taker seemed more suspicious of me than the police had. The driver was just about to close the doors and take off and I yelled loud in Croatian, 'vozac cakja!' which means, 'driver wait!' in a pure Croatian accent. Even the military police back in the lobby were laughing saying, 'Catch him! Catch that bus! Don't let him leave!' The busses seemed to have the habit of leaving customers standing on the sidewalk even when they were empty."

I replied, "It must be communist beauacracy. Nothing has changed since I left." I told him, "You must be proud of yourself Pace, slipping right through their fingers. I'm glad you are here. I was afraid I would have to take off from work to travel all the way to Europe somewhere in the Adratic and spend a hundred bucks just to throw a bunch of little flowers in remberance of you. I'm glad I didn't have to do that. I would have been pissed about that."

Pace asked, "Over me or the money?"

I said, "The money man, what do you think? The time lost on the job and those poor little flowers thrown in the salty water." We laughed like crazy knowing we had a bonding friendship.

Pace laughed and said , "Anyway a few hours later I found myself at an airport where I boarded a local flight to Ljubljana, Slovenia."

"It looked like you had a rough ride," I said, "but I'm glad you're here and happy that you are well. Good thing the military police didn't arrest you. I wanted to ask you, do you remember before you left we saw those people on television who volunteered to fight for Croatia?"

He said, "Yea, yeah, I remember."

"Well, I told him, they were all executed about a week ago by the Croatian military."

He stared at me with wide open eyes and a slice of pizza half way in his mouth. He spit the bite out on his plate and said, "Hey, what the hell is going on? Those people were fighting for Croatia and they got executed?"

I answered, "Well let's take three things from the information that I got. One is greed and glory instead of fighting for the victims, the Bosnian people. They want to crusade for Christianity in the twenty first century. The next reason is they disobeyed direct orders from the military command they were under. And finally by making the fatal mistake of trying to sell weapons to the enemy the Serbs, who they were fighting against. That's what I call being stupid. Especially stupid was the Spanish guy who was the editorial political writer for one of the major newspapers in Madrid. I was so disappointed. He of all people who had a knowledge of the world should have known on which side he should have been fighting for instead of joining the wrong side. He should have gone to Bosnia and fought with you and me, Pace. That would have been the noble thing to do. Now he's buried somewhere with no marker. It's like the good in life that you give is what you get back. He got back six feet of dirt and that's all.

"There are villians and victims and he should have joined the good side like you have done. He got his just dessert and not from Jesus or Muhammed or Moses. It was from the devil himself and he got served a mouthful of dirt on a silver plate right from the get go. Too bad he didn't get a taste of it when he was alive. A sober reminder that morality and immorality don't go hand in hand. The rest of the gang of mercenaries were all professional soldiers just like you Pace, no insult to you, but in this struggle in Bosnia they went wrong all the way. You on the other hand have proven by in siding with Bosnia that you are a true soldier in every sense."

"Oh don't flatter me, Angelo," Pace replied. "What do you want?"

"Just a promise that you'll stay alive," I answered. "I've already lost too many friends in Bosnia. At any rate all those volunteer crusaders are dead soldiers now. And guess by who's hand they are dead?"

"Whose hand is that?" Pace asked.

I answered, "Their own.Their own hands with their actions and deeds that led them to their own graves. It was from the Croatian soldiers bullets that they are dead, your friends from Saint George, Utah, who once tried to convince you into joining the very same group. Do you remember? I'm glad you never took them up on it."

Pace replied, "That was something to remember. They really wanted me to join. They were converts from Roman Catholicism to the Mormon religion."

I told him, "One individual's deeds can create the circumstances of life or death, for better or worse. So they did it to themselves. Croatia didn't need their professional assistance anymore. The war was just about over in Croatia and just beginning in Bosnia. Soldiers are, as we both know, in all parts of the world except ours, a disposable commodity. Don't you think that's right, Pace?"

"I hate to say yes, but you are right," he answered. "The only indisposable commodity in the military is a ranking officer. Do you know why Angelo?"

I said, "I would say to grow an officer into a full fledged winning and productive field commander takes a seasoned veteren who has had years of training and hard work. To replace a uniformed soldier all you need to do is just put a rifle in his hand and give him ninety days of mediocre training and maybe he'll go kill himself or someone else with it. The commodities are so plentiful that one has no reason to go too far to look for them. Every ghetto street, every ghetto town and every village are full of warm bodied candidates who have nothing else to do but join the army. The only thing they get to learn there is something they've already learned on the streets."

"What's that Angelo?" Pace asked.

"Don't cut me off, I am just about to tell you. Not to degrade a uniformed man, and not to offend any soldier since I have been one, but most of them have learned how to kill and hurt each other on our streets for whatever reasons they may be. When they enter that sacred gate which we call the gates of learning, about how to protect the nation, instead they find themselves to be learning what they have already started to learn in the streets. That is everyone is the enemy and to kill and to kill and to kill without mercy. Everything outside of the gate they had left in the world where they had once lived becomes their enemy."

"How did that happen, Angelo?" Pace asked.

I said, "The political ideology of the military and civilians are two different entities. One is a provider and the other claims to be a protector or that's the way it is supposed to be. It isn't that way. The protector is supposed to be the military and was created after all by civilian society. Since they are classified as protectors of society they believe that everything and anything that they think should belong to them does. The civilian, the provider and life line of the militaries suddenly have no say. Even the volunteers that join the organizations of the collective governments and armies are supposed to be just that, voluntary, to work for the better of the people. The whole purpose of the volunteer armies is to be free protectors for free civilian society overall. They are not doing what they are supposed to."

Pace asked, "What do you mean by all that?"

I answered, "The military should belong to the citizens because the citizens are the ones who provide everything for the military to exist. They should answer to no one else but the citizens. Who did you answer to when you were in Vietnam? And who did I answer to when I was in the military in Yugoslavia? It was to a single brain washing ranking officer who saw nothing good in anything but his own world of the military and wanting to teach how to destroy what the civilians were building. Why are you, I, or any good citizen with good intentions not allowed to visit military barracks or police on the corner streets or even the fire department to talk and share conversation and morning coffee with them?

"We are treated instead as if we are their enemies in most places of the world when actually we are their providers and life line to enable them to be what they are. It should be that way, we for them and they for us. Something is missing there. All of these services are supposed to be facilities for the people and suddenly the government is the owner of everything in every society from here to China. The cilivians always look for a change but any time that even peaceable attempts are made, the people who want a change for the good are considered enemies of the state right away. They find that changes are not acceptable. The only changes that are made are from inside the governments by the bureaucrats at the top that couldn't even find the states they are representing on a world map because they are so unaware of their own surroundings."

"Changes rarely happen in a peaceable manner but only through bloodshed. So unfortunate but true. Even our great American revolution has paid heavily for our independence through events such as the civil war to retain the right to be who you really are. A famous phrase that people have used through the centuries is, 'While the freedom walks towards you that you have been fighting for you may not live to meet or see that freedom, but there is hope however that the next generation may see it.' It seems like every generation from all around the world has repeated that same phrase of hope without having a happy ending. People try therefore to make changes democratically through the ballot box or at times when that doesn't work, forcefully through rioting and revolutions to bring about the change. Sadly it seems like a happy ending has never occured. Most of the governments are suspicious of any and all new ideas."

Pace scratched his head and said, "I don't know guys, I think you've lost me on all this."

I said, "Only a politician can understand dirty politics. I'm sorry to admit that I am a little bit of a dirty politician. I understand it although only as an ordinary citizen. I don't make decisions I only try to influence the decisions somehow only for the better of men just like you who do not or do not wish to understand it. And there you see that man is never free from anyone, even himself."

Pace said, "I think I've felt real appreciation maybe for the third or fourth time in my lifetime of experiences. During the Vietnam war in the Delta I came close to death quite a few times. Each time that happened I became more grateful for my family, friends and my country."

"You're not getting soft on me, Pace, are you? I asked him. "You just mentioned something about your country and I'm always the one who's telling you should be grateful being a citizen by birthright in a country like this and I should be as lucky as you to have been born here."

"Don't give me that, Angie," Pace replied. "Remember some time ago when you told me that during the Bolshevik revolution that in one of the speeches of Lenin's he was asked where the men felt most at home? And he answered without hesitation that home is everywhere where you have a roof over your head and your human dignity is respected. He said that is home and his home is in the Mother Russia because he had a roof over his head and he felt his freedom and dignity was respected.

"It's was proven after he died that not all the Russians freedom and dignity was respected. I think both of us are lucky because both of our human dignity and freedom are respected here in this great nation. Lenin never lived long enough to see his people walk in freedom because they never did. Perhaps their dream was shattered with Lenin's death."

I said, "Pace, I wonder when the people in Bosnia will feel that they have that human dignity and are respected by their fellow man?"

"Angelo, I just came back from there," Pace answered, "and their luck is running out. The only way their dignity and respect that they deserve will ever be given back to them is for them to fight for it and many will die."

I told him, "That reminds me of an old saying in the Balkans since the beginning of time, 'Seven Balkan men must die for one to live and eat well.' It's ironic, but that's the truth. I'm a Balkan man myself, but I'm glad I don't think that way. My father taught me that if I plowed the field or did a day's labor that I should do it well so at the end of the day no man would have to lose their life for one other man to eat well. All men should be able to enjoy the fruits from their labor. The war is a terrible thing. We have somehow found it necessary as humans to think space and time must be protected at whatever cost. As we are talking, Bosnia is in flames."

"Speaking of the Bosnian freedom fighters, here comes my friend Ramiz. He's in town and just walked in." Ramiz was smiling from ear to ear. "Let me introduce you him."

CHAPTER FOUR: RAMIZ' STORY

I introduced them to one another and told Pace that Ramiz was one of the wounded who was given treatment at the expense of our good people here in the States. I told Pace of Ramiz' horrifying experience and a close call he had from people he once called his best friends. Some of them had even gone to first grade with him and were like family to him sharing his childhoold bed, dinner plate, and most importantly, the love of his mother which she equally divided with all of them.

"She was quite a lady and a wonderful mother," Ramiz commented. We could hear the heartbreak in his voice.

Pace asked, "Is your mother still alive?"

Ramiz pulled a chair back slowly to sit down and join us and without looking at Pace he said in a very soft voice a shocking statement that his mother had been brutally murdered by the Chetniks. Pace regretted the pain he caused him by having asked.

I cut in on Ramiz to say, "Those Chetniks and Croatian Ustsaes were boys who had grown up just like ourselves to become men, and many of them left Yugoslavia many years before the war for whatever their political grievances were with Tito's government, economical or political. Obviously every one of them had some type of political difference with the previous government in Yugoslavia yet they still returned to do the unthinkable."

"As for myself, whose father was prosecuted and spent many years in jail, the system did not just prosecute the ones they had found guilty in those days but the whole family as well. But I didn't choose to raise up arms against innocent people and murder indiscriminately as they did, I chose to try to make a change in the system of the political structure of the country, but for me and the people that believed as I did, we were not given the chance. The illiterate and the misfits took up arms and started to plunder and kill instead."

"It's just like the slogan from the past communist world saying, 'Svi za jednoga, jedan za svi', which means 'All for one, one for all,' a profoundly dishonest and inane cliché no one with a sane mind could agree with.

"We watched on our televisions as the gruesome war was unraveling out of control as many different self-made military groups were forming. On the Serbian side was a notorious bankrobber and

murderer called Arkan who was bankrolled to do the dirty work for
Slobo, and became a leader of a group called the White Eagles.
On the Croatian side was a notorious group from Australia who years
ago called themselves young Croatian freedom fighters. Among them
happened to be my one of my friends, Peter, and an aquaintance, Mata.
Peter is a good friend of mine, at least he was. That is what I thought
of him."

"They came in by the thousands like flocks of black ravens
carrying lots of money in their beaks and with a will to die for their
mother land, Croatia. They came from Australia, America, Canada,
Argentina, Chile, Germany, and the rest of Europe to finally free
Croatia and for the first time give her a red and white checkered square
national flag to give birth to and call the new nation of Croatia, and
rightfully so. I firmly believe every man has the right to a nation and a
home but not to take away my own home at my expense to call his.
Everyone should earn all the good from all the work in their lives and
reap what they sow, as the Croatians had forgotten this one morally
important thing. Tragically as the war went on the men lost track of the
reason why and what they were there fighting for. Patriotism had gone
out the window and hatred conquered their hearts. Some good soldiers
went bad in this conflict."

"Without anyone in leadership who was experienced enough to
remind the men that they must obey that code of honor as soldiers,
again the soldiers went wrong, killing looting and raping, with the
confidence of no one to have to answer to and unchecked. They was
no one to remind them that the fight was not to conquer anyone or to
oppress. The fight was to release themselves from being oppressed and
conquered for so long."

"I could hardly disagree with their crusade but I have to ask
myself a question. How can they forget the reason they had come from
all over the world? Was it to kill, plunder and burn their next door
neighbors in Herzegovina? Or to instead try to help stabilize their own
country of Croatia that has already bled enough? The pizza maker man
became a president.

"I think the moral decay over many generations in Croatia has
proven again that it is leaderless. How can it happen that a pizza man
from Toronto is the president and leader of three million people? Was
he the most qualified candidate or is it just an old curse that has been
hanging over Croatia for centuries?   In a time when experience,

chrisma and a clear vision of leadership is needed, he is one of those who did not possess any of that badly needed magic. The ones who did and were truly qualified and capable such as Mr. Masich were shoved aside".

"When one can do no good he is capable of a lot of wrong doing. Tuzman let loose hundreds and thousands of armed Croatian militias to plunge southern Bosnia in blood." I pointed out to Pace that Ramiz was one of the rare survivors among the thousands who did not survive it.

Ramiz suddenly seemed to feel very comfortable with us and wanted to open up and tell his story from his heart and soul. We were eager to hear it. Ramiz a little shyly and adjusting himself comfortably in his seat looked up at us with emotion in his face saying, "I still bleed inside and thank God no one can see it and I don't know how anyone could help to stop that bleeding." Pace and I answered almost as one with the same thinking, "We are here to listen to your experiences, please go right ahead."

Ramiz began to speak, "Just this past spring I was looking forward to spending some time in the garden with my mother. I love gardening. I have more than two hundred bushes of roses in all kinds of colors, and some time ago I started to build a little water pond. I was looking to have it completed before the really hot days of summer hit. My mother was already in the garden pruning the roses. My best friend Adnan and I were still debating on where to go to and what to have for breakfast while my mother was doing her gardening."

"We finally decided we would go to the old town of Mostar and have a late breakfast there. So I opened the window facing the garden and before I could call out from the window and let my mother know we were going to old town and be back very soon, I saw a column of men in military fatigues walking towards our house. I didn't recognize where they were from or whether they were Chetniks, Croats, or Bosnians, because I didn't recognize their uniforms. We hadn't seen any military action in our area since the war began."

"I called out and asked my friend Adnan to come over to the window. He looked out and said, 'Man I think we are in trouble. Those guys are Ustashe, and the guy in front is the notorious Mate.'

"I told Adnan , 'Hey I know Mata. He is a friend of mine and we went to school together. He is from these parts here.'"

Adnan said, "Well I don't think he is here as a friend, I can tell

90

you that. It would be good idea,' Adnan said nervously to me, 'if you went downstairs and took your 9mm with you. I'll watch here from the window with my AK-47, and don't stand in front of Mate. Stay to the side so I can keep him in target range."

"Don't worry, Adnan," I said, but I heeded his caution and on the way downstairs I was loading my gun's chamber to make sure it was fully loaded and then I stuck it behind my back inside of my belt and hung my shirt over it with hopes there would be no shooting. I got down stairs and opened the front doors of my house. There I saw Mata and almost a hundred of his men in the yard with some of them standing on the main street leaning on a fence. I hadn't seen Mata for many years and he looked the same to me, which was mean, foxy, and untrustworthy.

He was still the same Mata I knew. He greeted me, "Hey Ramiz, my brother!' "Bogg, bogg!" which means "God be with you." He turned his back and said to his troops with his hand on my shoulder, "Here is a the Herzogovinian man I was telling you all about, a true one, Ramiz is a patriot."

I rose my eyebrows and took a deep breath and shrugged like I agreed with him. "'Mata take it easy," I said. 'I haven't done anything so noble to be such a great patriot, I only served in the army for a few years, an army I didn't even want to be in."

There was no reply except for some loud laughing, "Ha, ha, ha, ha!" and he opened his arms to gave me a hug and said, "We haven't seen each other in such a long time." It seemed he was older and wiser but one thing that never changed was that laugh of his. I felt a little awkward because of that gun in the back of my pants, but then I remembered he was carrying an M-16 and a pistol hanging on his leg in a cowboy holster and had a hundred men with him. He almost reminded me of General Montgomery. For some reason I didn't want to let go of my gun and kept my right hand on the handle of the gun on my back. So I hugged him only with my left arm, then he swung aside his American made M-16 over his back to free his arms and hug me. A second later after we separated from the dishonest feeling hug we looked each other straight in the eye and one thing crossed my mind."

I was thinking of all the beatings he got when we were kids because of the trouble I caused when we played soccer and stole cherries from the neighbors' yards. For some reason he always took the rap and took the blame without question or complaint. I still feel guilty about it when remembering. I'm glad now that I told him back then that I felt bad about it. Now I think it looks like pay back time for everything. At any rate I wasn't taking my hand off of my gun."

Mata was quiet for a second and looked at me as if trying to guess what I was thinking and said, "Ramiz my friend, I'm not here to get even with you for all the trouble you got me into when we were young but I didn't forget about it."

I said, "I was worrying about that just now, I admit I did get you into a lot of trouble when we were kids." I was laughing and looking down at the ground still kind of feeling guilty.

Mata said, "I also didn't forget you protected me from all the bully assholes in school and on the soccer field. Because of you I could bully back all the guys that I otherwise couldn't have done anything about when we were young. Remember that?"

I didn't have the chance to reflect on our childhood because suddenly Mata's mood changed just like an unpredictable wind that builds into a tornado. He cried out, "Auntie, Auntie!" With a look of affection he spotted my mother at work in the garden. Suddenly he turned and put his hand on my shoulder seeming like he had forgotten he was just had just been calling to my mother and said, "Ramiz, I envy you." Then with pain and sadness in his voice that seemed to be coming from his soul, he said, "I wish my mother were alive so I could do some good things for her like you do for your mother. Just look at this beautiful garden." He was staring with faraway look in his eyes somewhere off in the distance.

I told him, "We always shared my own mother. She loved you just as much as she did me," trying to snap him out of it.

Just as suddenly he gently leaned his American made M-16 against the fence and stuck his hand gently in his the camoflage shirt pocket and pulled out a lighter and a pack of cigarettes in an elegant looking package that were my favorite kind called Drina. I recalled we couldn't ever afford them when we were young. We had to get the nastiest tobacco ever rolled for a cigarette which the government produced for the masses, the only ones that we could afford. I can even taste them now just thinking about it. They would burn all the way from your throat into your lungs. We recalled those memories and laughed.

He offered me a Drina saying, "Ramiz would you care to join me? Remember we could never afford these when we used to smoke together?" "

I shrugged and thought for a moment back on a lot of our happy memories. I said, "Yes, I do remember that. They were happy days even though we were so poor."

Mata then reminded me of a funny thing that wasn't funny at all at the time because we had been sweating bullets because of a girl we both knew, and he asked, "Do you remember that little Serbian girl down the road that we both wanted for our girl and we fought over her and I was the one who ended up getting her but almost getting killed?"

I said, "Yea, I always wondered why she went for you. It wasn't looks for sure because I was much better looking."

Suddenly Mata seemed to be himself again as I knew him when he was a happy young boy when we were young and we laughed and he replied, "Do you have to remind me?" It was funny then and after all these years it's still funny now but yet it was very sobering.

Mata continued on smiling, "I was in the room hiding under her bed while her father was yelling and screaming down the hall swinging a tomahawk in his hand yelling, 'Milica! Milica! What the hell is that noise in there? What the hell is going on? Who the hell is in your room, girl?' I was hiding under the bed naked. Remember that Ramiz? I was holding onto my underwear and pants in my hands and shaking scared to death."

I couldn't help laughing and said, "It was funny alright but scary at the same time. Her father was one crazy bastard. I thought I was going to see you roasted over a pit with your scalp hanging over the fireplace for a trophy for Milica's father. You're still here so it didn't happen."

We laughed and Mata said, "When I peeked out from under that bed and saw him waving his arms with that tomahawk flashing through the air, man, I have never been more scared in my entire life. You know what I heard Milica's father had said at the time? I don't really think he was mad because he thought it was me who was there, I think he thought that it was you who was the one there, Ramiz."

"Spare me," I told him, "After thirty years you want to remind me what I was trying to forget? I think you must just have been jealous of me even though you were the one who was doing her. Well, there's no better time than the present to know who your real friends are."

Mata said, "I heard Milica's father saying to her in exactly these words, 'You little whore! I will not go for anything like this kind of embarrassment to my family! For you to have that jack ass circumcised Balija in my house, in your bed! I swear if I catch you with him I will chop you both to pieces!' all the while he was waving a sekiru or a tomahawk."

"Oh," I said, "It's a good thing you told me because that's a little more than what I heard. Get to the point Mata because it's not getting funnier. I know the bastard hated me anyway. He always said to me when I was a boy while he was holding a knife in his hand that one of these days he was going to circumcise me. I knew I was already circumsized when I was little. I haven't recovered from that fright to this day. I wish it was me that dated his daughter instead of you. She would be pregnant and have twenty children by now."

Mata laughed. I was trying to change the subject and said, " I was just about to have lunch now, I am hungry. We were friends then and we were kids. We had nothing real to rival about then. We are grown men who have been around the world. We know we know now what we missed out on and that was a lot of the good life."

"What's that we missed out on Ramiz?" Mata asked softly furrowing his brow.

I answered, "We have missed having freedom and money in our pockets but I think we both had one very important thing and that was the love of our families. Now as grown men here we are in for a big fight. The word is the Serbs have been plundering everything up north and heading toward us. I hope that is why you have come."

He didn't answer me and took out two cigarettes in his hand taking the time to put both in his mouth. He flipped a beautiful chrome lighter he had with his thumb and then gently brought the flame to the tips of the cigarettes. He was inhaling the flame from the lighter through the cigarette while his eyes were glazed staring at the flame. The way he did it made me feel like I was doing it instead of him, and I could feel the pressure extending in my chest. It reminded me of when we had smoked together in those worry-free days when we were young and in the safety of my mom's and dad's home.

"He lifted his left hand to the cigarettes and took a deep pull then slowly and gently took one from his mouth while holding it by the middle and extended his hand to me so I took it and inhaled deeply. He said, 'This is like old times my friend, this is just like old times.'

"My eyes were focused on him and his every move but my attention was not just on him but his many men that were standing around behind him and all strangers to me. I thought his gesture was a sincere one but I was kind of torn between being happy to see him and not too happy. There seemed to be something that was missing inside of me and him as well. I told him, 'Thank you, thank you very much. This does remind me of the old days and brings back the memories of when we were very close.'

"Mata said, 'I thought we were still close. What happened?'

"We are Mata, we are close, as close as the dew on the grass after a morning rain. These are difficult times we are experiencing right now and as you said it is good to know who your real friends are, especially right now. We have both grown up to become surely seasoned and mature men and we must choose what our priorities are and are not."

"Mata told me, 'You mean to tell me you have put our friendship on the back burner or just have hung it over the fireplace to dry out?'"

"I wouldn't say either one but if I have to make a choice then it would be in one of three places, the garbage, the fireplace, or on the back burner. You will find our friendship in just one of those places and that would be on the back burner for now but it can always be restarted at any time."

"You have sure grown up to be a really hardened man, Ramiz."

"That's true, Mata" I told him, "The only thing that didn't happen that I would have liked to happen was to be taller than you though." I stepped forward to face him nose to nose measuring him with my hand to his forehead and said, "It looks like we are just about the same height, I didn't outgrow you." We really laughed and it was one of the moments with him that I felt really comfortable with him and we both realized we were grown men with our own needs and with our own very different ways of life.

"'You have a beautiful garden,' Mata stated. 'Only here in our Herzogovina could a garden look like this and nowhere else do the roses bloom so aromatically sensuous and beautiful.' I looked at him and reminded him the garden belonged to my and his adopted mother.

I found out I was in for one more small surprise from up Mata's sleeve. He took the same lighter that he had lit the cigarettes with and leaned toward the roses with it in his right hand while he held onto a stem of a single rose in his other hand. He looked at me while holding the lighter to the rose and a short and sharp blade emerged from the lighter as a knife popped out. Mata then leaned gently and smelled the rose and said, "May I please?"

"I thought he was asking to smell the roses more and said, "By all means my friend, by all means."

"Mata replied, 'It's beautiful, I have to have it," and he snipped the rose off the vine with his knife/lighter. "Roses are the only thing from the plants that will talk to you if you listen carefully. Just listen to them sometime if you don't believe me."

"I was surprised to hear Mata talking like that because I never knew him to be very sentimental. After he cut the rose the blade disappeared back into the lighter. He smoothly slid it into the military camoflage pants pocket he wore and I had to admit he did look very sharp. I was almost fooled by the way he looked. He looked like a real general although he never was one. Then he stood up and brought the rose to his nose and took a deep breath to smell it and said, 'You can never fail to win any mom's heart even if you have already have won it and even by giving her one of her own roses from her own garden if you know how do it right.'

I told him, "I was wondering when you were going to get around to saying hello to mom."

"He looked at me and smiled and suddenly turned serious. 'It's your fault,' he said, while moving his hands insuiating in a sign language that I had been talking too much. Then with a cleverness and surprising charm that I never knew he had, he walked towards my mother smiling and greeting her, and he told her that she was always in his thoughts because of the way she had always treated him just as well as she did me when we were boys."

"He reminded mom he remembered how whenever he had a cut on his leg, arm or face from playing with me on the soccor field that she would wash and nurse it with the same care as if he were her own son. Then how she kissed it to make it better saying it would now be healed. Then he handed the rose to my mother with both of his hands positioning his body in a low bow as he did and said, 'I respect you as my own mother since I have no memory of mine and lost her when I was very young. You gave me the gift of knowing what a mother's love means and for that I thank you.'

"She was flattered and blushed in shyness. Her eyes filled with tears and in a shaking but strong voice grabbing on to his hands she told him, 'God rest your mother's soul, I will always remember her. She died not long after giving birth to you. The day when you were born and she left to go to Heaven, oh, how you cried as if you knew your mother was gone. I held you in my arms and made a promise to your mother that I would love you and look after you just like my own Ramiz. I held you as my own child and never looked at you any other way except in the same way as I do my son and I still see you in that same way.'

"She looked into his eyes as her own filled with tears and said, 'You two boys better look after one another, because I can't this time and there is no one else to.'

"Those were magic words my mother spoke and I think it broke Mata away from any bad attention at least for now. Then mom walked in the front door of the house without looking back because she knew that Mata and I needed to talk. There were important matters that we needed to discuss. Mother never questioned me and she hugged and kissed us both before she went inside. In all this time my friend Adnan was still guarding my life from the window."

"Mata, obviously you've come to see me," I told him. "What is it I can do for you?"

Mata answered, "I want you to join us. We are in a fight to save our country. We are all from Herzogovina and we need to save it from harm by the Chetniks. All of Bosnia and Croatia have been infested and plundered by them. By the way have you seen what happened in the city of Vukovar?"

"Yes, I did," I replied, "and it's heartbreaking. It looks just like Berlin after the bombing from the allies. Nothing has been left untouched by the Serbs. Every building, every house, every street and every bridge has been destroyed."

"Yes,' he said, 'and greater tragedies are still in the making. There are concentration camps holding thousands of our people.'

"Whose people?" I asked. "Whose people are you talking about, Mata?"

"I'm talking about our people,' he answered. 'The Bosnians, Herzogovinians, Croatians, and Dalmations. All of us need to stick together to defeat those murderous Serb bastards who chased me out of my home thirty five years ago from my beloved Herzogovinia. I'm here now to do some paying back.'

"I could hardly disagree with what he said and felt somehow convinced that we would be fighting for the same cause. I agreed to join his group. I finally looked up at the second floor window to call Adnan. I yelled up to him, 'You can come down now my friend, everything is fine!'

He stuck his head out the window in confusion like a fox out of its hole and yelled, "All right, all right! I'll be down!"

"I looked Commander Mata straight in the eye and told him, 'I have known you since we were children or ever since I can remember really. Your father told us once about us not being real brothers and we were both confused. If my own father hadn't confirmed it I wouldn't have believed it and my mother never said anything. I admit I bullied you sometimes but I always loved you like my brother. Wait for me for a moment while I go pack up and get my rifle.'

"He told me, 'Don't worry Ramiz, where we are going there are plenty of rifles available of any kind you should want, thanks to our friends from Chile and Argentina.'

"All right Mata, what gun do you have for me?" I was looking at him slyly yet with a smile in my eyes.

"I have a gun I know that you like and have always liked."

"I looked at him with surprise and a little doubt. I asked, 'How do you know what kind of gun I like? You must have done some homework because I don't recall that we have ever had the chance to talk about guns. When we were young we never talked of guns and we didn't serve together in the military. As I recall you served in the Australian military and I served in the Yugoslavian. If memory serves me right Mata, I received a letter from you in 1971 and my mother still has it in her cedar chest. It had a the seal of the Australian Royal Navy and you enclosed a picture that showed you on the deck of an Australian destroyer and looking very dignified. So what kind of gun you got for me?'

"Mata replied, 'It's a surprise and I'm not telling you now until we get to the barracks. Come on man let's not waste any more time cause we got to go. We have a job to do and a country to liberate.'

"Those were the magic words that I wanted to hear. Until then I doubted Mata and all his men. A country to liberate so that we can be free. The thought went through my mind like a rush of wind through the sails of a still ocean. Here we were as two men who wanted the same thing. 'I was hoping,' I said, 'to know exactly where it is we are going.'

"He answered, 'We'll be going over the old bridge just across the river on the outskirts of the old town.'

"We left and got going on our way. An hour later we found ourselves in what was always known as the Christian or the Croatian part of the city of Mostar and arrived at the camp. The southwestern part of Mostar was already being destroyed by the shells of Serbian militants, the Chetniks, and Croats alike. It seemed to me everyone wanted to destroy everything that they had taken so long to build. They completely destroyed a part of the city where the Bosnian Muslim population lived. At the time I didn't know it was Mata's soldiers who had been responsible for shelling that Bosnian part of Mostar across the river. I couldn't see a single window from the thousands that were once in the buildings of the Bosnian high rises of the neighborhood that was still intact. The destruction that had taken place just that day or the day before was mind boggling. It crossed my mind to hold onto the hope that none of the devastation I was seeing would touch my own villiage.

"We were ambushed along the way by every kind of resistance group there was that either fortunately or unfortunately we could not even identify. We fought heavily out by the old bridge for awhile in the hills from the barrage of attacks by the Serbian army, or perhaps it could have been a volunteer Bosnian army, who were using heavy machine guns and RPG's. We lost a few of our men."

"I asked Adnan to stay close by and hopefully we could make it to the garrison. We walked around the city in the tall grass to avoid being ambushed and so that we could keep an open field of vision all the way to our garrison.

"Before we reached the barracks I hadn't been sure exactly which bridge he had been talking about. Since we had left my house I heard a bridge mentioned a few times but no specific bridge by name. Then I found out that he meant the old bridge. I was sad and enraged at the same time. I overheard Mata recieve a call on his two way radio and it sounded as if it were coming from the high command in Zagrib. It was from the high command and with no doubt from the defense ministry. I could hear the person on the other end say, 'Best regards from the President!' and 'Bogg,' which means, 'God be with you.'

"The bridge has to go!' I heard him say. 'We need to get rid of that symbol once and for all.' I was puzzled for a second overhearing the conversation and at first just curious about what they meant. It didn't take long for me to realize as they kept talking that they were planning to blow up the old only bridge, the only one connecting to the old part of the city. Most of the hundred men behind us had heard that everything was ready and the next morning the bridge would be blown up at 1500 or 1600 hours and sent into the bottom of the river. They roared and were jubliant and some even fired their guns in the air. By the time they got to the garrison most of those men would not only ever not see that bridge or the city of Mostar again but their lives were going to be blown apart just like the bridge.

"There was a young man I noticed who always seemed to be standing next to Mata. It seemed he was always around Mata and trying to be low key and not to be noticed. I wanted to break down his walls and find out what he was really all about. I thought he might be a logistic officer, because he didn't speak any Croatian nor did he wear any uniform, but with no doubt he had good taste in clothes. He spoke German and English and I was later proved to be right in my observation of him and his behavior and actions. I thought to myself that by the day's end I needed to find out everything about this guy. Later I would have wished that the end of that day hadn't come.

"He was well organized, neat, well dressed, well groomed and very conserative in his conversations, except with respect to Mata on whom he focused all of his energy and attention. His opinions were only directed to Commander Mata, and Mata's reaction was the only one who seemed to matter to the young man. It seemed that in his mind no one else existed. He was very soft spoken and I could not hear as much as I was trying to without being too obvious of the conversations he had with Mata. He wouldn't allow anyone to see his mouth moving during conversation. Everything he did and the way he went about it seemed to be very important, secretive, and private.

"I tried to strike up a conversation with the man and it didn't seem to be working. You crossed my mind, Angelo, for a topic, thinking if he knew Mata that well maybe he knew you, although as it turned out you were bad luck for this situation. I thought he may know you or have heard of who you are. After failing at my first attempts to strike up a conversation, I said to him, 'Young man, I have a dear friend who lives in Las Vegas, Nevada that you may know of. You remind me of him in a way because his manner and style are similar to yours.'

"He stared coldly at me with his deep steely blue eyes and placed his right hand over his left shoulder dusting off imaginary lint from his cashmere sweater. It felt like he looked down on me. He moved his head slowly, 'Well, I'm sure he can't be just like me nor I like him. I assure you, whoever he is, we probably wouldn't even like one another. Maybe you should talk with Peter about this friend of yours, he could be his friend but not mine,' while again dusting on his cashmere sweater almost as if to brush me away. I was thinking, 'What a mother fucker you are,' but I kept trying.

"I told him, 'All the people I know who know my friend would rather have him as a friend than an enemy.' As he was trying to brush me off with his body language and tone of voice, something suddenly was happening and I had no chance to elaborate or try and get through to him anymore because all hell suddenly broke loose with the whistling sound of shells approaching closer and closer and everyone starting to run everywhere.

"There wasn't time to continue our conversation because at that moment it was just every man for himself. The shells were coming over the mountaints from Serbian cannons on both sides of the town of Mostar. They are all mortal enemies of each other, Serbs, Croats, and Bosnians. The Serbs and Bosnians seemed like they were collaborating to attack the Croats but that wasn't the case. The Serbs shells from the heavy cannons were coincidentally coming at the same time as the shells from the Croatian side of the city were.

"It crossed my mind that it was like devils and angels were sleeping in the same bed together. I thought, 'Can this be possible?' Not even Mother Mary could untangle this ball of yarn. I thought hopefully that they would run out of shells. That seemed the only hope that maybe even Mother Mary could grant. The shells that were blasting our compound from the Serbian side were in such a large number it was like they were just throwing M&M's at a children's party so the kids wouldn't run out of candies — only they weren't candies but highly explosive deadly projectiles that could blow a person into a million pieces.

"Everyone ran in every direction. Despite all the chaos and confusion I heard Adnan's voice screaming and calling my name, 'Ramiz! Ramiz! Where are you, you bastard? God damn you, get up!' In our horror we cursed God for everything, for it or against it.

"In a matter of seconds all that could be seen was the red dust from the powerful explosions. For some strange reason everyone was running toward the garrison and barracks that were a half a block away

101

across a flat open field that offered no place to hide. It reminded me of the ancient story of a Roman ship during the time of Marc Anthony's famous battle with the Greek fleet ,when one of his ships was damaged and one of his soldiers was trying to hold on to a bubble in the water to save himself from drowning. One could truly feel and see the desperation and will to survive. There were no rules. Anything goes. It didn't make any sense for them to run to the barracks because it was a perfect target for carpet bombing, a word invented during the bombing of North Vietnam by B-52's because there was no place to hide and every square inch was bombed. This was just such an occasion, only with a perfect barrage of shells from their cannons hitting every square inch of it. Anywhere you ran to was right into a trap with shells and explosions. The only safe way to run would be backwards into one of the holes where the shells had already exploded because it was not as likely to hit again in the same spot. It was a picture of pure panic.

"It seemed like the shells were falling and soldiers were running to the same place at the same time on a collision course of shells and human bodies. It seemed like the men were in race with the shells to see who would come in first at the designated target. It was almost like a they had a death wish but it showed only their inexperience in military training and fear of death and their love for life. The men were surely untrained and inexperienced. In this situation they showed that they were only mama's little milk boys and with no doubt in the wrong place and with the wrong ideas in the wrong fight, whatever they were doing maybe they should have been playing toy soldiers in a warm safe place but not real soldiers.

"The explosions, horror, and chaos were all around us and then in one instant we heard two huge simultaneous blasts. After those explosions I found myself gasping for air. Then I remembered that there were two military trucks full of explosives parked right in the center in front of the barracks. They must have just received direct hits. After the dust cleared I could see they were no longer there and there weren't any men standing around anywhere either. There were only huge craters and twisted steel everywhere.

"At that moment I felt like there wasn't any air left to breathe. I was gasping like a fish out of water with my hands on my chest and neck and trying to figure out what was wrong not realizing that I had been thrown about thirty to forty feet. I was lucky not to have been knocked out from one of the pieces of the debris or big twisted pieces of steel. Huge clouds of dust and debris covered the area. You couldn't see your hand in front of your face. Suddenly there was only deadly silence for a few moments, only you could still hear the echo from the explosions from the empty high rises echoing from the city and surrounding hills and mountains sounding like the distant bells of Notre Dame. I wish they had been the bells of Notre Dame or afternoon prayers from the Minaret of the Mosque calling the faithful instead of the Hell it truly was.

"After that short moment of silence the voices could be heard moaning in pain and panic calling for help, although the dust was so thick I could see no one. A real Hell on earth was right before my eyes. I felt something warm and salty tasting dripping on my lips into my mouth. I tried to wipe at it and also tasted the dirt mixed with the taste of my blood. I knew I was wounded but I didn't know how badly or where. I was in a state of confusion myself with no time to be scared. I was still trying to still my heart from the explosions and gasp some air of which there didn't seem to be enough left of to breathe.

"I tried standing up not knowing exactly where I was, then realized that I was not on level ground and had fallen onto something sharp. I gripped onto it with my hands. The dirt was was caving in under my feet. I felt sharp pains in my hands and fingers. I didn't realize I had fallen into one of the craters from one of the blasts the shells had made. I felt scared, not knowing where I was and not understanding why I couldn't see the sky until the dust finally settled and a clear picture of the devastation was emerging slowly in front of my eyes.

"Suddenly I felt as if I what it was I had been holding on for dear life to was a boot that belonged to someone and was giving me a sense of security in my state of panic. I heard the first human sound I'd heard in a while coming from a little above me calling, 'Oh boze moj!' which means, 'Oh, my God!' Through the strange deadly silence that I thought I was trapped in, suddenly I heard the sounds and the cries for help that were coming from all around me, calling out to the mother of God and crying, 'Help me, please!' It seemed I heard it in every language, Italian, French, German, English, and Castillian Spanish of the men crying out for help. Most of these men were not real Croatians. They were nothing but a bunch of mercenaries and killers.

"Without thinking I called out, 'Adnan!, Adnan!' Those were

the very first words I had spoken since the chaos began.

"Suddenly I heard a voice, very weak and racked with pain, barely above a whisper, saying, 'I am here, I am here.'

"I was so shaken up inside after the explosions and didn't remember where I was at that moment. I stood up and tried to compose myself and figure out what had happened and, when I looked around I saw all of the debris as I was standing inside of a big hole and I thought, 'Oh man, how did I end up here?' I realized finally that I was in this crater and holding onto a leg with a partial body still attached to it belonging to someone wearing a military boot and not realizing in those few seconds or moments that had seemed like an enternity, what exactly it was that I had been holding on to. By the time I had crawled out of the hole I saw that only half of a body was attached to that leg and for some strange reason I wasn't going to let go of it. When I finally came back to being myself again I saw what I had been holding was a corpse with only one arm and part of a face and I almost lost it. That was the most horrifying thing I've ever experienced and I instantly felt intensely afraid to die. I thought I had been alone in that hole but there I was holding on to part of a human body that had been torn up in in the explosions and had somehow landed into the hole I was or perhaps we landed together, but perhaps he saved my life. I couldn't recall right away anyone who had been around me or near me during the attacks but when the heavy grayish red dust had settled the picture of what had happened and the devestation was clear. It was part of the body of the blond boy I was trying to stike up a conversation with. I was not prepared for the reality of the aftermath of what really happened, and I was out of control with emotion for a moment and without a doubt felt like there was not enough air for me to breath.

"The boot I was holding was attached to the partial body that belonged to the handsome blonde boy who was wearing the cashmere sweater just moments ago, brushing the dust from it and ignoring me like I didn't exist. He was the logistic officer for Commander Mata who I was trying to get know. Maybe he had just saved my life. I was still in one piece and he was torn apart. I was horrified because I just saw him minutes ago and now I was clutching his mutilated body and holding it like a frightened child as if he could protect me or save me in some way. When I realized I was holding on to the half of a mutilated human body of a man who moments before I had been speaking with and trying to get to acknowledge me, I felt the

104

panic close in on me. I was clearly afraid to die. It's not a good feeling. I shoved the corpse away from me forcefully. I was revolted and cursed letting out a scream of pure terror and helplessness and thinking to myself, 'My God, What's next?'

"Not too far away lying half buried in a pile of rubble and mortally wounded was Adnan. He looked at me with a face that was so tired and full of pain and his eyes were glazed over but empty of any tears. His eyes were as dry looking as the desert sand and devoid of any emotion. He was surrendering to his fate and final journey of his destiny which I was about to learn. A piece of shrapnel that had flown from the blown up military truck twisted like a rope and tore through his abdomen like a spear, protruding out from his shoulder and neck. It was a gruesome thing to see. I ran to him and slid to my knees trying to hold him and to see if I could free him from the jagged piece of metal.

"He put up his hand saying, 'Well, it's about time you got here. What took you so long? Please, please don't touch me,' in a very weak voice devoid of any fear or pain and with a kind of calm acceptance. As I was trying to see what I could do, reaching out my arms wanting to remove him out of that rubble, he weakly held up his hand again to stop me and whispered, 'Please don't mess with my trophy.' I was confused at first and realized he was referring to the twisted metal that was pierced through his body like a spear. He gazed up toward the sky and he moaned, 'It hurts pretty bad,' but I thought that I saw in him that he was not afraid of dying. There was no panic in his face. He was accepting and had made peace for the hand of death that he was dealt. I don't think I have ever seen him more at his best, more calm, collected and at peace with himself. I was grief striken but felt a jolt of envy at the same time from the peaceful bliss that was coming from him. I knew I was feeeling more sorry for myself because I knew I was losing my friend.

"He held my had and with the last exertion of his breath he whispered, 'Ramiz, my friend, I am sorry we couldn't make it for breakfast in the old city this morning and now you'll have to go alone from now on.' Those were the last words my friend ever spoke. He died with his head on my right arm. The blood from his wounds and the wounds from my hands were mixed together. Back home that was a ritual that meant that were blood brothers because our blood mixed. I felt as though half of myself had died too.

"I was mad at God, and I called up to Him, asking, 'Where are you, God? Where are you?' There was no reply from God for me. I wondered and questioned why I was less important than Moses or Abraham were to Him. When they called up to God they were granted His attention and I truly needed His help. The only answer was a dead silence and a few of the very weak cries coming from the wounded. Adnan will live on through me in my memories."

At that point Pace and I were anxious to interupt Ramiz' story of his incredible real life drama. I said first, "Ramiz my friend, there is nothing more gratifying in the world than to be able to love someone the way that your friend loved you in his expressing of his last words to you. You are a fortunate man and we will all make sure that Adnan will never become one of the forgotten soldiers. Let us promise that we will not let it happen for him, as well as all our fallen freedom fighters."

Ramiz was deeply emotional as if he were almost reliving his experience but he continued on with his story, "I took off my jacket and gently lifted Adnan's head to put it under it for him . As I gently slipped it under his head I stood running both hands over my face, suddenly overwhelmed with grief. I felt like my chest was hollow and I had nothing inside. As I was grieving with unbearable pain like I have never experienced before I heard a faint voice coming from a short distance away where I stood next to Adnan's body. The voice was a faint moan in German, 'Please help me, please help me!' In all my pain his voice caught my attention and I walked toward it to see what I might be able do for him.

"I was mad, confused and devoid of emotions. Voices like his seemed to be coming from all around the area of the garrison. For whatever strange reason, I felt I had to go to that particular boy. I recognized the voice because I had spoke with him earlier just before we had got to the barracks. I remember him being a soldier of one day in the military of Mata's who had just arrived that very morning as one of Mata's newest volunteer soldiers, right before Mata came to my house. He played in the almost waist high grass making ocean waves with his hands as we were walking to the barracks together after leaving my house. A nice and innocent boy, a city boy who had probably never been in the country or seen such high grass in the meadows and yet he was armed to the teeth with a deadly machine gun hanging from his shoulder. He was to me just like a little boy and made me laugh while he played in the grass although his innocence as a young boy was being lost by ending up by being armed heavily and ready to kill. He had reminded me of myself as a boy.

"I asked what I could do to help him but I could tell he was too torn up and beyond help. I still felt no emotion and I couldn't feel sorry for him for whatever unexplainable reason. Perhaps I was too traumatized myself from all that had just happened. It was too much blood and death in a very short amount of time. He was barely seventeen or eighteen and strong in body yet in mind still a young boy who never got the chance to fully mature and become a man. Now he never would. How could his parents have let him come? Was it only his decision or did they influence him with their ancient hatred that was passed down over generations? And did they encourage him to come here and to kill or be killed? Whoever made the decision to influence him to come here, the boy paid the ultimate price.

"It crossed my mind that I should get out of the open area and leave that boy behind for now and find maybe a place where a shell had already exploded with hope another shell wouldn't strike in the same place twice. I don't remember exactly what I did after that. The chaotic situation kept continuing as everyone was talking in different voices, screaming, and yelling and cursing everything under the sun. Some of the guys were kicking rocks into the dirt in anger at their powerlessness to prevent what had just happened. The only thing I was sure of at that time was that vengence would come with no doubt. The healthy men were clearly thirsty for blood. I thought someone should step in to get things under control because everything was so chaotic.

"I saw with amazement a barrack still standing with all it's windows and doors blown out. I scratched my head in disbelief. For whatever reason the main building of the barrack was spared from being obliterated like everything else around us. I took it kind of personal, like why was that building still standing when everything else was blown up?

"The next thing I saw was Mata walking slowly from the main building looking collected and cool. He walked over to the podium that he always obviously used when addressing his men. The podium was built out of plywood and made for the commanders to address the troops to put them up on their pedastals. There was a tall man who was following behind Mata who appeared to be all business and looked strong, and mean with a red face seeming to come from his agitation about the ordeal. I thought I had heard of him before but couldn't be sure. My curiousity was piqued. I wanted to know if I knew for sure of him or maybe had met him before. I remembered then that I had heard of him, from you, Angelo. That man was your pal, the notorious Peter F. from Vukovar. You called him a half-breed with triangularly mixed blood of a German father and a Serb-Croatian mother. 'You couldn't get a better mix,' is what you used to say about Peter, and only the German blood gave him what it took to be a man. Unfortunately for him there wasn't enough German in him. He is a sorry and confused man and bitter about everything in life."

"Yes, that's right," I said to Ramiz. "You sized Peter up quite well. It's the truth. He is a sorry and confused man and I know just the way he is. He was never happy and never satisfied but would always say that he was content with what he had. I know that he's nothing but a untrustworthy low life no matter what. I never understood his idea of contentment. To me it seems like he's lost without any direction or goals in life. Peter always bragged that his inner peace and contentment would lead him to the road for success in his life. I know a few more losers who are people just like Peter The first projects they attempt become their very last and their very last turn into their first. It seems like then none of their projects ever get finished or their goals and final achievements ever reached. Their plans always somehow leak with holes or bleed from wounds. That was Peter. It seems the only goal he ever truly reached was to be good at hurting people under the orders from Marshal Tito. That is what he was proud of and bragged about and could boast about all day and every day without feeling any guilt."

Ramiz reared back to laugh then reflected and became reserved for a moment, then he went on, "That is the Peter I suddenly saw on the podium and he was yelling in his strong voice. I swear I thought he had a megaphone in his hand but he didn't and didn't need one. There were more than a thousand men astounded in confusion with commotion and chaos like they had never before experienced that was taking over the garrison, but Peter's voice commanded and got their respect in a matter of seconds. 'Gentlemen,! Soldiers!' he said in English, German, and Croatian. 'I command your attention! If you don't give it to me voluntarily I will take it forcefully, and believe me I will get respect one way or the other! I have a reputation and I insist and will command your respect!' Then he yelled, 'Attention,! Attention!'

"Everyone scrambled to fall in line by height and rank. The place that they were lining up was still littered with the many dead and wounded and all of the debris. It could remind one of being in a horror movie with special effects only they came from real explosions and not movie props. Peter got the attention he wanted and some of the wounded tried to line up but not with much success. Peter didn't look to care about them, but he only wanted that every able bodied man line up. At that moment Mata walked toward the patio and ordered his second in command to turn on the lights, put a stop to the chaos and help the wounded men and bury the dead before nightfall. I thought to myself that we didn't have very much time left before nightfall came. Mata took over the podium introducing himself telling the men, 'I am your commanding officer, Mata, as you already know. I want all the healthy and able men to start picking up the dead and prepare them for burial.'

"His orders were completed before nightfall. He definitely commanded the respect of the men. Everyone formed groups and with shovels, brooms, and a tractor, and they dug a huge hole just outside the main barrack for all those torn up bodies to be put into a mass grave. The sunset that evening looked red and wounded almost as if it knew what happened that day. We were done before the sun set, complying with Commander Mata's orders.

"For a strange reason the remaining men were turning to each other saluting with an old ancient Croatian gesture, saying, "Bogg! Bogg! Bogg!" It is considered a gesture of the strong and honorable men and warriors. It is not so much a word of a religious significance but more in the spirit of young strong men feeling the manhood of themselves.

"I found myself to be at the podium standing in front of Mata. It seemed somehow I was always near him and couldn't seem to get away from him. Through all the chaos and confusion Mata found time to introduce me to Peter. Mata reached out his arm and pointed toward me to acknowledge me to Peter and looked in full control of himself and very collected. He walked toward me saying , 'Peter, this is Ramiz, who is my friend since childhood and Ramiz this is Peter.'

"I greeted him in the same way saying, 'Bogg! Peter, it is very nice to meet you.' "Peter said, 'And you, Ramiz. I am from Australia and it looks like I beat you here by one day to join the troops.'

"I told him, 'Well at least none of us were late because just like Commander Mata says, 'We have a country in Bosnia and Herzogovina to liberate, people to free and a debt to repay.'

"I tried then to excuse myself so I could rush out and help any of the wounded in whatever way I could. I followed a voice I could hear calling for help and was surprised to find that German boy, and I was amazed to find him still alive. I apologized and told him I was so sorry that I had to leave before with the thoughts of Adnan on my mind. Though still alive, this boy was beyond anyone's help, even God Himself. The only thing to comfort me was my belief that when one is absent from the physical body he will perhaps then be in the presence of God the Allah. I did everything I could to offer him some comfort and gently put my left arm under his head and found myself wiping his forehead just as I did not long ago with my friend Adnan."

Ramiz stopped for a moment, and sighed deeply, overwrought by his feelings of compassion as he was retelling his story to us. His eyes were growing wet as he stared off into space somewhere seeing something far away like the events were occuring all over again that were forever etched in his mind and heart. It took him a moment to compose himself and continue.

"I felt mad and was asking the boy loudly, 'Damn you boy! Why you? You are so young. What are you doing here? This is a grown man's job and not for little boys!' I realized then that even grown men such as myself shouldn't be here either or anyone else. I could think of a thousand better places to be.

"I tried to move his arms because they looked twisted and I could see his bones sticking out of his torn camouflage uniform. I tried to move his legs out from under him. When I put my hand under his lower body I felt the warm pool of blood that was as thick as jello. He was still concious but showed no fear or pain in his face. His eyes were glazed over and he locked them with my eyes seeking some kind of assurance that he might live through this from me. I couldn't give him any. I just couldn't, as in my faith it is prohibited to lie to a dying man. A promise given must be kept and a lie never told to a man breathing his last breath. Trying to comfort him I asked, 'Where are you from? Why are you here?'

"In a heavy accent he said, 'I am from Germany and I came to help Croatia be free from the Serbs, but here I am dying instead.' I was right in thinking he was from a Croatian decent.

110

"I suddenly felt so bitter that I laughed sarcastically and shook my head and told him, 'You stupid little boy! Leaving your homeland and dying in a stranger's hands, in a stranger's land. Don't you know that dead men can't free anybody, and they can only imprison the souls of the the loved ones they leave behind?' He showed no emotion to what I had said. He only coughed a couple times and I saw small drops of blood coming from his ears, nose and mouth, whatever blood there was that was left in his body. The blood around him had congealed in mass as thick as jello. He beckoned me with his fingers to gesture for me to come closer. So I went to him and put my ear up to his mouth but could hardly feel any breath coming from him. Finally he weakly said, 'Please call my mother.' I don't know why but I taunted him and repeated his words, saying, 'Please call my mother.' I stood up looking at the glazed sky yelling with arrogance, 'Oh mother, where are you?' I then told him I promised I would fulfill his wish.

"Then I felt chills run through my body. That very day before I had been talking with my own mother when I was debating in my heart and soul whether I should join Mata and his bloody group of mercenaries or not. I hadn't planned on having to bury any of them or calling their mothers giving them news no mother should ever have to hear. So I promised to call his mother. I felt like my position was that of an undertaker. I felt that under the laws of nature no parent should have to bury or hear the news of the loss of their child, it should always be the other way around. This war and these people broke all of natures laws.

"The boy whispered weakly wanting to tell me something else and growing more weak very quickly, so I lowered my head again almost check to check with him and barely audible he said, 'Please don't leave me here.'

"I said what I was thinking out loud with rage that again was exploding inside me, 'Your mother must be a very beautiful woman but she was a fool just like my own mother was the other morning when you guys arrived at my home. Our mother's should have forbidden us to go but we needed to go and stand up as men.'

"His very last word whispered with a great effort were, 'I come from Mannheim, Germany. Will you please take me home?'

"I told him in anger, 'You are at home now you fool. I will bury you here where your mother and father told you was your home and that's why your little boy's body will be buried right here. It seems it

111

must be the wishes of your parents.'

"By then he had gone and I picked him up with my left hand by the chest of his camoflage, and looking around for a shovel, I dragged him over the field. I don't think I laid him down gently. I just dropped his body that only hours ago had been playing in that same grass while pretending to make ocean waves and making me laugh. Now he was dead and I was mad perhaps because I had liked the boy and felt pain of the loss for someone so young who I had barely gotten to know and whose light of life had just been extinguished forever. I had developed an attachment for him from our shared emotional agony.

"I started digging and was talking and cursing to myself without even realizing it. For some stange reason I was feeling a deep sense of loss. I pushed the shovels full of dirt in chunks of sod that were the yellow color of unfertile soil that wasn't good for anything except to be a thin layer to nuture a little scraggly grass on top. It's almost like cheating nature. No wonder there wasn't a single tree anywhere. I felt I was thinking out loud all of my crazy thoughts and next thing I knew I had dug the hole as deep as up to my nose. Why did a young boy like this come all the way from Germany to die? Why did it happen? Were his mother and father at fault? He had no damn business being here, neither did many other young men who came from around the world for this uncalled for obsene crusade. Most of these boys I doubt even knew where Croatia or Bosnia was before they came here. All they knew about it had come from their bitter parents.

"I kept digging until the hole was level with my head. When I felt the hole was deep enough I jumped out of the hole, kicked his body with my foot into the grave and said, 'Here this is what you wanted, your permanent home in Croatia! You might as well call it your motherland because you sure gave up your life for it. Too bad neither you or she benefited. I hope I live through the bloody chaos to deliver the news no one ever wants to find out, to let your parents know what became of you. If for some reason I am unable to, the earth will hold our secrets.'

"I flipped his body over with my foot into the grave that I just dug and he landed flat on his ass with his back against the dirt wall with his legs crossed almost like he had sat down to talk to me. For a second I thought, 'Why is all of this horror happening to me?' I swear to you I thought he came back to life. I looked at him and said, 'Man, you look like a good Muslim sitting down to drink coffee. Where did you learn that position? I didn't realize the native Catholics in the area had the same customs as ours. Maybe you converted to Islam.'

"I realized I had been conversing with a dead man and tried to regain some of my composure. Yet being aware that I was talking to a dead man still I couldn't help it and told him, 'Don't worry. I'll do what you had asked me to because it was your last wish.' Do you guys think I was going mad or just racked with pity for the boy?"

Pace answered him, "No man, going mad would be a very natural reaction to what you went through. He reached to pat his hand over the table with comfort knowing truly what Ramiz felt having experienced very similar things in Vietnam himself. Ramiz thanked him for understanding and said it was nice to know he wasn't all alone in what he had experienced and it gave him some sense of relief.

I had to interrupt for a second trying to lighten the mood and said, "Be grateful you are still here talking about it and have yourselves and me to talk to today. Many were denied to have another day to live just like this."

Ramiz then continued on still entrenched by the vision of his story, "I pitched down the shovel in that hole as a support so that I could jump in with him. There was something else I just knew I had to do but had to think about what it was. After I jumped back in I took a couple steps over to him and knelt down. I pulled a handkerchief from my pocket and gently wiped off his face and put it over his head. Then I jumped back out of the hole using the shovel to support me and faced his grave again. I pulled out the shovel and leaned on it limply and felt is if I were breaking down. Can you imagine, Pace, I was about to break down over the people who were there to burn and destroy my Bosnia and her people? I was overcome by my emotions and my anger at it all filled me with rage. It wan't hate and rage at the boy but at what was happening to me and what I was becoming. I felt I was not the same innocent and kind human being I had been just hours ago and was becoming just like them. I thanked God I hadn't had had to kill anyone yet. I was becoming as hardened as a steel beam. I cursed the boy not thinking that I knew he couldn't hear me. I was talking to his dead soul and asked him, 'Would you like me to say a prayer for you?' It wasn't all the young boy's fault because he had been taught what to believe in and stand for from the seed planted by his mother and father that they instilled in him, with the hope that perhaps it would not culminate with his death or anything bad, but deliver some good.

"I had joined a group of people without morals or direction or purpose for doing anything noble or good. I was a member of their group for one whole long day. That was a day that turned out to be a living hell on earth.

"So I asked the unhearing boy which type of prayer he would like, a Christian, Orthodox, or a Muslim one, since I thought I could do them all. I almost waited for him to answer and said, 'Aren't you gonna answer me you son of a bitch?' He was just sitting there getting cold. I was getting more angry when he didn't answer me. I liked him though and I was sorry that he was dead and that was the thing that was causing all my anger. Then I said to him, 'Since you're not answering me, I will just say a prayer in the hope that it's the one that you were baptized in.' I thought later that I was glad he didn't give me his preference because if he picked the Muslim one I wouldn't have known how to do it. I told the dead body of the boy that we would just face Rome with your last rites and a prayer. I buried him then. I was shoveling and slamming in the dirt faster and faster and didn't even remember leaving his grave.

"The next thing I was aware of I was wandering through the barracks in the ruins. The boy's death wouldn't leave my thoughts. I wondered again about his father and mother who were living somewhere in Germany. I thought they were likely to be in a beautiful, comfortable, safe home and living in peace and tranquility with plenty of time for everything. How sad it was to see one such as this boy that they had perhaps unwittingly sent to die. Instead of doing all the right things for their children it was all wrong for the one I had just buried in that unmarked grave.

"Did those perhaps hundred of thousands or millions of Croatian parents who left Croatia influence their sons by their own political and religious ideologies, the ones that bled their beloved Croatia for centuries after they had practically abandoned it becasue they didn't want to fight for it? Now they were sending the children to do their fighting. One of the biggest reasons for their failures was that they were leaderless. Their political idealogies for Croatia never came to be fulfilled at least up to now. Were these people the one's like this boy's parents, die hard patriots who were not willing to waste their own lives but were willing to sacrifice the lives of their children for the dreams that never came to fruition for themselves? Here again the laws of nature had been broken with the old burying the young instead of the young burying the old.

"So they sent the children from all over the world to the front lines in the motherland of Croatia to do battle and spill their blood so that their own dreams for Croatia would become a reality and they could be able to proudly identify themselves as Croatians once and for all. This particular action was taking place in the wrong territory of Bosnia and in Croatia and came to be an occupying force. They were unable to try to make a difference without the spilling of blood and now it's their home and their own blood that has been spilled. They wanted to bring glory to Croatia, a place that never had any except for in an illusionary way. Croatia was always being milked by the ones who were other than the people who were the true masters of the land for centuries. Their destiny was the same as my Bosnia and they always had been vunerable for being milked by others.

"Here they are still dying centuries later, and let's hope this boy who had ended up here will be one of the last. I hope that his death will not have been in vain. I hope his death will take away some of the hatred from the people's hearts, and most of all to give them strength to be able to heal the wounds. If that can happen in the present, then the future may hold promise for them and my Bosnia.

"By midnight that night there was nobody in the garrison except for a few men who were changing guard every few hours. After that long never ending night, finally by early sunrise I was still awake the same as I had been yesterday like the day never ended for me or did a new day begin. That morning I swear I thought the sun looked different."

I asked him, "What do you mean, the sun looked different, how could it look different?"

Pace said, "Angelo, just leave him alone and try to tell the story, I'm enjoying it."

So Ramiz said, "I'll try paint a picture of it. Perhaps the sun reflected on the pain of the events that had occured and we had gone through that previous night. I will try to explain by saying it looked like the sun was actually bleeding, just like my body and heart were bleeding. The sun looked like it was feeling the same as I was. Pace, I am telling you the sun was different. The way the sun looked and I felt were as one."

Pace interuped and looked at me to ask, "Do you believe that could happen Angie?"

I laughed and shrugged, and jokingly said, "Ramiz, I think that you might have been hallucinating and didn't have full control of your senses and emotions. Seriously I can empathize with you and feel your pain." Then I told Ramiz, "If you don't mind my interrupting for a minute, I wanted to tell you of something that reminds me of another strange phenomena about the sun intwining with the events, similar to your story."

Pace said, "Well, I don't mind if you don't make it too long. I would like to hear Ramiz finish the story."

I replied, "I promise I'll make it short. It's a story about Atilla the Hun in 410 AD while he was invading Europe. He was marching on his way to Rome and there was no stopping him. He was invinceable up until he had his encounter with the sun's magic and the slyest and cleverest Pope in history, Pope Leo, who had saved Christianity and Rome with his little finger and the gold cross that he wore on his chest."

Pace and Ramiz were not familar with that story and I did my best to enlighten them about this very true story. Atilla lost the chance he would later regret of historical proportions and the only chance he had in a battle at one time. Pope Leo knew of Attila the Hun's reputation and knew the sword and spear were not enough to fight Attila. He had his own bag of political tricks that he had learned throughout his lifetime although they would not be of service to him with his upcoming encounter with Atilla. A trick of nature turned out to be his saving grace and best defense from a disastrous encounter with Attila and his army. He knew from his experience and wisdom that he had to come up with a way as seasoned politician would, to be able to defeat Attila somehow.

The Pope took the task of saving Rome upon himself. When Attila was invading Europe a villiage priest accompanied Pope Leo as well as a couple of Roman senators who had arrived from Rome to meet with Attila the Hun on the banks of the River Mincio to beg him not to invade and destroy their homes. Right from the start nature was performing a miracle and worked in the favor of Pope Leo and performed some magic. Some historians dispute what happened although the legend of the story I think is true, just like yours, Ramiz.

"You see, Pope Leo had the problem of convincing the most powerful, arrogant, forty seven year old charismatic warrior, who already plundered most of the known world in fire from Asia to the

116

Italian Alps in the French wine country, to spare them from the same fate of those lands he conquored and not plunder the Italian penninsula and Rome.

"That little man Pope Leo, small in body but big in heart and mind, single handedly changed the course of history not only by his experience and leadership skills but with also with the symbol of a giant golden cross that was encrusted with rubies and diamonds and hung on his chest. The cross was a Roman symbol of punishment during those pagan times for anyone who broke the laws in Rome. Imprisonment was only a temporary thing for the convicts in the Roman empire. Their inevitable ultimate punishment was crucifixion. After Christ's crucifixion on the cross, the cross became the symbol for forgiveness of sins in the new religion that was fast evolving and overtaking western Europe. The cross Pope Leo wore was very impressive and Atilla must have found it fascinating. A gold cross that had a man sculptured who was in agony and nailed on a cross hanging from the Pope's chest must have vexed Atilla and in his curiosity he must have wanted to know all about it. The Pope didn't hesitate to explain his belief in the power of the Lord God. Pope Leo can be acredited in single handedly saving Rome from certain despair by the hand of Atilla.

"It looked like everything worked out to be in Pope Leo's favor. The Pope was impressive with his robes and gold cross he wore that Attila had never seen the likes of before. Even the sun was doing it's magic for Pope Leo as it shone on his cross causing it's reflection to blind Attila for a moment. The day had been overcast by clouds but they suddenly parted to allow the sun to shine brightly through them causing the reflection of the gold cross and star to cast it's shape in front of Attila .

"Everything was working in the Pope's favor. He wasn't wasting any words in convincing Attila that this was a sign directly from God. Leo's experiences gave him an edge to negotiate with Attila. Pope Leo used this opportunity to capitalize on the moment when nature's magic took the stage and performed her magic like no other. Legend has it that during the critical negotiations the heavy clouds broke apart to allow the light from the sun to break through, and is what we would call a modern miracle in religious terms. The sun shone brightly, almost purposefully to glare directly onto Leo's cross.

"Pope Leo quickly noted Attila's reaction and used the moment for the second time to tell Attila that this was a sign from the God of his new religion. Pope Leo told Attila that what was happening was nothing less than a message of truth from God and a sign for Attila that if he decided to wage war on Rome he would surely be cursed to Hell. In the end Attila decided not to plunder Rome and perhaps part of his decision was partly based on the time he had spent as a young boy in Rome and was the guest of his old friend and later rival, Commander Aetius.

"All of us at some point in our lifetime have seen the performance of nature's beauty on her stage on her own terms. We have no way to explain it and it becomes magical and deeply spiritual to us, if only for the simplist reason that it's something we can't feel or touch.

"That single event with Pope Leo brought out the vunerability of the real human in Attila the Hun. That mystifying experience was as equally imporant to know about him as his being unforgiving in the heat of battle. It showed that he was human after all and had a fear of the unknown as we all do. He was poor with his knowledge of politics but on the other hand he was still the greatest military strategist who earned the respect of his warriors each day by bringing them back home alive from the battlefields. That is the picture of a true warrior. One thing he had been sure of was that he wanted Rome for his own. If his army hadn't been sick with maleria, not Pope Leo or any of his magic nor anyone could save Rome. I could only say he was a realist. He was a leader who could not live without conquoring and fighting. The battlefield was the only life he knew or wanted to know, nothing more or nothing less.

"Pope Leo was a well seasoned politician as well as a visionary for his church, religion, and the future of Rome. The Pope clearly knew where he was going to go after his visit with Attila that day, and that was by the mountains of the Alps in Northern Italy. He went back to Rome knowing he had proved to be triumphant over the deadly and ambitious Attila. He also knew this was going to pave the way for the church to take over the empire of Rome and the moment he must sieze. For the first time the dark ages for the western world had began and the church and state affairs became one with disaterous conquences.

"Attila told Pope Leo , 'You may be a good magician, or really be your the messenger of your God which I have no knowledge of nor do I care. At any rate you did perform well today and I will not invade

118

Rome, your church, or your new God.'"

Ramiz was not very knowledgeable about history, it was a weak point in his intellectual capacity. He was intrigued by the way I told and compared the reality and the coincidental things of the past to the present and how they intertwine. Both of the places of our stories were not far from each other, only about two hundred miles apart. I felt good showing off a little of my knowledge in ancient and current history and politics.

"You can tell me whatever you want Angie," Ramiz said as he looked across the table at Pace for some support. He held out his hands as if to say, "Come on Pace, help me out here."

Pace said, "I wouldn't touch this topic with a twelve foot pole but it is intriguing, it was a great story and the truth, especially if Angie is telling it."

Ramiz continued, "Well, I'm telling you that on that day the sun looked like it was sick and it was red almost as if it had been crying. It didn't look the same as on any other morning when I have seen it. Continuously through that night shells were hitting around the barracks area. It was a one hell of a sleepless night. In the early hours of the morning there was total silence. By the late afternoon I could hear the powerful and deadly sound of explosives coming from the city. As the sun was high over the mountains the explosions ripped into the area of the garrison, and again I heard the sounds of the deadly dooming explosions and thought, 'Here we go again.'

"Angie, the explosion felt almost like my body had exploded too, it was that powerful."

"Yes, Ramiz, I am very familiar with those deadly sounds of explosions. I experienced that in Vietnam," Pace said.

Ramiz brushed back his hair with his fingers and continued. "It sounded like it was another direct hit on one of those stupid trucks that were loaded with ammunition that they had missed last night. Peter came out with a towel on his shoulder just as the explosions were going off from the area of the main barracks just like knew that would be the last of the explosions, calm and collected. He headed straight toward the water faucets and didn't look the least bit troubled by what had just happened.

"The next thing I knew there were quite a few men gathered behind Peter who had been waiting to wash their hands and faces of dirt from all the debris and blood from their cuts and wounds that they recieved from the barrage of attacks. I was there too trying to clean my own wounds. The sink was made of a giant hollowed log that was filled by water from a small stream up the hill and flowed through into the trough. I finally had gotten my turn and was trying to wash my cuts on my hand and face. We all needed to cleanse the grime, dust and dirt away from the previous night's situation of chaos. A tiny little mirror hung from a pole in one of the logs by the faucets where I was standing so that I could see my reflection. I didn't like what I was seeing. I saw myself as a man afraid for his life and wondering how many more chances he would get. I didn't know it but my fate was hanging in the hands of the man who was about to walk up next to me to wash the dirt from his face just as I was doing.

"Peter suddenly stood next to me and greeted me with a slap on my dusty back. It felt like I was hit with a bag of salt. We started to talk. I asked him if he knew what the explosions were that had just come from the direction of the city. I told him that my heart had almost exploded from the impact and I was hoping he would say we needed to leave. Peter laughed, rubbing his pitted huge red nose which one couldn't help but notice and said 'My heart felt the same. Don't worry, I'll let you know in about twenty minutes when everyone is lined up in the Pista drill field after the break.'

"By breakfast time we were all at Pista lined up waiting and wondering what we were going to today after yesterday's ordeal and the most recent explosions. I knew what I wanted to do but the only way I could do that was to try to get out of there alive and not carried out with my feet forward, so I accepted my fate and the circumstances of the moment. Mata and Peter greeted the troops saying, 'Bogg!' in one voice.

"Peter addressed the troops saying, 'We have news for you. We have done something that should have been done a long time ago. We are bypassing the traditional military inspection and the good news you have been waiting to hear is that the symbol of Ottoman and Islam has been destroyed. The Bosnians will have to build another bridge over the river because we blew it up this morning.' He was talking about the old bridge that was the only connection to our part of the city and the other side. He continued, saying, 'Now there will be no question where the border of Herzogovina is and who it belongs to.'

"Man, Angie, when I heard him say that now we will know where the border of Herzogovina was, my heart sank. That's when I knew I had made a grave mistake by joining Mata and his men. I knew I was wearing the wrong uniform and was going to be ahamed of it standing beside Mata. Mata declared the river as a border. He said, 'Everyone get ready. In five minutes we are moving.'

"The Bosnian defenders from the city of Mostar on the other side of the river, the part that Croatians call the Muslim side of the city, wanted to do some payback for the bridge they all had loved having been destroyed. The bridge was a loss for everyone because it was an ancient bridge and a monument. What they did to the bridge was of no purpose or benefit to anyone. It was only a bunch of destructive, mindless men who committed this senseless act and wasted a historical monument in the process to gain nothing but condemnation around the world. It was mind boggling now when I look back. The world cried over that bridge but didn't shed a single tear over the 500,000 slaughtered Bosnians."

Pace said, "The bridge was an unreplaceable thing of history and people are replaceable."

"How do you replace the people?" I asked and said, "Wait, don't answer me. I will answer for you. Maybe the Bosnians got a new name, the Barbarians, with no TV or radio or available hunting grounds because they are occupied by the Serbian forces and everyone is stuck at home being stupid and making more babies. Maybe that's what they should do because they will be wiped out anyways but after all I think they should fight and show the world they are not barbarians and show the world they can fight as warriors without commiting any crimes or harming any unarmed man or woman."

Pace replied, "That is what they have been doing, fighting like true warriors. I was there and am proud of them."

"May I please continue?" Ramiz said. "Whoever was in charge of that inane decision to blow up that bridge must have the brain of a pigeon and no respect for the value of the historical signifigance of anything. Shame on them for blowing up the bridge. It showed how blind and hateful men can be. It's the luck of being educated. That's all it is and I was as blind as my people were not to have seen it coming."

"During that time the Bosnjaks felt they had been betrayed by the Croatians and rightfully so. The Bosnian Muslim Bosnjaks just a few months before stood side by side with Croatia in the city of Vukovar, which by the way was obliterated by the Serbs, but we tried to save the rest of Croatia from bleeding to death from the Serbs. Now the very same people, who were are commrades in arms for the fight for Croatia destroyed ours and their own monument and entire city. We helped the Croatians fight for their liberation from Serbia. The Chetniks were bandits and likewise unmerciful, bloodthirsty bastards. This was the thanks we got for all of our good neighborliness we always had extended, particularly to the Croats throughout history.

"The Muslim side of Mostar started to pound and bombard the Croatian side with all that they had. The Croats obliged them in the same way. I thought, 'Boy am I on the wrong side this time. I hope no one ever finds out that I was part of this bunch of losers. I felt embarressed and ashamed. I found myself with my head in my hands sitting on the sidelines watching everything happen like a confused fan at a rugby game whose team was losing and being unable to root for anyone, even myself. This was no game, it was much more serious. In this situation it wasn't about being anyone's fan. It was about the destruction of my people and our country and being unable to do anything about it.

"Hell on earth broke loose once again. Most of these madmen had been my fellow countrymen. Now they had split into divisions that seemed to be trying to obliterate each other. They were bombarding one another until they ended up at the end of Hell. It seemed like Heaven and earth were exploding together. Military trucks filled with explosives received direct hits causing powerful explosions that were beyond belief. It seemed no one was in command that was smart enough to learn from just the day before and move those trucks that were filled with ammunition and explosives out of target range. All of it seemed like senseless dying. Again there were many men wounded in the same kind of circumstances as the day before, many men were lying unconscious or dead in the heavy dust and dirt covering the surrounding area.

"Through all of this chaos that I wished I wasn't a part of, a thought occurred to me. As I saw so many soldiers killed, I wished that perhaps now all of them should be dead and then many innocent families wouldn't be hurt by them. Their intentions were clear, to indiscriminatly target every apartment in the tall high rises without missing and with no mercy and to kill anyone and everyone. It seemed to me that maybe the Bosnian citizens of Mostar were not dying in vain and God was working in his mysterious ways to stop them from bringing total destruction to part of the city. Material things were leveled but the spirit of the people was raised to fight back.

"I had only one thought. That was to get out of there alive and survive that nightmare. Pure fear chilled me to the bone for the first time in my life. I am a witness to their destruction to try to keep them from doing what they planned to do, and barrage the rest of the city. Now they were preoccupied with their own troubles and survival. In two days I experienced more anguish and death than anyone could imagine, and for what? I had lost my best friend and found out the friends and neighbors I had grown up with were not my friends at all, in fact mortal enemies. That is a heartbreaking thing. The friend I had grown up with and thought of as my brother and who my own mother treated as her own son, was a prime member of a group creating concentration camps for my people, who once had thought of him and loved him as their own. Those people were the Bosnians, the Bosniaks."

Pace said, "I thought the Croatians didn't have any concentration camps."

"Don't kid yourself. They had them on smaller scales than the Serbs but no less oppressive. They were different all right. They kept Bosnian men is oil tank holders that some were about eighty to one hunderd feet wide with close to three hundred men at a time. Them smell of the oil, heat and the men was unbearable. Some of friends said they overheard the men talking saying that one of these days they would as Croats be embarressed by what they had done to the Bosnians. That was a truth that echoed through Croatia and that day has come.

"I could see no good coming out of it in any way or from any side that I looked at it . I felt an inner scream of anguish trapped inside of me at the reality of this tragedy that was happening around me. I felt like I was breaking down and my inner soul and spirit were going to give out on me. I ran to try to find a safe place to hide. I looked around but couldn't see anything because of all the dust and I stumbled many times over different kinds of rubble and debris. No doubt a lot of it was the dead bodies of men. I kept stumbling and suddenly found I had fallen into a crater about ten by thirty, the result of a direct hit on a truck full of explosives. It was yet another physical and emotional shock to me. I felt like I was falling forever down that hole. I had a brutal cut on my left eye from a piece of metal that was down inside the hole. I could feel something warm running down my face and felt pain in my thigh. The huge cut ran across my face to my left eye and had cut through to the bone. I tried climbing out of the hole and after a few attempts I found myself wandering around the battleground without any invaders but full of the aftermath of debris.

"After the dust started to settle I could clearly see the tragedy and hell that had just taken place yet again. I said to myself I had to get the hell out of this hell. Then I heard the music from the radio speaker coming from the commissary that was still playing the patriotic songs of Croatia. It was a particular song and the only one which was playing at that time and it is still stuck in my mind. It was by Miso Kovach called, "Proplakat Ce Zora," which means, "The early morning will cry." That is exactly what was happening. The morning did cry alot of tears of blood including my own and the song added even more heart break. It looked almost like an exact repeat of yesterday afternoon and now all these young men were dead too. It seemed like there couldn't be any healthy men left. It looked like someone had gone mad in a slaughter house, and for what? I wonder how much success they could have had if all of them had put their energy and efforts into trying to bring peace instead of war and killing each other? Expending that energy for all of that evil could have worked wonders if it had been diverted for the good. If Mata had joined the Croats in fighting the Serbs we could have saved hundreds of thousands of lives. Now we have to fight on two front lines of the Croats and Serbs. It was a simple no win situation. I can only wonder. Sadly we'll never know the answer to what might have been if everyone would have put down the guns and sat down to talk instead.

"Chaos and panic reigned the emotions of our few thousand men. The barracks were blown up and even the commissary and the kitchen that they had missed hitting the day before was the first thing they hit the next day. It looked like they had known that they missed our very important eating place before and they wanted to make sure we wouldn't be gathering around it tonight to talk about all our failures. They definintely knew what they were aiming for. Men were running in all directions. I remember very clearly thinking at the time that it was very strange, as though each of them had a different idea of how to escape the inescapable rain of the artillery. I found a little niche in some rubble and just sat down there watching it happen and this time I actually enjoyed it. I knew if one of those bombs did hit me it wouldn't matter whether I was running or hiding.

"After the bombarding stopped for the forth time the dust appeared in big red clouds like some kind dry ice fog that was set up for a dramatic stage show. Only this was the real thing and not a performance on a stage. After a few seconds I could hear men getting up and running in one direction or another but couldn't see them. About a half an hour later we counted more than a hundred wounded. Thank God I was only cut up again in places and only bleeding a little but I was alive and one of the lucky ones who was still in one piece and able to walk around. When that fact struck me I found myself thinking about my friend Adnan again and the young boy that I had to bury yesterday. My heart was pounding so hard in my chest I thought it would come out.

"Wounded and dead men were everywhere buried in the rubble of brick, metal, and wood. Some of the men were bleeding badly and this time I really wanted no part it anymore since I now knew what their true agenda was. I was beginning to wish for all of them to just disappear, no matter how or where. Wandering through the garrison I was filled with agonizing feelings of despair, not for the first time, I was learning how to accept the despair. Despite my anger I had to try to save some of them as a fellow human being if I could.

"I found myself again pushing dirt and using my bandaged hands as shovels. Each time that I pushed my hand into rubble and dirt I would feel the sharp objects cutting my flesh to the bone. I felt no pain or fear. I knew I had try to dig them out and even if I might only save just one man I must try and do it. I could let nothing stand in the way of saving these young men from dying. I was brought up in a faith that teaches we must be giving, compassionate, merciful, and helpful to the needy, sick or injured. I hoped I was doing my part. I felt like I was playing God right then and I if I could only dig one man out alive and save his life it would be worth it. Maybe I could even cause the one life I had saved to spread the message on to his people of goodness, kindness and that myself and my people are not the enemies of their people."

Pace spoke up, "That would be asking too much my friend, even from God. Too much blood has already been spilled and you and your people are to blame. They are there because they want you out of Bosnia. You are a noble man Ramiz, but noble deeds don't alway bear fruit."

Ramiz replied, "Anyway it didn't matter what I tried to do save them, it was not to be. I needed more than my hands. I needed a bulldozer or else miracles from God.

It looked like there was going to be quite a few corpses to bury. I don't know how long I spent digging but the only thing that I was able to dig out was a man's head and it wasn't talking. The rest of his body was still attached to him but lying trapped under thousands of pounds of heavy metal from a truck that exploded on him and a few other men. I cradled his head in my arms, gently brushed back his hair with my fingers, comforted him and told him he would be OK. Seconds later the strong grip that had been holding onto my hand relaxed and he held up two fingers like he wanted a cigarette. I lit a cigarette and held it up to his mouth for a puff. He wasn't able to inhale it although he looked at it like a life giving gift. As I was holding his hand I could feel the life start slipping out of him then his head went limp in my arm.

"I stood up and brushed my fingers through my hair not realizing how bloody and dirty my hands were and thinking out I said, 'Hey you, God, don't you think it's too much already?' I went on then to another voice I heard calling out. I was beginning to detest everything around me for a second. I wished I could just squeeze the life out of the source of all of this madness and make it stop. I wanted it to all end, the darkness, sorrow, and the memories from this time. I wanted it all to end right then and there.

"I stared without seeing anything and felt my eyes were traveling on an endless journey through space and time looking for God again as I had done a few times in the last couple of days. I wanted to talk to God and spun around in kind of a drunken way to look around me and saw nothing but death and despair. I thought, 'How much more of this do I have to see? Is there any light in the end to all of this maddness?' There was no help to be had from anywhere or anyone it seemed, not even especially God. I wanted to ask Him, 'Where are you and how can you allow these things to happen? Is man created to suffer in agony for eternity or is this man's own doing?' I couldn't hold back my impulsive emotions asking, 'God, why have you forsaken us?' I felt like Moses must have up on Mount Sinai, lost and confused but there was a difference between Moses' situation and mine. He had plenty of time to talk to God but for me it was a matter of life and death. I was looking for an immediate message and I didn't care if it came by telegraph or voice mail but no answer was coming. It's devastating to feel that you know there is no hope coming from anywhere, even from God.

"One thing I felt did come from God at that moment was the strength to compose myself and to be strong for my remaining fellow men that kept calling from everywhere for help in weak agonized voices. By now I felt I owed nothing to the cause of these soldiers but I still felt compassion for them. I embrace the teachings of my religion and the Koran that command me to be there and not walk away from one who needs help regardless of who it may be, even my enemies. I need to try to win their hearts. Through the quagmire of my emotions I heard their cries saying, 'Help me please, my God. Why me? I am dying and I haven't done anything wrong. Why me?' So I went looking for some way I could help.

"I was emotionally and physically exhausted, but still found the strength to do what I believed my moral obligation was to do. I was picking up the wounded men. Some of them had torn up legs and arms or were barely alive or not alive, blown to pieces. Then I heard a voice that sounded almost like the young boy I buried yesterday. He was crying unemotionally without any tears and calling for his mother. I went to where the voice was coming from and saw a young man lying in a pool of blood. I was near the water trough that somehow was still left standing and I ran over to wet my hankerchief and ran back to the boy.

"I knelt and tried gently to hold his hand but it was broken and he wasn't able to move it. I gently dabbed at the wounds on his face and mouth with my wet hankerchief. He opened his eyes to look at me and weakly asked for me to put it in his mouth. He seemed to light up for a second. I looked him over to see what kind of condition he was in and realized his body was like a dry branch that had been stepped on and crunched into a thousand pieces. I again found myself with this young man comforting him in the same emotional upheavel and roller coaster of emotions that I had yesterday before that bloody sundown.

"He was still conscious but I could see no fear of death in him. He wanted to say some last words as the other men before him had wanted to. I think his body was in shock but his mind still alert enough for a few seconds to deliver his last words of sorrow and know that he had made a mistake and had followed the wrong man in coming here just as I had two days ago.

"I put my left arm gently under his head and found myself again cleaning his face with the front part of my shirt that I untucked from my pants and comforting him as I had done with the other dying men. I reflected again on the senseless waste of lives. Here was one more of the many wasted lives and for nothing. For sure I think the boy probably had everything he ever wanted wherever it was he came from. Here he was dying in a land he didn't even know or belong to. I thought to myself, 'That's the way it is when you have everything but don't know or respect what it is you have.' That may be what happened to this young man. He may have had everything but didn't know or value it. I hope that he heard what I said to him before he died."

I interrupted him to ask, "What did you tell him Ramiz? Were you going to thank him for coming over to kill our brothers and sisters? He had no damn business being there. Neither did any of them who came from overseas, the Serbs or the Croats, those bunch of bloodthirsty bastards. They are both responsible for so many of our children who are murdered at their hands."

"No, Angie," Ramiz answered, "I didn't tell him anything like that. I told him I was going to bury him deep in the ground and drive a stake right in the middle of his grave so he wouldn't ever get out. That's all I told him only not out loud. I am still a forgiving man but not forgetting."

Pace laughed and asked, "Why did you tell him that? Were you afraid he would become a vampire?"

Ramiz said, "Well, I realized that we were not on the same side by the time the bridge was blown up and the shells were sent to my part of the city from my commrades. It really didn't make any difference to me if he lived or died since I knew I wasn't part of that team anymore. I wanted to play it safe and be better safe than sorry. I would be fighting against my own people if I stayed with them. I knew I had enough of this group and would be leaving the first chance I had. I did bury him like I promised all by myself. I put him over my shoulder and took him to an open field. I took a shovel and ax and started digging into dirt and every time I lowered the ax I said something to him just like when I talked to the other boy I buried. I'm not sure what I was said. I was mad. I was mad about the loss of my friend and not getting a chance to properly grieve for him and mad about not being sure of what the extent of the losses were around me and across the river where my home was.

"I dug just a little tiny hole for him. I don't know how long it took me to dig, but it wasn't too long for sure. In this particular area the dirt was like some type of clay that was always naturally moist and could be carved in any way you wanted. I dug his grave which came out an untraditional grave for him without intending to. He had said he was sorry and he had been following the wrong people. I thought that would be the way he would like to be buried after admitting that he had been wrong in being here.

"I looked around and saw everyone else was occupied with their own digging and nursing their wounds. They were trying to recover from the psychological trauma of all the shooting and blood around them. No one was talking with anyone. Everyone was in their own personal world passing by each other without seeming to see one another, just lost. I finally realized they were all a bunch of sorry losers who were losers before they came and have proven it now. They all deserved what they got.

"No one was paying attention to me or what I was doing at his grave and I kind of pushed his body and then I really kicked it until he fell down into the hole I made. I swear he didn't fall flat down but into a crunched position right on his ass just like the other boy did with his legs landing being crossed. I don't know if it just happened or because of all his broken bones. I doubt he had a bone that was not broken. I kicked clods of clay until the hole was filled and each time one fell over him I felt I had hurt him because that clay dirt was so heavy.

"I knew I asked this dead boy all kinds of questions also but the son of a bitch didn't answer me either. There I was again at the task of undertaker that I never applied for. I kicked at that dirt as hard as I could. I was just angry and getting angrier because I could see myself becoming just like them and I didn't like it. They were cold blooded. Now that I look back it's a good thing they never got the chance to see their wishes fulfilled with all that blood from innocent people on their hands.

"My thoughts and my heart again wandered to his mother and father. 'Did they really know that he was here? Was it by their doing and had they shaped him to be ready to kill at a young age and be willing to be killed, or was it by his own will that he was here?' I knew myself to be a compassionate man and felt I was losing my compassion and didn't like what I was becoming. I blamed it on these men. I didn't hate the dying man or feel such rage because of the way I had buried him or by the actions of my childhood brother and friend Mata who was jubilant about ordering the blowing up of the bridge that I had loved so much. Mata and Peter gave the reason the bridge was blown away as that it was a symbol of the Ottoman Turks. Islam hadn't bothered him while we were growing up and sharing my mother who had taken care of him as her own. On the contrary my thought on the bridge was that it was a symbol for prosperity and unity for all of us that the Ottomans had left as a gift to us, Serbs, Croats, and Bosnian Muslims alike. My heart grieves for all of us.

"I didn't cover the boy's face with my hankerchief like I did with the other dying men. I hated what I had become because of what these men did and were trying to do and still planned to do. Now I knew I must do everything possible to make sure they didn't succeed. As a Muslim I couldn't think of a single Muslim prayer, to ask God for help to stop the destructive mission of these madmen.

"When I was burying these men I was able to pray for their souls for them in their own language and faith. I felt again compassion and mercy for their dead souls and wished we had met under different circumstances as fellow men, even though I doubt now that they would have had the same feelings for me. For the young man I just buried with no name on a stone that never was erected, that was the end of his story and he thus he became just one more of the forgotten soldiers.

"It seemed many of these men were like they were because they had been brainwashed and shaped throughout their childhoods by their parents' and families' ideologies, opinions and failures that they talked of every night at the table over dinner. It's sad to think their families sharing and conversations over meals at the dinner table were wasted in such negative thoughts and energy instead of in love and compassion for human kind. This is now the final result from their upbringing, they are dead in a strange land. They heard it all through their young lives so much that it became ingrained in them that a man should be willing to give up his own life for no good reason and be willing to hurt another who had never caused him harm. In this case it was the Bosnian Muslims, ethnicly identified as Bosjnaks, who became victims of this madness. Two hundred and fifty thousand men, women, and children were killed, thirty eight thousand of them being children. The wounds and pain inflicted on the Bosnian people, not even God could heal, I can honestly say.

"When I will be able to see children playing in school yards with echos of happy laughter, screaming and playing in pools of water from the last evening's rain, and the parents who are leaning by the fences and walls waiting to take their children home after school? When I see that again, I will know that time has started to heal the wounds. Although those wounds will never be healed completely or any of those dead children brought back. We can never forget what happened to us. We may be strong enough to forgive one day but we will always remember, and our strength and education should give us the insurance to live to grow old.

"The irresponsible and hateful parents of these soldiers had raised their sons for one main purpose, to do the dirty, inhumane, ungodly and unearthly, filthy work that they weren't able or missed finishing doing themselves. Again innocent blood was spilled. I only can call it innocent because the ones I had buried I had only known them for two days and hadn't seen them kill anyone, only be killed. Maybe I should be grateful I didn't witness any of their killing like most of my brothers and sisters in Bosnia who witnessed their own children and loved ones being slain by men with similar ideas as those of Mata and his men.

"I thought, 'Did these young men just have the desire for an adventure that they now have paid for with their own lives?' I was wishing they had asked me first before they came here. God knows my advice would have been much more honest and accurate than their parents was. Perhaps if I'd had had a chance to advise them it probably would have been in vain anyway. If I could have had the chance to teach them anything it would be rose gardening instead of playing with guns, just like I was doing when the soldiers came to my mother's house. Perhaps then they would have had the opportunity to grow old.

"These boys' role models were nothing but drunken old men who were failures at everything they did in their lives and they left their countries, villages, and towns. And now their only salvation was in the unfinished glory only these boys could bring to them. That was not to be because most of them were dead instead. These drunken disillusioned old men who many times called themselves stateless over a beer or shot of whiskey, had fed their hatred to the young men. They kept their theories alive over drinks in bars and cafes while looking at the portraits of their heros from World War I and II, their role models who had failed them and each generation all throughout history, time and time again. These old drunken men who hung around the taverns had nothing good to show for themselves but the blood of the innocent up to their shoulders, and that is why most of them left their country. It was a chain reaction that started centuries ago, of failures in the so called leadership that left a trail of poison behind and continues with their ideology of hatred to this day.

"Once again the Croats and the Serbs were holding up the portraits of their heroes Ante and Draza and passing them on through the villages and towns of Bosnia.. Those men were the symbol of butchery as much as Hitler, Stalin, or Mussolini. No one should be proud of any man like that. The uniform of those days of vengefulnesss and hatred was back. All the symbols resembled those which had motivated the massacres of World War I and II. The Croats had the Ante Pavelic potraits and the Serbs had their notorious Draza Mihailovich potraits. Each man brought nothing but shame on their people. The Croatian leader died in exile in Argentina far away from his own people. The Serbian leader got his wish and was executed on the orders of Marshal Tito, a man my Bosnian people helped install to power and had fought over four years in World War II to help defeat Hitler's army. While we were fighting to save the Serbs and the Croats from being occupied by the Nazis and Facists, which the Serbs were teeming with as well as Croats, we were fighting along with Tito to put one nation for all people. Our Bosjnak population paid a heavy price from the Serb Chetniks.

"Tito managed to orchestrate and bring the Serb and Croat communist parties closer together by creating his little communist government called United Yugoslavia and the losers in that were the Bosnians, because they were left out of the picture and not even recognized as a territory or a republic for the people of Bosnia who lived there. It was a deep dark hole for my people. He was making sure by the time he was gone there would be nothing left for the Bosnjaks, so that his dream for a bigger Serbia and some dreams of a bigger Croatia would materialize and then live as a confederate Yugoslavia and his statues wouldn't get torn down like Lenin's in Russia did or Hussein's in Baghdad. Fortunately none of his plans fully succeeded. My people throughout Bosnia and Herzogovia today are planting the gardens and roses like we have done for thousands of years with the genuine help of the new Germany and their leadership, the people of Italy and their leadership, and the people of America and their leadership, and finally the United Kingdom was able to jump on board but only after the defeat of John Major by the current prime minister, Tony Blair. He was willing to see the injustice being done and showed courage by joining along with Bill Clinton to send out the troops and confront the butchers in the Balkans who were Milovic and Tujman. They were men that had made a promise to destroy us from the face of the earth. They had bloodied their hands, hearts, and souls with blood from our children during World War II and now again.

"With no doubt we now know that their dinner table conversations were to create the blueprints for this tragedy. The events that were happening in Bosnia had been woven like a spider's web over a long period of time, and it was looking like she would keep weaving it for a long time to come unless we became strong opponents then. Perhaps if we stay strong they will show restraint, and respect for us from the example of our strength, and will not even think of doing the unthinkable again.

"The kind of senseless and hateful conversations over the dinner tables and glasses of whiskey, God forbid, probably even took place at the Christmas Eve dinner. They wanted to free themselves from their own failures and wrong doing by bringing wars to these young men and turning innocent little boys into monsters instead of good citizens and neighbors. That wasn't enough for them. Two of the most wanted murderers on the planet today are fugitives who are hidden by Serbian Orthodox churches and their representatives that preach forgiveness and a stronger and healthier life for their people and nation with a Bible in one hand and a sword in the other.

"That is the cause of the downfall in that part of the world. The leaders carrying the sword and the Bible which do not mix and never have. They both have powerful sharp edges and are capable of destruction beyond our understanding. We wonder how God could grant wishes to a people like that and allow them to succeed. There should be no healthy life for them or ponds to fish in or rose gardens to prune until they truly seek forgiveness and realize how much they have wronged others. It is not man who can grant the forgiveness, that is to ask from the higher power. The only ones who realize that are the ones who carry the Bible in both of their hands and do not know the sword. Perhaps even I could be the one to help teach the repentant ones about the rose gardens and teach them how to prune them, it was not to be, at least not yet.

"The criminals only wanted to leave their mark and have their names in the history books no matter what the cost, even if written in blood. So be it. They have succeeded in that with shame. It was written in blood by sacrificing their own children and murdering thousands of Bosnian children. Now they are answering for their henious deeds with plenty of time for reflection in prison and committing suicide in shame. The latest one to die in prison was Milosevic. Perhaps it was a sucide or a murder. It's a time of shame for the nation of Serbia.

"After I buried the man I found myself retracing my steps and going over to the water trough again and I felt dry and thirsty as if my mouth was full of sand. I needed some water and I felt a sense of being safe and secure there listening to the running water dripping in through the trough bringing me back home for a moment by the little stream that flowed past my house. The trough had protected and saved my life by absorbing the explosions since had been standing near it during the ordeal of the explosions. I washed my wounds and the dirt off my face and hands. Being there again hearing the water and using it to wash was a good comfortable feeling like it was the water used for baptising a good Christian in the Jordan River where John the Baptist was baptized by Jesus, or the water used by my prophet Muhammed to wash before praye,r or by the pure water of the small springs in this good and innocent earth. It sure felt good to splash the water on my face, baptism or not."

I interrupted and looked Ramiz straight in the eye to ask, "Don't tell me you are switching from the Minaret to the bells of the Vatican?"

Pace laughed loudly, "If he was going to do that he might as well switch to Saint Gabriel who was the messenger from God to the prophet Muhammed of the Mormons, It would be closer to home for you."

We all burst out laughing looking at one another. We were three men with very diverse lives and religions but very close in that identity as humans who commected with each other long before the religions evolved.

Ramiz sounded defensive and almost shy from feeling outdone by Pace and my jokes, although we were trying to make him feel more comfortable relating his story and give him a little break. He said, "Of course not, don't be silly. I've got nothing to be ashamed of about my religion especially since I don't know that much about it."

We chuckled at his humor even though he hadn't been joking. I thought his answer was very innocent but clever. He wouldn't elaborate on anything he wasn't one hundred percent sure about but he was ready to die at any time to defend his religion. It was strange phenomena but justified in a way. I laughed and asked, "What is your religion, a new holy water? No, but seriously," I told him, "not knowing what direction the road is going always brings destruction and tradgedy. Just like in Bosnia before the war, we didn't know whether we were Bosnjaks, Muslims, or what else and we paid heavily because of it. Next time you identify yourself with something you think you're sure of, you had better make sure you know what you are in for. I hope you will now learn more now first about your culture and then about your religion. If you are willing to die for it, it would be nice to know exactly what you are about to give up your life for."

We all laughed but it really wasn't funny. I was serious about what I said. You should always know what you're willing to die for if you are willing to die. Dying men can't continue to make a difference but we can learn from their mistakes and only the living and healthy can make a difference and continue laying bricks of hope where the dying have left off.

Ramiz wanted to change the subject of religion and go on to tell me a story about something that had happened that involved him and my long lost friend Peter. "Really Angelo, am I gonna be able to finish my story? What I wanted to tell you about is that I found myself standing in front of a man who was from the Gold Coast of Australia, the legendary Peter F, who I was about to get to know. He is a friend of yours, Angie, isn't that right?"

Pace interrupted and said, "Yea, he sure is all right. I met that character."

I said, "I never really trusted Peter, but for some reason I have always called him my friend. Yes Ramiz, I guess I can say that we were once friends but I'm not sure if we were friends for financial, political reasons or if it was that we really were just true friends who had been had both been living on the edge at the time and enjoying what we were doing without quite realilizing what the consequences at the end of the road would be. We needed each other to help us to accomplish our respective tasks."

Ramiz said, "Angie, I think I am ready to listen to you talk now. You and Pace have been patient with me doing all the talking so far."

I told him, "Don't worry about that, Ramiz. Pace and I are good listeners, and we're paying attention to your tragic and triumphant story and you have our attention. Your stories are intriguingly gruesome. It is also satisfying that you also are actually here to tell it."

Not understanding, Ramiz asked, "What do you mean by that?"

I tried to elaborate and explain in plain English as best as I could. I told him it was good having him here, and that he was healthy and not wrapped in a cast or missing any limbs from his body or six feet under without a marker. He smiled shyly showing his appreciation.

"As I was telling you before, my friend Pace sitting here next to you, who is called, The Warrior from Utah in Bosnia, is a freedom fighter for the Bosnian people and also an intelligence agent, but not full time."

Ramiz asked curiously, "What do you mean, not full time?"

"Our American government has a way of recruiting people when they need them and this time this is where Pace was needed, especially because of his Mormon faith. It was obvious he would be more trusted than a Serb from Chicago. Don't forget that Pace has been the only one from the Christian world that fought for the freedom of our people. Perhaps he has a good reason and his own history of his people has taught him because his own people were once oppressed a few centuries back and told to leave their homeland. Right here in this great land of America there has been plenty of injustice done and there were wars and killing . The Mormon faith evolved in the old world and the horrendous persecution followed the new faith and the people packed up and left for the new world looking for the freedom of worship and to free their hearts and minds for a better life for themselves and families. It was not to happen at least until they arrived in the land where they planted roots and a new state was born and is Utah that is one of the proud fifty states in the union."

Pace stepped in, "Angelo, I was waiting patiently for you to finish, but I don't appreciate your comparison of myself with a Serb."

"You are missing the point, Pace. The government wouldn't send a Serb nor trust them enough to send them over there for the sake our own national interest and for the long time secutity for this nation. They would sell us down the river to the Russians. So, you are the right perscription pill for the naval intellingence and the CIA and the Pentagon too. The day will come when your selfless sacrifice of going to Bosnia will be recorded in the pages of history as one of the daring

136

contributions to the cause of both places, Bosnia and America. So, I am not comparing you to the Serbs. When we have no use for people like you we dispose of their services and they fade slowly into the untold pages in history.

"But I promise this story will not fade away untold. It will be told since I believe there is much the future generation can learn from all of us by this endeavor and in saving three million people from being slaughtered. That is the whole nation of three million, one million people have already been slaughtered. God knows by the time this war is over, who knows how many people will be left alive. The Serbs are determined this time to get rid of all the Bosnians. Our government has not yet decided if they are going to protect and save the Bosnians or let them drown in their own blood, at least the remaining ones who are still alive."

"I'm sorry Angelo, I didn't mean to offend you," Pace replied.

"How could you possibly offend me when you are trying to save my brothers and sisters? Maybe I am the one who might have offended you. I couldn't even think of doing that. The only one who has truly offended you or I or any decent human being around the world is Butros-Galli, that bigot, the true Serb lover."

Pace said angrily, "The world knows Butros-Galli is the most prejudiced man against the Bosnians but no one does anything about it yet. The ones who want to are too poor and hopeless. By the time our politicians locate where Bosnia is on the world map I'm afraid it will be too late to save it."

"Wait a minute Pace, you want to tell me President Bush doesn't know where Bosnia is, being a U.S. ambassador to China and also the U.N., a CIA director and Reagan's vice president? Isn't something wrong with that picture? I think it is old fashioned American lobbying. Maybe Pat Robinson, Jerry Falwell and Billy Graham made the call or maybe one of the Israeli lobbyists. You can't have Bosnia in the middle of the Christian Europe, what's wrong with you Mr. President? Even if he wanted to help with the influence of those religious leaders who are commanding respect of millions of people he'd have to really think twice to do it. Perhaps he regrets now that he didn't do it. The creation of the religious faiths are much younger than the evolvement of human life. He had the opportunity and he blew it but no one could take his experience away as a diplomat."

CHAPTER FIVE: AN HISTORICAL PERSPECTIVE

Speaking of wars in America, during the Civil War there were many great men, and two of the great men who were once childhood friends and West Point Academy graduates, were unique and special in their own ways. They both became seasoned politicians and military leaders and one became a great president. Their visions and ideologies for the nation took them down two different roads that divided the country.

General Lee had become leader of the southern states. General Grant become leader of the northern Union army during Abraham Lincoln's presidentcy. Each man fought and believed strongly in what he was fighting for. They each believed their fights were for a just cause. Hundreds of thousands of men died for things that they believed in, their principles, their honor, and a country to call their own, with the confederate flag or the stars and stripes to represent a country they will be proud of. One flag would reamin flying at the end of the day, and that is still the stars and stripes.

Both men could not be right and win even in this great civil war but many men who followed and believed in General Lee or in General Grant paid dearly with their lives to honor those beliefs. Perhaps we are a better nation today because of it. The north claimed a fight for the dignity of all men. The south with General Lee had a different preception of dignity and freedom for the human man. That was to free ones who look like us that were white and enslave anyone who looks different, strip them from their God given rights and dignity to be humans, and force them all to pick cotton so the southern elite could have plenty of time to drink fancy wine and good French champagne. The right way did prevail with General Lee's ultimate defeat.

By this time I knew that I had grabbed Ramiz' attention with my little story of American history and the civil war. I continued on. "In the duration, many thousands of men died that today we worship as heroes regardless of whether northern or southern. They all helped to create a union and nation that stands proud and respected. The price we paid during the civil war was not in vain.

"The loss of life in Gettysburg sparking President Lincoln's address probably made it the most painful and passionate speech that he or any leader in the world ever had to give. The casualties were clear and enourmous to ignite such a passionately powerful speech by the president. It was a wake up call and a turning point for America to become one union instead of a divided nation.

"Where does my beloved Bosnia stand in her civil war, Ramiz?" I asked him. "Bosnia is not in a civil war, Bosnia is being attacked by her neighbors. It would be an injustice to call it a civil war, as it resulted from aggressors attacking a peace loving people. Will the people unite after the war to forgive and forget? Or will it break in pieces into tiny reservations? Oh, I have my doubts, Ramiz, I have my doubts."

I told Pace, "Let me tell you something about Ramiz and my country's history. I have told you Peter and I were acquaintances during the post cold war when Russia was communist, Yugoslavia was socialist, and Tito had an iron grip over the people of Yugoslavia."

I told him that Tito was feeling insecure in his position and having many sleepless nights since he had opened the borders in 1962. Tito had recruited and trained people like Peter to try to prevent his sleepless nights. Peter and the people like him were supposed to make that possible for Tito."

"There was massive unemployment under Tito's regime during the 1960's and 70's in Yugoslavia. The unemployed were highly educated. Tito's government was unable to fulfill their promises to the educated masses and provide jobs for them in order to have better lives. There was no future for them in Yugoslavia. Tito realized he couldn't deliver on his promise, so he opened the borders and the people were free to leave. He had hopes that in so doing it would prevent a form of revolution to overthrow his government and perhaps cost him his life. It did work for him.

"He promised they would have the chance for better lives in the new world and be protected by agreements that he would be personally involved in and drafting union labor contracts for them in the nations they would go to work in. It would cover country to country throughout Europe wherever they found employment. It was in the fashion of an organized union, although controlled by Yugoslavia and Germany, Italy, France, Holand, Austria, and the rest of western Europe. Tito's allowing all of these healthy, able and educated people to leave was a gold mine for western Europe.

"The system in Yugoslavia that he was running was a form of

semi-socialism and semi-Stalinist. The system did not allow economical growth to create the jobs for the hundreds of thousands of people that were skilled in many different professions in potentially highly productive fields who were anxious to be productive citizens. There was no future for them in Yugoslavia.

Western Europe in fact was in very short supply of skilled labor and needed a masive numbers of skilled workers for them to continue growing and be as advanced as they planned to. Yugoslavia was just a place that the west was looking at to supply them with available skilled educated labor, and Yugslavia had numbers in the millions of highly educated people. They requested that Tito open the door for his people to work in the western world and get paid well for it. Looking back at this deal, it almost seemed like an organized crime labor contract. Tito the bandit and the rest of western Europe was the nice guys helping to rescue all of these young people. That's what he did and it was a smart thing to do, not that he had a choice. It was a one way street.

"Tito's cleverness had won him the guarantee of wearing the royal crown for life rather than getting overthrown by a possible revolution. The offer from the west to employ all of these people was a dream come true for Tito. He was sitting on a keg of power ready to explode and he needed to get rid of that pressure. He clearly saw gains without any risk of loss. He used his new investment of human bodies that promised a return in profits of forgein currency of astronomical numbers. He exported his people and in return allowed foriegn currency to be imported enabling Tito to extend his lifeline and his totalitarian system of ruling Yugoslavia. Life was looking up for Tito and his lackeys but at the same he unknowingly became an undertaker and was digging a grave for himself and his country. Within a few short years, Yugoslavia became as rich in the communist world as compared to America, in the western world. They were importing everything and exporting nothing. The dollars and the marks were flowing and they were hardly producing anything.

"He had no choice even if it was a very smart choice, but to open the border in 1962 and let the people go and look for a better life all over the world. In the span of one year more than two million people exited the country, the lifeline of the nation. Any smart man would know that his heart had fallen out of his chest and you could say there was no match available for a transplant. The nation was dying. By seven years time ten million healthy productive citizens had left.

Only grandma and grandpa were left behind. Even though he knew what was happening he truly must have believed what he did was the right thing just to save his own skin. He figured the ten million could come back and vacation just like they did do.

"He was clever enough that a few years before he opened the borders, he had recruited thousands of new agents he predicted he would need to safeguard his regime and his presidency. He trained the agents well to do his dirty work outside of the country. Each of the agents were assigned places all over the world in order to monitor the labor of people that he had allowed to leave for employment. This way he could keep tabs on the loyalty of the masses of his people who were living outside the country. Many who had once wanted to see him overthrown were now hesitant to join any groups on the outside with all of these agents spying on them so they continued to be slave laborers and send the money home to their families in Yugoslavia every day. In the meantime Tito was hunting, and enjoying life on his private island of Brione, where he had created his own private safari with the sweat and blood from the people working outside of the country. Now that's what you would call one sharp dude.

"One important thing that he failed to realize was that he actually was losing much more than he was gaining. The healthy, young, intellectually skilled labor force had left the country. What was left behind was a question no one was asking, or were too blind to see. It was that only the old, poor, and handicapped were left behind. Most of them were old warriors from World War II still living in their glory days and counting and shining their medals, telling their stories and waiting for their pensions to come at the end of the month, sadly not knowing that their children were not going to be coming back, just as I never went back to my father but sent letters with checks in them to him in the mail. He came to accept it after awhile along all the other parents. The innocence of their lives didn't allow them to figure it out and as long as they received some letters, postcards, and checks from their children it was a comfort to all of them.

"That was Yugoslavia of the late sixties and early seventies. Everything started to go to hell. The factories were closing and there was no economical prosperity or growth. The cash was still flowing in, however, from the sweat and hard work from those who had emmigrated to the west. Houses and palaces were being built everywhere, with no one to live in them. They were sometimes used only a month out of the year as summer homes to one of the thousands who had left there some years ago. That became a tradition that exists even today.

"The revenue from the foreign currency coming into Yugoslavia was more than anyone could dream of, including Tito himself. It really made no real difference on the whole for the state however. Only some of the elite top individuals profited personally. Society on the whole in the country lost by losing so many of their capable and educated citizens. Obviously it should have been forseen the system would collapse. The country managed to create enemies of their own citizens both internally and externally. All the groups were working to destroy the country and hoping to benefit from it's destruction. My people were watching all of this on the sidelines. It was a fatal mistake once again.

"Tito was the beneficiary of all this for a long time, but he died a few years before his empire went down in ashes due to the foreign currency coming into the country and the lack of growth and production inside the country. One could argue the survival or failure of Yugoslavia for these or many other reason. One I'm very certain of is that he promised the Serbs they would be crowned the kings of Yugoslavia after his death. They were fool enough to believe him. I think he must have known the Serbs could not lead themselves, they must always have some outsider, just like Slobo, their very last one. He was a Montenegrin.

"The new leadership with Slobo at the helm of the country didn't need any enemies from the outside. His thoughts were, 'The holy grail is right in the palm of my hand and I'm not passing it up.' They were their own worst enemies and were on a path of total destruction. It was a country of corruption like none other in history. Millions of people had their savings confiscated. Slobo knew what he was doing. Tear the country apart and keep all the money. Of course he didn't have the intelligence to think of the consequences of it. Each state within the country worked on its own terms without any regulations of the federal government and no one to answer to. Once more there was a mass exodus of educated people. Belgrade had flooded the country with their currency of dinars. They were buying the dollar and the German mark for any price to exchange their dinars. The black market was thriving and inflation was out of control. The only other comparison I could make would be that to what occured in

Argentina with the bank scandals and the military government in charge and an inflation rate of eighteen hundred percent. How stupid could he be to not see how those people of Argentina paid with their lives?

"Milosevic was becoming filthy rich. Tobacco and drugs were two of the many commodities that were under his control. There was only one other thing left for him to do. That was to become truly Slobo the Terrible and fufill his life's dream and his predecessors life's dream. It has been their dream ever since their defeat by the Ottoman Empire on St. Vitus Day in 1389 when they tried to get rid of the Muslim faith in Sanjak and Bosnia while claiming to crusade to save Christian Europe from Islam.

"I realized then the man was insane and couldn't figure out why the rest of Europe didn't see it. The Chancellor of Germany was the only one who saw it and said the man must be stopped. I was astonished and even breathless to learn that in 1984 and 1986, President Tuzman of Croatia had worked on the blueprints along with his mortal enemy Milosevic to do just that. Here were the twenty-first century crusaders repeating the steps of the past that no one could be proud of. It was Richard of England, and then Phillip of France, and now it was Tuzman of Croatia and Slobo of Serbia. It is ironic.

"The crusaders story was told as one of a shameful failure. The Ottoman army the Serbs fought in Kosovo on the Black Plains was not a Muslim Islamic army as the Serbs claimed. There were all more than 65% volunteers and the paid men from every walk of life such as Austrian-Hungarians, Polish, Czechs, Slovacs, Moldovians, Bulgarians, Greeks, Palestinians and Jews from what was then Palestine, today's Israel, as well as their own Serbs and Montenegrins. For the Christian world to belive Serbia's claims of saving Europe for the second time from Islam is a very uneducated presumption in such a world full of education and information. By now Slobo had robbed all the ordinary citizens of their wealth and masses of the people were left with nothing. Only a small number who were very educated and yet very corrupt and in cahoots with Slobo prospered. Here in the states there were people collecting money for Slobo, a hundred dollars for each Serb. A Serbian man by the name of Dushan asked me if I would like to contribute. I said without a second thought, 'Of course, how much do I have to give?' He said, 'One hundred dollars, Angie.' I pulled a hundred out of my pocket and said, 'Here I hope this will bring him down.' He was surprised and grateful that I gave him the money but too stupid to realize what I had meant.

"The remaining people were like a flock of sheep for whom no one cared just like Dushan. There was a chain reaction of collapse and the mistrust between the republics. The ordinary citizens were ignorant enough as always to believe in what the leadership told them. Production of any industry was down forty and fifty percent. Agriculture was at it's lowest point in history since the 1800's and everything was being imported. There was one story of a company that bought some products from Japan but they wouldn't sell them only one item so they had to buy some toothpicks along with it and they did even though they didn't need them.

"Everyone was scratching their heads and saying they thought Yugoslavia was supposed to become an economical power of the eastern and communist world like a new America in the west. How could they have been so blind? It was a shiny apple on the outside to the world but rotten to the core on the inside from being eaten away by the two worms Slobo and Tuzman.

"All around the world the immigrants who left former Yugoslavia, specifically Serbs and Croats, formed new radical groups consisting of the old and new. An underground resistance was surfacing demanding changes that eventually got through, but which brought nothing but suffering to all of them. The days of the former Yugoslavia were becoming shorter and shorter. Some of these groups were young Croats from Australia and some were Ustashas from America, members of an old right-wing political organization of Croatia.

"A Serb group from the other side was the legendary Chetniks. They could easily be compared to Bin Laden and the Taliban in Afghanistan, using the same methods of control with misery and destruction and the leaders of their Orthodox church heading them. These are people who are proud of being notorious for killing and raping women and children. Translated to English their name means bandits, murderous thieves that are capable of nothing good. Their treacherous ideas throughout history have never done anything to benefit the people of Serbia, as they have proved undoubtly that they are not capable of thinking right or creating anything that they could be proud of.

"Finally a group of young Bosnian freedom fighters emerged,

the Bosnjaks, who were not that well known among our people. Their ideas were not well known nor were they supported by the people. During the formation of this organization the only thing they wanted was for the Bosnjaks to be recognized as full fledged citizens and Bosnia as their homeland. The group with a clear vision for statehood for the Bosnians in confederation as Yugoslavia had been formed 1962. No one from the organization ever asked for Bosnia to be an independant state, only to recognized as a state land of the Bosnjaks.

"Forty years late we now know what the reaction from the Serbs and Croats were and the brutal and tragic final outcome. Civil war broke out in the country between the Serbs and Croats with Bosnia once again finding herself in the middle. The Bosnian government that was leagally accepted then by the Bosnian people was headed by Alija. Alija and his government were aware but lacked the military and political to recognize the danger we were in and refused to believe what was really about to happen to us as a people. They were unwilling to recognize the grave danger we were in and the problems that were coming for the country, problems that I and others could clearly see as a time bomb that was about to explode in our faces. We were about to be exterminated. Everyone else was taking up arms in Bosnia, both the Serbs and Croats, while the Bosnians were being disarmed and placed under an embargo by the UN for them to be slaughtered.

"It was just as I had predicted long ago in 1962 when I had an argument with my father about what would eventually happen to us. I hoped he didn't live to see it. Unfortunately he did and I wasn't proud of proving him wrong. A trail of tragic events were woven into a web like that of a giant spider that had been weaving for over the last hundred years. Even that would be truly an understatement. History was repeating itself once more.

"The last attempt to exterminate us was made by King Alexander of Serbia and his lucky general, Draza Michalovich. This butcher was later executed for the atrocities he commited that were too much even for the communists. Draza paid with his life by the hand of Tito, his former partner in crime. One had to go and that was Draza. There wasn't room for both to rule. His execution left Alexander the so called great king, stateless and for a good reason. He didn't believe in the country he was ruling anyway. Anyone who doesn't have loyalty to their true homeland doesn't deserve to rule over it and he found it very easy to leave. Alexander died in disgrace in San Pedro,

Caliafornia.

"The demands of the Bosnjak people were not that extraordinary. After the war they only sought equal recognition by the state of Bosnia as citizens in confederation with the state of Yugoslavia. Bosnia was called Bosnia but the people were not recognized as Bosnians, only as minorities of the Muslim faith who lived in the confederation of the state of Yugoslavia.

" All they received instead was to be murdered or be imprisoned. Most of the young intellectuals were put behind bars for quite a few years inside and outside of the country. The plan by the Serbian government and Tito's regime was to eliminate the young and healthy they thought might be a threat to them. The wheels of torture had started spinning and our bright and young were disappearing. The only ones missing them were their families. At special times over holidays and dinners in the homes of our people many chairs at the dinner tables were empty and only hopes were there that they would be back to fill them again but they never were. Those were the only wishes of all of their parents that never would get fulfilled.

"The Bosjaks realized that somehow and some way they had to work this out and show patriotism again for their country, they being the ones who liberated Yugoslavia and helped Tito get where he was to become president. Even then things were still getting worse. They had hoped as Bosnjak's that their participation in the new Yugoslavia would stop the continuation of the killing, abuse and the misplacement and confiscation of their private properties.

"The abuse and torture of our people just went underground with a different system and in different manners but by the same people. The status quo is still the same. The Serbs are ruling us again. The cycle of uprooting us has never stopped. No matter who had been sitting in power Tito, Alexander, or Milosevich, it just seems the burning torch has passed hands and the fire is still burning as much as ever.

"Most of our young Bosnjaks never got the chance to experience jail and time behind bars in which to think and organize as Mandela did in Africa. They were murdered and butchered wherever they found them, and their families were more silent than ever for fear of more of the same slaughter. The young Bosnjaks needed time and space to grow and evolve but it was never given to them. The chance they rightfully deserved like the rest of the citizens to blossom fully to realize their potential for a nation they belived in was not to be. It was always a dream that we would be as one and integrate our people in Yugoslavia. At that time there was no other choice to dream any other way. God forbid, an independent Bosnia, like I dreamed and told my father. He told me I should be put in a straight jacket. I told him, 'Don't worry dad. Unfortunately you may live to see it, exactly like I tell you, an independent Bosnia and the world will learn to live with it because we are people who have contributed to the world as much as any other society. That's where we have a chance as a nation.'

"The Serb and Croat organizations inside and outside the country enjoyed all the privleges from Tito and were not treated as harshly. He wouldn't dare offend them, especially the Serbs. They were not murdered on every street corner by the Yugoslavian government watchdogs, who numbered in perhaps the thousands. These were men such as Peter.

"Just the idea of the Bosnjaks being known as a formidable force like the Chetniks or Ustashes put Tito's government into a state of panic. By Tito's paying too much attention to the Bosnians he ignored the true threats posed by the Chetniks and Ustashes. They wanted his head on a platter but wouldn't know quite what to do with it even if they had it. Lucky for him that they were so disfunctional as a unit, both politically and stategically, that he was able to die naturally as an old man. That should tell us who is running Serbia now.

"As we all know, the Bosnjaks were never treated as full fledged citizens during Alexander or Tito's rule of Yugoslavia. Yet the Bosnjaks had always been considered moral pillars of the country of Yugoslavia before and after, perhaps because of their creativity and education. Even the mention of the name Bosnjaks and their possible recognition of Bosnia as their homeland brought panic to the government and to the rest of the country, and was unthinkable and would be as bad of a thing as voodoo or black magic."

Pace then asked, "Angelo, how can that happen that a people are repressed in a country and strangely also considered pillars of the country that hold it together?"

"I told him we were like trees blossoming to bear fruit at the end of the season, but we were always shaken of our pollen too early and we were not allowed to bear all of our fruits. Enemies of ours were always there to shake us up so that we never reached our maturity. During this war they have killed thirty eight thousand children. The buds flowering that once were our children never got the chance to blossom.

"Even after everything that has happened, in a quiet way we still have our morally strong foundations. We thought we were the glue that held Yugoslavia together all that time. We mistakenly refused to believe that the Serbs and Croats were looking at us as criminals who had been sentenced to life, criminals hoping for the country to collapse so we could be set free. That is the way the ordinary and uneducated as well as the intellectual Serbs and Croats saw us, as a threat to their livelihoods.They think we are the ones to blame for for their own misfortunes and failures over the centuries that anyone could name at least a thousand of.

"We were always the most highly educated people and ran every branch of civilian way of life of the country's except for the military, which was the gravest mistake we made. We are paying now for it with our lives. They have guns and we have pencils and paper. We should have the power of both also since we are capable and have understanding of the power of both. If we had that perhaps we would have used it wisely and the mothers wouldn't be wearing black scarves of sorrow over their heads. That surely would have been a triumph. All because we as men failed to see that we needed both the pen and the sword to succeed to prevent the grief of the mothers, ours and theirs.

"The Serbs and Croats love to march in uniforms, and their police parade in the streets. We were the ones drawing up the blueprints and working tirelessly to build an infrastructure in the country to have lives better for all of us. In other words we were doing the thinking for them every day so that they could have time to parade. Again they proved they were incapable of thinking for themselves. Our ideas of freedom were different from the Serbs and the Croats, perhaps because we have had so much suffering. They liked someone making decisions for them and telling them what to do so they didn't have to think. We didn't. We liked to have freedom in our hearts, souls, and minds and to able to think for ourselves. We wanted that for everyone including them. For the Serbs, it was impossible to teach.

"It would be just like an ancient Bulgarian joke. A man killed his friend while on a trip in a caravan. When he appeared in front of the judge he told him his camel had killed him. The judge got mad and asked him to prove the camel did it. The man said to the judge, 'If you give me one year of time, I will prove it to you and bring the camel to court to prove it.' Everyone thought he was crazy including his lawyer. The judge said, 'Ok you wise man. I'll give you one year, just tell me what you are going to do in that year.' He said, 'I'm going to teach the camel to talk and she will explain everything.' The judge laughed and said, 'I'll have the hanging party ready when you come back with the camel. Now go.' In front of the courthouse the people watching told the man he was crazy and asked him why he just sentanced himself to death. He brushed them off and replied, 'In one year I am hoping either the judge or the camel will be dead. Then I'll be a free man because that was the terms.'

"In the situation of Bosnia the only way we can be free is by educating the Serbs to appreciate their lives as we do in Bosnia and then I think peace would come. Our idea of a country prospering is to be as one unit. We were the nation's conscience. We look as a good example to be the line from Abraham Lincoln's Gettysburg address that says a government should be 'Of the people, by the people, and for the people.' That is the essence of our thoughts for Bosnia. Perhaps some of the words in Lincoln's speech were expressions of his own personal pain he felt for his nation.

"In this situation the ideas from our Young Bosnjaks political party went over with them like a lead balloon that would never float or like an ocean with no tide to ever splash up on the shores. That again was unexperienced leadership of the Bosjnaks.

"They saw it as us cutting into their pie, and they didn't want to share any pieces of that pie. The land of Bosnia belonged in their minds to them, the Serbs and Croats and we the Bosnjaks must disappear. We were left with one choice, to fight or die. Unfortunately we choose neither because of our belief in our status that we thought we held being intellectual people and as high society people that didn't need to settle things with guns. A pencil and paper was the thing for reasoning with. Boy, were we wrong. We should have known better than that. Whoever told anyone you could grow beautiful flowers without good soil, water and a lot of tender care?

"We Bosnians thought because we had a quiet moral respect and didn't go shouting from rooftops, we thought that as long as we stayed at a nuetral stance and appeared as a bridge for the two to meet through us to reconcile their differences, the Serbs and Croats would be at peace and not war and at the same time spare ourselves from being engulfed in the flames that we had nothing to do with. That was another grave mistake we made again and we are still nursing the same wounds that we did a half a century ago. Again our tragic history taught us nothing. How easily we forget. We got our asses fried again in the same scalding, burning pan. When will we ever learn?

"During World War I and II the Serbs and Croats tried to obliterate each other from the face of the earth. We found ourselves right in the middle of it. When they were tired of killing each other and with nothing to be proud of the little reasoning and sanity they had went out the window. The only way to save face for them in front of their people was for both of their leaderships to again blame it on Bosnia for being the root cause of their fighting. Sadly masses of their uneducated people believed it and picked up sticks and stones and pitchforks to massacre their neighbors once again and again our most powerful tool, the pencil and paper didn't work. I still hope we will prevail with it one day.

"One officer of the Austria-Hungary army that participated in trying to obliterate Belgrade was none other than Tito himself. He sent the cannon shells day after day and month after month to the streets and neighborhoods of Belgrade. We as the Bosjnaks did not participate in trying to obliterate either one and wanted to remain neutral. We were the ones who always believed that Serbs and Croats should try and live in harmony and peace together. It has been our belief through every conflict then and today."

"There was one problem however. Each conflict brought to the Serbs and Croats astronomical despair and a great loss of lives. The Bosnians were the ones who had always tried preventing it while observing the tragedies on the sidelines favoring neither side and helping the misplaced in despair and the rebuilding of the ruins.

"As many times before, the Serbs and Croats would look back at what they had done to each other and both sides could see themselves as clear losers just as they were. The leadership wouldn't dare admit to their people any wrong doing during the conflicts because that would be a lynching for themselves. They wouldn't come to terms with the truth and admit that each party of their respected countries were to blame for the agony and destruction, so they blamed who else but the Bosnians. They would save their skins again. They couldn't play ball without the football. They needed somebody to blame and Bosnia has always been right in the middle of the two.

"During World War II when they were killing each other like

there was no tomorrow, the Bosnians tried to protect the families and were true good neighbors of both the Serbs and Croats. Their children were never murdered by us. We were making sure the factories, farms, and ranches kept going and produced enough so all of us would not starve. No matter how much we did it was never enough.

"They were busy killing and we were busy feeding the families. It seemed they thought that their evil deeds must be done today or the sun would not rise tomorrow, and they wanted to be sure they got them done today. On the contrary the Bosnians all throughout Yugoslavia were the ones that protected all of the people regardless of their religion or ethnicity. The Serb Chetniks and the Croatian Ustasha alike were nothing but bloodthirsty butchers. They plundered and destroyed everything in their paths. How then could our own Bosnian people be blamed for the treacherous roads they took to their own destruction?

"History again has been repeated in this latest heinous aggression first against Croatia and then against Bosnia. The Serbs and Croats were killing each other while we were the ones with an open door and safe havens for the innocent during this latest aggression. The Serb and Croat families were not running from Bosnians but from their own fathers, brothers, neighbors, and each other. After the Serbs and Croats were tired of fighting each other they turned to the Bosnians who again were armed with pencils and paper and no guns.

"The notorious Croat Brother Satan from the monasteries on the coast of Dalmatia and Herzegovina came back once again to do evil deeds. He was covered with blood as he was chopping off heads and the men were singing their national songs and hugging and patting each other on the back with bloody hands in approval of each other and of what they had done. How patriotic they were doing it in the name of mother Croatia. Satan was back. Only this time it was Mata and his Croatian gang and Arkan from the Serbian side.

"Once again the Serbs like the Croats had Satan with them too. This time it was Slobo and Arkan doing the Serbian dirty work. Serbia is still a fascist state. Croatia in her fight for a new life is marching on the way towards hope for democracy. In Bosnia we are still at war and on the march for liberation to the gates of freedom. One state has become three. Bums, murderers, and drug pushers have infested the country. There is no one with authority to protect the children. Bosnia is truly in a fight now more than ever for survival.

"Throughout the history of our people we have been good fathers and neighbors. This is truly a test of time. The roots, trunk, and branches of our tree are just about to dry out. We must take drastic actions as we did before to save ourselves. We must get rid of the bums, murderers and drug pushers that are driving Ferarris, Lamborghinis and American SUV's in our country and give them the chance to be honest citizens. We must bring morality to the level we had once before. Otherwise our tree of hope will die. We should be happy with our progress, but never satisfied. The moment you are satisfied with your success you are doomed for failure. You can be happy as a professional gardener, but never satisfied until every last rose has blossomed into a beautiful full fragrant flower. Our people deserve no less. We have paid much more with our blood to let illiterate drug pushers who haven't more than eighth grade educations driving red Ferraris and Lambroghenis through Bosnia in whatever business they are in and let these kind of people tarnish and destroy everything good ever done. Too many lives have been lost for the drug pushers to run free and terrorize our people but for the dream of hope and security from this kind of immoral conduct of some people not even citizens of the country.

"We have the right to have the dignity we deserve and which after all is a God given right. How can we see ourselves as neighbors now? Are we compared to madmen who need straight jackets and heavy gloves to keep from hurting ourselves or each other? I'd rather provide straight jackets for the madmen and aggressors who I see as insane. Unfortunately we never succeeded in preventing them from harming themselves and we as rescuers found ourselves getting hurt also.

"Tito came into power because of madmen. They were the road to the bridge for his success. When they were burning, killing and raping, Tito was promising a good life for all. Boy, we were wrong in joining him too. We should have been fighting for our own survival and not everyone elses. I hope we will do that the next time there is a fight and we will take care of our own first."

"The Chetniks, Ustashas, and Fascists were the madmen who were Tito's mortal enemies but at the same time his ticket to power. Tito called us and we responded one hundred percent and joined the army of Partisians to help bring justice and freedom for all the people. Again we had joined the wrong party. Tito never gave Bosnia a clue about what he had in store for us. That was as we know now, to uproot us from our land and make us disappear just like the turbulent waves from the ocean wipe the sand on the beach away from the shores. It almost worked.

"From 1912 to 1990 more than six million people have left or else died in the land of the Bosnjaks, Bosnia and Sandjak. We found ourselves on every corner of the globe being stateless and drifting around the world trying to find an open door to settle in where we would be accepted. Hopefully we could save, share with and bring our rich and healthy traditions and mosaic of culture from our beloved Bosnia that we had for over a thousand years. The rich moasic culture of our people has with no doubt brought enrichment to other cultures we have settled into. Finally we are getting recognition as true contributers of this beautiful world we all share. Our contribution has been one of those small dots in a postive way. I can say proudly that I am happy we didn't use guns and forget about our pencils and paper. Our contributions have only come through pencils and paper and not by looking down the barrels of guns. The world has finally paid attention to us and recognized and finally accepted us such as we are.

"As you, Ramiz, and my friend Pace here and the whole world for that matter know, the Serbs are eliminating our people from the face of the earth and not for the first time. This is just history repeating itself. At the end of the nineteenth century and beginning of the twentieth the world was in turbulent and chaotic times and we were in the eye of the storm and paid dearly for it.

"World War II wasn't much different. Our parents and grandparents hoped that would be the end of it. Sadly they were wrong. It's the same status quo of discrimination, butchery, confiscation of property, stripping away personal identies by changing family names, being unable to practice the faith you believe in and all the other dispicable things, like burning women and children after tying their hands with wire around bales of hay.

"Under the new regime in Belgrade, communism was a promise for a better life and justice for all. Tito's tutor, Milovan Djilas, made sure that the promises made during the war to us and the rest of the people would be delivered. It was delivered all right but only to one of the groups. That was the Serbs, and Orthodox Montenegrins who shared their religion. We were left out once more.

"We never saw it coming. They were running politics and the

military and we were running everything that was supporting the politics and military. We were like workers for the queen bee and we were feeling happy to be doing it for awhile. We were happy until it dawned on us we were not a part of a whole unit but merely being used as slaves. If you were lucky and able to leave you escaped over the border to any country to the west. Many of the mothers and fathers cried for the sons and daughters who left and were never to return. The vacancies left by the ones who fled were soon filled by their brothers and sisters and the string of slavery was not broken.

"During the 1960's up until the time of this current war one group of people who had escaped across the borders, and were lucky enough not to be killed while crossing the border, never had any thought of returning. Those were the Bosnians of the Muslim faith.

"The Serbs and Croats were free to come and go as they pleased. The Serbs used the leniency afforded them by Tito to freely travel back and forth. On the other hand, the Croats were not anxious to break the traditional bread with Tito and his Serbian regime and bury the hatchet. After all, he was considered a traitor by the Croat people since he was Croat himself and let the Serbs run everything for him. Obviously the Croats found themselves from the outside looking in with no recognition or participation in their country at all and were bitter with Tito with feelings of betrayal. One should wonder what the real Bosnians felt about that. They were betrayed one hundred percent by Tito and the communist party.

"The Serb Chetniks and Croatian Ustasa, with Ante Pavelic on one side and Draza on the other trying to obliterate each other, found themselves bleeding to kingdom come and counting the notches in their gunbelts. When they were through counting their bloody notches they discovered their notches were gained by the loss of the lives of their own people . They had no one else to blame it on and they saw Bosnia as an untouched target sitting right in the middle of them. They unleashed themselves on us like a bunch of hungry rabid mad dogs. We were not prepared or ready to defend ourselves in 1945, for the simple reason that we were fighting facism and the all the able men were in Tito's army.

"Now in the twenty-first century the ways of killing have not changed but one new difference has surfaced. Most of the men doing the killing are very educated. The phenomena I have discovered during this war and not just in the former Yugoslavia but throughout the world, is that the men who are commiting these heinous crimes I see as men not capable of the kind of fatherly love displayed at home. Perhaps they were not brought up with any. I see them as predators that I wouldn't even compare with any animal predator in the jungle, ocean or on land. It would be insulting to every one of these predators. I see them as ones in love with bringing pain on the innocence of humanity. That is their reaction to nature's beauty, to reach their own perverted orgasams. The flame from this kind of orgasam must be extinguished. It is our duty after all not to let those flames burn in ecstasy for their triumphs.

"It's been four years of hell for Bosnia and Croatia in the same sense, with most of the Croats being ashamed of their participation of a million people being killed and many others misplaced all over the world. The number of Bosjnaks was three and half million people, one quarter of whom vanished. I almost feel I should mourn for my existence because I will be exterminated if I don't do something to perserve my Bosnia, but we are a very proud people and it would be shameful to mourn for myself.

"Perhaps this time my neighbors will see through the burning and looting of the destruction of our nation. This destruction that took place scarred our landscape in this nation like a bear that clawed a tree leaving deep gouges. If they could reflect on the beauty and richness our nation possessed at one time, perhaps the ones who led the cause for all this destruction would be the first ones to find a place in their hearts to realize the wrong they have committed to that beautiful moasic that took over two thousand years to develop since before the time of Christ. Sadly that will probably not happen until the patriarchs who are the church leaders will preach redemption and forgiveness and admit they need as the faithful to try and reflect on the wrongs done. If that would happen with the patriarchs then it would be easy to convince the masses at the Sunday gatherings.

"We as a people have contributed much to the world, and our neighbors can learn from us. We are part of nature and know how to live in harmony with it. We are like a stream that never dries. We are like the wind that never stops to help pollenate trees to assure each flower recieves generous pollination for a good harvest at the end of the season. Most of all we are neighbors that you would never have to have any fear of for your child. If there were rain our faces would need no washing by it because they are all always clean and our hearts are pure and thoughts genuine. Our vision is one with the hopes that as our neighbors you would trust in us as we hope to trust in you although it can't always be.

"Peter, who I regretfully once called a friend, is one good example of a poor neighbor and a gardener cultivating bad seeds in his mind. He didn't grow any roses in the garden of his mind but bullets that brought death to many. That was Peter, the gardener of dead flowers, along with many others like him that surrounded him. Peter along with murderous monsters like Arkan and Seselj, assured that many thousands of mothers never again knew a dry face with no tears.

"Night after night after dinner during the family's traditional gathering there always seemed to be an empty place left at their tables and suddenly there would be tears coming from a mother or sister who was missing her son or brother. There was always someone near to comfort and help them get through their grief and promise a false hope to see their loved ones home again soon but knowing in their hearts there really was no hope for that happy reunion.

"The heartbroken mother would sit at the window by a little kerosene lamp with a weak glow of light but enough to keep her knitting her little gifts while she imagined hearing her child's voice coming down the street or his footsteps hurriedly running up the stairs. Then they would hug and rejoice and she would give him her gift that she put so much labor of love into of the little socks and sweaters. She worked tediously hour after hour knitting it for them in their absence. They were nothing but empty dreams but she would refuse to believe it. The voices would never be heard.

"These mother's stories were the same throughout the villages and towns. The mother would be holding her knitting making a neck scarf for her long gone daughter or son, doing the tedious work night after night with barely enough light to see by the little lamp. Each time she pulled the yarn through the needle her emotions guided her somewhere far away in the unknown that she would never walk to in her mind she would rather work by the weak light the lamp with her old weary eyes. She would glance out the tiny window hoping to see a glimpse or hear the voice of her child coming home but again she saw nothing of what she wished for and her hopes were empty. Yet she continued to knit and knit. That little flame in the kerosene lamp still would burn like it was just about to go out only not just yet.

"They would presevere regardless with hope, and the morning

of a new day brought new hope and they would busy themselves with something else to do to prepare for their children's return. They would bake all day in old fashioned ovens for hours a special treat called Gurabija. They wrapped the cookies in soft cloths to preserve the aroma and wonderful flavor that was similar to that of pisnelles and then they would place them in a beautifully crafted wooden chest to save their freshness and take out when the children returned. The cookies were baked hard and dry and were preserved to be as good as when they were first baked.

"Since the fall of the Ottoman empire first with the crowning of King Alexander of Serbia to Tito up to now in the new millinium, our mothers have known no peace. Heartbreak is a part of their lives. Black, white, and brown scarves have become the common fashion in recognition of the loss of their loved ones.

"In the same valley of our hometown and across the countries of Serbia, Montenegro, and Croatia, the Serbian mothers don't have to sit by windows and hope for hopeless dreams to come true. They are blessed in knowing their children are safe and sound throughout the western world and able to send them those beautiful hand written letters of news. It was a huge contrast for the two mother's types of dream. One got to be proud of her child's success and the other only had the hope one day of having tears filled with joy from seeing that her child was alive. I would call this a double standard even from God.

"Why is it some seem to be favored and have so much privledge from God while others have nothing? For fifteen hundred it seems God's favortism has gone to the Orthodox Slavs that they never took full advantage of. From the ancient Greeks to the Romans and the Austria-Hungarians and French, not to mention five hundred years of Ottoman Turks. All of this contributed some good directly to the Serb culture. Yet they were incapable of running their own house. Is it circumstances and has nothing to do with God or is it God's will and the opposite? To create the big ball of yarn first you need many sheep, and you need to know how to keep them happy and producing enough wool. Then go through the process with painstaking hard labor that requires expertise and knowledge. Then you will create that big ball of yarn. To inherit that big ball of yarn and have it start unraveling takes very little energy and an abundance of stupidity. You could say the Serbs possessed plenty of that. In all of this time of over a thousand years they have never been a master of their own home and my ancestors had no hand in it to be blamed like they were.

"In the Bible of Christianity it says to turn the other cheek to your enemies. I believe in Islam that says the same thing only phrased a little differently, exhorting compassion and mercy for mankind. Are we as individual men to play God and judge others for the injustices and crimes we have been wronged by? Or are we supposed to wait until God in His time does it Himself? If history has taught us anything, I think the interpretation of the Bible and the Koran is that you should love your neighbor and be compassionate and giving even if your enemies are doing you injustice. If you get hit with rocks that are thrown at you while you are offering them bread, there seems something wrong with that picture. In examining some historical facts no further back than the time of Christ the picture of the dishonesty in man has always existed.

"In the old and new worlds of America, Europe, Australia, and Africa, each time new lands were accidently discovered in the then unknown world they were not uninhabited but had people already there living and thriving in peaceful civilizations. All of them had received and welcomed the newcomers with exitement and open arms, offering bread, and being excited and comforted in knowing they were not alone on this huge unexplored planet. Their excitement soon turned to disappointment, and tragedy was brought on them. Instead of returning the kindness, we took from them and then looked down at them through the barrels of muskets, and over the edges of sharp swords and long spears.

"The events occuring in Bosnia were no less evil than that was. Turning the other cheek will make you another tragic statistic. Sharing bread with your neighbors is done only through strength from the heart and soul. Anything less than that will invite repeats of murder and extermination.

"Ones who never cared about the idea of turning the other check were ones like the Serb and the Montenegrin children who had no reasons to do so. Their exsistence was never threatened.. They always had a home and country to call their own and yet always tried to dim our lights of hope in Bosnia to call it our home. What is it that makes them so unhappy in their own homeland? Perhaps it is their laziness, carelessness and they are bad gardeners who want something for nothing. There is an ancient joke in Serbia and Montenegro. When the Serbs and Montenegrins go to bed at night and wake in the morning they stretch upwards and sit at the edge of the bed feeling tired and not wanting to do anything the rest of the day. One could call it being lazy or not having any concern about doing anything good for the day.

"These are the people who wanted to take away what we built and were building for our children and our futures. I would have liked to tell them, 'Roll up your sleeves men, and don't sit there on the corners of your bed. There is much do to in life to make it better.'

"The hopes of our people should be in no one else's hands but our own. A repeat of the murder, rape, and genocide should never be tolerated to occur again. Respect and trust should come voluntarily. They should hand it to us on a platter eagerly. We deserve and give nothing less and should expect nothing less from our neighbors.

"When we weren't strong enough as a unit, there was mass emmigration and forced eviction from our lands and homes. It became a tradition over the last hundred years for the families of our people to celebrate and recognize their children becoming young women and men and to throw a big party for them when they they came of age and were ready to leave. They were going on that same repeated journey that there was really no other option for but exile to the new unknown world. It was a choice I had to make and experienced myself. Every person that was at my party on that night, no less than a couple of hundred, touched me or shook my hand and wished me good luck. I told them all this was a five-year plan for me and I would be back and to think of it as just like my being away on a mission to a gold rush. Most of those before and after me had the same ideas.

"I found over the five years I had been gone I felt distanced in my heart from my birthplace. I missed the love at times of my immediate family, friends and my childhood but then I would realize that all of my beautiful memories were as fragile as a drop of water on the palm of your hand. They weren't enough reason to return, not even the treasured memories like those moments when my mother and father would come to wake me in the morning to have Turkish coffee with them. That aroma of the coffee was blended with the love of my parents yet even those recollections were not enough to drive me back. A few drops of water on your palm can never quench a deep thirst.

"Forty years have gone by now and I lost all my desire to return at all. I found my new home in a land that accepted me and gave to me everything I had dreamed of. My mission for the gold rush has become a reality. I hoped that every child that had that dream as I did to got to a new world and found what I did. The hopes and then the fulfillment of liberty and a healthy life were enough reason to never look back again and most of us or maybe all of us never returned.

"As time went on our letters home to the old world were written less and less, dwindling off until they faded away like a season of the year had passed without being noticed. The aged or elderly of the familes that had said goodbye to the young ones suddenly weren't around any longer to read the letters and one more reason for them not to write. It was one more step in distancing ourselves from our birthland and at the same time digging our new roots deeper in our new adopted homeland. Some of the generation who stayed behind were left with an empty space in their heart for the young who left home, knowing that we would not ever be returning.

"Each season of the year brought change in her own natural way, but tradition never changed or faded. Through the changing seasons people carried on the rituals of that season especially before the harsh coming winter season when there was always someone preparing to leave home. There wasn't much else left to do after that during the long winter nights, after all the crops were harvested and safely stored for the upcoming long winter, and the young had left for the new world. They would repeat that ritual of previous years and the families visited with one another time and time again from early in the evening until late in the night to exchange any news from their loved ones.

"They would take out the worn wrinkled letters they had been carrying around in their pockets to bring there and read them and tell only of any happy news or little success stories from their loved ones. They would talk all night with no time taken to pause afraid there wouldn't be enough time to tell their story during that night. They would drink Turkish coffees and Sljivovica, a traditional home made plum brandy. By late night or early the next morning they would have mentioned the names of hundreds of young men they had not seen in years but still kept fresh in their memory. They would describe each one of them from when they took their first steps and as boys up until the day they left.

"Throughout their conversation over the night there would always be someone that was thinking about his or her own child and shedding tears. Suddenly everyone would notice the tearful person and would focus all their attention on reassuring and comforting him or her. By early morning the special pinsell cookies called gurabija were all eaten by the group instead of the ones that they were meant for. All they had of us was those wrinkled letters, but they were comforting. Some of the parents discussed while eating the cookies how much their child had either loved or hated the gurabija cookies.

"Each passing night and season they were aging and being robbed and distanced them from their children who by now had their own families and had become providers. Most of us don't notice the span of time and think about when we will meet the invisible final wall at the end of life's wheel of fortune. We should be thankful that nature doesn't grant us the ability to see where that invisible wall is, and how soon the wheel will stop spinning.

"For the new generation in the new world, life was much different and there wasn't time for talking of cookies. It seemed life was like being on roller blades all the time only much faster there in the new world. In the old world the same saga lived on and the night following would be much the same as the previous one. They would hold the hope that one would be returning home and knock loudly on the old heavy pine wood door and in an excited voice call out, 'Hey, Gazda!' which means, 'You, the owner of this home!' It is used as an expression for ones who return home after having been away for a long time to show respect for the owner of the home.

"The great land of America wasn't built by ones who went there and then left just so they could return to their old world with their riches. It became the nation it is because no one did go back, just as I and people before me didn't. There was nothing to go back to. The people who destroyed the dream of that little lady and many others, sitting by the window with the candle as tears ran down her face were Tito and his trained bloodthirsty killers that roamed all around Yugoslavia and the world making sure those children would never come home. The old Yugoslavia and then Tito and his men were the chief architects for all of the broken dreams."

After listening raptly to my tale for quite a while Ramiz asked, "Do you mean, Angelo, that they killed all those people?"

"Hell yes, Ramiz, that is exactly what I meant," I answered. "These people have hands soaked with our blood. Their intent was to exterminate us and remove us as obstacles. Somehow we were always in their way. Some of the architects for our removal now are Milosevic,

161

Peter F, Arkan, and Seselj. It seems their ideas came from the notorious and the late Rankovic, former chief of state police who was Tito's right hand man. I had the misfortune of meeting Rankovic once when I was hospitalized at the VMA in Belgrade for treatment of some wounds in December of 1968. When I met him he looked exactly as I had pictured him to, a Chetnik from head to toe.

"I remembered a story my father had told me about him once. He had a hand in the lives of one thousand men who were tortured in the city of Pec. On the outskirts of the city there was an old mill that was not operated by the wind but by water. It was similarly operated like today's modern turbines in hydro dams. Rankovic conceived a heinous plan of torture using this water mill. He tied people to the top of the wheel which would spin up to eighty miles an hour. The ones who came out of it alive were never the same. Thousands were victims of this especially unusual and cruel form of torture. The ones that did survive had loss of memory, loss of their body muscle control, and they trembled constantly like having Parkinsons disease.

"It was discovered many years later that kind of torture affects the inner ear canal and the three inner ear bones. This would cause many disfunctions of the whole body. Rankovic invented this way to torture, and it gave him his only orgasam of pleasure. Others like him have hurt many of our people as well as their own during the communist era, but mostly it has been our people and the Albanian Kosovars that have been the victims. The internal security police left by the late Tito are still delivering deadly blows to our people.

"Those same men who worked for Tito found themselves after his death suddenly without jobs and their prestigious licenses to torture and kill in jeopardy. Right away they were recruited by Serbian President Milosevic and some were recruited by Croatian President Tuzman. The thugs who thought they would be unemployed found the recruitment to be welcome news and now had an even better unrestricted license to kill with no one to answer to. More killing was demanded by their new boss Slobo and all the better.

"I helped a niece of Milosevic when she really needed it during my work with immigration, to help her make sure she had her work permit and the first step towards legalization. I didn't know at the time that I was helping someone whose uncle would become a butcher of historical proportions in the twenty first century. She had spoken highly of her uncle as a compassionate man.

"At the time there was mass destruction in the city of Vucovar by the aggression of the forces of her Uncle Slobo, self declared president of all of what was then Yugoslavia, commmanding from in his office in Belgrade. I wanted to explain to her that the way she was seeing her uncle protrayed as a good man was a far different picture from what he was doing and we had yet to see his true colors. One thing that struck me in her conversation was her confession that some of her immediate family had a history of committing sucicide when they became a certain age. I didn't comment on it at the time but it crossed my mind with hopes Slobo was at that age and would get rid of himself and be doing a great favor to the world and maybe we wouldn't have to be going through all of this. But then perhaps I wouldn't be writing this book now.

"The girl ended up moving to San Francisco, which is where I met her, and she completed training to be an engineer. The man I had met her through was one of my fellow Montenegrins, Vajo Raicovic. He had joined Arkan's White Eagles during the war in Bosnia and later was killed by Arkan himself for betraying him and also killing many of his men while trying to clear a path for himself to reach the ranks closer up to that of Arkan. Unfortunately I even helped this bastard get legal immigration into the United States, but that was before the war. If I regret anything I did during that time to help people immigrate this was one case I truly regret.

"All of this activity by the former Yugoslavian agents from overseas connected to the gathering of these losers in Yugoslavia to be fighting on two opposite sides, one with Tuzman and the other with Slobo. This time instead of working together many of them found themselves on opposite sides killing each other. That was good except that my people in Bosnia were too ignorant and refused to believe that they would land in the middle of this fire and sooner or later to be taken away as trophies. The Bosnians had no plans of defense. What made them think that this time would be any different from previous times is beyond my comprehension.

"I couldn't even convince my own father that this is what would happen and we had heated debates over it. He left town without us saying goodbye to one another because he couldn't admit that he had been wrong. I could understand my father's point of view with his being one of the leaders of the communist party and believing that all people could live in peace and tranquility. He fought most of his life for that belief and paid dearly for it. It was a noble thought and I never held resentment towards him. I just wish he had been right and everything had been true that my father believed in and there wouldn't have been all of this bloodshed. It was sadly not true.

"Peter and all of these ex-patriots of Yugoslavia were part of this old terror and now part of the new and more fashionable terror. On the front lines with him were Arkan, Seselj, and Vuk Drskovic, the rugged looking and degenerate dirty bastard that rooted with a Serbian flag in his hand and inpired thousands of Serbs through his nationalism. He led the murderous bastards to loot and kill, with full approval through the media and Serbian propaganda that trampling on Bosnia was the correct thing to do. Vuk's party time was short lived. What he thought was easy prey proved not to be. Bosnia is still alive and well."

"When my friends were flying over Belgrade with British and German Tornadoes, US F-16s and F-15s, and never forgetting our US carriers with the F-14 Tomcats, this bastard Vuk cried on Serbian TV begging us to stop the bombing. I won a bet I had made with Vojo, one of Arkan's boys. I bet him that they may have been laughing at the time but that they would soon be crying in the days to come. I reminded him many times that Serbia and Montenegro needed no enemies when they had friends like him to lead them.

"The only thing that was important to them was their status of employment. That didn't change, but only their boss, because one died and another took over. Their idea of killing was to terrorize the old, young, and the weak. In the first stage of their invasion of Bosnia, one incident that occured, committed by one of the militias from Serbia and Montenegro's White Eagles, was that of a young girl who was raped and mutilated. They cut off her ears leaving in her pierced earrings which were 24 karat gold in Turkish lira. They took both pierced ears and sold them in the capitol of Montenegro to the highest bidder, who paid one thousand marks. That was just one of the many brutal gruesome incidents these men were capable of and did. They never had the guts to meet our men and soldiers on the battlefield. Obviously they could only prey on the weak and defenseless.

"All of these men got their just due mostly by killing each other just as Vojo did in Belgrade while trying also to support his drug habit. Milosevic killed Arkan and the rest were all being tried at the Tribunal in Haag for their henious crimes.

"The patriarchs and head of the Serbian churches have yet to acknowledge their direct participation in all of this. They carried the Orthodox Bible in one hand and gunpowder in a barrel with a short fuse in the other already ignited. It is a sad day for God if He understands any of this in human man. The image for God as great being displayed in these kind of men is no doubt a red flag for a black future for all of mankind if that therefore is the truth.

"These men with the love of darkness continued all through this war doing what they obviously learned from their ancestors and did what their fathers, grandfathers and great grandfathers had done before. My father taught me this was a new world with a smarter and brighter generation capable of not repeating the atrocities of the previous generation. He was wrong. They are smarter and brighter yes, so now our existence is even in more in danger than ever.

"These vultures received the call through their Othodox churches to come to mother Serbia to defend her from the infidels in Bosnia. What a crock of sand that was and is. They had forgotten these same Bosnian people fought on the front lines with the Serbs in the Kosovo plains and lost their lives along with the Serbs to help them in their defense. Throughout history we fought shoulder to shoulder with them to keep their freedom up until the last war in 1941. Each and every time the Bosnians had a tendency to forget what these people had done to them in the past. Perhaps this time they will not.

"If the only way for us be good neighbors is with the barrels of guns, then so be it. I hope my father and all the fathers throughout Bosnia and I as my father's son, will never believe innocently like our fathers had that nothing bad would ever come from the other side of the hill with the thoughts there would be no need for guards on the hill to watch. When we got the news from the other side of the hill it was all bad news for us and we were not prepared to receive it. There were no guards to protect our families. The hill was unguarded. By the time we thought to do something to protect ourselves many had already died and were dying. The rivers, streams and meadows and horse barns, houses and even the cemetaries were full of the mutilated corpses of our people. Most of the ones who did this came from overeseas, America, Australia, Germany, and some naturalized citizens, some born here as well as others. One man bragged openly in the American magazine Time, that if America gets involved in the war in Bosnia he would go to fight against America. He was either an American naturalized citizen or American by birth of Serbian descent. These were the misfits of society, drug addicts, rapists and murderers that were raping our children and killing our brothers and sisters all through Bosnia.

"It wasn't enough that they did the damage and killing that they did over the last thirty years outside of Yugoslavia. They had to come back and put the icing on the cake and sad to say it's a bloody cake. Where do we go from here?

"As I said before, Tito was the mastermind who created a superb group of people that wouldn't ever leave any traces of blood from their dirty work to connect them to the crimes that they were committing all over the globe. They did leave some traces of the bank robberies they pulled throughout the western world which netted them millions. Most of them were wanted by the Western governments, but there was nothing for them to fear because Serbia was their safe haven. It was the law of the wild west. You could commit a crime in one county and go to the next and be a good guy and the sheriff would welcome you because he wants a cut from it.

"In this instance Milosevic made sure he would get his cut from those robberies and Arkan was happy to oblige. The next logical thing for them to do was steal luxury vehicles, not in the hundreds but in the thousands. As one can now see the Porches, BMWs, Mercedes,Volvos, Ferraris, and Lamborghinis in some cases are being driven everywhere in former Yugoslavia. How could these citizens all afford these kind of luxury vehicles? One robbery did go wrong by some of the descendants of Serbia in America at a famous Lake Tahoe resort in northern Nevada. The casino wasn't robbed but a bomb did explode and do tremendous damage and suspects were arrested and prosecuted.

"These kinds of criminals are just one example of them having a lucky rabbit's foot. Many of the criminals can consider themselves lucky and no one could prove them guilty of their crimes. One could say maybe then they lived happily ever after.

"A lot of governments turned a blind eye to the crimes, not wanting to cause any conflict of diplomacy with Serbia and the rest of the European governments. There was an American of Serbian descent who claimed to be a veteran of the U.S. Army who was interviewed in Queens, New York, just after he had returned from Bosnia during the first stages of the war. He declared allegiance to Serbia and their murderous militias instead of the country that had given him everything.

"There are two differences between him and people like myself and my people. One is we always remain dignified as human beings and the second is being loyal to our country and never biting the hand that feeds us. That means being loyal to the country that has given you everything. All through the war in Bosnia as an American citizen of Bosnian decent, I place my allegiance as always to what is in America's best interest and to making sure the independence of Bosnia is in America's best interest. It is a long term investment for America with big future returns, stategically, politically, and economically and the world will be much better off for it.

"America will never be better off being betrayed by her citizens such as this Serbian American war veteran protrayed himself. It was painful to see such a display. The love of his orginal roots overrode his idea of patriotism. In this situation he was lynching America and throwing her into a deep well of water to suffocate her all for a country with a history of oppression which was the reason for his own father to run from it and make sure his son would be born in America and have a better life. How could he possibly justify those actions? There is no justification of his support for the oppressive Serbia that his father ran from and for him to join in the army of Serbia against the men he once served with, the American soldiers.

"I did my part to stop the traitor bastards who betrayed the honor of our military and what our forces stand for which is freedom and defense for the weak. The man from Queens that bragged to fight against America if we went to Bosnia was just that kind of traitor. I want to question the motive of our justice system about why this man and others like him were not questioned and made to answer about their affiliations with Serbian forces and which groups and how and why it was they were standing on the side of the enemy when American forces were in Bosnia with some of those in uniform giving their lives for our country? Is it possible that these traitors added to any of the casualities of some of our soldiers?

"Betrayal and changing loyalties were common under Tito in Yugoslavia. Men were going to the tables that looked like it had more bread on it than a banquet of Julius Caesar's. In America we don't have to compare tables. We have the stablity and all we have to do is protect our interests by bringing countries such as Bosnia and Croatia in our corner as participants of a free society and not with men such as the ones Tito had tutored as assassins and spies.

"Tito's agents numbered in the thousands. Some years later after I had left Yugoslavia I was approached by Peter himself and offered the luxury and privelege to join this club. I weighed the pros and cons in a matter of seconds and to be on the winning side would be to not join but not break my string of contact with him either. It was easy for me to decline. My people were the victims. How could I possibly do that and be betraying my own people? Quite a few of my Bosnjak brothers were insiders as members of this exclusive club, and looking back now they have nothing to be proud of.

"I wanted to protect the interest of my Bosnia from the people who were just like Peter, but I liked to keep my enemies near by so that I could keep an eye on what they were doing. Each time I felt I was very close to the fire and some of my people might get hurt. I tried warning them every time but failed to convince any of them about the danger until the war broke out. I thought it was a smart idea to keep the enemy in range so I might know what they're up to every day.

"The people's enemy were not the members in Tito's exclusive communist club, Peter, Seselj, and Vuk, who were considered the good guys, but people like me, who saw the dangers that were in store for us in those days. Most of the community considered us as traitors to Yugoslavia. Peter and the thousands who were like him inside and outside of the country were trained to be eyes for Tito and were his watch dogs."

Pace stared at me curiously, paying close attention to everything I was saying and patiently he asked me with disbelief, "Angelo, I don't understand, is that similar to our CIA?" His concern was showing in his expression and tone of voice.

I answered, "No my friend, not like the CIA. That would be an insult to the CIA who fight and protect for our freedom as a nation from the internal and external enemies. These people were cold blooded murderers who were trained to watch the immigrants from Yugoslavia. If any of them should step out of line which in their view would be by displeasing Tito, who had so much power he thought of himself as the crowned king, then they would be killed and the body never found. Peter was one of those guys with that blood on his hands up to his shoulders.

"Pace, just take a look at this guy here now. Take a good look at Ramiz. He could consider himself the luckiest guy on the planet just to be here drinking coffee with us. Ramiz is a fortunate man who genuinely appreciates the second chance God gave him to be alive to tell the story. I will say that our friendship has been much stronger since he was released from the hospital. We are older and wiser and have learned to be greatful for each new day. How he had survived during his ordeal in the city of Mostar is beyond me. What do you think Pace, is it a miracle?"

"No, Angelo," Pace answered. "I wouldn't call it a miracle. I would call it a will to survive beyond the suffering and pain and having a love of life that can still be sweet. Nothing can be more of a compliment to a human being's body more than to have an understanding of the privledge to be born and to live your life to the fullest. The ultimate compliment to life is to grow old and be able to reflect on your life knowing you had made a contribution to a better life for all."

"Well, my friends," Ramiz replied to us, "I sure can say that when I heard my name being called on that day in Mostar I considered myself to be lucky, even though I was lying in a pool of blood and buried in dust that covered half my body. I was telling you before, Angelo, about the encounter I had with your friend Peter."

I interrupted, "Excuse me Ramiz, but he was never such a friend who I would be comfortable leaving my children with, even for a few minutes to go get a pizza pie. He was only really an acquaintance that I shared some similar interests with, whom I thought I should keep accessible so that I knew when he was planning to come and kill you, Ramiz, and every one of you. I've told you all these years about this type of guy but you wouldn't beleive me, thinking I was out of touch with my mind. At least now you know I wasn't crazy. Anyway go on and tell me what happened that day. I know what happened to you, and Pace would enjoy hearing it."

Ramiz was silent for a moment as if composing himself after my revealations about what I knew was going to happen to our people. Finally he said, "Well, after I buried that little Neo-Nazi..."

Pace interrupted him, "Wait a minute." He burst out laughing and slapped his hands on the table saying, "You mean to tell me that there still are some of those so called Nazis left? Angelo was telling me about this Croatian guy from California a few years ago that was preparing to deliver a bomb to the Yugoslavian counsel office and blow himself up. Wasn't he a member of the Ustasha group, Angelo, the Young Croatians?"

"Yes," I told him, "he was, to my knowledge, as that's what his brother Branko told me. The Ustashas have nothing to be proud of because they were clearly associated with SS Nazis. They were the ones who were killing Jews and everybody else they considered to be in their way. So tell us, Ramiz, about what happened when you and Peter met up at the water fountains?"

Ramiz went on again, "Well, I was washing my face and trying to reflect on everything that just happened. Peter was cursing Mother Mary and God and everyone else yelling, 'Those fuckers are gonna pay for this!' For some reason I pulled my head up and turned to look right at him. We kind of glared at each other. The only thing I remember saying to him at that point was, 'Peter what happened? You are bleeding.' Then as I remember he put his left hand up over his brows and eye and then looked at the blood on his palm.

"When he saw the blood he became enraged and started pacing in circles faster and faster like a dog looking for a place to take a dump that couldn't make up his mind. He started yelling and cursing, 'You mother fuckers you! Fucking balias! All of you Serbs and Bosnians! We should surround you and your Serb brothers with a Great Wall of China so you can kill each other until the very last one! If any of you are left then we'll finish you off!'"

"I asked Peter, 'What's the matter, short on memories right? I thought you told me your mom was part Serb.' His temper really flared. 'Fuck you Ramiz, I know who I am, I don't need you to remind me!' I walked over next to him and grabbed his wrist wanting to sock him right in the mouth but I didn't because Mata wouldn't have backed me up and I would have been a dead man. Instead of knocking him out I told him, 'Peter your eye needs looked at because you're bleeding.'

"The cut on his face looked almost like he had been in a boxing ring but nothing too serious but that kind of cut can bleed a lot and some people bleed more than others, especially when emotional. He pulled his wrist out of my hand and said gritting his teeth in anger, 'It won't be you who will be looking at it, Ramiz.'

"OK Peter, maybe you should call up Angelo in Las Vegas,' I told him. That really set him off. It was a little lethal injection for me. I didn't know you were on bad terms and it seemed there was no love left between you and Peter."

I answered, "I don't think so since the last time I ever saw him I told him I would cut off his genitals if I ever saw him again and stick them in his mouth."

"Oh man, I really did it then," Ramiz said. "The last thing he wanted to hear was your name. He kicked at the dust with his boots waving his hands in front of his face. He went to the barrack that was still standing after all the explosions. He was cursing and slammed the door going into the barrack. I thought the door would fall off it's hinges, as broken glass was flying everywhere.

"When he stormed into the barrack that had become a temporary command post, I heard someone trying to get Peter's attention calling him shouting, 'Peter, Peter! There's an urgent call from Australia from your daughter and ex-wife. They sound hysterical and are crying!'

"I heard him reply, 'My ex-wife? I don't have an ex-wife, Mister. It's always been my wife.' Peter is one of those people with a face no one could forget. He has a red complexion with white splotches on it and a nose shaped like a wild giant mushroom in the forest, that have a rank odor when ripe, with a giant square body that compliments the nose. A perfect example of nature's specimens gone all wrong."

Pace asked, "What do you mean by a specimen gone wrong?"

"Well, Pace, Peter considered himself as an Aryan Anglo-Saxon man. Doctor Mengele went wrong on making Peter an an example for the pure Aryian race. There are two types of men from the Anglo-Saxon race, the good looking ones and the ugly ones. Peter was an ugly one. A face like his is hard to forget. No one could love it but the perhaps only the mother that gave birth to it."

Ramiz interupted and said, "Hey, I'd like to finish my story if I can. I was still standing by the water trough when Peter stormed out from the barracks washing up. He leaned over the water trough still muttering to himself to splash water on his face a few times making his cuts bleed heavier and causing him to be more enraged. He was vigorously rubbing his hands over his face and head. I was confused for a second wondering how I could help him and his bleeding eye and wanted to know what was going on. So I asked, 'Peter what has happened, what's going on?'

"He looked at me and said, 'Why do you want to know, you

fucking balija! Just so you can feel more satisfied? I've had enough of your crap!' I told Peter, 'I just wanted to help if I could but you're a hard man to even talk to and it looks like you don't need any of my help.' He was waving his hands in the sky and raking his fingers through his hair over and over in such a rage that his shirt came untucked from his pants and his fat belly hung out and then his pants fell halfway down his legs and he looked disgusting. He said, 'My son is dead! Only twenty years old!' He was trying to tug his pants back up and tuck his shirt in.

"I felt really bad for him and told him, 'Gee, I'm so sorry,' and I meant it with the utmost sincerity. He turned to stare at me and yelled at me, 'Fuck you, you fucking balija,' calling me that for the third time now. 'You're not sorry!' he yelled. 'You're all alike. To you it's just another dead Croat!'

"I told him, knowing I was pushing the envelope, 'You better make up you mind what it is you are, a Serb or a Croat.' It was only him and I there still playing with water at the trough. He wasn't far from reading my mind though. Then Commander Mata came out. He looked worried about Peter and tried to calm him down.

"The next thing I knew Peter had his hand on his Belgian gun that is capable of firing fifteen rounds in half that many seconds. A hand gun like that feels more like a machine gun instead. I thought for a second that he was pulling it out to shoot me because of the way he looked at me. Mata told Peter, 'I don't think Ramiz met any harm. He was just trying to comfort you,' not knowing what I had said to him. I doubted that he was hearing what Mata was saying to him. I had hoped that my childhood friend I called brother and now my commander Mata would stand by me, but it wasn't to be. He stood by his Christian brother. I tried filling in then saying, 'Look Peter I really am honestly sorry about your boy. I only hope the news was a mistake.'

"Shut up, you fucking bastard!' was Peter's response. 'If you say one more thing I will shoot you myself. I'm not sure who brought you here but whoever it was ought to know I'm about to get rid of you for good.'

"I didn't need to reply because Mata was standing right there. That comment had overdone it for me. I wasn't about to take anything more from Peter. I shouted with my finger up in his face, 'Peter you are an ungrateful miserable creature! Your problems are your own and for your information I wasn't forcefully brought here, I volunteered. Its true because Commander Mata came to my house and we talked because of our childhood friendship. I believed in Mata so that's why I joined. And here you are now trying to preach at me your true colors which I don't want to hear from a little miserable red headed ape son of a bitch! You are just reaping what you have sown. You came all the way across the world just to blow up that bridge which meant so much historically to all of us.'

"His reply to me then was, 'It wasn't the Christian Rome that built that bridge, your Turks did it.' I told him, 'No Peter, you're wrong. Our people built that bridge, Croats and Bosnians alike.' I was getting into his face and feeling assured because I was armed. I continued, 'The Romans could not have built that bridge. There was no Roman Empire at that time, only the Ottoman Empire. They had reigned over this part of the world for half of a millenum. Don't be ungrateful to them. Their presence enriched our culture and educated your sorry ass, at least in some ways.'

"Peter's response was, 'I don't look to the east for a prayer but only to the west and to Rome.'

"My temper was flaring again and I said to him, 'Peter you are a fucking baboon and I doubt you even know where Rome is. You are an illiterate, ignorant, and arrogant man.'

"Our argument was accelerating out of control, at least it was on my part. For some reason I felt alone and empty but still felt confident with my piece tucked behind me in my belt. The thing I wasn't aware of at the time was that my piece wasn't tucked in my belt as I thought, and Peter had noticed while we were talking and both felt comfortable and I was washing up. I had left my gun lying over by the water trough. I had the feeling Peter wanted to tell me something and that something was off but he never said anything. Perhaps he was pushing my buttons then since he clearly knew that I would have nothing to challange him with if it came down to it.

"Our argument was verging on being physical and I was wanting a physical fight and I wanted to teach the bastard a lesson. It didn't cross my mind that I might have needed my gun to confront Peter since I was in prime physical condition and could have kicked Peter's ass as well as many of the others with no doubt. That was my first mistake. The wind was picking up and the heavy red dust was filling the air and that didn't help matters. It was a stupid mistake that almost cost me my life and shows the inexperience of people in times of crisis. I was green and Peter was seasoned although I know I had more heart than Peter. My own heart almost got me killed. It seemed everything was unraveling out of control and heading in the wrong direction, in this case directly at me.

"Suddenly Peter was acting over confident and blew up yelling at me, 'Fuck you! You son of a bitch, you! You are nothing but a balija and I will get rid of you right now if you don't shut your mouth!' He reminded me of little tempermental high strung Mexican chihuahua dogs and I wanted to kick his ass so bad. I didn't want to keep my mouth shut like I should have and I knew I could take him. I wasn't intimidated by him at all. My pride was much bigger than he could know."

Pace interrupted to ask, "Do you regret you didn't just swallow your pride, Ramiz?"

"Hell no!" he answered, laughing. "I thought he didn't have it in him to shoot and kill me and he didn't. I'm still here, but boy was I in for a surprise. Angie, I should have talked to you before I made that assumption, and asked you what kind of man he was."

I told him, "Ramiz, I wish I were there to warn you about him, although it probably wouldn't have helped."

"Hey Angie," Pace said, "What kind of friend are you? Here was a man about to be killed that you didn't even warn him about. What kind of people do you hang out with?"

I said, "Ramiz never called to ask me that day, what he was up to or ask how it felt to get blown up by a nine millimeter. I should know, I've had that experience before. It isn't that bad when you live through it." We all cracked up laughing because now we all knew.

"I know one thing for sure, if it had been just the two of you alone there, just you and Peter, you could be sure he never would have pulled a gun on you or shot at you. He would have walked away with his tail between his legs but that doesn't mean you shouldn't watch your back. He is a resentful and unforgiving man. He wouldn't have the guts if he were alone with you. And the fact that he knew your gun was wrapped in a towel about fifteen yards away. That and the only other reason he would have shot you is because he had a lot of the Ustashas around him. Even if I was there, knowing you, I probably wouldn't have interfered. I would have just shot his sorry ass for shooting you and reminded you to always have your gun with you and not walk around without your underwear on to flash your ass and going to the shooting range without a gun. That was pretty dumb my friend. Wouldn't you say so?"

Ramiz acknowledged that I was right in my advice and if there was a next time he would be at the shooting range wearing underwear and tight pants, shaking his head he replied, "It was a dumb thing for me to do, leaving my gun behind on the water trough. You can't lose your virginity more than once in life." Ramiz humor again made us really laugh. "Next time I will be sure not to ever leave my gun anywhere. A gun can be your best friend."

We all laughed at his sense of humor. I told him, "I know your character though and you wouldn't have even allowed me try to try to save your little tiny butt."

We all burst out laughing again, having fun remembering together and not forgetting how fortunate it was for Ramiz to even be here. We accidentally tipped the table over spilling our beer and sodas all over our pizza pie. That didn't stop us from finishing it anyway.

We were more exhilarated to celebrate Ramiz' good fortune and feel our gratitude that he survived that ordeal. The experience for all three of us was definitely a sobering reminder that a man who I could have at one time call a friend could be of an altogether different breed just like Ramiz childhood friend, commander Mata. They are the men who are truly a breed of a predatory type. He is like the proverbial wolf wearing sheep's skin. Ordinary honest people would not see the danger from the ones like them, and are not on gaurd for defending themselves and many have paid with their live due to their naivetee. They can be fooled by their masquarades of seeming harmless but yet they are deadly as they have proved. Guys like Peter take full advantage of that and don't let anyone or any opportunity slip through their fingers. They are simply dangerous and can even be deadly as Peter was for you in your case, Ramiz. Under those circumstances he used his advantage to try and hurt you and our people as well."

He replied, "I reminded Peter right before he shot me about a story that you had told to me, Angie. You had told me about Peter calling you once in Las Vegas from the Gold Coast of Australia because he needed a favor from you. You didn't turn him down or curse him about it. You fulfilled your obligation as his friend and helped with what he was asking and that was to legalize his brother in law, sister, and their three children so that they could settle down

legally in the United States. As you told me also you never charged
them a dime. I reminded him that you visited his family in their new
homes in New York and Connecticut to make sure the children were
set in their schools and that his sister and her husband had gotten jobs.
I told Peter that he was an ungrateful man and a bastard. I asked him if
he would have enough balls to call you a balija too, which is a
degrading insult, after all you had done for him and his family."

I told him, "Ramiz, when you want to help someone with
something from your heart you don't look for a profit or any payment,
the satisfation in your heart is your reward."

Ramiz continued, "Well, Peter didn't look so tough or proud of
himself after I asked him about that. He didn't care for anyone to know
about all that you did for him and his family since everybody thought
he was the big shot from Australia, especially Mata. I pointed my
finger at Mr. Bigshot and said, 'You're a nothing and a nobody and I'm
not gonna cave in to that crap from an asshole like you.'

"His hand reached down toward his gun. When I saw that I
thought he must have really had it in him and wanted to have a
shootout and I really wanted to oblige him. The next moment I went
for my gun and realized it was not there but a long way away sitting
over on that stupid water trough wrapped in a towel. What an
embarrassing moment."

We all laughed and couldn't stop to say anything for awhile.
When we recovered finally Pace anxiously said, "Well, sorry, please
continue. This is getting pretty good. Then what happened?"

"There were about fifty men surrounding us armed to the teeth.
If they had been wearing sombreros they would have looked like
Pancho Villa's gang ready to watch a cock fight, and my one man show
was the only cock there and a losing battle was about to begin, and
they looking eager to see what would happen next. It wasn't that they
were necessarily rooting for either one of us but I stood alone on my
side and it looked like I had no fans from the group since they knew
the only shooting would be coming from one side and they were smart
to not stand in back of me. I had an open exit to run behind me if I
wanted to get shot in the back. Everyone there also knew I didn't have
a gun except for me at first and we had our audience with Peter and I
as the stars of the show and it was about to begin and it was about to
be over in a few seconds.

"I told him he was an ungrateful man in front of all those

people that really didn't know much about him and to them he was a mystery man yet he commanded respect if only for the reason that he was Mata's right hand man. When all the soldiers heard what I reminded him about what you did for his family it seemed his ego was hurt in front of all those men. Peter's face looked red and puffed up like a bad white liver from a slaughtered sheep. He was so enraged that he went ballistic shouting, 'I've had enough of you, you fucking bastard! My son is dead and he was probably killed by one of your fucking people!'

"I replied to Peter, 'I don't think it was by our people unless they were trying to collect a bill you owed them. Our people did go after you but not your boy. Maybe he was dealing drugs with those Serbo-Albanians and the deal went bad. You know how it is in Australia and America. It's the wild wild west. If your gonna play you have to pay. Everybody shoots from the hip.' That was the last thing I had the chance to say.

"I saw him reaching to pull out the gun at his hip and could see the barrel of the gun pointing straight at me and the the spark of flame coming straight from the barrel of the gun. Everything seemed to happen in slow motion. I could clearly see those flames from the barrel of the gun coming straight to me as he fired it over and over. He ended up emptying his gun in me and I was hit six times. I think that is he was a pretty poor shot that out of the sixteen rounds in his gun he only hit me six times from five to ten feet away. Maybe it's because his hands were shaking too much from being an alcholoic for so long.

"I felt I was doomed as the explosions racked my body and I saw myself starting to go down. My knees didn't buckle but I was falling forward hitting the dirt hard. It felt as if I were falling forever into an empty space and time. My eyes and body felt devoid of any emotions or pain yet my mind was aware of what was happening to me. By the time I did hit the dirt I could only see the clouds of dust and thought, 'That son of a bitch just shot me.' I felt I was drifting outside of the world I knew. I clearly felt I was dying. I wasn't breathing. I could feel the air pushing out of me but not coming back in. My whole life was passing before me through the eyes of my mind. Strangely then I found myself breathing, with a sound like wind blowing through a tunnel. The sound scared me. However I still didn't feel any emotion, not pain, anger or sorrow. Somehow I had surrendered to whatever was meant to be but felt at peace with what was happening without trying to have any control over my consciousness or the overall situation."

"Well, my friend, I think that's what the sensation or how it feels to be dying is. I know myself," I told Ramiz, "because I had those same sensations in a harsh winter morning on January 13th, 1969, at two o'clock in the morning. I was shot and wounded and thought I was dying or actually maybe was dead, but who knows? I'm still here anyway and you are too and we're not dead."

We all burst out laughing at once. I asked Pace, "Hey weren't you ever shot in any of those place you've been like in Vietnam or anything?"

He replied, "No, I didn't get shot."

I laughed and said, "You mean to tell me that with all those mad men that were shooting at you from every angle you didn't catch a single bullet in all those years? You must have had some damn good hiding places."

His temper flared for a moment then he caught himself and told me, "Well if my bullet proof vest hadn't caught a few of them maybe I would have been. Anyway Ramiz, I am glad you're still here, even though you didn't have a bullet proof vest."

Ramiz turned to me and asked, "Angie, is it true that during the beginning of the war in Bosnia that Pace and Peter both were guests in your home in Las Vegas at the same time?" He was asking me but wanting Pace to confirm that.

I replied, "Yes, my wife Mankiu had cooked a memorable dinner and Pace was the guest of honor. I wanted to introduce Peter and Pace to each other so that they would be acquainted. I was a traveling man at the time and I wanted to introduce Peter to know someone that I knew and was important to me. If the two of them got to know one another I thought I could also get more information about both of them like who they were really working for. It didn't take me long to find out. I thought being a double agent was complicated enough. With these two I would be a triple agent. I also thought Pace could be a good companion for him as well as a friend and company to each other when I wasn't around. However Pace really didn't like Peter much. The only thing they had in common was in their triple agent titles. "

CHAPTER SIX: A DINNER AT HOME

During that particular dinner event I needed to leave to go to the store and pick up some things my wife needed to complete her preparations for dinner. Going to grocery store is one of the things I'm not to good at and probably the last place you would find me. This time was different, I didn't mind going. By the time that I had gone to the store and came back it looked as if Peter and Pace had struck up a pretty good rapport trying to impress one another with their triple spy titles in the short time I was gone.

I dropped the goods in the kitchen for my wife and stayed with her for a few seconds, holding her from behind her waist and kissing her gently on the neck, thanking her for as always, being such a great hostess.

She replied softy with love and sincerity, "I do it all for you, Daddy, all for you." She likes to call me Daddy because the children do. I leaned over her to open the cabinet door of the bar and pull out a crystal bottle of Louis the XIIIth cognac. I knew it was Pace's favorite and that he could not drink it at home because his wife was very religious and it would have hurt her feelings. She's a beautiful lady and he obviously loved her very much.

He has an excuse now and then to indulge in Louis the XIIIth with me. I always felt I was the one who was committing the sin, since I am supposed to be a good Muslim but my friend Pace made me look and feel good because he would drink me under the table anytime. I thought it was the right occasion to treat my Mormon friend Pace from Utah, and Peter who had traveled all the way from the Gold Coast of Australia.

This was the third visit I'd had from Peter in a short period of time. He said this time it was just a personal visit with no strings attached. That was refreshing to hear for a change. When I received his call from Australia to tell me he was going to be coming I had asked him what it was this time what could I do for him? Peter said defensively, "Hey, can't I just call up my old friend and just visit an old friend who's always been there for me?" It was flattering to hear but that is just not Peter. "Angie I just want to visit with you this time."

I told him, "Peter, I don't believe that for a moment. I know you better than that and I just don't believe that. You wouldn't even visit Saint Gabriel in Heaven if a feather wasn't there to tickle you at the end of your journey. So what is the trouble this time? You seem to be in a hurry to get out of Austrailia."

He replied, "What's the matter Angelo, don't you want me to come and see you?"

I answered to him, "Peter, now you sound like we've been having an affair. Am I dreaming or are you for real? Get a grip on yourself and talk like a man Peter. I wouldn't want people to get the wrong idea. It could be embarrassing." Peter was acting like himself again and starting to lose his cool. He never could accept my compliments very well." I told him, "Whatever the reason your leaving Austrailia in a hurry is, just promise me that this time you'll make a clean getaway and not be traveling impersonating a rabbi or a priest, OK? I would like you to travel just as Peter, a crystal clear Peter. Do you think that's possible?"

"Oh, come on man," he said. "I've got a new idea. I think I'll be an Orthodox patriarch."

I told him, "Well, if you're a patriarch, then I'm the damn devil himself." But he did actually make that trip with the papers as an Orthodox patriarch.

"I'm going to Colombia for a few days to buy some gems," Peter said.

I asked, "Are they real ones from mines or the ones like you acquired in Zurich from that Russian general of yours, the ones you told me about that were made at the Mir space station?"

He laughed and replied, "Don't worry Angelo, these are real. I'm leaving to begin my travels tomorrow and I'll be making a stop over in Colombia."

I joked, "Gee Peter, it's a good thing that I don't do any drugs. You're not going to pick up a couple kilos there are you?"

He seemed a little uncomfortable but said, "No, this is just a legitimate business trip. I should be in Dallas within five days. I have an important meeting there with you know who and I'm going to meet with some very important people in Central Intelligence." As you can tell, Peter was always very secretive. He could keep a secret like a cracked barrel holds water.

I didn't at all doubt he was going to meet with some of our agents because he had had previous encounters with them that I had come to learn of. When he was in San Diego for a meeting while the

Serbian navy ships were bombarding the city of Dubrovnik, he encountered some of the same agents I worked with and I knew during the Croatian independance war from Serbia, although he was unaware of that. We made sure that whatever story he told them would be double checked and analyzed, and I would participate in that. In those days Peter was heavily involved with intelligence and with the United States who were trying to shorten the war in Croatia. We all knew that he was a heavy sympathizer of Serbia. Precautions were taken to avoid any mistakes of giving him anything valuable he might take back to Serbia. The only thing he took back to Serbia was the fact that Bosnia would not get the support of the western world, which the Serbs already knew.

"I could say that all succeeded in achieving our personal goals and my main goal was foremost to teach our intelligence how the communist world thinks and how the communist soldiers operate. If that could be conveyed to our troops, it would save the lives of our boys. That was my priority and second to that it was Bosnia. I have never had second thoughts about my convictions in those regards. Peter, Pace, and I all had common goals but saw them differently because of our varied backgrounds. I wanted to ensure the casualties of that war would be at a minimum. It seemed Pace's ideas were more strategical and political. Peter wanted the whole pie and two forks without sharing with anyone. The Serbs and Croats got to be the winners and the Bosnians got to drown. I saw the beginning of the conflict to a long journey and my participation in it could be beneficial if I was smart enough to see where and what my priorities were. They were in the interests of the USA. I tried to make sure that our American boys would come back home safely and unharmed more than anything. I did feel for the Croatians but I felt that I owed them nothing. I owed everything to our military forces and I did everything that I mentally and physically could to make sure harm wouldn't come to any soldier in the U.S. uniform.

"Peter had questioned me a few times about my patriotism and why it was I would like to see Yugoslavia torn apart, although it was already on a path of destruction without any help from me. My answer to him was simple and easy. I told him that most communist party members were eating well back when I went hungry and the communism that he loved so much kept me hungry — not that I think I would have been any better off under the royal crown of Alexander.

Those royalists again are repeating the cycle of violence that they feel they hadn't finished during 1912 and 1941 thru 1945. Then and now they are guilty as charged for trying and succeeding to some extent, in exterminating my people of Bosnia.

"Ironically, my father was one of the many architects who helped create the bloody Yugoslavia that you seem to love so much, Peter. He thought our people would be safer under it," I told him. "Don't go feeling too sorry for your communist pals. Just look what they are doing now to Croatia. They are blowing up the walls of the ancient city of Dubrovnik and wiped out the city where you were born Peter, Vukovar, along with thousands of their people. It's beyond me how you could support those bastards."

Peter was looking down at the ground and didn't have the courage to look me in the eyes because I wasn't about to listen to any of his crap.

"The Serbs were on the road as they always were to destruction without a system of checks and balances. The whole country of Serbia became one blood thristy gang. Croatia has gotten enough from the Serbs. The US finally decided to supply Croatia with sophisticated weapons via Germany, Italy, and Slovenia. Tuzman and the Croatian forces were ready for a pay back to the Serbs. Almost three hundred thousand Serbs laid down their weapons and ran across the border from Kraina to Bosnia.

"Belgrade was too far to run to and Bosnia was right there. A million and a half of them flocked like locusts to Bosnia and guess what they did there? All the able bodied men who were in uniform in Kraina found new weapons waiting for them in a Serb populated area of Bosnia, especially the Banjnja Luka area. The Serbs clearly resented Bosnia sympathizing with Croatia. They didn't hide their feelings and were sending the message that the Bosnians were going to regret it. The Bosnians were fool enough not to take them seriously and did find themselves regretting that. The reason they gave for it was that that they blamed the Bosnians for their losing the war in Croatia. Sore losers always do find something or somebody to blame for their losing. Serbs were notorious for blaming someone else for their own mistakes. This time the reason was again the Bosnian Bosnjaks.

"This was the beginning of the end for Bosnia, with the invasion of almost a million Serb refugees from Croatia. It was a clearly clever strategy from the Serbs stand point and there was nothing Bosnia could do about it being part of the one country of Yugoslavia. People could go wherever they wanted to seek saftey as refugees. This move was not for their saftey but a more of a strategic move than anything so Bosnia could be taken over. It worked and it did happen. Hardly any land was controlled by the Bosnians. Every able bodied man of Serbian decent was recruited to plunder Bosnia into fires of hell. The Croats were free from the war but Peter believed that the war was not yet over. He then joined the Serbs. He moved from one chair to the other by joining the crusade of the Serbs over Bosnia. That was a disappointment for me.

"Croatia finally got her wish and declared independance. In just a matter of days President Tuzman of Croatia was already looking to enlarge to expand the national perimeter for a greater Croatia at the expense of their most loyal neighbor, Bosnia, that had bled with them every step of the way until they gotten their independence. It was a real slap in the face to the Bosnian people.

"Most of the world saw the Croats' invasion in the territories of Bosnia as being immature and stupid. His actions as a leader caused him to lose prestige as leader of Croatia. He was fighting for his own survival and the survial of his nation of Croatia yet blind by violating the integrity and soveriegnty of Bosnia and her people. The Croatian leadership showed ineptness and inexperience. Instead of helping Bosnia contain the war and the tragedies that were about to occur they instead waged attacks in Herzogovina in the southern part of Bosnia to annex for their own. It was in violation of international as well as their own moral codes if they had any. None of it mattered to Frnjo Tuzman. He gave the Croat miiltia the green light for going on rampages of killing and destroying and to form concentration camps. It was the ultimate slap in the face for the Bosnian people. How does someone recover from that? Everything was happening so fast that they had arrested hundreds of thousands of people with no place to put them, so they used old oil reservoir containers that were as only the width of half of a football field with only ladders up the sides for getting in or out, to keep our people imprisoned for the duration of the war. One can imagine the heat and humidity of those containers. The smell from the reamains of the sludge of the black oil heated by the sun above must have been a living hell on earth.

Ramiz replied, "That's not all so horrible. Man has a natural ability to adapt to any conditions of his enviroment given the time in order to survive. A lack of water and then food is the biggest killer. Man can adapt to anything else."

I answered, "President Tuzman of Croatia adapts well too by the use of his creativity."

"It was later revealed when the news leaked out that long before the war began President Tuzman had an urgent secret meeting with the self proclaimed president of Serbia, Slobo Milosevic to decide how to carve up Bosnia between them. I wonder where Tuzman learned how to carve things? Oh, I remember now. After he was stripped from his rank and kicked out of the army in Yugoslavia he went to Toronto and got promoted to pizza man. I guess maybe now he considered himself to be a professional slicer.

"He must have met up with Milosevic, who on the other hand was a banker by trade and now thought of himself as a seasoned politician. The only thing he needed to learn was how to slice and carve and Tuzman had answers for Slobo. Tuzman told him they would be able to cut the cake and eat it too when they applied their skills together in Bosnia.

"These two fools must have believed in what they were doing and that it was all good and right and they could handle it. They were two grown man who thought they were playing with marbles without realalizing the marbles were sticks of TNT that would blow up in their faces. And at the end it did. They did do a good job unfortunately at the beginning of the war. They not only sliced and carved the land but the whole population. In fact they almost exterminated us.

"Looking back at the Bosnian conflict the only man who finally rose to the occasion to save Bosnia and that I could thank for his efforts is President Clinton. There may be many who might disagree that his actions helped saved Bosnia. Looking carefully at how the ball unraveled in Bosnia, without Clinton's order for our air force to blast the Serbian forces in Bosnia, in a very limited way yet effective, we would have been doomed to hell. Without that single selfless act from President Clinton there would not be Bosnia today and we would just be history period and the dreams of President Mitterand would have came true.

"Honestly at the beginning of the war I had doubted myself that any leader in the western world would support independence for Bosnia. Most of the Christian world had been busy working up a new phenomena of faith that has been spreading like wildfire especially over the last forty years. Groups of evangelical preachers in every color and shape were politically and fanatically faithful to their new ideas in faith of being born again. The radicalism of Islam along with these new ideas of faith left no room to give one another for the understanding of one another. Demonizing and the bashing of opposing faiths has created a wedge between the new Christian faith and the ancient Islam faith of the middle east. A prime example of these historical changes of society in changing in peoples heart and minds how they see one another is the evangelical preacher Pat Robertson, who was cheered by many Jewish rabbis around the United States for bashing Islam and helped in that way the new Islamic faith in the United States which was hardly known of then but with the help of the constant bashing Louis Farakhan became well know with his new nation of Islam organization,.

"The conflicts of the two faiths became three and was unavoidable. We know who won and who lost. The middle eastern peoples' passion of love and hate have no in between. We in the west know how to love and hate and know how to strong enough to bend in the strong winds without breaking. The new radicalism of Islam became the big loser of this conflict.

"During this war in Bosnia most American people didn't know where Bosnia was only that the Bosnian people were Muslim. By the time we educated the masses of Americans and most of the politicians that the Bosnian people were Europeans and direct decendants of some of us, although it is true they were praying to Mecca and not to Rome is the only difference between them and us. But that name of Muslim rings with steryotypical connotations in our heads as strong as bells of the northern dam. The Muslims can go to hell, and who cares? Let them disappear. Thank God somehow, someone got through to win the hearts and minds of few influentual people in the media and politics. That moment of education succeeded which was a good moment of fortune for the Bosnian people but a disappointment to Butros-Galli who truly wanted Bosnia off the map.

"Their religion was the reason for Bosnia finding herself in the middle of these two forces. Because of the association with their identity of Islam their status of European heritage that they treasure went out the window. Sadly they were seen in the eyes of western world as Palestinian bombers, not as their one of their own kind and fellow European citizens since the beginning of time. I would call that most misfortunate for the Bosnians. It is a tragedy and a selfishness showing how easy we can turn on our own kind and one another and misunderstand everything we are all about as fellow men.

"George Bush Senior was running for re-election and somehow he didn't have the time to take up the issue of Bosnia. He didn't particularly care if Bosnia became an independant state in the heart of the Christian world. The prime minister of England, John Major, had hoped the Serbs would win and obliterate the Bosnians from the face of the earth. However his former boss who put him in his position, Margaret Thatcher strongly disagreed with his view on the Bosnian political crisis. Ironically, he didn't mind childless English people adopting orphaned Bosnian babies after the Serbs had killed their fathers and mothers.

"The U.N. Secretary General Butros Galli confirmed by his statements, what I had feared. He wasn't about to let anyone interfere with what the Serbs were doing. The world divided in two blocks. The Muslims for the Bosnians and the Christians for the Serbs. It is ironic that not all of the Muslim nation were for Bosnia. Never the less the U.N. at that moment had become a Christian body representing only the Christian world as did most of the western world unite with him. Bosnia was surrounded by a ring of fire. Bosnia was denied the fundamental God given right to defend herself.

"The war was raging in Bosnia at the same time of the presidental elections in the United States. Kadafi of Libya, Hafiz of Syria, the prime minister of Israel, Saddam Hussein of Iraq, Slobo of Serbia, the aggressor who was waging the war and his accomplice Tuzman of Croatia were having orgasms in the meantime over the atrocities in Bosnia. In Washington we were about to get a new president who was hardly knowledgeable about anything further away like London, Paris, and Jerusalem, and perhaps Moscow also. But Bosnia and Serajevo? God help us.

"Unless the new president realized what and where Bosnia was and how important it could be for the future to us, Bosnia would pay with their lives just as they did. After all my wish came true and President Clinton was the one to ride in on white stallion and help pull Bosnia out of the pits of hell. I saw President Clinton as our only hope because of his open mindedness toward religion and he seemed to be a universal man. I realized he had a broad intellectual capability and had a healthy curisoty for recognizing the important issues around the world and that was a blessing. I was right, thank God. He found himself fighting to bring members of the U.N. to the right path and to do the right thing and represent every citizen of the world as they should, but it was to no avail. The new president was in a fight against the U.N. and his own country's senate by himself. No one could agree about what to do or not do in Bosnia. One thing they did agree on that President Clinton I saw thought was morally wrong. That was to fatten Bosnia with international food donations and then let the Serbs go ahead and slaughter them. It was going on day in and day out. The U.N. would donate the food and the Serbs would donate the bullets and death. President Clinton finally decided he had to do something. He tried to lift the arms embargo with Senator Dole as the architect for the plans so that Bosnia could be able to defend herself. No matter what he did the U.N. wouldn't budge. The U.N.'s gates weren't opening for Bosnia. I asked myself a thousand times, 'What is the U.N.'s purpose? Is it only a selected bunch of intelligent crooks who sit in chairs in plush offices playing God?'

"I have never seen anything good come about from the U.N., not only in Bosnia, but Rawanda, Zaire, Ethiopia, Zambia, Afghanistan, Palestine, Israel, Northern Ireland, and on and on. Not forgetting as well the newest victims in Chechnja or the bloody civil war that has been going on in Sudan for the last thirty years, or to forget Liberia on the African continent. There is injustice and oppression in our own hemisphere. It exists on every continent.

"I think and ask myself, 'What has happened to the leadership in and around the world?' We are used to by now the third world leadership by nothing more that the misfits of their societies. What scares me the most is the western world seems to be slowly decaying in the same path to being virtously leaderless which is a very scary thought. When President Clinton rose and saw the injustice, hope erupted not just in myself but many people around the world that there are leaders who care and that there is hope for the world. We will not repeat Phillip and Richard's mistakes. There will be nothing to be proud of if we do repeat them. It was a good thing that we didn't. Perhaps it was just a curse left by King Richard and Phillip, but not strong enough to take us down the same road, and that in itself is a triumph. We have learned from their journeys on bloody crusades of how senseless it all was. However we shouldn't suffer by perpetuating their bloody sores and mistakes. It would be wise to let bygones be bygones. Whatever Richard's ideas were while he was crusading, even though they may have been noble, when he applied them they ended up turning into blood baths with no accomplishments. One thing it accomplished two thousand years later was that division of the two faiths that has reawakened and cost half a million lives. Until someone realizes it, it's all wrong and for nothing.

"I would think the minds of men in the time of King Richard were handicapped by the complexities of the new emerging faith. Yet I see us in the twenty first century with Bosnia, Rowanda, the Palestinian and Israeli crisis of over the past forty years, Russians and Chechynas, perhaps we are even more barbaric than our predessors were. Our rationale is totally out the window. The moral values in any of these wars do not exist. For fourteen hundred years Islam has flourished. Perhaps it is only for the reason that the religion has always been a private and personal thing to each individual. Suddenly things seemed to have changed. The religions and state have become one. The western world has preached that since the beginning of Christianity until the early eighteen hundreds. That put the western and Christianity in the dark ages while Islam flourished. Now everything has suddenly shifted. Christianity has separation of church and state and everything seems to be flourishing and nothing has been the same.

"The world of Islam on the other hand has been imprisoned by the integration of religion and state. They could not see that it was the same problem in the Christian world since Pope Leo had united church with state affairs. It took seventeen hundred years to realize that it was all wrong and it was not good. The Muslims are right now occupying that same dark hole of hell the Christians left. Chruch and prayers should belong at home and the state obviously should be by itself as it exists today and over the last three centuries.

"The picture is clear that these two separate bodies should not interfere with one another. One may say the bride and groom are happy when they give one another the respect for their own space and independence. Islam on the other hand picked up where the Christians left off from the dark ages. Religion and state has become on,e creating a state of confusion. Everything has gone wrong since then and I see no end in sight. Eighty percent in the Islamic world are illiterate. Men with a limited knowledge of their surroundings and masses of uneducated people have nowhere else to turn except to God or a to a mythical world.

188

"I have more questions that I contemplate. 'Where is any hope going to come from? Is there any light at the end of the tunnel? Does the tunnel have an end?' The long historical tunnel with only one exit at the end leads directly to Bosnia. The west has developed and life has flourished and Bosnia was and is one of the participants of it but not noticed by her distant northern neighbors. Islam is obviously seen as a rival to the western Christian world but shouldn't be. It should be on the contrary, complimentary. The two should dance together harmoniously and give us the gift to reflect on the good lives we have, in the past and present with a clear vision for the future. We tend to close one eye not seeing what we really need to and feel with half our hearts and that means cheating ourselves of the beauty, decency and the honesty that is taught in both faiths."

"This is one of the prime examples of feeling with half a heart. It seems it makes it much easier to do wrong. The so-called civilized world abandoned Rawanda and quarantined Bosnia so that they could be easily massacred by the Serbs and Croats alike. These new crusaders claimed to be fighting to save Christianity. What was sad to me is that is looked like a new crusade. That was something I was hoping not to see. I wanted every western man, woman, and child to prove me wrong. What is wrong with this picture and this world? How can this be? Had I been forsaken by my fellow man?

"It took them a while, but I must confess it looks like they proved me wrong. They did come to the rescue, all of them, even the one who had paved the road for Milosevic of Serbia. The world was finally ashamed of their own lack of care for their fellow man."

I was waiting to hear a confession from Peter that he should have a change of heart and join the rescue of the victims instead of supporting the villians but he said nothing. That was disappointing and I was just about to lose it. "Can you answer my questions for me, my friend Peter?" I asked. "Am I wrong and don't know what I'm talking about? You're a genius Peter, a man of the world, a bright man that has seen justice and injustice done. Oh did I just call you friend? Do I kid myself to call you a friend, man who supports one of the most gruesome butchers on the planet today? Maybe it is best if you keep your thoughts to yourself and don't tell me how you really feel. I don't think I could digest it. You are an experienced man of the world. You always have an answer to everything but maybe it would be bettter for your health if you skipped this one too. So what is the answer?"

Peter stared with surprise at me and how serious, angry, and concerned I seemed in expressing my questions and opinions to him. Peter dodged my questions which was smart on his part. He did say, "I owe you at least some kind of answer after all the years we've known each other. At this moment I'm in a very personal internal war. I hope you won't be disappointed as my friend by the time all this is over."

I brushed him off. I knew he was in his own conflict with himself and one of his wars had just ended and another personal war was just beginning which was the conflict in Serbia and Bosnia.

It was obvious to me and I knew now he wanted to crusade to free Serbia but from what that was I don't know, maybe from that sucidal maniac who who was taking the country on a road to hell. No one was attacking them. They were the ones who were the aggressors. He wasn't going to admit his plans to me. He was portraying himself still as a patriot of Croatia. I didn't doubt that as he already proved that to me but at the same time he wanting to be a patroit of Serbia's, hanging on his mother's apron strings. He was proving he was capable of stretching beyond the limits. Peter was like new rubber that was just harvested from the tree and not processed. What you see is what you get and I knew Peter better than he knew himself.

I found Bosnia to be right in the middle of Peter's assessment of the Croats and Serbs. It looked to him like the Bosnians were blocking the path of either one of them to become a greater Serbia or a greater Croatia something must be done to get the plans to succeed. The answer was that Bosnia must be gobbled up and that we must disappear even if it included his friend Angelo, whose wife at that moment was preparing a dinner like he'd probably never had. Whatever friendship and trust that was there between Peter and I was disintergrating. I know on my part it was a for sure thing and happening fast. He wasn't going to be a babysitter for my children anytime soon.

Peter was trying hard to get off the subject I was pushing and starting telling me about his trip from Australia which he said had taken him directly to Colombia and from there he had flown directly to Zurich. I didn't think that that made much sense and that he was lying to me. It wouldn't have been the first time. He did not go to Colombia. He had flown directly to Zurich to meet with some bloodthirsty warlords. He then went to Lubljana and from there to Zagreb where he had met with President Tuzman and the minister of defense. They both

190

signed a brand new and recently published history of Croatia as a gift for him for the espoinage services that he had provided during the war in Croatia. It seemed like he could not wait to arrive in Las Vegas and bring the book to show it off and that it was signed personally by the president and Defense Minister Ramlik.

Whatever route he then took to fly to South America he somehow had ended up going to beautiful Colombia after all. I verified it from the phone call recorded on my statement from Sprint that I received after that. He spent at least a half a day in Cali just off the coast of the Pacific Ocean, a beautiful place that I am familiar with, and one of my favorite towns. I had taken a tour for seven days back in 1986 on the river Magdalena all the way down to the Caribbean Sea to the city of Barranguilla.

Colombia is a unique counry with unique people. It is like no other South American country. The native people are warm and friendly. They are a mixture of the natives and the early European settlers that blended together into a civilization and has evolved into a very beautiful nation. Their tradition and culture is very similar to mine in Montenegro and they believe in that ancient law of justice of an eye for an eye. Their way of life reminded me and took me back to ancient beliefs of Montenegro and the laws of the land. That brought me right back to memories of my ancestor's land. My grandfather served that type of justice himself to preserve dignity and honor of the family and was the tradition that guided our peoples lives since the beginning of time. Our cultures are enriched by our belief that we must live by that ancient law which has enhanced us and built our characters as men and as a nation. One should be able to reap what you have sown and earn what you have gained by the sweat of your brow. When we must carry the swords their blades are always sharp with no mistake for what they will be used for, to defend our sacred honor. There's not much difference in the ancient laws. No wonder I felt right at home there.

Peter could be described with no doubt as a deep rooted, strong, cultured Balkan, southern Slav man with a raised in a culture and tradition very similar to my own. He was also able to identify with the Colombian people. Our heritage from the Balkans identified us closer with the Colombian people and most of South America. It seems that our two cultures are not drifting apart. Instead they lean on each other like pillars at the same time and are complementing to one another sharing a strength and traditional way of life with a closeness and respect for the family unit. Peter must have found himself very comfortable there also at least from their traditions if not from his own personal character.

I asked Peter if he had had a good time in Colombia and he answered, "Just like I'm sure you know already Angie, it's a beautiful country. I always feel so at home there I know I promised you, Angelo, I would come to see you. It just took me a little longer to get here than I thought it would."

I told him, "That's all right Peter, I wasn't going anywhere and it's good having an old friend here."

Mankiu said dinner was ready and we should go on directly to the table. The dining room in our home reflected my taste and the indoor framing and decor was accented with mahogany and pecan wood that really brought out a warm and relaxing atmosphere that made one feel like part of the family. From the dining room across the hallway was my personal library where I spent a lot of my time. My home was a beautiful exclusive ranch home with breathtaking views of the city and surrounding Redrock and Warm Springs mountains. It was nothing like the little house built from a solid stone wall in which I had grown up as a child. I wonder sometimes if had orginally been built as a military fortress or a house. The walls were unusually thick. In the winters the walls would drip with sweat from the humidity. It was uncomfortable and unhealthy. On the contrary the summers were very different. No matter how hot it was outside the many windows in the house provided circulation and it was much more pleasant, unlike the winters with the constantly wet walls. And I can't forget that fast moving noisy creek beside our home back in the little valley of Gusjnje in Montenegro.

We didn't want to lean on those wet walls but there was plenty of room in the hearts of my parents to lean on for the love of their children and our family which is something that all children need from their mothers and fathers. I remember those days when we did not have any electricity and would sit by a gas-burning lamp at night to do our homework and rush to finish it before sundown. We only had that one kerosene lamp in our house so it was always a race against sundown. I now look at my own children and reflect on the love, care and attention that I had received from my parents, and I only hope I can only be as good or even as close to a parent to them as my parents were to me.

The food that my wife had prepared that evening for my friends and I looked like one of the feast of Julius Caesar's. My wife set the table exquisitely like never before. Champagne was served first, Louis Roederer crystal, 1986.

I called for my friend Pace to lead the way to the table. Peter wasn't going to allow that to happen. He jumped ahead to the kitchen and asked Mankiu if he could help out with anything. He loves the kitchen and messing around in it.

She replied, "Yes, you could do the dishes after dinner." We all just laughed.

I went to sit at the head of the table. Directly behind me hanging in the middle of the wall was a black and white portrait taken of my mother and me as a boy of about four years old. It is the only picture that I have of my mother. I picked up my glass to make a toast to my friends turning to my mother's portrait. I looked at her as I have done many times before with love and respect in my heart and my eyes and repeated the same words that I have many times before saying, "Thank you for giving me life and for being there every moment when I really needed you and your presence is always felt whenever I need you still."

I found both my friends were very emotionally touched looking shyly at me but not because they felt like strangers in my home. They were a little taken aback by my tribute to and the respect for my mother that I have. Perhaps they identified with themselves and the way they felt about their own mothers. They both simultaneously made a comment about my mother's face saying that she looked like an angel with a face that every mother truly should have.

I smiled at them and said, "Every true mother has a true mother's face. For me my mother has the most beautiful face because she is my mother."

In the meantime Mankiu brought out three more fine and pretty pricey bottles of wine from my collection, a French from the Burgundy valley, Le Montrachet Marquis de Laguiche, Joseph Drouhin 1989, and an Italian Barolo Riserva 1986. The bottles were already uncorked. A red wine should breathe for at least a half an hour to bring out the body of the wine, and I like it that way.

Did we get drunk from the wine or lose the importance of our conversation? No. Did we finish off all of the wines? No. We just had a variety of wine to enjoy at the table. It helped us in a way to appreciate how fortunate and lucky we were and just by being able to be where we were in that place and time. We silently reflected for a moment in our thoughts on the turbulent times in the rest of the world.

We ate and talked touching on all the things that were individually important to us, our businesses, health, the opportunities we've had and the risks we were taking in order to succeed in our lives, and not to forget world politics which we all loved talking about passionately.

Peter warned us, "I think there might be a pretty good desert on the way." My wife brought the dessert out to the table along with my little daughter Nadira helping her mother to carry the desert plates in her tiny little innocent hands, looking for some approval for helping out. Of course she got it and all of the attention. Then she was only three years old and every time I talked to her I momentarily forgot about everyone else in the house. She knew where her seat was on my lap and most of the time she sat there all through the dinner and rubbed my chin and neck with her tiny little hands and I truly could see I was madly in love with her then and I still am and have enjoyed every moment of it.

My wife smiled broadly and said, "Well boys, you are in for a treat today. I made many phone calls and worked very hard in creating this masterpiece, baked Alaska cake." Everyone applauded her knowing how much labor it takes to make something like that. She said, "My husband has talked so highly of you and knowing you myself I wanted to give you a special treat that is not just an every day dessert." She is no doubt a fantastic hostess and reflects a true picture of a happy loving family. She cut the pieces of the cake so huge that no one was able to finish it. She said, "There is one more thing that I almost forgot about. My husband's favorite dessert wines from California that I'll bring out in a moment. The wines we had with dinner are some of my husband's favorites too. He usually opens a bottle and pours a full glass for himself but never even finishes that one glass during dinner. Luckily we have a neighbor who knows my husband's habit and enjoys the wine but is not allowed by his wife to drink any at his home. So he checks in every now and then with us. Uncle John is a loyal neighbor, we can always count on him to knock on our door to check on the status of the wine.

I said to Mankiu, "Don't worry, Mom, our neighbor John will be by tomorrow afternoon for sure to take care of any of the open bottles. Old man John always makes sure it doesn't go to waste, since

194

his wife won't let him drink at home."

Pace said, "Oh, he must be Mormon."

I said, "No, Johnny is not a Mormon, he's German but his wife is Mormon and very religious. One of these days I'll probably get in big trouble from her because John always returns home drunk."

Mankiu got the wine and said, "This is a California after dinner dessert wine." She poured some for us all in sherry glasses.

"Well what's the name of it?" Pace asked.

Mankiu answered, "I don't know. It sounds like an Italian wine. I don't care for wine but I will have a glass of this. Angie told me that the name of this wine is Dolce Vita, means sweet life."

Peter was feeling humorous and replied to Mankiu, "Don't worry Mankiu, I don't expect you to be a wine connoisseur because I know in China they only serve that plum wine."

I had to come to my wife's defense and warned Peter he better drop it or he was going to look like a fool. I told him she was better than I was at wine tasting. I said, "I wasn't talking about the wine being sweet when I told her that anyway, I was talking about her, but she missed the point." I scratched my head looking at her and said, "How did you miss that?" Then we all laughed. Mankiu had quietly poured our wine and we the drank some Dolce Far Niente. Everyone made a pleasurable sound and showed how delicious they thought the wine was by their expressions. Their look of approval was like one of those pictures worth a thousand words.

Peter was not hesitant to compliment my wife and thank her for the memorable dinner experience. I felt he really meant it from the look in his eyes and by his body language and from the sincerity of his voice. It looked like Peter had finally broken down to show the real human side of himself that I hadn't seen in awhile. Of course he was changing as he was growing older. I truly think we all become more humble and more appreciative as we grow older.

Peter told Mankiu, "I am flattered, Madame Koljenovic, you are a beautiful lady. I hope that your husband appreciates everything that you are."

She answered, "Mr. Peter, I am my husband's wife and your friend. I was pleased to have you as a guest in our home. I appreciate my husband for his strength and knowledge and that he is a good provider and father and also the most wonderful husband. When I think about him I feel as if nothing in the world could harm me and we have our beautiful daughter and another child on the way."

"Wow!" he cheered. "Am I going to be one lucky godfather or what?" He went to Mankiu and hugged her like he'd known her all of his life. After all Peter was a man almost sixty years old and Mankiu was only twenty three, which was the same age as Peter's daughter. I didn't mind him giving her a hug, patting her belly and promising to change diapers as the godfather. With no doubt in my mind at least at that moment, I felt his intentions were genuine. Even I, Angelo, a man who has traveled every corner of the world, could be fooled for a moment by a man like Peter with his charms, but never for long and not long enough enough to get burned.

Mankiu asked us if we would like to retire in the library and go to my study. I led the way and we all three thanked her again almost at the same time. As we passed by the kitchen in the hallway we all could hear the familiar sound only made by an espresso machine and boy we were ready for some of that. A few moments later there were three espresso's garnished with lemon peels and sterling silver spoons next to them. We all mixed our coffee twisting the lemon peel in our coffe that brings out the real body of espresso. Pace stretched and said, "I had better not tell my wife that Mankiu really treated us this good tonight. She'd be very upset unless I get a piece of that cake to take home to her." Of course Mankiu was ahead of him and had already packed up a whole dinner as well as some desert and a toy for his little boy, Madison.

I replied, "You better not tell her about your having any achohol. She may not let you come back here anymore and I don't want to lose a friend." Then we all laughed.

Mankiu walked into the room and asked if I would like her to take our daughter upstairs so that my two friends and I could get down to our business that brought us together there after all. We were three men who had three different views of the world but all three of us were working toward the same goal. However I still wonder exactly whose goals they were and who would benefit from them, just certain indivuals or everyone? At least that's what I wanted to believe, to make the world a better and safer place for all of us using the strengths and triumphs from each of our faiths to perhaps help steer the world for a safer tomorrow but I knew deep in my heart that it was good thoughts but would never go any further than that room..

Both Peter and I were very interested to learn more about the

196

current situation in Bosnia since the war in Croatia was coming to an end. I was very curious to know if Pace had the chance to do any investigating regarding the Serbs' rebellion in Croatia. I wondered what effect it would have on the flight of the people and also on immigration. What would happen if the Serb civilian population had to move suddenly for safety from the attacks by the Croatian forces? President Tuzman had promised they would attack Kraina unless the rebels disarmed. From the border of Bosnia by the sea all the way up north to the ancient forest of Kraina, there were almost two million Serbs leaving with their families on the Croatian and Bosnian sides. Bosnia would be the only safe haven for them if Tuzman did what he said he would do and that spells trouble for Bosnia.

In the Croatian community here in the States a topic of talk in every church, business, and home is that every Croatian wants every Serb to leave Croatia, this time dead or alive. It makes no difference to them. Their patriotism has reached a point of having no rational thought. Every Serb is guilty in the eyes of the Croats. The Serbs just had to go. I knew this would have a great impact on Bosnia because the Serbs had nowhere else to go. Belgrade was too far but Bosnia was right there to accomadate the Serbs from Krania. Someone would have to pay their being evicted from their homes and that the would be the Bosnians. One million Serb refugees eventually flocked into Bosnia on wagons, donkeys, tanks, and trucks and they brought plenty of military hardware with them. They made themselves at home in eastern and western Bosnia and united with the rest of the Serbian population that was in Bosnia already and braced for war against the Bosnians. Their territory of Krania needed somehow to be compensated for and Bosnia was a good place for them carve to it out.

Croatians from all over the world raised more money during the war than God has hair on his head. The money coming into Croatia was in astronomical amounts totaling in the billions. They had no shortage of contributors. However the contributions are having no effect. At first it didn't look like it was being used for investing in the economy or any of the rebuilding. It looked like most of the contributions were just vanishing somewhere. Tuzman must be buying up the pizzerias around the world with the money donated and he was fast losing his prestige with world leaders. Whoever was managing the donations, it didn't look like they believed in Croatia, at least at first. It would be interesting to know what did happen to all that money the

Croatian people sent from overseas.

The city of Knin was just minutes from the ocean with a population close to one hundred percent Serbian and had close to three hundred thousand inhabitants. Krania was considered in the eyes of the Serbs as a Serbian autonomy inside of Croatia that was left over from Tito's era in Yugoslavia and Alexanders before that. Both Alexander and Tito wanted to please the Serbs, and the Serbs developed the attitude to be a self governing community existing like a state within a state. It looked like independence for Croatia was assured from the international community and was coming fast. The Knin Serbs wanted no part of Croatian independance and the rift of conflict grew wider. Croatia wasn't going to put up with any of that nonsense rebellion in Knin.

Knin blossomed over the centuries and the good life had gone to the people's heads. The local corrupt leadership wanted to separate them from Croatia and unite them with the so called mother Serbia and it backfired on them. The newly armed Croatian army with American tanks moved in on Knin and a million people suddenly found themselves homeless. They crossed the border into Bosnia and it was an invasion of Bosnia and immediate new war involving another state. For Bosnia to absorb and to place one million people in homes in three days would be impossible and they were not given the chance to. Karadgic had his own plans and already planned to evict or kill all the Bojnaks so he could have his new Republic of Serbia leading them on the road to a greater Serbia but only in his stupid mind. It looked like a trade deal that was made between Tuzman and Milosevic. He lost Knin to Croatia and he needed to compensate for the loss so Bosnia and Bayna Lufa were his logical choice. He ignored the orginal agreement with Tuzman to break Bosnia in half. Slobo wanted it all now. Bosnia looked like some easy hunting for Slobo and again that was his mistake.

For the Serbs, they had a choice and they chose to leave even though no civilians were in danger and leaving Knin was like losing a part of their souls, or so they said. How could one make a statement such as that when their evacuation was voluntary? I think if one believes that his home is truly his home he should never leave it, not even in death. Obviously the Serbs didn't believe in Knin as their home so they packed up and left. I look at their behavior as like being little red scavenger crabs on the bottom of the ocean. They are too lazy to build their own homes and will not hesitate to invade the homes of others at whatever cost. In this instance the Bosnians homes were invaded in the hundreds of thousands by the Serbs. Most of the inhabitants in those homes in Bosnia were killed and a few could consider themselves lucky to have escaped. The Serb scavenger was happy but only for a very short time until the American Navy and Air Force got involved together with the Bosnian freedom fighters.

The Serbs thought Bosnia must now be brought together and become to part of Serbia, and the Muslim population had to get out of the way. Nationalism become part of their daily lives once again. Bosnia suddenly became a nest for the notorious Chetniks and a killing field for the cause of Serb nationalism. Their claim was that they were the gaurdians of the Serbian church. Suddenly every Serb had become a nationist and blood thirsty. If they were the guardians of the Serbian church, then all the loss of life and the atrocities that they committed were approved by that church. On the contrary the Chetniks were nothing that they claimed to be. If that were indeed the truth, Serbia wouldn't need any other enemies. The Chetniks would be all the remedy for their incurable sickness that they'd ever need. They are going to have to deal with the Chetniks who were and still are lowlifes and misfits of the Serbian society and Serbia will have to confront that in time if she ever wants to be a part of the community of nations.

I can't recall any historical instances where any Serbs could be proud of any of their contributions because there aren't any since the time the Chetniks started to be ambassadors for their people. Most of the Croatian and Serbian problems seemed to have stemmed right from Knin, not counting past conflicts but at least in this particular conflict that has torn the Yugoslav republics apart. Knin was the seed of that germination. Who had the key to opening the door for Croatia to declare her independance? The Knin rebellion was that key.

Pace was exicited and anxious to share his recent experiences and adventures. He had plenty of them to share with us about everything that had happened during the time he had just spent in the Balkans. We talked of the ancient cities of Dubrovnik and the city of Zadar, birthplace of Constantine. He was a ruler of the eastern Roman empire and son of the mother who was a main force in creating Orthodox Christianity. We also talked about many of the other tiny small resort places on the coast of the Adriatic Ocean.

We were all absorbed in our conversation about the creativity and advancement of man since the beginning of time, and the birth of new religions and how much good has come from it, but also how much evil has come from the political manipulation of the people by by religious leaders, as all of the good has been tossed out the window. The greed and struggle for more power by using religions to control the masses became the most powerful tool to use for dividing, weakening, and the conquering of human beings and at the same time insulting the human mind along with it. We take it all in stride even though we know everything about it is myth.

Looking back over the past two milleniums and the recorded facts in history, there has been no ruler, king, president or emperor who succeeded in sustaining power or fully controlling the masses of the people or the lands without using religion as a prime tool for controlling and creating conflict.

If that is true then the flag with green colors of Islam representing the young and the future has no hope, and the words of loving your neighbor as yourself that is written in the Christian prayers has no worth. The principles of Islam and of Christianity have been violated by those to whom these two faiths have been entrusted with the responsibility to uphold and be guided by it in the way it was meant to be interpreted. Instead it has become a tool to use by the very few for insulting the rest of the intelligent, healthy minds We have allowed that to happen.. There is no hope for man's salvation until the religious leaders have a change of heart and become rightous themselves and the ordinary earthly men who look for salvation will follow. There is at this time no energy left for the hope of salvation for us all. The institutions are being used to divide rather than unite. How blind and heartless that can be.

I will not lose hope however. I am lucky to have a man sitting by me whose faith is as young as he is. He is a Mormon, and whatever he has been taught up to now seems to be the right thing. Perhaps we all can look at his example and be brought back to our senses. I'm not saying the Mormons are the perfect ones but with no doubt they are good neighbors and good citizens on this little planet of ours. Simply said, I wouldn't fear for mine or my family's life by having him for a neighbor or by having a glass of cognac or a cup of old fashioned Turkish coffe with him, which we both do enjoy very much. Here again we are two men with two very different backgrounds yet with very much in commen even if it were only cognac and coffee. Yet the connection between the two of us which was most important was our connection to a love of life.

Why can't these principles and natural laws be guidelines extended for the rest of humanity? It shouldn't be that hard to do. The mind as a highway that allows you to travel distances as far as you can imagine and extends hope into a future as far as you can imagine. In the historical manuscripts that I have read, nowhere has it been written by any so called prophets that a few were given the right to deny the masses of humanity those rights that were given to humanity by the supreme power of the universe. Just by who those few claim the right was granted to them is unknown to me. It was only obvious they are claiming to be obeying the word of their God, as well as my God, and your God. That has been the trouble brewing on the horizon since the first days two milleniums ago.

When I look around me I consider myself to be fortunate and lucky to have had and still have the opportunity of sharing the beliefs of my faith with so many different men and women. I can see hope in every one for a better tomorrow. I have traveled the world and have seen much good in many people. All of the beautiful people from every walk of life never cease to amaze or surprise me and how different we all are from one another. That is the beauty of us all. Not even two of us on the whole planet are exactly alike, especially in our thoughts. We all may see one single cloud in the sky but not in the same way no matter how hard we try to. Each one sees it in his own way. That is how we may see the heavenly gates and the hereafter. For me the hereafter is right here and no one has convinced me yet there is anywhere else. My heavenly gates are opening the door of my home and feeling the freedom that was granted to me by my constitutional rights as a citizen. This freedom was not delivered by God in the sky but was delivered by the ordinary man that inhabit this land that saw the need for a constitution to guide the people and make each person feel equal and worthy of themselves. I dare to say that God didn't right that, Thomas Jefferson did along with many other ordinary and visionary men write this document that profoundly effects my life today. I am able to perform from sunup to sundown for the good of my family and the promise of a better tomorrow.

Neither I nor anyone else has a right to deny anyone the choice of where to plant a tree of hope. It's only common sense I should know that I would be benefitting from the tree's shade so why should I object? The difference of our thoughts and how we may see things should not make a difference or break us apart but only bring us closer together.

I found my friend Pace not to be just different but passionate in his love for his family and his country yet he was reserved about something introduced to humanity no more than two millenniums ago, that was Christ and Muhammed, and before then Abraham. After all it looked like they were ordinary men with every day problems to solve for themselves and their tribes if they wanted to sustain and survive themselves as leaders. Abraham as one of them had a real crisis. His tribe was in economical disarray. He needed a solution in order to keep it together and survive as a leader. As we all know he came up with one that was not very successful except for himself and not the tribe. I would characterize these men respectfully as the Godfathers of the last two millenniums whose influence in the pages of history are not yet finished. Until now so much human blood has been sacrificed directly from the seed they had sown and we have harvested everything that they planted. We have used it with such disregard of what it was it really intended for. They were immune to thoughts of failure and they were way ahead of their times. If I see them as immune to thoughts of failure perhaps I am right but for them believing in us and that we would not fail them, proved wrong.

If there was one thing the prophets all sought for sure it was to make their mark in history as they did. If there is one thing these men were aware of it must have been that they knew they were making history and changing the world. Since the time of their deaths every con artist in the world has used the recorded experiences of these noble men as a reason to benefit themselves and their own personal agendas and not what was truly intended by these three noble historical figures.

After debating over pagan Biblical history Pace, Peter, and I exchanged ideas about the war, current politics and the turmoil in the area which was also profoundly affecting the rest of the world. We tried to analyze the interests of the three parties who were engaging in nothing less but the destruction of each other. This current conflict in the former Yugoslavia is one of those bad connections where one more bad con artist is turning the events of the history into something for the benefit his own self. Slobo is right on target in the name of protecting Christianity. There is a conflict like a repeat of the battle between David and Goliath. Bosnia was certainly not Goliath. How could they be when they were armed with slingshots? Serbia on the other had rightfully deserved the name of Goliath.

The Bosnians I see as naked. Perhaps they are in this situation because they believe their neighbors were of the same character as they with a love of life and family. Although that was not the case. Their Serb neighbor was everything but. One could say the Bosnians found themselves to have lost their underwear and could only cover their nudity with their hands to protect their dignity. It is a sad chapter in history just as it was in 1941 and in many other similar tragic instances before that. This is one more black page nevertheless in the history of man.

Strangely I found myself during the heated debate between my friends, with my knowing that Peter was no friend of Bosnia, in my own home where I should feel the most comfortable, instead feeling like I had to defend Bosnia. Perhaps I hoped to give Peter a lesson in history. I almost felt I was pleading my case in my own home. In a way maybe I was since Bosnia was toothless and as defenseless as a brand new born baby. What I'm trying to say is Bosnia had no arms whatsoever to defend herself with. She was at the mercy of the West and the rest of the hopeless Islamic world who in many ways failed themselves in the last century as a unit that was once comprised of tradition and strong families. The Islamic nations are in times of turbulence, unrest and upheaval. This didn't seem a time when they could help Bosnia in any way, politically or militarily. Their autocratic self formed governments did not speak for their people. The heads of the states did not represent the masses of their people. The legitimacy of support from the Islamic world leaderships was never justified by the Western world since frankly the Western world never had any respect for most of the Islamic leadership around the world except for a very few. I would not shy away from mentioning their names, Maylasia, Turkey and Pakistan. Perhaps they have earned their way in the nations of community. For me it was the hope of the Christian world to have a change of heart towards my Bosnia. Without it there would be no Bosnia.

It was just as I had hoped that my invited friends would help me spread the message. I had invited them to be my guests to reaffirm our bond of friendship over dinner and a glass of wine. Ironically I found myself on the defensive, trying to paint a clear picture of what they already knew. It was like telling Picasso how to paint. It was like trying to remind the professional what he already knows and is.

Both my friends and I agreed clearly and knew who the victims and the villians were. Did that make any difference? Pace was feeling sorry for the people. Peter seemed to have different ideas. He may have been feeling sorry for the people but I felt he still wanted them out of Bosnia and he thought we should take a trip to Anatolia, dead or alive. I was surprised that he knew where Anatolia was. Someone must have told him the geographical location of it. Peter didn't say it in so many words, he was very careful but I could tell where leading by his mentioning that there were so many Bosnians in Anatolia now. I reminded Peter that Bosnia was my home and we were there to stay and I wasn't going to Anatolia anytime soon or ever. His ideas on who the land of Bosnia belonged to would not be shaken by my proclaimations. Hate and compassion were having a conflict in him with no doubt and he was still being very careful not to step over the line at least in my own house. Perhaps he thought it would be very improper. I think it was because he ain't got no balls.

Like Shakespeare said, "To be, or not to be." That was the question for Bosnia as a nation and a people. Does she belong in the heart of a Christian world as a new born Muslim state? Of course not and that is not what we're trying to make it, but why not leave her to be just as she always has been? Bosnia has been a beautiful jewel and a mosaic of beauty and progress for all the races and religions. It is what has made Bosnia special all throughout history. But no, some of the irresponsible nations have to give the Serbs the green light to crusade for whatever that may be, justifying their shameful actions and now we are all embarressed of them. Every chance has been given to the Serbs to wipe the Bosnian people off the map.

The blueprints from 1984 that orginated in Belgrade were finally surfacing and Bosnia got put on the grill to roast in flames at full blast. The true colors and intentions of the Serbs and Croats were clear and were finally coming to bloom for them. The Christian world and some of the Muslim world were in agreement with Croatia and Serbia to carve up Bosnia for a greater Serbia and greater Croatia. They clearly hadn't given a thought about what would happen to us. When the question arose on the battlefield the Bosnian people woke up and realized the slaughter the Serbs and Croats prepared wasn't only for a few but for all and they organized and resisted.

Finally the West and some of the Muslim nations and also the head of the U.N. , Butros-Galli, who crusaded openly along with Henry Kissinger, one of the respected Jewish leaders and a former secretary of state, all wanted to get Bosnia out of the way and deny her the right to membership as a nation. Mr. Kissinger was a lead pragmatist to deny Bosnia membership in the U.N. as a nation. To Bosnia's good fortune Slobo and Tuzman failed them badly. The French president, Mitterand, was so upset by it that he had to make a trip personally to Sarajevo to see what kind of resistance this was and how come a two hundred and fifty thousand man Serb army could not conquer a little city of a couple of hundred thousand people.

John Major of England was so disappointed that he broke relations with the former prime minister, Margaret Thatcher, who had been his idol and mentor, because she was for Bosnia but Major was not, and the relationship between them deteriorated to nothing. The mentor that she was to him was no more and Tony Blair was elected to prime minister and America got a new president at the same time.

After all this the light at end of the tunnel was starting to shine for Bosnia. Resistance grew stronger and the oppressors were leaving the territory in massive numbers and they all had blood on their hands, from the ordinary farmers to the school marm who today is serving a life sentance for war crimes in Haag. Butros-Galli returned to his native country to be in seclusion, possibly broken hearted that the Serbs did not fulfill his dreams although they did break the jar spilling a lot of blood. The Israeli government has yet to redeem themselves for supporting Serbia in the aggression on Bosnia. Again they must have been disappointed and they turned their backs on Serbia, which they thought was the right thing to do in support of the Bosnian freedom fighters. I say better late than never. Their good gesture was in sending a C-130 American made cargo plane full of medicine and doctors to see if they could patch up the wounds they helped contribute to in the first place.

The world grew tired of watching the gruesome pictures of the war on TV and they demanded justice for Bosnia and punishment to the aggressors. The call was just. Ordinary people around the world were questioning their leaders and how this could have been allowed to happen and still be going on. Leaders around the world were being pressured by the citizens to do something. They were doing something all right and that was to put the pressure on Slobo to finish the job fast and clean, but he was useless. How could you expect anything to be done by Slobo either good or bad? From the tree he grew up from nothing good could happen, only bad. That was a disappointment to his supporters but a blessing for Bosnia.

The next thing that happened was the leaders who had been die hard supporters of Serbia had a change of heart because the Serbs, as the losers that they are with their true colors starting to show, made them realize they had been supporting a bunch of heartless criminals and that it was the right thing to do to finally start giving Bosnia the support she deserved. And they finally did. The final glory days of the Serb's that would tip the world in outrage was when they massacred nine thousand people in Srebrenica, the youngest being only ten years old. The loving parents around the world saw that as the final straw to breaking the moral codes of conduct. They went to the streets by the millions all around the world to demand answers to how this could have been allowed.

It is very easy to answer that question. It was the blue helmets wearing U.N symbols who were the ones who opened the door to the Serb's ten thousand strong army enabling them to walk into the city of Srebrenica without having to fire a single shot and pratically being welcomed by the U.N. commander and Serb sympathizer as many of them that there were. One was a Canadian commander named Mckenzie who had been accused of rape by some Bosnian women and being a spy for the Serbs. This kind of behavior of men in uniform claiming to be crusading and protecting should be unacceptable in communities of nations where decency should be a law of the land. I hope Commander McKenzie has a daughter who can be proud of him when he tells her about his deeds, especially the rapes of the young Bosnian women. All the while the U.N was convincing the city to disarm themselves because they would be protected and there was no need for arms and so they did. Butros Galli must have been very happy and his evil spirit growing like seaweed inside himself.

They presssed on with their army killing more than ten thousand in one day. It became a bloody tear that ran down every decent human face around the world. The responsible leadership around the world had no choice but to stop the slaughter which the ordinary people around the world were starting to demand. If I am to thank anyone for saving Bosnia it would be people like my friend Pace and all the next door neighbors around the world who thought the world would be better off not to take Bosnia to a slaughter house but save her so she could continue on with her contributions.

The conflict involving Bosnia occured right after the Serbs and Croats dueled it out and the Serbs lost. A rematch was called not with Croatia but with Bosnia this time who were not even looking to be contenders. The Serbs were merciless in Croatia and the city of Vucovar was totally destroyed. It was comparable to Berlin after the allied bombing or Stalingrad after Hitler was finished with it. The city of Vukovar was overrun by the infantry, Serbian army Russian made T-73 tanks, Russian Mig airplanes and helicopters. They unloaded all they had on them and blood flowed like the river Sava or the Danube. The people who were able to ran for there lives and those who could were fortunate enough to run inland to the city of Zagreb and live to see another day. Ones who were unfortunate and were not able to flee never lived to see another day. The dead and wounded were not numbered in the hundreds but the thousands. Some people compared Vukovar with Hiroshima after that horrific and unfortunate day, remembered forever in history in the way she was brutally destroyed.

Peter and I once both served in the same army and I asked Peter if he remembered the allegience we had given when we all had sworn to never raise arms against the people of our country, but to always protect them from any harm by internal or external invasion. I reminded him I had kept that oath but he had broken his a long time ago.

He said to me, "Only a fool would have kept that oath." Then with a cleverly fast retreat he said, "I was just kidding Angelo, I know I don't have a lot to be proud of since I left Yugoslavia but I believed in the country and you didn't. You had a reason not to and I have good reason to believe in the country since my father was a German soldier who was given the chance to live in Yugoslavia and marry and have a family."

I told him, "Yes and to give birth to a misfit like you. I'm just joking Peter, just like you. Since you're in my home I have to be nice to you. Your life story is very complicated. Was your father half German or all German?"

Peter replied, "I'm sure he was enough German and Yugoslavian anyway. I love that Yugoslavia."

I answered, "I'm sure the difference is that I loved all of those people in Yugoslavia and you Peter, loved the system and the party with it's plates full of food. You are just a fake just like the rest of them. And don't try to change the subject Peter. We were talking about the pledge of allegiance to the people. Do you remember what it was all about? I remember from that pledge that no officer could order his troops to fire arms against any of the citizens of the country."

I was raising questions to Peter and Pace during our conversation and it was turning into quite a heated debate at times. We were agreeing and disagreeing about what happened to that code of honor and how and where good soldiers could go bad, even here in this great nation, in their duty of serving and protecting. We all had different ideas of interpreting the meaning of it.

I brought up to Pace the trauma and the events that had occured during the Kennedy and then the Johnson administrations during the height of the war in Vietnam. The ordinary citizens were happy with the way things were but the politicians wanted something more and they got it with twenty years of a war and nothing to show for it but sixty thousand dead young Americans, and it was all for nothing. Johnson decided not to run for reelection which was no loss for the nation and Nixon was an antidote the country didn't need either.

Pace said, "I'm afraid our country had almost become leaderless then. I mean in the sense that of now knowing a world existed outside of America and that we should have been dancing with it and not trying to blow it up. Then we went to Indochina to pick up the trash the French left behind when they ran away, and it only took us twenty years to do it. Ironically we didn't get the trash picked up but created more and left it there."

I said, "Don't blame yourself too much, Pace, as the Russians were dancing and trying to help you blow it up at the same time. So you were not at fault by yourself."

"I know, I know, but we really did need a Vietnam. I could say there was the good and bad fallout from the turmoil of the Vietnam era in which has yet to be all played out."

I said, "I think in the future Vietnam will prove to be a good economical ally to us."

"Maybe, maybe, Pace said. "Perhaps in the generations to come but not in mine. We lost men every single day in Vietnam but during that time the economic boom in the U.S., the ones lucky enough not to be in Vietnam, life was very good and millionaires were being created every single day off the blood of the American boys who were there dying to protect us from so the called threat of communism which in reality we had nothing to fear. The children of these newly created millionaires had more money to spend than God has hair on his head. When you have so much without having worked for it you are bound to experience everything that exists that there is to experience on this planet. And so it was a cultural revolution. In China it was Maoist revolution and in Russia it was still the Bolshevic revolution. Here in the states it was Woodstock, Bob Dylan, hippies, flower children and rock and roll, and not to forget the sexual revolution. Every mom and dad from the fifties thought their children were bringing the world to an end with morality out the window, and surely the country would not survive with this new generation. After all the turmoil we are here as a healthy, powerful, and prosperous nation that carries a big stick that all our neighbors are more afraid of than ever before."

I asked Pace, "What do you know about Woodstock and those raggedey looking children from that generation by just looking at how they dressed?"

Pace jumped in and said, "Oh, they are now the senators, congressmen, mayors and presidents and CEO's of all the major business in the country. They are all the people my mom and dad were afraid of. At that time in questioning the government's actions was legitimate in demanding the government stop the war but it was as many politicians said that democracy only worked through the ballot box and not from stone throwing and violence with drugs and rock and roll."

"In the sixties the U.S. government was in crisis and in chaos because of the movement of the hippie culture, Vietnam, Cuba turning communist and the missle crisis it seemed like nothing was going right and the younger generation was seen as anti-establishment and the government was not going to stand for that. The enlistment of volunteers in the military was down to none so the draft was introduced and the principles of freedom and democracy were swept under the rug. The freedom of democracy was gone. Whether you agreed or not with the war you still had to go."

People saw Vietnam as a full scale war but the government refused to admit it and called it police action. Every third U.S. family had somebody by then in uniform except for the children of the politicians. If any of them were in uniform it was as firemen or in the National Guard or Coast Gaurd and they felt safe at home or they moved to Canada. This was the perception of the average American citizen who had a son or daughter in Vietnam. Looking back no matter if one's son or daughter was serving their country in uniform at that time it was still an important duty to pay for your country.

Civil unrest in the eyes of the government was becoming more and more unpatriotic and inexcusable especially when it came to the war in Vietnam. One day that happened that was interwoven in these events for the National Guard will never be forgotten. The national guard had to make changes from protecting citizens and started shooting the citizens. Boy, were we in for a surprise and a shock. People were scratching their heads. I thought we were a nation of law and order that you had the freedom to express yourself in without fear of being shot. Law and order got tossed out the window by the bureaucrats in the White House.

There was an unfortunate incidence of intolerance that happened at the Kent State University in Ohio. The National Guard went heavily armed to the university campus and ended up blowing a bunch of students away just because they were demonstrating. Thank God they didn't drive a red car. In those days you wouldn't drive a red car on the street because anything red was considered to be sympathizing with Bolshevic or communism. Freedom does have a limit, even here in the states.

I made my point to Pace by saying, "My understanding is, Mr. Pace, and if I am wrong please correct me, the National Guard was established to protect people from any internal harm. The National Guard's duty is to protect the country from internal unrest or enemies at the same time allow the people to express their constitutional right to voice their opinions of agreeing or disagreeing without causing physical harm to anyone. Isn't that what freedom is about, to be able to express your feelings and opinions as long as you don't hurt anyone?" Ironically I had to remind him of the constitutional rights and the First Amendment that he was born to enjoy.

Pace said, "Angelo, you're bringing back memories of a most painful time in my life. True, I was in Vietnam while the National Guard was in the states doing their job but somebody screwed up on that regretful day. The unthinkable occured and I remember it very well and with great pain."

Students were demonstrating their patriotism and the love for their country and expressing their opinions of disagreement with the

210

government on the issues of the war going on in Vietnam in the way that they best knew how. They were slain by the ones who were supposed to be protecting them. Their rights as well as all of ours were with no doubt tarnished for years to come. The memories of that tragic moment are still very fresh in the minds of the American people.

I told him, "Listen Pace, this again is another example of a good soldier that went bad and carried out the orders of an incompetent commander who had taken his own personal patriotism to the extreme. Who are these people that take our constitutional rights in their own hands? They play God in their little uniforms with their little stars and stripes on their shoulders. They forget their job is to serve the people.

"Only in communist Yugoslavia were non members of the communist party automatically considered the enemy of the state. We had an army that was supposed to protect all the people and the nation and protect the international borders but we had the city and the state police who were watchdogs again of the non members of the party which was about sixty percent of the population and they needed to kept in line by all of these state, federal, and military police. By law every citizen is to be issued a passport at birth by a so called law that people were not even aware of and for those non members of the communist party it meant nothing anyway. None of the citizens was ever issued one. If you needed one you had to go through hell to get it or possibly grease a palm to get it and with a lot of grease.

"I first saw a passport myself when I needed to go overseas and I had to pay for it myself by shaking a hand and greasing a palm. During my time in the military and before that I never had a need for a passport nor was I ever offered one. I'm still amazed and it boggles my mind why they allowed me to be in the circle of the ranking members without ever asking me to become a member of their party."

Pace and Peter agreed that the tragedy in Ohio was unprovoked and with no doubt a grave mistake on the part of the National Guard's leadership. That campus massacre in the United States during the Vietnam war was something that should never have happened or ever should be repeated. "It was a display of the incompetent leadership of that particular ranking officer," I declared. "No one else should be blamed."

Peter was clearly split emotionally on the issue of the war between Croatia and Serbia. Somehow, even though it is his birthplace and his hometown that was destroyed to the ground he was hesitant to put the blame on the villains that destroyed it, the Serbs.

I looked at him and said, "If I didn't know you any better, Peter, I would think you were crazy or just too young to understand the tragedy and the consequences of what has happened in your hometown Vukovar. Maybe I just overestimated your intelligence but you are not crazy or too young to understand. You must be blinded by your love for Serbia and that's a scary thought and I hope I never find myself in that type of position and not understand the fine balance between right and wrong. A few hundred thousand people were killed and their homes and churches were systematically blown away and destroyed. How could you sit here and pretend like nothing happened?" I asked.

Pace was clearly taken in by our heated debate and the way I pressed Peter. As usual Peter was looking at the ground like he always did when he knew in his heart he was wrong. Shrugging his shoulders without saying anything wouldn't answer me.

Pace spoke up wanting to change the subject and save the day. He could see how I was getting on Peter's case. "What else are we men who have fought in wars supposed to talk about anyway? We don't know how to talk of anything but wars. It seems like our whole lives are consumed by them."

I looked at him and laughed out loud and said, "I couldn't agree more. I promise I won't let this consume my life's thoughts. I will try to enjoy whatever life there is left to me. I will never forget the past but I am not going to live in it."

Pace continued on with his ordeal in Vietnam. "I just want to say as for my country, when we went to Vietnam, it was a whole different thinking by our government. There was a spread of communism and our government was afraid after the French got deafeated by the Vietcong in Indochina."

"Please Pace," I said, "Spare me from the French. They got their asses kicked. When have they ever won a war anyway? I think America went to Vietnam because of their inexperienced yet very cocky leadership that misunderstood the world in general and had the misperception that America was the only ones to be the world's gaurdian angel which also made them dangerous. Who has the right to rule anyway, only the ones who are capable and know how? I think America learned fast and now they have a high seat in the game. I would compare it to a man supervising and watching a baccarrat game. His chair is high above all the players and the table so that he can see all the action and call the shots. America is in the very same peculiar position and the stakes are high and they better know how to lead. Respect doesn't come cheap but only with a lot of hard work even if you have to step on people's toes. Strength and character go together."

Pace said, "You're just too smart for your own good. That can be dangerous to you health."

I told him. "I'm a patriot and I love this country and I think it is about time for us to really lead the world." I said, "Let me just name a few things that the old America got involved in with little foresight or knowledge. For example, the Russian Revolution, the Spanish civil war and in South America, Chile, Argentina and Cuba to name just a few of the countries as well as their leaders such as the Shah of Iran and the Iranian revolution. I could go on and on.

"America got sucked into the Spanish civil war when they crowned a fascist as President for life. They had protected him all this time. He died happily ever after and was buried honorably as a fascist in Spain. We have supported some pretty notorious characters such as ones as none other than the facist Franco, Mussolini, Marcos of the Phillipines, and the Emporer Hirohito of Japan. We even tried to save the Russian czar from failing."

Pace said, "It seems like you're trying to insult my intelligence, Angelo. I know who those leaders were like Franco. After America lost the bases in Tripoli and Libya we didn't have a choice but to support a guy like Franco. Because Spain was very strategically located we needed to increase our presence in the north African continent and Spain was as good a place as any."

I reminded him, "America thought they needed Spain as a military base and sacrificed the freedom of Spaniards for forty-eight years. America was keeping Franco safe long before the trouble in Tripoli and Bengaza in Libya. Can you justify denying a whole people their freedom just because our government thought only Franco could secure our military presence in Spain? That's crazy, it makes no sense. Our bases would have been in a better position without Franco there than with him. Just as it has been proven, we had better relations after that bigot Franco was dead. Spain and the U.S. became much closer as allies. Spain's not Africa. It's a massive strategical piece of land overlooking North Africa that borders the Mediterranean and Atlantic Oceans. You can see Africa on a nice clear day from the Spanish peninsula."

"Vietnam was a very different thing," Pace replied, with disagreement in his voice and looking uncomfortable the way I was describing American military adventures around the world during that time but not disagreeing.

I wanted to make it clear however that the spread of communism must be stopped without a nuclear disaster. One could honestly say we were very trigger happy then. I continued to stress to Pace saying that the beginning of the Vietnam war was nothing but misunderstandings and a lot of ego that was involved and put us into a deep hole that took two decades to get out of. At the end of it we got absolutely no benefits only huge losses of life and communism was already deteriorating from inside and not because of any pressure from the U.S. The credit should only be given to the ordinary people from that communist world in getting rid of it. People just like me that know the brutality of communism from their heart.

Pace said, "Those full-bellied, freedom loving patriots easily sent our boys across the world to be killed to assure their fat existence, people like Kennedy's Secretary of State, Robert MacNamara, and then Henry Kissinger, who was nothing but a Manhattan bookkeeper at the Rockefeller Corporation. Kissinger was juiced in by the Rockefellers, who were a nice wealthy Jewish family that wanted to be one step closer to the White House, and so they made him Secretary of State during the Nixon administration. He had charisma in relating to the Europeans because of his European culture and for sure he could talk like no one else."

I interupted him, "Yes, Henry reminds me of Milovan Djilas, the young charismatic Montenegrin who was solely responsible for molding Tito into what he came to be. You could say Henry Kissinger was also molding a couple of our presidents and helped make Isreal a nuclear power using our tax money and with a great help that was orchestrated by England. I think they are regretting it now. Of course they would never say it out loud. They wouldn't want to offend the Israelis."

Pace couldn't wait, "I agree. The Jews are the best lobbiests and hijacked our politicians in a way."

I asked, "Wait a minute, what do you mean by that? Nobody gets willingly hijacked and it's illegal here."

"The Jewish people are the greatest participants in the community and every day society and are one hundred percent participants at the ballot box. The rest of us take that for granted. That's what I meant by hijacking politicians and now you know." Pace answered.

I laughed and said, "I will remember that and promise to cast my vote every election."

Pace and Peter found that very funny and laughed. Pace wanted to say his piece of mind about his dislike for Henry since the time he served under him in Vietnam. "It was never stated that Kissinger was really a Jew. He was always presented to be a German boy and he never acknowledged that he was Jewish at the beginning of his political career. They always said about him that he loved soccer and was from Germany."

I said, "You mean to tell me that if people knew he was Jewish they would have objected to his becoming Secretary of State?"

Pace answered, "Not neccessarily, but I personally never liked him and we had much better and more experienced candidates than him for that position. The influence from Rockefeller showed that politics have no boundries."

Peter didn't like the way our discussion was heading especially when we pointed to the fact that comunism had fallen from the inside since he had been living well under comunism. He didn't want to accept the fall of communism from it's own self destruction and wanted to put the blame somewhere else and that was the West.

He stood up on his feet holding his snifter of Louis XIII, which he couldn't have gotten in Yugoslavia but only at my house and it was free. His hands clearly shook while he was trying to straighten his collar, which he had the habit of doing every minute or so especially when he found himself losing control of a conversation. He turned red as a beet taking a sip of his brandy and it seemed to go down the wrong way almost choking him. I pounded him purposelly pretty hard on the back. I told him, "Don't go dying at my house Peter. The damn French put too much sugar in the cognac. Seven hundred dollars for a bottle of sugar water you shouldn't choke on if it is real Louis XIII. I wouldn't want anyone to suspect me of killing you because probably nothing I say would clear me."

"You are a wise guy Angelo." Peter coughed out. He didn't find it funny and whatever sense of humor that he had seemed to be gone.

Pace wasn't much help to Peter because he was loving all of it and he asked, "Peter are you OK?"

"Not really," he choked out. "This time Angelo's pushed the envelope too far. Tito is what he grew up to be and what he was."

"Yea, a damn butcher," I thought to myself, not wishing to insult him anymore than I already had.

Peter was obviously shaken up with good reason. His bread basket and paycheck with Tito was gone. I already knew that Tito was his idol. In his eyes Tito could do no wrong. I told him, " Peter I don't why you're getting so upset. You have two new employers now he and are working for Tuzman and Milosevic."

Pace couldn't help jumping in, "Oh perhaps you'll get a big fat pay check at the end of the day if you live long enough."

I said, "For now it's for nothing else but a slap on the shoulder and words of praise from them, 'You're a good boy Peter.' Maybe his thanks will come later." I   I told him, "Maybe if everything goes in your favor Peter, maybe you'll get that dog bone to chew on for the rest of your life, but If I were you I wouldn't wait for that bonus because it ain't coming. These two losers don't have anything to buy it for you with. They will only take from you and that's it. Tito on the other hand, I think was a little bit better of a patron for you. I think you are missing him already."

Pace wise cracked, "That is such a sad story."

Peter said, "Shut up Pace. What do you know about Tito?"

"Oh, not too much, except that once we had a lame cow with only one teet that Tito sucked off of for forty five years or so. Russia was Tito's other lame cow with one teet. He managed to suck them both to death and the bastard lived to tell the story and laugh about it. Now because of that his whole country has left him and been blown up in pieces. His second highest achievement was in a pretty primitive trade as a tool machinist in a pretty primitive country. As far as I'm concerned he was doomed to be nothing. His biography was writen by Englishmen instead of his own countrymen. He thought nothing of you or anybody else in Yugoslavia, Peter. I guess somehow Tito's life changed one-eighty when he joined the Austrian-Hungarian army. He actually participated in the invasion of Serbia and fired quite a few shells from the Austrian cannons at Belgrade. Then he joined the Russian Revolution to save the Russians from Czar Nicholas' butchering of his people. What a noble man he was. Did the real Tito return from Russia? That is a question yet to be answered."

Peter was turning as red as a baboon's ass. He said, "You do surprise me Pace. Your knowledge of history is not bad. Angie has gotta be involved somewhere here."

I put up hands, " My hand are clean. I can't take any credit for Pace's knowledge of history but I admit he is giving you a good lesson. One thing I could say for Tito and his ordeal in Russia is that the real Tito never came back. I think Russia is where Tito was killed and replaced by a Ukrainian that looked like him. The new imposter wasn't missing any of his fingers like Tito was. He had them all and he wasn't speaking the Serb or Croatian language either. The imposter was very fashionable unlike the real Tito as well. The real boy probably never got the chance to own a double breasted suit and if someone gave him one as a gift he wouldn't even know how to wear one. He owned probably one pair of shoes and one pair of pants. The shoes were probably Roman moccasins and I don't even want to think if he possibly owned a pair of underwear, not that I really care.

"The real Tito never ruled Yugoslavia. Obviously the imposter needed a tutor, someone with a high vocabulary in the Serb and Croatian language. There was no better man for that job other than my charismatic fellow Montenegrin, Milovan Djilas, a dedicated ideologist and communist. He was just what the doctor ordered. Stalin created the new Tito so that Yugoslavia could become a republic of Russia.

"The new Tito of Stalin's creation suddenly had a change of heart about becoming a part of Russia. He liked the position he was in and must have thought, 'Hey why should I give this up, I feel pretty good here so let's just keep it.' He had surrounded himself with people who were hungry for power just like he was. He paid them well and they kept him protected. It also made it possible for him to get a honorable burial with a state funeral and a tomb built for him. All of this coronation and his good life happened in the same city that he had bombed to hell as an Austrian coporal. What a twist of fate.

"He brushed off Stalin and survived it. How many people could say that? He executed forty five thousand people in a months time in 1948. Whoever he thought were followers of Stalin and not his, he executed or had exiled. He sent thousands to the Naked Island in the Adriatic to their deaths. He remained in Belgrade, safe in his twenty square kilometer cage filled with about twenty thousand of his personal military, that I was once honored to be a part of myself, called Tito's Guard."

Peter interrupted, "So why did Djilas never reveal that Tito was an imposter after he was kicked out of Yugoslavia?"

I answered, "A smart man would never do that, admitting he had been a fool. Who would believe him anyway? He would have been called a traitor too that had supported a fool without roots or any kind of bloodline as a southern Slav. So there is your answer." Peter was furious and steaming like a hot red pepper.

"One thing I could say about this guy, Peter," I told him, "is I wanted to have his suits. The imposter Tito had a unique and expensive taste in his fashion style. When was our real Tito ever so fashionable? And Tito's children from his first wife had no resemblance to this Tito. The real Tito was a poor boy who never owned two pairs of pants, socks or shoes. He was born poor and died poor somewhere in Siberia with Stalin's thumb choking out his life. I wonder if a marker was put on his gravesite? Probably not."

"You sure know everything, Angelo," Peter finally said. "You know I went to school in Belgrad for intelligence service."

"Yes Peter, I know you went to school over there, you've been bragging about it a long time." I told him. "Do you want to tell our friend Pace what your expertise was when you graduated from Tito's so called criminal academy?"

"No, Angelo but maybe you should tell him," Peter answered.

I replied, "If you insist, Peter. Where should I start? I wouldn't want to disappoint you and leave anything out about your filthy job."

It seemed we were in a real debate this time and our friendship was going out the window. I was starting to lose my temper as I got in his face and said, "You've asked me if I was a Mormon or a Muslim before just because I have a Mormon friend. I have friends of every faith including you, you smart ass. Have you decided what you are yet, Roman Catholic or Serb or just a humble decent human being? I hope I get a straight answer this time but I assure you it really doesn't make any difference to me. It would just be nice to have the truth of any kind from you for once. I am trying to be polite because you're a guest in my home. You know my culture and tradition instructs me to be polite. As I remember you're traveling with documents to be an Orthodox priest this time spreading the good gospel of God's word to the world. I'm just quoting what you said. It seems like you approve of what the Serbs did and what they are doing in Bosnia right now, killing thousands of people and raping them."

Peter replied, "Well, America did the same thing in Vietnam with the killing and burning and looting," cleverly trying to change the subject while moving around in his chair like he had a live worm in his ass."

I said, "We are not talking about America right now, Peter. We are talking about Bosnia and your and my ancestoral land."

Peter had tipped the scales the wrong way with Pace too. Pace told him, "Peter, I wouldn't say we were in Vietnam for the purpose to kill, burn, and rape the women and children. We went to Vietnam for the very reason to prevent something like what is happening now in Bosnia and that it will never happen in this country."

"What exactly do you mean by that?" Peter asked.

"I mean we were there to stop the evil from spreading," Pace answered. "We pulled out of there but won the war anyway and kicked their communist asses every day. They were weak and we were strong. What Serbia is doing in Bosnia has been brewing and in the works for a long time. It has just come to a fruition recently and people are paying a heavy price with their lives."

Peter asked, "How do you know it has been brewing a long time?"

Pace replied, "In case you have forgotten, I have just come from there. I'll tell you something else Mr. Peter, about something I heard with my own ears that was quoted by a lady who was there, word for word. Her name was Emira, she was one of the Bosnian fighters along with her husband and daughter. She told us what happened when the Chetniks raped a girl and tore her stomach apart. The girl was a young woman who was no more than twenty years old and was gang raped by twenty Serbian bastards. She was pregnant also. After they had gang raped her they cut open her stomach and took out her baby. They slaughtered a calf and removed the belly of the calf and put into the young womans belly in place of the baby and then sewed her up so she would still look pregnant. They were bragging and saying that she looked better. The question I don't have the answer to is what they did with the baby. That gruesome story was the talk of the town and all the villiages in Bosnia."

"So don't push me Peter," Pace stated, "because this is not my house; it is Angelo's house, but I'm still not obliged to take any crap from you. I can only tell you Peter, that what the Serbs are doing to the

Bosnians is a nightmare. It'something like I've never seen in my life and if you want proof I have hours and hours of tapes here I brought for Angelo that are documented right from the front lines."

Peter said, "Oh, those tapes are nothing but propaganda."

Pace replied, "So I guess you already have your mind made up anyway Peter, about who the victims and villains are. I know who the victims are. The Bosnian people are the victims."

Peter said, "Hold on a minute, Pace. I never said I was supportive of all of the killing. I am supportive of the old Yugoslavia."

Pace said, "Obviously you are, you were eating good in the old Yugoslavia."

I told them, "I don't know, gentlemen, but my people are not suffering for the first time. All of this prosecution and killing has been in the works since the times of Alexander of Serbia in 1912. Only the guards have changed. The ideas are still the same and the blueprints for our destruction are still as strong as ever in the minds of the Serbs, and Peter is a very naive man as I have always known him to be. If I didn't have a code of honor I would give him a bullet right in his forehead right here over my dinner table although it would dishonor my name, family, and culture and tradition. I will take it as his just trying to provoke and test your devotion toward the cause in Bosnia and I shall leave like that for now.

"If Tito was a Croat and a real Croatian born boy, I bet that he would not have tried eliminating us during his last forty years of rule. Maybe he would have oppressed the Bosnjaks, my people, but not try and uproot us totally from society as his predessor King Alexander tried to do."

Peter's argument for Tito was a waste of time. I told him, "He was not the real Tito, he was an Orthodox Ukrainian and as far as I'm concerned the case is closed. If you want to debate it you can tomorrow. As for me, I am not debating this subject any longer. I will say that Djilas was the new Tito's lifeline. He was teacher, tutor, planner, and public relations man to Tito, and knew he needed to transform Tito into what the people expected him be. Tito knew he needed to tranform himself into the real Tito who came to be a mythological living legend that never intermingled with his citizens. I believe he was an imposter who wanted to wear the real Tito's shoes that in reality were only Roman moccasins that were the poor boy's shoes."

"Who do you think was the new Tito then?" Asked Peter.

I answered, "Well, I think you should know, as you hang around those people more than I do. I think it was that sharp Ukranian good looking boy who was chosen by Stalin. It was the man whose funeral you went to in Belgrade a few years ago. Do you remember?"

He replied, "I did go to a funeral and it was an experience."

I said, "It was nothing like what you guys experienced when you killed our people all around the world, was it? Or did any of them even get proper funerals? How many souls can you account for when you go to Hell, if you ever get there?" I wanted an answer. I was losing my temper.

"Well, Angie like you have said, gentlemen don't tell."

Pace spoke up and said, "All right girlie Peter. It's girls who never tell their secrets either but the boys will so they can brag about it."

I interuppted and said, "Pace don't push Peter to brag about it right here in my house because he may get hurt."

Peter didn't like that. He turned as red as a bell pepper. He is naturally pale but his face was bright red and puffed out like a bulldogs. He said, "You are some two faced dudes and I don't know what you mean by that."

Pace replied, "Let's just say that if you were one of the guys or shall I say dudes, that were in Vietnam with me, I wouldn't have let you stand behind me. I would have made sure you were in front of me so that I could keep an eye on you."

I laughed, I mean really laughed. I found what Pace had just said genuinely honest and at the same time hilarious. I asked Peter "Do you know what Pace meant by what he just said to you?"

"I guess you're going to tell me no matter what. I'm a prisoner by my own choice in your house. Maybe I should go get a room so that I can feel as free to talk as you guys are."

I said, "Come on Peter. My house or a hotel room wouldn't make any difference. You're a wimp when it comes to straight talk. Don't worry about it because my house is open for you. You have the keys and are free to come and go as you please like you have been for years. Please don't tell me you don't feel at home in my home because I do adore your children as much as my own and hope that you feel the same about my family. Do you, Peter?" I asked and laughed a little. "Oh, and by the way, don't get fresh with Mankiu anymore by rubbing the baby in her belly. I don't want anyone who is a fan of the White Eagles and Arkan rubbing my wife's belly."

Peter turned and asked, "What are you trying to tell me, what do you mean?"

I said, "You need to wake up to the real world, Mister, because you are a cheerleader for the team who are the biggest murderers of the twenty first century right now." I was trying to bring him back to the real world since he was confused and starting to lose it. I told him, "You are lucky your children are grown and no longer live in Yugoslavia any more."

Peter laughed fakely and said, "Well, I hope I'm still a candidate to be godfather to the baby since I have no grandchildren yet."

I said, "Peter we'll talk about godfather but you won't babysit for sure." Deep in my heart, after the conversation we just had, I knew I wouldn't leave my children with him for any moment. He had lost my trust that night.

I said, "I want to make sure you understand what Pace meant Peter, when he said how he would feel being in Vietnam with you and I'll tell you what my advice would be. Don't go on the front lines with him because he will shoot your ass. It appears he doesn't quite trust you and I think he is right not to. The two of you wouldn't do well together on the front lines. You are still a hard core communist, Pete."

We all laughed and Peter took it all in stride. He was a man with a lot of preseverance and it ended up being a great evening, and something for me to remember, that the man I had called a friend for many years was nothing but an enemy of myself and my people. It was not such a surprise to me really, in my heart I'd always know it but didn't want to admit it to myself. Peter said to Pace, "I hope there are no bad feelings or anything was taken personally over our political debates tonight."

"No, no, not at all," Pace replied. He was squeezing his fists together, cracking his knuckles and looking somewhat uneasy. "I told you before that Angie is my good friend and I hope we will always stay that way."

Pace just laughed sarcastically, "Ha, ha, ha. You will always be around Angie as long as he has something you can scrap off the plate for yourself."

We said goodnight and Pace left for home and Peter said he

would like to try to get a couple hours sleep before traveling. I asked if he'd like my help packing before he rested. He declined and packed for the trip he would be making early in the morning to the Gold Coast of Australia.

At eight o'clock the next morning the bell alarm was ringing the sound to wake up. Mankiu had already brewed the coffee and the table was set for breakfast. As Peter was descending the stairs, he saw Mankiu pouring orange juice into glasses. He greeted her good morning with his strong voice in Chinese saying, "Jo sun, Mankiu!"

She thought in a way it was funny that a white man spoke her language and said , "Peter, you speak better Chinese than my husband does."

He replied, "All of my neighbors in Australia are Chinese and speak nothing but Chinese. There was no way to communicate except to learn it myself."

He asked me at the breakfast table why I wasn't more fluent in Chinese. I said, "Well Peter, I look at it this way. Before I married Mankiu I had only eaten rice three or four times in my life and had drank tea hardly at all. Now I find my eyes are starting to shrink and stretch sideways. You know what that means my friend? I am beginning to look Chinese and so I thought I better quit eating any Chinese food or speak any Chinese and stick to only Mankiu herself, and just forget the food and the language and the prune wine."

We all laughed loudly and ate our English muffins with eggs and cream cheese. The coffee filled the house with a delicious aroma. On way out the door on our way to the airport I asked Mankiu for to-go cups of coffee so that we could enjoy it on our way there. She was happy to comply, flattered from all our compliments.

Peter seemed truly emotional as he expressed his appreciation to Mankiu for being a fantastic hostess. Maniku did not hesitate to remind Peter of our conversation of the previous night. She said, "It would be nice if you could save just one child in Bosnia Peter. I don't think it is too much to ask and I think you owe it to my husband and for the sake of your own children. Part of last night's conversation I couldn't help but overhearing and it makes me not so sure you are capable of being a true godfather to our children. I only hope you were joking around with Pace and my husband. If not you have plenty of time to redeem yourself. We can talk about the godfather topic another time if we see each other again."

We were then on our way to the airport. He didn't respond and seemed to feel embarressed. We parked in front of international customs so he could check in.

We said a brief goodbye to each other and the last words I recall Peter saying were, "Angelo it's was great to see you. I hope nothing ever comes between our friendship and I look forward to seeing your baby soon. I think you are a very lucky guy."

"Oh," he turned around and said, "I almost forgot, I have something for Mankiu." He pulled a white envelope from out of his pocket. He handed it to me and told me to promise him I would give it to her as soon as I returned home.

I said, "Peter, I will be your personal pizza delivery boy straight from here to my house to make sure she gets it. I hope your not trying to get fresh with my wife."

He said, "I love that girl as my own daughter and besides, I'm too old for that."

Just before he crossed over to customs he turned to excuse himself from the officer for a moment and looked me straight in the eyes. His eyes were filled with worry for some reason. He said, "I didn't like that son of a bitch with us at your house last night. I think he was trying to intrude on our friendship."

I replied, "You're not jealous are you, Peter? That's kids stuff. It's obvious that you're not a man who likes anyone very much."

Peter replied smiling, "But I do love you."

"Well," I smiled back waving him away with my arm, "I don't carry a piece of meat on my back just so you can have a bite when your hungry, so you must have a better reason than that to love me. You'll have to give me the real reason."

He laughed and said, "I'll call you from the air after we take off and tell you what it is."

I said, "Well, don't leave me hanging too long. I don't want to lose any weight over why my friend's sudden proclamations of love came for me after all of these years. He must have been feeling guilty about something, possibly all the stupid shooting off of his mouth the previous evening."

Of course he has told me many times that he loves me and I am his best friend. He was especially grateful when I provided for his sister and other members of his family's immigration papers in only practically a few hours time right here from Las Vegas so that they are now able to live free, be educated, and be full participants as American citizens and live that dream life that would never be possible to experience in Yugoslavia even with Peter's connections.

I threw my hands into the air and said in my final parting words, "Don't worry Peter, your friendship will always be safe with me. I know you love me because I am the only one with enough guts to give you a hard time and tell you exactly what and who you are. You know I'm not too shy to tell you that, Pete, whether it's compliments or critisism. Either way you deserve it. You told me yourself that you're not afraid of the truth so don't complain. Now go have a safe a trip and don't worry about calling me from the plane because I have so many things to do today."

He waved and I waved goodbye and was on my way home. Twenty minutes later the phone rang but I didn't answer it because I knew it was Peter. I didn't answer because I was busy and frankly a little tired hearing Peter's nonsense and I had lost some respect for him last night when he finally showed his true colors.

I almost forgot about the envelope to give Mankiu. I went back in the garage to retrieve it from my car. I came back to the living room with my hands behind my back where Mankiu was standing and told her, "Listen girl, Peter gave me this envelope to give to you and said I shouldn't open it, only you." Laughingly I told her she better tell me what was in it. She was surprised about it and put her arms around me and kissed me. It was a perfect opportunity for me to show my thanks to her for being such a terrific hostess to my friends and a wonderful wife that was so respectful to me. I told her all that as I handed her the envelope. She said that after hearing his talk of last night she didn't wish any gift from him as she opened the trash and tossed it in. I had to be at Caesars Palace to meet a friend, Ken Breezy, so I kissed her goodbye.

CHAPTER SEVEN – PACE THE WARRIOR

The next time that I saw him, Peter asked me, "How is your friend Pace the Mormon warrior doing?"

"I see you're being sarcastic and still sore from the meeting we had with him, but the warrior is very well, thank you," I told him. "Let me tell you about a time during the African campaign of the early 70's."

"What about it Angie?" he asked.

"It was when you were digging for the gold in your nose, Peter was in Zimbabwe, Mozambique, Namibia, Botswana and the notorious war torn Angola. The Mormon warrior that you just asked me about and I crossed each other's path with the same people who had wanted him hanged, and for good reason too."

I told him I had been in those areas selling guns with the Italian boys while Pace was trying to protect and help the white regime survive in a black world that had been oppressed by the white man for centuries. I got the chance to ask Pace for the first time in all the time I'd known him why he chose to work with the white regime in Zimbabawe and what was then called Rhodesia.

In January of 1971 I flew from Rome into South Africa where we settled down in the capitol of Pretoria in the heart of the town at the Holiday Inn. The next day we went to their festival that had been going on at the time. There were thousands of people from all over the surrounding areas attending the festival, wearing colorful and beautiful costumes. On that particular day the weather was not very favorable. In Africa it was the winter season. There were broken bottles and shattered glass everywhere and somehow I had stepped on a piece of sharp glass and cut my foot, such that it required about ten stitches.

The white Africano doctor who treated me at the local hospital said that an hour earlier he had treated a white man with white hair who was from Salt Lake City, Utah, in America. I laughed and commented that I bet that he wasn't from Salt Lake City but from some God forsaken small place that an American bald eagle wouldn't even want to fly over. Maybe he was a wild man from Mount Zion park. The doctor found my comments so funny that he laughed.

He said, "You better quit being so smart so I can patch up your foot."

226

I apologized, and said, "I'm really sorry doc, I didn't mean to distract you from your job."

He said, "Some doctors don't have a job, just a duty to save lives. Don't you forget that. The next time you go to a doctor you might appreciate it more."

I didn't want to let him know I had experience with doctors and did truly appreciate them. I was just having fun with him. I asked him what the name of the guy he had treated was and that maybe I knew him. He said, "I can't pronounce his name but he was on the front page of the newspaper today about his fighting in Rhodesia for the white regime. He is a handsome devil."

"Doc," I said, "I don't find men handsome or pretty, just arrogant and ugly. They all look like gorillas to me, and I don't care if they look any other way because I just want to have all the girls."

On that note the doctor got a little bit purposefully rough with my wound and I got the message fast. I thought I had better keep quite at least until he was done patching me up. Suddenly he said, "Hey wait a minute. I've got to get you a copy of that newspaper so that you can read about your friend from America." I looked at him silently. My expression was questioning why would he would think that American guy was my friend. Maybe he thought that all white people were fighting on the white side against the blacks.

We had been selling guns to Mogami's guerrillas in Zimbabwe along with my friends Claudio and Renauto. It was Renauto's connections we used on this trip. The doctor's conversation with me made me think for a moment that maybe we may have been getting set up for selling guns to guerrillas, but it was not so. To experience the injustice the African native men endured from the white Africanos in South Africa and the rest of the continent could make one's hair stand on end, and was a scary thought. I experienced it first hand in my own country but nothing like in the country of South Africa. God forbid, to be oppressed like that. Imagine that at all of the state public facilities and parks that were supposed to be available for all the people in the community's use had signs posted at every entrance or bench to specify that the use was for only whites, and separate for blacks segregated into different facilities. Even the restaurants, restrooms, and drinking fountains were identified as being only for whites or blacks.

The doctor called for his nurse to please bring him the morning's paper from his desk. He was anxiously waiting for me to unfold the poorly folded rumpled newspaper to see the article that he wanted me to ingest on the man from Utah. There on the front page I saw the lion soldier from Utah, my good friend Col. Giles Pace.

I said to myself, "What is he doing crusading for the white man coming all the way from Utah to South Africa and Zimbabwe?" I hadn't realized that I had been voicing my thoughts that loudly. My friends Julio, Claudio and my Tunizian friend Siki were standing near by while the doctor and I were discussing the news on the front page of the paper.

"Why are you so concerned? You act like you've known the man all your life." Claudio said. "Why do you look concerned?"

I laughed, "Ha!Ha! I know many men like him. I think we are following in the footsteps of Che Guevara, the Cuban revolutionary was visiting here for sure in the recent past in the Zimbabwe area.

"Look at my buddies Claudio and Julio," I told the doctor. "They would die for me and I would die for them at any time." The doctor wanted to know what I thought about a guy coming from America to fight for the white regime, since the Europeans were definitely siding with the black Africans. He looked at me strangely seeming to want to look to me for support but none was forthcoming, then or in the near future. I wanted to tell him I was here to fight aginst the white regime, but I didn't and I couldn't unless I wanted a lynching for myself and my friends. I did agree that the man looked pretty impressive in the picture in the newspaper.

I told the doctor that I felt I was in a just place there but my so called friend from America was with no doubt in the wrong place. It was a different time and place then.

The doctor was surprised but not shocked by my bold and direct opinion. I read out loud a paragraph from the newspaper article on Pace. It was from Mogabi himself, a leader of freedom fighters. I considered him to be no good by what I'd heard from others and from reading the Che Guevara manuscripts about him years later from his own personal revolutionary manuscripts published after the death of the legendary revolutionary. Guevara was a south American native finding his fate decided in Bolivia and fought along with Castro in Cuba. He became the second in rank as a revolutionary leader next to Fidel Castro. Castro felt too crowded by Guevara and got rid of him by sending him around the world to spread the gospel of Castro and his revolution hoping that he might get killed and not come back. Castro's wishes later did come true.

Guevara and Mogabi had spent some time together and during that time Guevara observed him and later said that Mogabi had no future as a leader because he wasn't a man of the people. Mogabi was only for Mogabi with a big body and no brains just like his boss Castro, only Guevara didn't know that at the time.

I believe in order to make a judgement about anyone in a position of leadership, as in this instance as Guevara did with Mogabi, he should have had a personal contact with that leader and used his own experience and knowledge to make his opinion or judgment on them. Guevara was right on target. Mogabi was everything a leader should be. He was even worse than Gavara thought and had proven that. Zimbabawe is in a state of chaos as opposed to the period when in the seventies before the fall of the white regime when they were the bread basket for the African continent and an agricultural power to be reackoned with. Today under his leadership they have turned into a nation of beggers."

I concur that my Italian friends and I made a good judgement that day in Swaziland at the doctor's office when we voiced our support about Mogabi and not our new American friend, Pace. It wasn't really so much support for Mogabi but for the human man's freedom as much as our own.

In this particular point and time Pace was fighting for the oppressor, who were the white regime better known as the white Africanos, and not the oppressed people, the native Africans. On the contrary I am a non-denominational crusader who has always wanted to help the weak. It feels good to be just in the eyes of God and especially the people.

The articles headline on the front page of the newspaper, if I can recall correctly that was called The Gazette said, "A white boy has come across the ocean to save the oppressive regime of Eon Schmitt who was the Prime Minister of then Rhodesia, now Zimbabwe." The doctor translated the article for me, being glad to show his skill of the Italian language since the paper was written in English and I was not yet fluent in it then. He continued to read saying Mogabi's statement in the article regarded this white lion from America, and said, "I will cut this white man and perform an inhumane ritual on him in the cruelest way possible. I might even cannibalize him and cook him for a roast on bamboo sticks."

He must have had some good enough reasons to do what he wanted to do to Pace. I thought it was funny when Mogabi said he was going to roast Pace and eat him. I said in the presence of the doctor and my friends who were standing in the doorway as we were leaving making my last wise crack, "I wonder what Mogabi is going to do with Pace's balls?" We all laughed.

The doctor replied, "Maybe he will dry them up and use them in the tribal war dance decorations." I thought I was a wise guy but the doctor's remarks were even lower.

I laughed and said, "Here I thought you were a nice guy, Doc. I'm not coming back for any more treatment from you but you really got me on that one. The Africans are your people and you are theirs and whatever you guys decide to do with Pace's tools, just don't eat them. I know that may be a delicacy here but it's prohibited to eat them in the states unless they are the balls from a slaughtered bull." I repeated again just to be a wise guy once more, "Don't eat them because I wouldn't want to lose a good doctor before I leave here."

I then shook his hand while sliding a good tip in it. The hospital was government owned and there was no bill to pay so my friends and I thought it would be only proper to tip the doctor. I was paid the day before for my armory merchandise in British pounds. I tipped the Doc one hundred pounds for his services. That was equivalant to three months wages to most of the workers there. He hesitated to take it but I insisted since I already slid it into his hand anyway. I wished him luck and we were on our way to Pretoria and to the Holiday Inn hotel to our room on the sixteenth floor.

Our room had a beautiful view overlooking Queen Victoria Boulevard. I felt hungry and tired. I couldn't wait to get cleaned up because I had a date that night with a girl I had known for almost a year and saw every time I come to Pretoria. She was a receptionist and hostess named Athina at the hotel of Scandinavian and Italian descent with a truly Greek name, making her a perfect blend of beauty. I shook hands with my friends, Julio, Renato and Claudio and Secke and told them, "Boys," and I repeated it in Italian, "Ragace, you are on your own tonight. I'm going to have dinner with my blondie Athina tonight at the steak house and make sure that you guys take your time to come back home late." Luckily they hadn't come back all night but did leave a message for me not to worry, they were having a good time themselves. I really wanted them to enjoy themselves because they had been working really hard all month especially my friend from Tuniz, Secke, who wasn't able to accompany us everywhere that we went because he was of color.

We stayed ten days in Pretoria, the city I would have liked to adopt as a second home in South Africa, but I knew this trip could very well be my very last one there. We were starting to get noticed too much by the South African secret service and the military police. We didn't want to end up dead in a ditch or in an unmarked grave. In those days that could have very easily happened. We boarded a plane that flew via Tunis City into Rome, my favorite place. We landed at the Fiumicino airport, today called DaVinci airport near my hometown on the outskirts of Rome by the ocean, Lido de Ostia.

Years later I sat in my home in Las Vegas, married with children and having dinner with this same man, Pace, whom I just barely had missed meeting back on that memorable day in the hospital. He was doing something then that I didn't approve of and wouldn't ever have done myself in helping the white Africano's oppress their fellow citizens. If I had met him then I probably would have broken both his legs and made sure that he never made it back to the US, and then turned him over to Mogabi so that he really would dry his tools for decoration.

Looking back now, I'm glad that we didn't meet that day. Now that I know him, I know we both do think alike and see life as God and nature has really meant it to be. We are both willing to fight for the underdog and clearly understand what it is that we are fighting for without a second thought. We have not always been on the same side, but we are the same kind of men, I hope I can say fairly.

I have met his lovely wife and beautiful little boy, Madison, who was four years old at the time. I held him in my arms and loved him as my own children. We became the closest of friends. He was ready to risk his life to help my people in Bosnia. There was no stronger reason for me to feel a bond with him as a brother. After all, one mother couldn't give birth to all the brothers. This is the best way, to have a friend you can consider your brother.

Giles Pace was a true hero in risking his life for people he didn't even know but saw as victims and wanted to do something about it. A hero is a hero, no matter if he is awarded a medal or not for what he does. Most of the time, recognition for heroism only comes when their funeral provides the photo opportunity at their final farewell and the medal given to the grieving wife or mother. Though Giles Pace was decorated for his heroism in the Vietnam War, his heroism in Bosnia went unnoticed and without recognition. Maybe somewhere in Bosnia today, someone remembers him, and is still grateful for what he did. I hope so, because I still remember.

In 1992, Pace was in Bosnia in early opposition to what was already clearly a deliberate and systematic genocide of the Muslim people of Bosnia by the racist Serbs of Milosevic's regime, at the hands of their dog packs, the jackal chetniks. Though most people in the rest of the world saw only what was happening in Sarajevo as the whole story, the fact is that the worst of it was happening up in the isolated highlands, away from the cameras, and away from any kind of help.

The UN, and at that time sadly also the US, were all agreed that the Bosnians should not be permitted to obtain military arms, so as to prevent war from happening there. All that did was to make it impossible for one side to fight, and that side was the one that didn't already have a big military machine. A one-sided war is more accurately called a massacre, or genocide, and yet that is what the world was accepting in Bosnia, so as to avoid having to take sides with Muslims against the Serbs who were running what was left of Yugoslavia, under Slobo the puffed-up little would-be fascist, Slobo with his Bosnian final solution.

Pace was up in the highlands trying to get through from Split on the coast to the rural area around Tuzla. Though the cities of Bosnia, like Sarajevo, are as modern and sophisticated as most in Europe, it is fair to say that life up in those highlands is still very much like it was a century ago, or two centuries ago. The people are certainly not stupid, and they are educated and often well read, but their lives are those of the simple home farmer, which are the way they have been since the beginning of civilization.

The land is beautiful, and very rich, but it is terribly rough, with high rocky crags and steep canyons, narrow passes, heavy forests, and eroded gullies. The weather is wet, both in the hot and cold seasons, and when there is no ice, there is mud. Paved roads are very rare, as are power lines and telephones. People spend their time digging and irrigating, fixing old walls and fences, weeding, planting, and harvesting, tending to their livestock, mending, cooking, and cleaning every day, as it has been there for centuries. It is a hard-working life, but a rich and rewarding life, full with family and culture, and they appreciate it.

Outside of the narrow fertile valleys where their families have lived for so many generations, they become refugees, and strangers even in the rest of Bosnia. Wherever they gather as refugees, they know the Serb army will eventually round them up, and take them away. To the north and west lies Croatia, and they know they are not much loved by Croatians either. It wasn't so long ago that the Roman Catholic Croatian Ustashe were rounding up Muslims along with the Jews on behalf of the Nazis whom they admired and served. To the south lies Montenegro, the land of my own childhood, but a land where Bosniaks are even more a minority, and the last Yugoslavian state still loyal to Serbia. They know there is simply nowhere to go. They cannot even flee, but into other jaws.

If the trucks Pace was trying to move up through those narrow valleys had been loaded with weapons, he would have been shot at not only by the local bandit gangs and by the Chetnik patrols moving through, but also by the UN troops, if there had been any around. The truth is, he was carrying canned baby food, some basic anti-biotics, and powdered milk. The rutted wagon tracks that passed for roads were a constant obstacle even to the double-axle all-wheel-drive heavy delivery trucks, especially when the weather started getting bad, and you could skid off the road on ice in the morning, and be up to both axles in mud in the afternoon.

Pace didn't go through the valleys and passes armed with a tank and a squad of men. He was the security himself, one man with a basic assault rifle, a Russian AK-47. He pointed out that it was a lot easier there to get ammunition for that one than for an American M-16. "I would always return fire," he told me. "You couldn't tell who these guys were, sometimes in Army uniforms, sometimes rough cammos, or just street clothes. Whenever their patrols were in the area, they would usually take a few shots at us. I always fired back, and they always just backed off and waited until we were out of the area. Then they just went in and did whatever they wanted to."

It was all too clear what they wanted to do, and they did it every time they came into a new area. The local people were just farmers, nice hard-working people who just wanted to be good Muslims, and not Mujahideen. The rest of the world didn't seem able to tell the difference, and the Chetniks didn't care what they wanted to be. If they weren't ready to try running away as hunted refugees, all they could do was to stand on their porches, nice old men, their wives in old frocks and sweaters, young men with only shovels against the Kalashnikovs of the Chetniks, and of course the young women, the girls, the most helpless. All they could do was stand there and be rounded up, and let the Chetniks do what they wanted to do.

It always started by knocking a few of the men around, and then by giving the women the chance to help their men by cooperating, and providing a little friendly entertainment for the troops. As soon as mother was spread on the table being stuffed like a plucked goose, then sister and daughter were taken too, and when sooner or later some husband or father objected loudly enough, balls were cut off, throats were slit, and men were shot. All of this that the Chetniks were doing should have been known was coming, and for whatever reason they refused to accept it, leaving their own fate in someone elses hands.

There were no secret objectives that were suddenly revealed, no awakenings for the unsuspected horror. Everybody suddenly understood what was happening but too late to be saved. Whatever had to be said to the news cameras, or to the parliaments, the courts, or the committees of the world, the truth was without question. This was an extermination, and sooner or later all of them would be beaten, rutted upon, shot, gassed, or gutted, until there were no more of them.

"Why was I the only one around there with a gun?" Pace asked. "I was permitted to be there only because I was just bringing milk for the children, and some medicines. But I ask you, what good is it to bring in milk to keep them alive, if they are only going to be rounded up by the Serbs and killed? The people talking about letting humanitarian aid past the embargo are hypocrites, just trying to make themselves look good while doing nothing, like people getting their picture taken throwing food over the walls into a concentration camp. Until somebody goes in there with enough guns to control the place, you're just keeping them from starving so they can be executed.

"It is a terrible fact of all human life, much as we would like to temper that fact with things like reason and compassion, that in the end the last word belongs to the guy who can kick the other guy's ass." That was where it all began for Pace. "We learn it on the playground at kindergarten," he said, "and it's true right up to the atom bomb. The last word is always the use of superior force. We hope that power belongs to somebody good, like the teacher who has the paddle and keeps order at recess, but somebody has to have it. In a situation like Bosnia, that power boils down to one thing."

I knew. "Guns," I said.

"Yes. To paraphrase Mao, survival issues from the barrel of a gun," he said. "These were not some strange science fiction movie places, they were people's neighborhoods, their farms, and communities. If those Bosnian farmers had been well armed, they would have had no trouble defending their homes together against the invading Serbs in Army uniforms, or against the marauding Chetnik packs."

He knew how I felt about the Chetniks, and how they operate, like packs of dogs who raid a farm at night, hitting in the dark, robbing, killing, and running, and always the raping, the raping.

Pace asked, "Why didn't the people such as yourself and people like you warn the people what was coming?"

I did, not only once, but every day for almost forty years. Every day I was called a traitor. I am finally redeeming myself from being any kind of bad guy in the eyes of my people that I still passionately love and tried to spare from the agony without being able to convince them of the danger. How could I convince any of them when I couldn't even convince my own father of the danger coming?

Even if the world had decided to move quickly to stop the Serbs in their genocide, the action they would have to have taken would be to send in troops who were armed better than the Chetniks and the Serb Army, and to have either kicked their asses or run them off. Then they could have taken the time to arm and train the local militia in how to defend themselves, and then they could have departed. Either way, the one single factor that actually made all the difference was who had the guns. Denying the Bosnians access to guns, when they were faced with guns, was simply being an accomplice to the crimes of Slobodan Milosevic. The United Nations were full participants in that.

I have carried a gun in the course of my colorful career in Las Vegas, and I have been in many situations where having the gun meant the difference between life and death. I am personally very aware that if someone takes my gun away from me, and I am in such a situation, then that person might as well have just shot me himself, as he has taken away the defense of my life. As a naturalized American patriot, I respect the wisdom of the Second Amendment. As a combat veteran, I know like Pace knows, that there is a point in any human conflict where there is no substitute for having the guns. Whatever the laws or the reporters or the churches happen to say, if you do not have the guns, then you put your women on the table, and you bow your head and kneel. That is no way for a man to have to protect his family. The Bosnian men found themselves with their pants down and no guns and that's all.

Pace showed me pictures he had taken standing in the middle of a beautiful long paved airport, apparently abandoned in the middle of a wide open area. "Look at this. This is Tuzla airport. This beautiful modern runway is only eight kilometers from where these people were being starved out and rounded up, and the UN was keeping it closed to all air traffic. If they were so humanitarian, all they had to do is just give permission for volunteer relief teams to use it. They wouldn't have to do anything else. We wouldn't be running a gauntlet line of tanks and bandits and Chetniks through the mountains trying to get a few truckloads of baby food into Tuzla." He looked like he wanted to hit something in frustration. "No. They said the airport couldn't be used because they couldn't guarantee the safety of airplanes landing there. To hell with that, just let us take our own chances. Angie, I know lots of guys, and lots of them are Vietnam veterans, who would fly hot missions in there in a second to run food and medicine to those people, if they weren't afraid of getting shot down by some UN hotdog in an F-16."

"Or one of Slobo's Mig-21's," I added.

"Yeah, it makes me wonder which side the F-16's are supposed to be on," he said, wryly.

I replied, "Maybe they are on the side of Butros Galli."

"What do you mean by that Angelo?"

I said, "Butros-Galli is Egyptian Orthodox, remember that, it means a Christian Orthodox, a Serb who would do anything to help Serbia get rid of the Bosnians as it is. Don't be surprised Pace, I'm not by what is happening."

He shrugged and said, "Sorry, I thought I knew everything."

The subject of the guns would come up again, and all too soon. I didn't know if there would ever be anything I could do to help the Bosnian people, my people. One thing that taught me for sure was watching the gallant Mormon warrior Giles Pace struggle to do something real and worthwhile for them, and to see his memory swallowed up by the chaos without a footnote for his heroism. I had decided that putting my time or any other resources into trying to get politicians or others to create more humanitarian aid was simply wasted energy. That was just fine to do, and bless the people who were doing that, but it was too clear to me that anything that could be done to really help the Bosnians would have to be directed toward getting them guns. Until they had guns, all of us who said we wanted to help them were just stroking ourselves.

CHAPTER EIGHT: A MEETING IN LAS VEGAS

Ken Breezy, a good friend of mine from Caesars Palace called me the night before to tell me he was back from Cancun, and he had brought a box of Cuban cigars. He said if I didn't come and have lunch with him, John Coletta and Reno Armani were going to take the all the cigars. I thought I should go because after all Cuban cigars are illegal here. You can't get them anywhere, but you can find plenty of them through friends if you want to. Believe me they are expensive too. I was ready to pay for them at lunch but they wouldn't even let me buy lunch or the cigars.

It's customary in Las Vegas for high management to be issued numbers on which to authorize any complimentary food, room, and beverage for certain guests as well as to use for themselves. I was always treated as one of the VIPs by them my friends. It was more of true friendship between us rather than just being one of the guests.

The guests that qualified for the comps were the high stakes players and such key customers. I was treated by that criteria since I was like a member of the family in our close circle, and which made my money practically no good in any of the hotels. I didn't really gamble at any games except when I got the occasional urge for baccarat. Then I would don my best suit and spend twenty-four hours at the table. It was great fun, but I'm happy to say not something I did too often or tried to make a living by. I was never really considered as a player but as a friend more than anything. That gave me a feeling of being important too, and respected by my friends there, especially by my good friend John Gallo, the casino manager then at Caesars Palace.

After lunch Kenny, the boys, and I enjoyed the fine Cuban cigars. He made sure that he brought a humidor box to ensure the cigars' freshness. He excitedly regaled us with tales of his short vacation at a San Lucas resort in Mexico. I reminded him that he had called me already to brag about what a good time he was having.

As close as friends that we considered one another to be to each other, we were walking with our arms around each other's shoulders. We walked out to the patio that overlooked the pool area. Caesars Palace didn't have just any ordinary pool area like just any ordinary hotel. It was truly a beautiful one of a kind pool area. The decor with Roman Rulers and the Greek goddesses statues and the pool and waterfalls themselves were absolutely breathtaking. The scene was a recreation to bring about a feeling like no other. You could easily feel like you were at the Victoria Falls in Africa or any other majestically beautiful places around the world.

The Primavera restaurant overlooked the entire poolside area with a great view and with the tables for outdoor dining. One could easily imagine just how it must have been in the actual times of Julius Caesar and his palace. There was no other place like it with a replica of the original Spanish Stairs in Rome. Each time that I dined at the Primavera it took me back to Rome and this day was no different and I felt like I was running around the collisium in Rome like I had in the early sixties. This day was even better walking with my friends Kenny, John, and Reno. The décor, pillars, columns, genuine marble stone statues, and architecture all reflected the history and power of Rome before and during Caesar's reign when he had ruled from the coasts of Dalmatia and northern Italy with the many statues of the gods and goddesses.

I have always found the faces of the Roman emporers fascinating, especially the one of Emperor Nero. He was a drama player in Roman times, and he became an emperor to be respected and feared, athough he had previously been known as an actor which was then considered a frivolous occupation. Nero was capable of wearing many different faces. Perhaps that is what has fascinated people over time, especially him and Julius Caesar and Augustus.

Every time I visited Caesars Palace to have lunch with my friends it was always at my favorite place, the Primavera. The Roman artwork was engraved into the high cathedral ceilings. It always gave me a trip down memory lane to my favorite city of all time, Rome. The statue of Nero was one of the many statues that added to the ambience of the room. It became habit for me after the many times I dined there that when we were sitting at the prime table that was private and secluded, and was always reserved for us with the statue of Nero that was right next to our table looking almost as if he was guardian of our table. Given his reputation one could easily think he was. Our table had a house phone that was always available for our use with a long cord so you could be free to walk around as you talked. At that time there were no cordless phones. I started finding myself whenever I was talking on that phone starting to gently rub Nero's nose and wipe his eyes on his statue and almost combing and brushing at his stone hair with my hand. I realized later that my hand was full of dust. As I talked on the phone I would also speak a few words to Nero telling him we need to do something about the dust on him.

My friends found that a little strange. Once they asked me why I did that, and why I was talking to him when I did that. I told them he was my favorite emperor and a man of great wisdom and maybe he would share some of it with me. I thought it might come in very handy. Reno laughed. Of course John and Kenny weren't much help to my cause. Nero was not the kind of emperor that you could go home and brag to mom and dad about. He was ruthless but wasn't capable of understanding just how ruthless he was. As much as that was his own fault it was also as much the fault of the Roman senate and the people closest around him. When you are holding so much power in your hands you need someone to help you distribute it evenly. He had no help to do that. I think in that he was not entirely to blame.

I purposely made it my habit never leave the Primavera without making sure to visit the statue now for the benefit of my friends, especially Kenny and Reno. I would rub his nose, wipe his brow and rub the hair on his head with my hands. I asked him, "How is it that you managed to live two thousand years? Could you share some of your wisdom with me? Is it just from one's will and determination and because he wishes to be remembered and to leave something behind or is everything just coincidence? Perhaps it was both."

On this particular occasion I wasn't standing by Nero alone. I didn't realize that Reno had been standing next to me while I was performing my non-sacred ritual. Guess who had sent him over. It was Ken Breezy, who was the capo and director of operations for Caesars for the past twenty-seven years. He was dying to know what kind of ritual I performed with my friend Nero. He asked me before what the hell I had been doing over by the statue and I replied, "I'm not telling you Kenny, I'm just admiring an old man."

Ken said, "You were talking to that statue, I saw you."

I laughingly said, "What are you trying to do, trying to make me look crazy or something? At least I'm not talking to myself. Maybe you should go talk to him because I think he'll answer you too."

"No, no, please. I was just curious and if I didn't know you any better I would think that you were talking to yourself."

"Of course I wasn't. How could I? I was standing right next the man."

I patted Kenny on the back so hard on purpose that it made him almost cough. I told him, "Not yet Kenny, don't worry. I, your friend Angelo, am pretty healthy and sane."

This time he sent Reno over thinking that he could really find out what the hell I was really doing by that statue of the Emperor Nero. Of course I had the phone in my hand every time. Now I was starting to think Kenny was jealous beacause he couldn't get Nero to talk with him. Maybe when he tried Nero ignored him because he wasn't a full blooded Italian and half Irish. I asked Kenny before he left as a joke, "Are there any bad feelings between you and the Emperor Nero? It looks like he not going to talk to you."

I said to Reno jokingly, "Can you imagine, poor Nero has had to look at this half Italian and Irish boy Kenny every day for twenty-seven years, six days a week, ten hours a day. Almost anyone would get tired of that except for his beautiful and respectful mother who gave birth to the old man who I call my friend and truly and deeply have alot of respect for. Reno was standing beside me watching me talking to Nero while I was gently touching his face. I told my friend Reno that it seemed like I was the only one that ever cleaned the statue up. There was always dust on him and I wanted him to be clean. As I was wiping under his eyes I said to Nero, "I must figure out how that I can live as long as you did." Since Reno was standing there I laughed holding my ear up to Nero like he had answered me and I said, "You mean to tell me I will become famous for sure?"

Reno laughed and said, "You're just plain crazy."

I told him, "Reno please don't interrupt. Can't you see I'm having a conversation with the emperor?"

He shook his head and walked back the few steps to our table and started cursing Kenny. "You and your big mouth Kenny, you just can't leave things alone."

Reno told him, "Damn you Kenny! You set me up with that crazy guy over there to make me look like a fool. Why don't you go talk to him?" Kenny brushed him off, shaking with the effort of trying not to laugh. John laughed with tears coming to his eyes.

When I finished my talk with Nero I returned to the table and I couldn't help thinking on what Nero's influence did and how it touches us today.

Reno seemed clearly touched and almost emotional from the attention I always gave to Nero's and also the rest of the statues. I think it was because of his own heritage, he is a proud American-

Italian boy. I wanted to break his trance he seemed to be in so I asked him, "Reno since you are the president of this hotel, why don't you tell the maintenance to pay more attention to the statues? Forgive me, I don't mean to intrude in your business but they do look sad from not being cleaned."

Reno said, "Jesus, Angelo, you are making me sad and feeling guilty by talking like that. Did you hear yourself talking to Nero?"

"Of course I did and I know exactly what I said, but you should be talking to him as well as the two others next to him, Augustus and Caesar. You're the one making a pretty damn good living off them."

"Angie now your really pushing it."

Kenny started to leave the table saying, "It's getting hot in here."

I stayed sitting so he couldn't get up to leave.

John said, "Now don't push him Angie, you might start to piss him off."

"I meant every word I said and my conscience is very clear too," I told him.

Reno said, "Damn, Angie, I was starting to get too emotional for a moment and you were pissing me off but you are absolutely right.."

I said, "You should have noticed, he was your emperor as well just as much as mine."

Reno said, "You don't believe in that reincarnation stuff, do you man? You're starting to freak me out."

"No, Reno, I don't believe in that, that's for sure. I do believe in the trees that bear fruit every spring. You can figure out the rest of it."

Reno asked, "You mean to tell me that Nero might be my great, great, great, great, grandfather?"

I said, "Maybe. Why not? You do look like him."

We laughed and to my surprise Reno reached over and picked up the phone to ask for the superintendent of casino maintenance. In a matter of moments the lady who was in charge of that department appeared at our table. She said, "Mr. Reno, what is it I can I do for you sir?"

He stood up and said, "It's nice seeing you, Helen," and then shook her hand holding on to it. He said, "Helen it is not I that needs something." He pointed over to where the statues were, walking her over to the statue of Nero. He gently put his hand on the head of Nero as he spoke with Helen while alternately looking at her and at the statue.

She nodded her head as he was talking and then he finally released her hand as she promised to promptly take care of what needed to be done. On her way out she said, "Goodbye, and I'm sorry I had to interrupt you boys."

I still wasn't about to let Reno off the hook yet. I was paying close attention to what he was doing. I said Reno, "You've been discriminating against our ancestors. You forgot about the care of all of Nero's friends and rivals that are here also."

"Oh shut up, Angelo. You're starting to make me think like you now." He shouted across at the bartender, "Luigi! Could you please bring another round of espressos here?"

"Yes, sir! I would glad to." In a few moments we all had double espressos with shots of black Sambuca with the two coffee beans in them.

Reno said, "By the way, where in the hell is our lunch?" He turned to grab the phone again. I heard the operator say, "Yes Reno, how can I help you?"

He had a funny way to introduce himself. Even though everyone knew his voice he still liked to show his clout and so would announce himself every time by saying, "This is your president and director, Reno. I forgot to tell Helen," he continued, "All of the statues and not just the one of Nero must be cleaned every morning when maintaince comes in." He thanked her and hung up. "You see Angelo, what I have to work with? Even the operator thinks that we once went to first grade together."

I said, "Don't worry Reno. You show your authority and they know who's boss. John and Kenny do anyway and they better if they want to eat and get their next paychecks." I thought maybe that was a little low but I didn't elaborate.

He looked at Kenny and John and then at me for a sign of approval from us for a job well done and trying to flex his authority some. He puffed out his chest from the satisfaction that he was feeling having just doing something that was really important.

I could tell people around us were looking at us curioiusly which happened many times before. They probably thought we were lucky people without any worries in the world who ran the gambling casinos like a gang of mobsters wearing thousand dollar suits, getting doted on by royal service and attention. We could have been in any scene of a worry free great movie.

Ken finally had the chance to ask Reno what the hell was going on here. He said, "I thought that you were going over and spy for me to find out what this crazy guy Angie here is doing over there talking to that statue day in and day out. Then there you are talking to that damn statue. What the Hell is going on here? Is that statue alive or something? Could somebody fill me in on all this?" He furiously puffed on his cigar. He bellowed, "Chef, where is that lunch?" The waiter had been standing and waiting for us to settle down so he could serve us. I wonder what he must think everytime he would see us coming. But after all he always ended up with a generous tip."

"No Kenny, nobody's not going to tell you anything," Reno replied. "Ireland wasn't under the Roman Empire, so Nero probably won't be talking to you anytime soon."

"Well I hope so. I look forward to hopefully growing old so I'll have plenty of time." He puffed out his chest and said, "My mother is a Sicilian so that should qualify me."

Reno brushed the air with his hand and put his fingers to his lips. "Shhhhh. I heard the Sicilians were decendants from Egypt and Spain."

That didn't sit too well with Kenny. "If it wasn't for Sicilians the rest of the Italians wouldn't be in America with their mobster reputations."

"We really thank you Kenny and have a lot of gratitude."

I said, "Oh John, I think this is the final straw between Kenny and Reno but I hope they can reconcile their differences."

Then Reno said, "Can I have a cigar please?"

Kenny was pleased to oblige and all was forgotten for that moment.

We were all enjoying our cigars, but Kenny just couldn't let it go at that. He looked over to Colletta and asked, "Did you notice when these two guys were over there talking to that statue?"

Reno told him, "Shhh, Kenny! Don't say that too loud. Can't you see all the people in this restaurant looking at us like we're a bunch of crazy mobsters? They'll decide to eat at the buffet tomorrow instead if they think we may be here again. We shouldn't scare people by having conversations like this."

We all laughed and Reno finally closed the conversation by proudly announcing, "Gentlemen from now on my ancestor's face and his pals will be shined every morning with tender care." We all applauded for success finally.

Many of the breakfasts and lunches I've had over the years with my friends always ended up to cost me much more than if I had just picked up the tab instead of being comped. There were three us that morning and I left a big bill for each one of us. You knew you were the talk of the town with that kind of tipping but money wasn't really an object.

I never dreamed my life would become so profoundly enriched in every way with every day. I picture the prosperity I was experiencing during the time of this fast moving good life as something similar to the same kind of feelings of someone who was unprepared for a sudden severe thunderstorm with heavy rains, flooded streets and water running out of control in all directions. It was a rush but was not intimidating, in fact I liked it and it made me feel like somebody successful and deserving of all the new experiences both materially and in my friends.

In the good old days in Las Vegas it seemed everyone had a share of the pot of money and money was everywhere. I wouldn't say everyone was making an equal share but everyone was doing pretty well. In those days there were no lower, middle or upper classes. Everyone seemed to be living the high life. It was a state within a state with special privileges having pure silver coins in circulation as currency found only in Nevada and nowhere else in the entire world. With my income I could afford the most expensive clothing I could find, fast cars, living in a hotel most of the year, the beautiful girls around me, and didn't have to be shy wining and dining my friends all the time. I found my softest spot was the girls and there was no shortage of them. Vegas was the place to be for that. Looking back now I feel am a very lucky man. I got to do it all my own way and enjoyed it very much.

Along with my business in Las Vegas I needed to travel to faraway places many times and I flew around the world. I went to Zurich, Hong Kong, Kuala Lumpur in Malaysia, Bali, Sydney Australia, the East Indies in South America, the Bahamas and many more places all over the globe. My business with immigration took me to all these places and I had a blast meeting people, some I had never dreamed of meeting but at the same time I got the opportunity to change the lives of many people for the better. I could truly say the experience was a dream come true for me. When I was a boy growing up in the communist era the chances of experiencing gestures of generosity from anyone was zero to none. Now for me to be able to help others through my job was a great feeling.

A special place that I had really wanted to go to and did get to go to with my friend Elliot, was Dhaka Bangladesh. We first flew into New Delhi, India and spent four days there. From there we flew to what was once called East Pakistan, now called Dhaka Bangladesh. We spent a few days meeting with a few people on immigration business and then we boarded a 747 Pan Am jumbo jet headed to Islamabad, Pakistan. We spent a few days in the capitol and again it was only for a very short time. We drove south to the coast of the Arabian Sea to the hustling, bustling city of Karachi. We chose to take the drive on the banks of the Indus River that was a fantastic experience.

Our driver was an awesome host even for the very little money he charged. The driver wasn't just a driver but with no doubt also an educated historian and for whatever reasons he was a taxi driver.I thought that was his own business. We found ourselves to be having the experience of our lifetimes. We traveled many places, towns and villiages that were close to highways. We went to the places that European man came from and also a place one of the best leaders from that period was born who ruled over the then known world many millinuems ago. His and his forefathers empire stretched from the banks of the Indus River to the shores of the Danube River and the Black Sea. Driving along the banks of the river I reflected that throughout all of history perhaps they are our forefathers. It was an awesome empire and was the land of Cyrus the Great, his fathers, forefathers, and the generations of kings after him.

The traveling I did then gave me greater appreciation for the world surrounding me and more of a hands on experience of knowledge than I could ever buy for any amount of money. However much money it would have cost me if I had to pay for those experiences I know it wouldn't be possible.

I am lucky to have had the experiences and helped so many intellectuals at the same time to come to this country. I understand that the street really does go two ways. America did need their skills and they also needed America to be able to have better lives. I saw it as being a win-win situation. Now as I try to put this chapter of history onto pages, my country of America twenty years later has again found herself in crisis with ten million immigrants and the leadership of this country not having a clue of how valuable these people can be for our country. They have forgotten that we are all children of immigrants except for the ones we called savages, unfortunately, but I respectfully call my brothers and my fellow man. They are the only ones that you never hear complaining. Perhaps they still are connected to the land and the earth as much as their forefathers were.

The people that I met in Karachi were skilled and intelligent. That's something that the United States could use very much. I helped to bring it about as I had done before. Of course it is worth mentioning that the immigration program was approved by Congress and the Senate of the U.S. a few years earlier. It took a little time for the program to catch up to the masses. I and many others who were like me were the ones filling the spaces and the final gaps for the program to work. I had one goal and that was to fulfill my obligations for the program that was approved by Congress. The able, skillful, and highly educated in all fields were the ones I sought to bring into the states. Each time I met with these intellectuals or groups of intellectuals I tried to help them understand about what they would find and might expect of their new life in America and picture what it would be like and how their lives would be different. I really wanted to pave an American road to freedom for them so they might not have too much of a culture shock when they arrived in the states. I wanted to help the transition be easier for them and most importantly to understand they would have the precious freedom that they really had never known before. I tried by personally relating my own experience to them.

This unique group of intellectuals were anxious and excited about traveling but also a little scared even being grown men yet for all of them it was their first time away from home. As one by the name of Amir said to me, "I am going in search for a piece of bread and a roof over my head on the other side of the world."

I replied, "Amir my friend, if I may call you my friend, only in the states will you get that loaf of bread on the table and that roof over your head and that precious freedom you have never experienced here in Pakistan although it is a democratic nation but far from comparison to the states. Perhaps after you leave you will never want to return to

Pakistan like the rest of the two hundred and fifty million immigrants who came to America and never returned to their forefathers homelands."

Amir gave me an hug filled with emotion and he said, "I hope you are right."

I responded feeling the emotions and patted him on the back and said, "I'm sure what happened to me will also happen to you and that is having a good life with prosperity." I had accomplished my mission and they did get to come to the states.

They are the very people today who are doing the kind of work such as that of an ordinary kindergarten teacher, or the scientist who makes it possible for space shuttles and the lunar satellites to travel beyond our planet and into space. The very people that I worked with in coming to this country have become productive citizens and guardians of society. I can proudly and humbly say that I am gratified by what I have tried to contribute to my adopted homeland. This reflection of my experience has given me more leverage with my friends like Reno, Kenny, John, Jimmy Paxton and many others besides of course, friends like Pace and Peter. It is a great feeling to be looked up to and respected.

As we lunched at Primavera the waiter came over to our table with a phone and plugged it in the wall. He said politely, "Mr. Angelo, there's a call for you from a man who says he is a friend of yours calling from Zurich, Switzerland." I knew right off it was Peter on the line.

"Hello, Angelo!" he brayed.

"Well, hello Peter!"

"Listen Angelo I hope you have a few minutes, there is something very important I want to tell you about."

"Go ahead, you have my full attention Peter."

The next thing out of his mouth was it's about Alija, a gun runner from Bosnia and the former chief of police, the type Peter loved to hang out. "I know already about what your new venture is about Peter, with the notorious illiterate former chief of police," I thought to myself without saying anything, because I wanted to hear Peter confirm what I already knew.

Peter continued talking, "He is a great guy. You've got to meet him. He's running semi-trucks full of guns to Bosnia from Austria and Slovenia and through Croatia, and is making tons of money."

I replied to Peter, "He must have one hell of a connection to be traveling through three different countries without any problems and no one asking questions. He must be greasing a lot of palms with no doubt, that would be the only way he could reach Bosnia with the guns. Unfortunately they aren't going to the Bosnians but the Ustashas and the Chetniks. The Bosnian people are paying with their lives so that Alija can get rich. Don't you think that you should rather be taking the guns to the Bosnian fighters so the people can defend their families rather than selling them to the Chetniks and Croats for a profit?" I asked Peter.

Peter laughed sarcastically when I told him Alija was getting rich from the blood of our people and he would have to answer in the end for his dirty deeds. He interupted me saying, "This is just business, Angie, and we got a big deal in the works." He said that his friend Alija made this fantastic deal with the Chinese government in the South China Sea on the island of Hainan for building a dam to generate electricity.

I asked him, "To generate electricity for whom? Don't you know that island is totally unpopulated? It is a beautiful island, there is no doubt about that but nobody lives on it except the Chinese military and their families. It's not because it's an unhabitable island but just because the Chinese never considered the island as a place to live. Why would you want to build an electrical plant there? I am familiar with that particular island and that area. Someone's conning you in this project and making you look very very stupid."

Peter replied angrily, "How do you know all this?"

"First of all there is no major river or lake on the island to supply the it for the kind of project you're talking about."

"Angelo, I guess you are just too damn smart. We can build the plant with the help of Alija's money."

I answered, "You mean with the blood of Bosnian children as money. Maybe the Chinese governer will allow you and Alija and guys like you to move there. That would be more productive because it would get your kind off the streets and the world would be a much safer place."

Peter blew up. He said, "I love you, Angelo, and you're my best friend. I would never talk to you with such disrespect. I have done nothing wrong. Please just hear me out."

I told him, "Would you get to the point, I'm in the middle of my lunch." I knew there were small towns and villages throughout that island but overall there was nothing spectacular about it except for some beautiful sandy beachs. I told him,. "I don't see any of the two billion Chinese people stampeding over each other trying to move to that island. It's not far from the major populations of Hong Kong, Hanoi, Vietnam, or the city of Nanxing and even though it is surrounded by all those metropolitan cities it's still a world away real civilization. The biggest activity on the island is the Chinese Air Force and their little primitive base with a bunch of primitive airplanes like the Mig-17 and Mig-21. Coincidentally, just recently one of those Chinese Migs collided with a U.S. A-11. The Chinese pilot died and the U.S. plane crashed almost right into the Chinese military base. Had you heard about that Peter?"

"No, I never heard about it but the whole damn world knows about it," he replied smartly.

I said, "Well, I guess we could consider that as an exciting thing that happened on that island since its creation. Now you are going to go and build a dam to produce electricity. That's great news. I think you're being conned."

"I'm telling you," he replied. "I have his power of attorney Alija gave to me from his bank in my hands right now that gives me the right to negotiate any deal with anyone regarding any business ventures or building projects such as this power plant."

"Peter," I said, "Either you are conning Alija or the Chinese people are conning both of you. Why you just bring it to Las Vegas and we'll build a strip joint and we could call it the Cheyenne Club."

"Quit being such a wise guy Angelo. You could have built a club like that years ago but you didn't want to."

"But really on a serious note Peter, let me remind you that just recently people from around the world scraped their pennies together to donate to the Bosnian government for buying food, clothing, medicines and perhaps some guns to protect them from being butchered by their enemies. You're telling me your friend Alija has enough money to go build a power plant on the island of Hainan on the South China Sea? If that's the truth and has any basis at all then Alija must be out of his freaking mind. He should spend that money to save lives in Bosnia since we both now Bosnia is about to anihilated. I hoped and thought you were smarter than that but at the same time I know you are a shrewd businessman and a barracuda. You sink your teeth in if you get the chance in anything that will brings some flavor to your mouth, but I think that this time you've been taken and played for a fool. Alija seems like he is smart and dangerous but what he wants from guys like you is to help keep him alive by stringing you along with funny deals that are unattainable like this so that when a real opportunity comes for a deal he will be the only one who benefits from it. When that kind of deal materalizes you will get left out, that's for sure. Like all the guns he's been running, have you made any money off that?"

He was silent for a moment and said, "Well, no, not yet."

"See there you are. I always thought you were smarter than that, obviously you're not."

Peter was pissed off at me by my painting a clear picture of Aljia to him but he managed to keep himself in check because he knew I wouldn't take any crap from him and since we were thousands of miles away across the ocean on the phone all I had to do was hang up on him. I wasn't convinced about anything he had told me. "Angelo, I'll fax you that power of attorney if you don't believe me. I'm telling you this guy has a lot of money."

He was good on his word at least on that issue and he had faxed it to me later that day and when I came home the document was there alright. It did look legitimate. A day later I received a call from Peter, who wanted to know what I had thought about the document. He was happy to hear that I believed that the power of attorney was genuine. I did want to know more about this shady character friend of his than what I already knew of him of which none of it was good. What I knew of him and what he had done was that he betrayed my ancestors' people and had made himself wealthy on the blood of my Bosnian brothers and sisters.

People in Bosnia were desperate for help while Alija was living a life of luxury in Luzano and Zurich. I questioned Peter on how Alija was able to aquire six to nine semi tractor trailor trucks that each cost at least three hundred thousand or more. Somebody before the war that was important and very rich had to have been paying for that to set Alija up now to be doing all of this. There had to be other parties involved either indirectly or directly using Alija as their front man. That was my thoughts.

Peter elaborated a little more by telling me about a close friend of Alija's who was a former soccer player in Croatia that happened to be the brother of the Minister of Defense in Croatia, Mr.Ramljak. Peter said, "Someone within the Bosnian presidency could be backing Aljia, but I'm not sure just who."

I told him if Aljia is a friend of Ramljak's then he certainly hasn't any blessings from the Bosnian government since the territory where he is selling guns is not controlled by Bosnian federal forces but the Croatian militia, specifically ones like Mata's under the control of Ramljak. I asked Peter if Fikret Avdich might have some connection with Ramljak and Alija and they if they were all in cahoots.

"No we're not. Fikret is the one with the real connections."

"Who? Peter I'm dying to know."

"OK Angie, it's Slobo and Belgrade who are his backers."

"It's a sad day for Bosnia and the Bosnian people, Peter. Fikret betrayed everything that we as the Bosnian people believed in and that was to be as one people and one nation. He broke the bond of trust by betraying us, walking away from us to join the enemy along with his men. This will always be remembered as one of the saddest chapters in Bosnian history, to betray his own for his own very personal benefits."

"I'm sorry Angelo. I didn't mean to give you any bad news."

"That's alright Peter, I've learned to absorb such news already and this too shall pass hopefully without rememberance."

I suggested to Peter that when he got back to Croatia that he do some research on these characters and how they really got to be where they are. Mostly I wanted him to find out who all the backers were. I told him I would appreciate it if he would do that and I would pay back the favor like I always do. I said, "After you find out all of that for me, I have an idea that could fill your lifetime dreams and get you very rich, Peter. It does seems like those people you are dealing with have a lot of money. They should be sharing some of it and I know a way to make them share. I'll leave you on that note, Peter. I hope you will ponder over these important matters that we've talked over and we'll talk again sometime by the end of next week." I went home hungry because by the time I finished with Peter my food had gotten cold and I hadn't even realized my friends had already left and I was alone at the table.

A week later on Sunday afternoon, I paid a visit to dear friends of mine, the president of the Riveria Hotel, George Maxson, and Jimmy Paxton, the executive of casino operations there. Over the years we have all always been there for one another.

We were having a late lunch in one of the Riveria's restaurants, the famously known Del Monico's. Since my friends, Jimmy and George were executives of the hotel it was only the smart thing to do and to take advantage of the privleges of their so-called comps of R, F and B, which stands for room, food and beverage. The privilege, however, always seemed to cost me much more because of my generous tipping than if I were just an ordinary paying customer. They both knew I loved them as true friends. The word "can't" did not exist in their vocabularies. I am very fortunate to have friends such as them.

It wasn't unusual for the house phone to ring quite a few times at our table during our meal because all the awesome responsibilities Jimmy and George had in the gaming and hotel operations of the entire property of the Rivera. Their average take in revenue would always be an awesome amount, perhaps a million or more. Obviously George and Jimmy had highly responsible and professional jobs to do. They received calls at all times from many departments, yet they always seemed to find time for me. After already having numerous interuptions, this time when the phone rang Jimmy looked at me with a gesture of his face and said, "This time it's for you, Mister."

I asked him to ask who was calling.

So Jimmy said into the phone, "Hold on Nancy, and let me ask him if he wants to take the call?" It was Peter who was holding on the other end of the line. Jimmy replied, "Angie, here, you talk to the operator."

I said, "OK, I'm always looking for some excuse to talk to Nancy the operator anyway."

"Angelo, honey," she said, she was always a little flirtatious, "There's a guy who says that has been calling and paging you all over town trying to find you. Do you want to talk to him, honey? He says his name is Peter."

"I'd rather talk to you but go ahead and put him through, Nancy." We laughed together.

"He says he is calling from Zurich."

"Oh great, I've been expecting him to call. Please go ahead and put him through. By the way Nancy do you like the flowers?"

She said surprised, "Are you the one who sent those flowers, Angie? I'm gonna kill you!"

George was laughing from across the table and said, "Don't

253

worry," as he dug out ten dollars to tip the bus boy for bringing him a bottle of water, "Angie didn't pay for the flowers."

"Just shut up, George. Can't you see I'm trying to score some points here? You just blew my cover."

Nancy ignored George's wise cracks and said, "I'll see you at six after work," and then she put Peter through.

When I answered the phone it was the same old Peter all right, the one who won't let you get a word in until his mouth got too tired. I tried in vain a few times to slow him down by saying, "Peter, Peter, slow down," but without having any success. I kept on listening with my hand over the reciever so that I could still talk to George and Jimmy until Peter was finally finished talking and thought maybe I was no longer be on the line.

Finally he said, "Angie are you there? Are you listening?"

I answered, "Yes Peter, I'm here."

He said, "You have to come to Zurich. I have a plan." That caught my attention and that's all I remembered about much of his supersonic talk.

"What's it all about Peter?" I asked. "What is so urgent that I need to come right away? You were just here anyway."

"Angelo I have two projects in mind."

"What are they Peter?"

"In a few weeks a transaction will be made and I'll be working for the people that are doing this transaction."

"I'm listening and you have my full attention. Who are the people, and what transactions are you talking about, Peter?" I asked.

Peter replied, "The people involved are retired NATO Generals who are very powerful and influential. One is from Scotland, one from Frankfurt, and one from Lozano."

I said, "Peter, if two of them are NATO's and one is from Switzerland, then he couldn't be a NATO General."

"All right, all right, Angelo, so I got confused. Anyway these people claim they are providing nuclear triggers for Pakistan."

I was already aware as well as the rest of the world that Pakistan was trying to enhance their nuclear program. I told him, "Peter, I hate to sound ignorant but I really don't want to comment on it. I am aware through the newspapers and media of Pakistan's interest and their desire for a nuclear program. I am really not comfortable in how little knowledge if any, that I have on the science of the nuclear field and it's hardware, triggers and devices that you're trying to tell me about but am willing to learn if your able to teach me anything about it."

"Don't be a wiseguy Angelo."

"I apoligize Peter, you have sparked my curiosty however and you've got all of my attention. Please don't think that I'm saying your lying, Pete, but I'm not so sure about all of this that you're telling me."

"Listen, man," Peter responded. "I have no reason to lie to you, and I'd never lie to you. Have I ever lied to you in all the years I have known you?"

"Why should you, Peter. I keep the red carpet under your feet at all times. Why should you lie to me? You would have too much to lose. You know that you are on an open phone line right now and anyone could be listening in on about what you have been talking about,. That would be considered treason, trying to sell nuclear triggers to a country that everyone is trying to stop from having them. You and those retired NATO generals are trying to sell to them. That's a violation of international and any state laws of any country you are a citizen of and is asking for big trouble. So tell me where do I fit into this transaction?"

"Your buddy Alija is going to be coming to Zurich," he said.

"Listen Peter, you got it all wrong. He is no buddy of mine and this is getting too personal. I'm here right now having lunch with my friends and they're starting to look at me like I might be some kind of a lunatic or something, talking about nuclear triggers and crap. This conversation right now isn't productive or professional. Why don't I call you when I get home? Until then you'll have plenty of time to digest everything and put it into better perspective. In the meantime I'm going to enjoy lunch with my friends and their company. Pakistan can wait for their nuclear chase and hopefully it will be used for peaceful purposes as well although I think they just want to counter with India's nuclear arsenal. That is a dangerous endeavor. "

"OK, Angie, but I didn't like your wise remark about that red carpet though."

I said, "What's the matter, you asshole? Are you blind, haven't you seen it yet? I think somehow and somewhere you're missing the point of what true friendship is about and far I've gone to extend mine to you. Well, goodbye Peter. We'll talk again tonight"

When I returned home it was about seven thirty in the evening.

I hadn't really thought much about my conversation with Peter. It didn't make much sense to me and I know Peter is sometimes a dreamer who likes to exaggerate things. Something suddenly flashed into my mind. Just a year before I was in Pheonix Arizona and this young man named Shoka whom I liked a lot and I had lunch at a restaurant in Tempe that he worked at on Mill Avenue in the American West building called Frescotti soon after I had arrived in Phoenix. The restaurant served truly fine Italian cuisine, with good food, wine and women staying in your memories. The friendship that I had with this young man had really started through our fathers friendship. When we finished lunch he took me on a ride through Pheonix, the Tempe area, and Scottsdale. The next thing we knew we were sitting in front of the headquarters of the Motorola company. I owned one of their very first giant telephones. To my surprise he asked, "Angie, do you know why I brought you here? There is a Pakistani general here in town and he's looking for a connection inside Motorola to be able to buy the advanced computer software that they make. I think you may be able to help out."

My temper flared, "You stupid kid! Don't you know what you're saying? Our country is practically in no diplomatic relations with Pakistan right now . We are holding one hundred of their F-16 jet fighters that they paid for and we are not delivering them to them for the exact same reasons you are talking about. You stay away from that general if you don't want to find yourself in a place you'll regret." He didn't like my tone and getting in his face. I was kind of hostile toward his suggestions to me. I don't think he understood the importance of it although he did tell me he would take my advice and not see the Pakistani general who was asking about a connection with Motorola. After that lunch I never did hear from him again.

This incident along with the conversation I had with Peter seemed to be connecting somehow now to make some kind of sense. Now I realized Peter's conversation was more serious than I thought and my meeting with Shoka at the Frescotti Restaurant that day, I could really see now that Pakistan was really looking to inquire and advance their nuclear technology. They were eventually successful by their persistance which paid off for them even without the help of Motorola in Pheonix.

Shoka was just an honest and hard working young man without any experience in any kind of diplomatic or political fields, especially

256

spying, and I didn't want him getting hurt or be a help to threatening our national security at the same time. He was nothing like my friend Peter who was seasoned and capable of wrongdoing in almost every way.

That night when I got home from the Rivera, that puzzle surely started coming together to me and Peter was credible in what he talked about earlier. I was so deep in thought that I didn't take the time for my usual habit that my culture requires. It is our custom to remove our shoes at the entrance to the house and put them in their proper place in the shoe closet at the entrance of the hallway. I walked all the way to the bedroom without removing my shoes. I needed to say hello to my wife and hug her and to see my little baby girl. I wanted to say hello, kiss her and play with her but then my wife reminded me about my shoes. I said, "Never mind about the shoes," and hugged and kissed them.

The phone rang while I was talking my pet language to my little girl. My wife answered and brought me the phone saying it was Peter on the line.

I was anxious to hear the details of his story but not the usual exaggerations of his, all I wanted was the plain facts now so I could connect any links between his story and what happened in Pheonix and then determine how real his story was real or not. I looked for a comfortable place to sit down. I was already tired of hearing Peter's talk although I knew it was not a waste of my time but in the back of mind I really felt like telling him off. I thought better of it and held back because I knew I may need to keep check on what Peter may be up to especially considering his Serbian patriotism. I needed to make sure I kept him on a tight leash that I was holding on the other end of in case I had to, like the old saying to keep the enemy in sight so that you know what he is doing. Peter was not really a friend anymore nor an enemy just a guy of some interest at this moment.

If keeping informed through him perhaps would enable me to save even one child's life in Bosnia or help prevent any nuclear disaster between India and Pakistan it would be worthwhile and then I would deal with Peter. Neither in Pakistan or Bosnia however could I claim any title for success except to perhaps save any life of an American soldier, that after all is what I was working hard at doing.

My wife handed me the phone and before I could even say hello he started talking loudly, "Angie, are you there? Are you there?"

I said, "I am here Peter, and don't worry because I'm sitting down in case you want to drop any more surprise bombs on me. How are you?"

"I'm fine," he replied. "I have decided I won't tell you anything more on the phone." Before I had a chance to ask why not he said, I'm just going to come there and pick you up."

I said, "Now I'm glad I am sitting down. This must be the real deal and not one of your hallucinations. I've been analyzing your story and you seem to be for real this time."

"Trust me, I am. I'm always for real, you asshole, you just never take me seriously."

I said, "You want to apologize to me now for calling me an asshole or later when you get here so you'll be able to kneel down when you do it?"

"I apologize."

"I accept. Where are going to be going, Peter?"

"I'm be there there to pick you up in Las Vegas."

"Peter, right now we are going nowhere, get to the point, you seem like you're out of your freaking mind. What is wrong with you? You sound like your choking and gagging on your own words. You don't sound like you're OK."

"Angie I think you are getting too smart for your own good." he growled. "Where are you learning all those smart English words?"

"Since you left Las Vegas I moved into the community college. I ate and slept and studied English so that when you called me I could show off to you my fancy command of American English. I was always better at English than you were anyway, Peter. You only have one advantage over me and it's very insignificant."

"What is that, Angelo?" he asked almost triumphantly, eager to hear what that was. "I am listening."

"Are you sure you want to hear it? " I asked.

"Yea I'm sure."

I said, "All right if you wish to hear the truth about yourself, fine but remember the truth always hurts." I whispered into the phone slowly, "I hope you are sitting down. The truth is you have a body of a Canadian moose but the brain of a Venecian pigeon."

He yelled, really ticked off, "You son of a bitch you! I hope that was some kind of a joke, but I know it wasn't."

"Come on, you know I'm only kidding but it's still the truth but

I have never held it against you. With a big skull like that you must have a brain in there somewhere and believe me you have proven it to me before. You can think when you're in a tight spot. Don't worry, I really wasn't insulting you."

"If that is not an insult, you must think that you are pretty damn smart then," he said.

Another thing that I said to Peter is, "When you and your generals are done running around trying to get your nuclear deal together for Pakistan, I think all the while it could be that they are just using you for decoys. In this kind of transaction I think money is not the object, Peter. When will you be flying in to Vegas?" I asked.

He said, "I will be leaving here in six hours and be in Las Vegas in about twelve hours from then. I be flying into Cincinnati and change planes for the flight to Las Vegas on United. You can pick me up Tuesday morning at ten. I will call you from Cincinnati and let you know what my flight number is."

The next day I went to McCarren airport to pick up Peter. When I spotted him he looked so excited like he was a newlywed groom instead of the same Peter I was used to. He couldn't wait to start talking. I thought he must have something important he was busting to tell me.

We shook hands and hugged and slapped each other on the shoulder and back. Then something very unusual happened. In all the years that I've known Peter he always slapped me hard on the back and squeezed me hard with a bear hug to show me he was strong he was but his handshake had always been weak. This time he kissed me on my checks in the traditional way of acknowledging true friendship. I was almost blown away. For a second he thought he would propose. When I squeezed his hand firmly which was they way of my handshake, only for him it was extra hard, he would always complain. I loved to see him cry and complain. I asked him, "What's the kiss for Peter? I hope it won't cost me too much."

He responded, "Can't I just be myself just one time with you Angelo?"

"By all means Peter, perhaps it's time you do."

We went to the car with his luggage and Peter told me, "I am not leaving here without you."

I told him, "Peter, stop getting fresh with me."

He said, "Quit joking with me."

I said, "There is something I haven't told you about yet. For the second time I am being indicted by the Federal grand jury because of my dealings in immigration with thirty seven different charges I didn't do. As you know I am already on probation with house arrest for one year. I still need to prove the trouble isn't my doing and I'm having a pile of trouble over it. I'm going to need a good lawyer and get much smarter and fast if I'm going to come out on winning on this. There will be to be no less than forty or fifty criminal charges against me. It's going to be a challenge to prove I am innocent and it's going to cost a lot of time and money. I have already lost a few friends over it. People that should be defending me are just fighting for their own survival. I need to be a very good boy now. Before I appear before the grand jury I have to show that I maintain a regular full time job and support my family."

I took a job at the Excalibur Hotel with my friend Max Hamilton but it only lasted for about six hours. I started the job that afternoon at the Italian restaurant in the hotel. The first three hours my body was there but mind was not on the job. Max showed up in the restaurant to make sure that I was doing alright. Guess who was with him? John Morocco, my old friend who was now the director of operations at the Excaliber and a man I had always respected. I respected him for being a capable man and the kind of guy I would like as a friend and I would want to socialize with. Something happened that day that made my life flash before my eyes. Just weeks ago I had been on top of the world and now here I was attending to guests in the dining room. I realized we weren't on the same kind of levels, maybe a few weeks ago yes, but certainly not now. I was tending to the guests in the restaurant with plates and there he was standing there, the director of the entire operations. I wouldn't say we were the best of friends before but did seem to we had a great respect for each other at least up until this day. It seemed whenever I did speak with him we always had plenty to talk about with a lot in common. We both knew we were living well and life was good. Whenever we did run into each other we greeted each other warmly with respect and friendship.

When I saw John Morroco he was standing next to the reservation desk at the entrance to the restaurant with Max Hamilton, my good friend and looking over at me, with no doubt he was wondering, "What's this guy doing here?" I could see it in his face even from across the room. His expression on his face was saying,

"Angelo must be falling on hard times.' I had run into him recently at the Fashion Show Mall on the Las Vegas strip while he had been doing some shopping with his lovely wife and I was with mine while we were passing each other on an escalator. We went back down to say hello and talk a little. We both felt glad to see on another and we were both looking like a million dollars. We exchanged greetings and shook hands on the same level professionally and attitude wise and shared a couple of laughs. At that time we said we would get together sometime soon and have a glass of the red wine that we both like, but we never did.

Tonight in the restaurant John was surely surprised to see me. I think he probably thought if I needed a job I should have come to see him although I wanted to land a job all on my own. I hadn't asked for Max's help in getting this job. John didn't bother to come over to say hello, nor did he show any reflection to acknowledge knowing me. Perhaps he was right not to. Max walked over to me and asked, "Angie, how's it been going so far? If you need anything, just call my office." John still stood by the reservation podium in the restaurant looking over at us. Max told me, "John is over there by the front door."

I said, "I'm aware of that." I was looking at him in the same regard as when I knew him before but John stood there probably thinking just as he had asked Max, "What the hell is he doing here?" He told Max to tell me he would see me later but I decided not to wait around.. Later I found out that Max had made a bet with John that I couldn't last one day. Perhaps that was the reason John didn't bother coming over and saying hello. I had thought of walking over to say hello to him. Then I thought better of it because I was at a disadvantage and he should be the one to approach me. It then occured to me that John was a man with pride and principles and wouldn't dare want to make me feel worse than I was already feeling. I was already feeling small. That was the character of John Morocco. John and Max left a few moments later without John's ever saying "Hi" or "Bye" to me.

After John and Max left the restaurant I wasted no more time, walked up to the manager, gracefully apologized, but told him I just couldn't do this and I had to go. Now I had to think about what I was going to do now about the grand jury. I went home to pick up where I left off. I said to myself, "Angie, you haven't lost everything, your soul or you pride. Money you can get back anytime."

"You see Peter, that is why I'm in quite a quagmire right now,"I explained to him. "People that I had once recieved a lot of respect from were not there for me now. It seems like I'm losing friends like a full cup of water that has a tiny pin hole in the bottom and they are just dripping out. I just wanted you to know that I'm about to be in for the fight of my life and I could even lose my privileges as a responsible father and my citizen's rights, those are the things that I live for. For example like yesterday, I felt a loss of pride in front of my friends at the Excaliber. I'm in no mood for anything less but solid concrete discussions about anything this time, Peter. Be serious before you start shooting your mouth off to tell me your blueprints of how we can get rich quick. Within the next few weeks the grand jury will decide to indict me and I will have to surrender my passport and I won't be able to travel anywhere. I'm doomed."

Peter asked, "How do you know all this?"

I told him some officers from the federal U.S. Attorney General's Office of Micheal E. Barr had shown up at my restaurant, the Prima Café in Summerlin. We had a long and frank conversation. They told me I was going to be indicted if I didn't agree to meet with them and give them my full cooperation. They wasn't much I could do to help them decide what to do with me since I knew no more than they did only confirmation was definitely needed. The grand jury would decide if my story and theirs matched. They showed me some papers that were signed by Federal Judge Pro.

"Have you spoken with a lawyer, Angie?"

I answered, "What for? I know exactly what they want from me and I know the laws pretty well and feel I am on the same level as them professionally after all I work with naval intelligence in San Diego, and Michael Barr, the federal prosecutor knows that. Whatever happens, this may save me from having to go in front of the grand jury. They would only serve me with an indictment and give me a court date, then I will consult a lawyer. Until that time it would be best if I work one on one with the prosecututor's office. Hopefully in the end it will the best move I will make. I am hoping your sister's family that I provided the immigration papers for will stay safe just in case I am unable to provide any further assistance they might need."

Peter asked, "What would happen to all of those people you helping with immigration if you are indicted?"

"I was promised in exchange for my full cooperation that every application I processed previoiusly would be safe since all of them are genuine."

"Man, your not your telling me your willing to stick your neck out for all those people including my sister?"

"Yes, I am, it is the only right thing to do. What I was doing was the noble thing to do. People will know when you have done the right thing. Remember when your sister and her children came to see me here in Las Vegas for help getting their immigration papers? I took the whole family into the immigration office and got them their temporary documents within a couple of hours. It was a great feeling to help your family and see them so happy. It made me really happy that I was able to help make a difference in their lives."

"Come on Angie. You're getting a little sentimental here. Seriously I am really sorry to hear of your trouble that you're having lately. I hope there is something that I can do to help you," Peter said.

"Yes, if you have nothing important to say you could just keep your mouth shut."

He turned and pointed his index finger at me and said, "Listen Mister, you had better be nice to me."

"Why is that Peter?"

He looked me straight in the eye, "Because I may be the only one that comes to see you in jail." Peter clapped his hands laughing like he was watching a dancing monkey at the zoo. His demeanor seemed to change suddenly and then somberly he said, "This is really serious. Did they call you by the name Angie in Yugoslavia?"

"No asshole, they called me Meljace, which means Angel."

I was telling Peter that some time ago I had a cocktail and dinner meeting at the Riviera with a man from immigration, Jose Luis Lopez. He had been recently promoted to the assistant regional director for the western region of INS and over time through immigration we became to be good friends. That night we almost got into an argument over the dinner check. He wanted to either pick up the check or else allow me to pick it up because he could not accept the dinner being comped for him and it could cost him his career. I told him he was invited as my guest and they would not accept my money there and I usually just sign the comp slip because they won't let me pay, I told Jose.

"I'm sorry but if you sign this check for our dinner, since I am a high ranking of officer of the INS, I will have big time trouble," he told me.

George Maxon, the president of the hotel came in and asked if there was some sort of problem, and why we were paying for our dinner. He said, "Angie, when you come here you are my guest and you don't need to dig in your pocket for any money because it's no good here. A lot of good customers come in here because of you. By the way, Philip Lou from Macau has been looking for you."

I said, "Please, George, let us just pay this one time because Jose Luis here, being a federal officer of INS is not allowed to accept a comp since it could be interpeted as a gift or a bribe."

That night Jose Luis warned me as a friend that if I didn't stop doing what I'd been doing by bringing too many people to INS then I was going to be in big getting in big trouble. He said, "Some others are being indicted for doing the same thing that you are only the difference is that they are doing it crookedly. You may fall with them because of their dishonesty. You as well as them are being watched under a magnifying glass and I'm telling you this as a friend off the record. The government is playing hard ball and wants to take everybody down. Attorney General Meese is really pissed about all of this. He's looking at it as a crooked scam." He told me Attorney General Meese was ordering everyone connected to this program to quit or get arrested.

I told him, "That's not right. What's he trying to do, shut down the whole program? I hardly am representing any people from Yugoslavia. I work internationally just as I was instructed to do. I am the only who has been bringing the bright, edcuated, and healthy into the country in the exact way that you guys instructed it be done and by all of your rules and regulations. Remember the meeting in Barbara's office with the director of the INS, Sprat, and when he read the instructions that came directly from Attorney General Meese? He thanked us for taking on this endeavor and wished us the best of luck. We did it legally and with your blessing. You guys practically begged me to take the job. Why now should I be getting in trouble for it?"

He replied, "I guess that's the way the government works sometimes even though the taxpayers have saved a billion dollars or more by the bright, young, healthy and educated that have been brought into our country, but this is still off the record."

I said, "That's thanks I am getting. I spared them thirty years of education and agony. I brought in the educated and skilled by the hundreds from all over the world. Today there are people creating and making America more productive and competitive around the world. Why is there not any gratitude shown to me for that?"

"Well they let you become a citizen. I guess that's the gratitude."

"Should I thank you for that Jose?"

"No, but if you want to I'll pass the message to the highest authorities."

I said, "You mean you'll give it to Attorney General Meese? If your going to do that, just let him know I am innocent of these charges that he's preparing and he doesn't even have to thank me. That's alright though because I'm not asking for any thanks just please tell him not to throw away the key on me like he told Inspector Kelley from his office he would do."

Now there I am thinking I'm going to have the fight of my life. All the the so called friends of mine in and outside of immigration were turning their backs on me and not even answering my calls. They thought I was going to get fried and I hoped they were wrong.

Peter asked, "So what is going to happen with you, man? You should come with me."

"Come where, Peter?" I asked. My mood was changing fast and I was not being too friendly with Peter.

"You can come with me to Australia. We could live there and in Switzerland."

"And do what?" I asked. "You have forgotten that you can't go back to Australia."

"Yes, yes thanks to mine and your friends Nenad and his brother," Peter replied.

"Besides Peter, you haven't even told me everything concerning your ordeals there and why you don't won't to go back. You are a drifter Peter and I don't want to be a drifter with you. You just want a companion to drift with you. I'm not about to do that."

He laughed sarcastically and said, "Fine. I'll just come and visit your virgin ass in jail and bring a big banner to hold by the fence that says, 'Angie is a virgin,' then all the convicts will know your ass is pure. Then you'll be in for some trouble Mister."

"Are you trying to tell me something about yourself, Peter? If so, I really don't want to know. My eyes won't ever end up looking like Bambi's nose you bastard, and I'm won't be going to jail. I don't think that jail is for smart people like me."

Peter said with worry in his voice, "No really Angelo, I care about you and this is serious. You should think about what you're going to do."

"I have thought about leaving the country," I said. "They told me if I were convicted I'd probably get thirty five years but with good behavior I maybe would get out in seven to fifteen. I always thought prison was a place for no one to be in, especially human beings that are truly meant to be free, unless they are serious menances to society. I don't think I belong in that catagory. Man made laws have sometimes violated the boundries of freedom, not just for us humans but all creatures on this planet as well.

"I have tried to put my thoughts together collectively to weight my losses and gains carefully and have seriously thought of just packing up and leaving. I was ashamed of myself later for even thinking like that and didn't want to tell anyone that I was thinking about doing that. I love this country because it is just and fair. If I have done something wrong then I will be prosecuted. If I haven't done anything wrong I need to prove it and I think my innnocence should be very easy to prove. I'm going to stay and face the music. In the next couple of weeks a grand jury will decide whether to indict me or not. If they do indict me it would take a little while to go to trial. If they don't nothing will change except that I'll be out of the immigration business for good as fifeteen other people will be out of a job including two lawyers, but not my friend Elliot. I need to do a 360 now to reorganize my life. I'll have to get my offices closed up including the one in Baca Raton Florida. After all I have family, a wife and a new baby right now. I need to be at home with them to learn Pooh Bear and Barney music. I'm in transition with my inner self and I like what is happening very much. For the first time in my life I look forward to coming home and for the first time since I have been on my own I have slept in my own bed every night of the week instead of having to try to remember the address where I was living at the time. So, this is a great feeling for me that I am not about to let be changed."

"I haven't seen your son Neli, where is he and how is he doing?"

"Neli is doing great and probably out chasing the girlies."

"He must be taking after the old man." Peter said and he laughed.

"He's living on his own now and has a wonderful job. I am very proud of him." My life with Neli still hasn't reached a point where I have been able to fully reconcile my inner personal feelings with the love I have for him. Looking back to his childhood during my own wild youth it reminds me of that song by Cat Stevens, "Cats in the Cradle." It's kind of a sad feeling relating about when the boy needed his dad around and he was hardly there, always rushing to do this and that. Now the son has grown to be a man and the dad wants to spend time with him and the boy has no time for the father because of the business in his own life. I remember the lyrics, 'When you coming home dad? I don't know when. We'll get together then. I know we'll have a good time then.' It seems some of those good times with him passed me by like a train going down railroad tracks. And just like the ending of the song, 'My boy had grown up to be just like me, and tells me, "We'll get together soon, dad." He loves chasing the girls and for now his job and that is his life."

Peter said, "I love that boy. He always takes me around to the great swinger clubs here in Vegas. I can't wait to see him."

I said, "No wonder I never see him when you're in town, you pervert. Let's get serious now."

Finally we were pulling in my driveway and standing in the garage of my house.

"Oh, it's good to be back in Vegas," Peter said stretching his arms over his head.

"All right Peter, grab your luggage man, and we'll take it upstairs to your favorite room."

"I love that room Angie, it has the most beautiful views of the Las Vegas strip and the Red Rock Mountains that you can see from out the windows."

I said, "When you finish unpacking and get cleaned up, come on down and relax. Mankiu should be home soon and she'll fix us a late lunch."

"Angie, I think I'm getting hooked on this town."

"Yea, so does everyone else and I'm one of the fools but I love it here." We both laughed. I said, "It is good to see you again. I hope we can reconcile some of the differences we've had at least in your heart Peter."

"Yes, I've been thinking about that alot too since I left last time and how what I had said was inturpreted and I want to tell you I truly do not feel that way."

"Peter, you have your lifetime to prove it and perhaps you can reedem yourself since you feel that way, not for me but for yourself."

He was anxious to talk not even bothering with unpacking. I sensed he was anxious to explain himself and try and correct what he called our misunderstandings and what he knew had offended me the last time he visited me. He just walked with me and put his arm around my shoulder which was not like him as we were going down the stairs.

"Ok, Peter, there must be something important you really want to talk to me about, just watch your step because it's a long way down. I wouldn't want to be accused of killing someone in my own house. That would be a shameful thing, especially if you didn't do it and were accused of it. I think you've made a long trip to see me and you will have my full attention."

He rubbed his palms together looking a little nervous and unsure of himself but smiled and said,"OK, you always surprise me Angelo. If you had talked like I had to you without using my common sense like the last time I was here and had taken it in the same way that you probably did, I don't know if I would have welcomed you back to my home again, as you have me."

"Well that is the difference where the men are separated from the boys. It's nothing personal, let's just leave in the cookie jar for now and I hope I don't end up with any broken cookies and crumbs."

"Angelo, I was thinking about having some of that Louis the XIII first? Do you have any left from the last time?"

"Go ahead Peter, you know where to find it, please help yourself."

There he stood looking very much at home with his snifter full of Louis the XIII that was left over from his last visit. "Ok, Peter," I laughed loudly. "I think you have made a long trip and it wasn't just to see my pretty face." I took out a brand new crystal bottle of Louis the XIII and got another snifter glass for myself that had the gold letters engraved on them with, "Family of Koljenovic." They were especially made for me by a man named Paulo in Mission Bay San Francisco that I met once and who owned a fine crystal shop there.

A few minutes later I toasted Peter, "I hope your trip produces the fruit of your labors even though I know you hate laboring too hard. I'm just glad for you that your labor of love is more of the mental kind than physical, just handle it right."

We both laughed and Peter said, "I may be slow on my feet but I'm a fast thinker."

"That's been your main problem all the years that I've known you. Sometimes your mouth is faster than your brain. Maybe you should try to find a balance and you'll come out ahead."

"I know you're right Angelo."

"Well, I hope this is a good project that you are thinking about that made you travel ten thousand miles to tell me about, and I'm looking forward to hearing all about it."

My friend Peter seemed unusually comfortable but ready and very eager to tell me about this idea of his that he wanted to be part of but had yet unfolded it or even had it figured all the way out and was still a mystery to me . I thought, "Boy, this is probably one big mistake but I'll keep my word and listen until he's finished." So I told him, "I'll make us a couple of Turkish coffees. How about it?"

"By all means. I would love to have one. It goes good with the Louis."

While I waited patiently on the water to boil in the old fashioned copper Turkish coffee jar, Peter was becoming more nervous and seemed impatient to spill it out to me. He had a habit of rapping his knuckles on the table with one hand and sticking the middle finger from his other hand up his nose when he needed to unload whatever was on his mind. You would find yourself hungry seeing Peter in that condition because you would want to throw up anything you had in your stomach. It was a bad habit. I laughed and politely said, "Don't break the table Peter. Just relax, you are at home now. Maniku will be home soon so just relax and hopefully she will be in the mood to cook a good dinner or if not we can go out. In the meantime our coffees are ready and I'll go get them."CHAPTER NINE: AN ADVENTURE WITH PETER

Once he got started talking, I have to admit, some of his story sounded crazy, some of it adventurous and appealing, and some of it troublesome, really troublesome. I needed to put the whole conversation into a strainer to sort it all out. I kept mental notes on what I thought was worth discussing later with him and kind of tried erased to what I sensed was just his usual big talk and exagerations and what was real. It took some time to sort all of it. The troublesome things are what I wanted to discuss with him first.

"Did you think I was talking about dealing with those generals?" he asked me. "You know me, all right – you keep saying it — that I will deal with most anybody, and I figure if somebody can afford to buy guns, he has a right to use them."

"Peter, your're contradicting yourself and what you said last time but go on."

"These guys have buyers and real connections to trade with countries that want to aquire nuclear weapons."

"Just what countries or country are you talking about?"

"Like I told you before, Pakistan has been on a shopping spree and I think my friends are going to be the ones who deliver."

"Yes, the question is what will they deliver Peter? And what makes you so sure it is weapons they are selling, and not nuclear power technology?" I asked him.

"Everybody assumes that if a Muslim country wants nuclear technology that they must be trying to make bombs. Even if that was so we should take it at face value for the simplest of reasons that throughout of Islam there hasn't been any civilization the Muslim world have even thought of anihiliating. I think the world doesn't have anything to fear from the Muslim nation becoming nuclear. Perhaps then they can realize that they are better without it than with it."

"What these people are offering is the trigger devices. Their only use is setting off atom bombs. Your friends, the generals are very irresponsible people and the consequences of their actions could have long term negative effects for generations to come. I remind you Peter, and those should also already know that the hostilities between India and Pakistan don't require nuclear weapons, it requires special surgeons to cure the disease of hatred between these two great nations and sadly I don't see the cure. I would say Pakistan needs nuclear weapons like I need a rock in my head. So just what is it you are planning with these generals?" I asked Peter.

"I think they need to be taught a lesson," he answered. "They need to be killed."

"Easier said than done. Perhaps you should know that better than anyone Peter." He was talking about murdering three people, retired military generals. Peter claimed he was working for some kind of engineering group in Zurich and that they were selling parts for the development of nuclear bombs to Pakistan.

"What else is new? Pakistan has already tested one

underground nuclear device with the blessings of the Western world. I'm surprised why the sudden shift by the West in supporting it. I think it is smarter to support Pakistan now so there won't be some kind of accident that brings a disaster worse than Chernobyl or Three Mile Island."

Peter was persistant and shrugged off my concerns and he wanted my full attention on what he had to say, which was understandable after traveling twelve thousand miles. So I did give him that attention and it was getting interesting. He described exactly where the generals offices were located in Zurich in deatail, just how far that he had to walk from his hotel down a hill step by step across the bridge of a lake and past the only grocery store there, that looked like part of the bridge like a floating barge. Peter described that after he crossed the bridge he would go down a hill and then turn down an alley to the left where the buildings were connected closely like sardines in a tin can. On the fourth building to the right of the alley in that building up on the third floor was an office with five rooms that all the generals shared as their office. He said they were more like apartments than offices.

Peter said, "I think you could easily get away with committing murder there."

"You mean to tell me that the walls that seperate the buildings and each room are made of brick or stone?"

"Yes! Yes! That's precisely it! It means they are sound proof. I knew you were pretty smart, you've never failed me Angelo."

"Wait a minute now, you act like we were partner's in crime and we haven't done anything like that together, at least not yet I haven't been foolish enough."

The way that he was explaining it to me was convincing me of his story and that the players were for real. I wasn't sure however if they were capable of actually producing the so called parts that detonate nuclear devices. I asked him, "Where are they making these, and where are they coming from?"

He answered confidently, "Made in Switzerland man, where do you think? The Swiss general is head of one of those factories that are making this stuff. "

"Wow, that's pretty heavy but I'm not surprised. Congratulations to Pakistan," I replied solemnly. My thoughts went back to October ninth when I wrote a letter to the late Senator Patrick

Monahan to state my displeasure of his branding Pakistan's nuclear program as a future Islamic bomb. I wrote him that is no such thing as an Islamic bomb. I wrote to the senator quote, "Was the Hiroshima bomb a "Christian bomb" because Truman and Roosevelt were baptised Christians? It is demeaning to Christianity and is insulting to the memory of Christ to say that weapons of massive slaughter can be an expression of Christianity. There is no way that an obscene bomb could be called Islamic There are no Christian poisons or Jewish bayonets."

The retired ranking officer generals status and connections in their respective countries left me feeling open minded of the possibilty that they were capable of delivering what Pakistan was looking for.

I didn't see anyone who was waving flags and volunteering to arm Pakistan with nuclear devices, nor was anyone making any effort to convince them that they did not need that. Then I thought it may be worth it to check this out further and out try to find out more of the truth. I wouldn't have to try hard convincing anyone of what I found out. I already had some credibility with the government here, and even though I was having some trouble at the moment it still couldn't stop me from doing what was right. I realized I knew no more than anybody else except for the difference that I was a participant in the ongoing game and most were only spectators who were waiting for the full picture.

I thought of discussing it with some of my friends in intelligence in San Diego, but I felt that there probably wasn't much new I could tell them they didn't already know. Looking back now I think that was a mistake. I could have tried convincing them I did know a little more than they did know but I was afraid I'd end up looking like a fool. Unfortunately I had no concrete evidence of anything to offer them except the three generals who would have denied it and Peter who was a flakey as a dry leaf in the wind. Peter was trying hard to convince me and was persistant that it was something we should cash in on. I was reserved with him on his suggestions. I knew the only right thing for me do was to stop these generals and Peter. I told him, "Just let me digest this a little, Peter."

"I need you to come with me now to Zurich Angelo."

I said, "Well we will see."

"I want you to come with me," he said, "and I want you to know there will be a surprise package waiting for you in Zurich, a guy from Bosnia."

"I don't care for surprises and never have. Who is this surprise package?"

Peter had been talking so much and for so long he was starting to drool white around the edges of his mouth. I politely handed him a napkin and another cognac, and said, "Maybe you should drink some water, I think your drying out. You're in the desert after all."

He took it and thanked me while he wiped his mouth. "Alija is the surprise and he is one tough guy who could be mistaken for an undertaker."

"You mean a grave digger or a grave robber?"

"Don't be so sarcastic Angelo. That's just the kind of tough guy he is. His bodygaurds were those long black leather coats."

I told him. "That's very impressive. Aljia is an African dog, a hyena and a scavenger, and from what you've told me he is becoming rich from the blood our people and he will have to answer for that sooner or later."

"Well, I know Angelo that he is selling a lot of guns and I wouldn't mind a piece of the action."

"Listen Peter, maybe I can help you out for that dream to come true for you. I will go along with anything you ask but not by myself. We can share whatever it is you want to do but on one condition, you make sure that we have a meeting first with this guy, this Alija."

"Yeah, man, now you're talking. You remember that I told you that he authorized me to represent him by giving me the power of attorney. Wait just a minute, hold on please."

Peter ran upstairs and returned a few minutes later waving a paper in his hand saying, "Here it is, take a look at it! It's for real. It has his name, Minister Alija Delimustafic, and is sealed by the bank, notorized and has his signature dated May 17th 1993." The power of attorney gave Peter the right to negotiate on behalf of Alija in way he thought beneficial to him by having that piece of paper.

I laughed and said, "Well, I guess we can go and build now in that God forsaken island on the shores of the south Gulf of Tonkin in mainland China just like you said. The best thing about that island is on a clear day you can see the capitol of Vietnam."

"You mean that island is that close?"

"Don't worry, the United States Air Force and their B-52's stopped flying over there a long time ago, thank God. Like I told you, just make sure that Alija is there Peter and I will be there with you."

Peter did not hesitate while holding up his snifter glass to toast our venture and then he stood and went straight to the telephone and dialed the international connection number that was in Vienna Austria. Peter had called that same number before from my home when he was making a call to Alija and had told him where he was calling from but I had never spoken with him before. "Hi, this is Peter calling from Las Vegas. Is Alija in?"

I could hear a lady who answered the phone in a very soft voice that sounded like she had been sleeping. She said, "Peter. I'm sorry, Alija is not in. He is in London and won't be back for a few days."

Peter asked, "What's he doing in London?"

She replied, "He's on some kind of bank business."

"Well, tell him I'm here in Las Vegas now with Angelo, and we're going to be in Zurich soon," Peter told her.

By this time my wife had arrived home with our baby. I greeted her at the door and lifted the baby carrier out of her arms. I honestly forgot all about Peter for a moment. I snuggled my little girl, kissing her and waking her from sleeping. I told Mankiu the same thing I said every day since our baby had been born. I told her I couldn't help it and knew I sounded like a parrot but I thought our daughter had my mother's same shining black hair. Maybe it was just because I love my mother so much I couldn't see my daugher any other way. Now that my baby daughter is growing up her hair does look very much like my mother's. Anyway after a moment I remembered about Peter being there because he was getting excited and called out, "Where is my Goddaughter? Where is my Goddaughter?"

I said, "Be careful, Peter. Don't you dare drop her."

"What do you think, I don't know how to handle a baby?"

I said, "Go ahead and give the baby back to Mankiu, I think she wants to bathe the baby right now. Let's get the hell out of here and go and get something to eat." I suggested, "How about Caesars or Bally's?"

Peter knew where he wanted to go and chose Bally's. I had treated him there before and he felt comforttable and familiar there since the last time we were there and he got the royal treatment from my friend Lario. I rang Bally's and asked the hotel operator to connect me with Lario's office in food and beverage. Before she would connect she asked to let him know who was calling. I introduced myself to her and Lario was immediately on the line. "Hey., Govinito! How the hell you been? Where are you? Are you here at the hotel?"

"Not yet but I should be there in twenty minutes or so. Peter from Zurich is in town and we would like to eat dinner at Barrymore's."

"It will great to see you Angie, and I'll have my maitre'de have your table ready when you get here and I hope I can find a few moments and join you for an espresso after dinner."

"Thanks, Lario I would like that very much and.if you speak with your lovely wife before I see you, please tell her to give the children a kiss from me and I'll be seeing you soon then." .

It was five thirty by the time we arrived at Bally's and we were just in time for a good dinner. I was ready for some of that homemade bread, a baked potato and filet mignon with a dash of blue cheese cooked in the center and a good bottle of wine. It would be just the thing to hit the spot. I was also looking forward to seeing Lario. I knew he would be happy to see me too, and it would be mutually gratifying. Everything that I have learned about the restauarant business I learned by watching Lario who is a master of his work. Peter ordered his usual twenty ounce prime rib.

Peter was anxious to continue on with our discussion and thankfully we had the corner booth which was private and secluded. He told me he wanted to go to Lozano as soon as we arrived in Zurich and thought we might be going to Croatia also. That was the original Peter I knew, always running ahead of himself. His mouth worked faster that his brain.

"Let's just enjoy our dinners and then we'll talk about Zurich, although I know I won't be going to Croatia with you," I said.

He never could stay in any one place too long. He had to always be on the move. I was thinking.that my friend Pace and I also had that in common with Peter but I would never admit my wanderlust to him. We all needed action, adventure, and challenge. It was an integral part to all of our characters.

Dinner at Barrymore's was fantastic. Lario did make it to join us for espressos afterward. I didn't know it but it was the very last time I ever saw him. My troubles were just about to begin and all of these good times would be distant memories.

The last time that I had spoken with Peter before his arrival in Las Vegas that night I had told him that if I saw him again I was going to rearrange his baboon butt face to look like a real baboon's ass, which would be a big improvement for him and he could consider it a free gift from a one time good friend. The best way to picture Peter was as a big red-haired strawberry-nosed craggy-faced guy with a body as square as a box with his head sitting right on his shoulders and a hard on attitude that assured he would not make but lose if he had any friends. That was the real Peter.

Being an American comes first to me and close upon it's heels is my deep feelings for that cluster of quarreling states and cultures that was once called Yugoslavia, where he and I both have our roots. We were pals once, compatriots, conspirators, and co-adventurers of international intrigue. When Peter and I made our moves on our adventures, we weren't fully aware of the effect our actions might have and how they could influence the eventual break up of Yugoslavia as a nation that once was and also that many lives were hanging in the balance. Of course we weren't the only players or the main players, there were many others, perhaps even more dedicated than Peter and I to the same cause, yet not the same cause. Peter was always for saving Yugoslavia and I wanted it to be torn apart.. It would be fair to share the blame and responsibility of the outcome. These adventures and the fight for what we believed in as individuals in is what had brought us together. It was for a common purpose although in the end we found ourselves to be on opposite sides with the blood of the innocent covering our forefathers' land. I always knew that Peter and I were plainly on opposite sides although we both were playing the game and I suppose it is fair to say that those are the things that drifted us further apart and I won.

Peter is a few years older than I am. He was one of Marshal Tito's first cadets of bounty hunters during his reign of Yugoslavia. These were secret soldiers who slipped in and out of many countries all over the world, investigating, intimidating, and sometimes assassinating people who had left Yugoslavia but whom Tito still considered of being dangerous to him and his communist Yugoslavia .

There were hundreds, perhaps a thousand recruited agents who were just like Peter, to ensure Tito's survival and protect him from his one time citizens that now he now saw as his mortal enemies from outside and inside of the country. A small number of Tito's special agents became notorious, such as the assassins Arkan and Seselj. These dark men built their reputation as the undercover agents overseas for Marshal Tito. Peter was one of the team members. Arkan is now dead, having met his fate in his gambling establishment in Belgrade by being pumped full of hundreds of bullets that tore into his body. It was a message from his best friend Slobo Milosevic. Seselj's luck was a little better. Slobo was sent to Haag to await trial before he was able to do the same thing to him.

That young Montenegrin Vojo Raicevic, no one thought was capable of doing what he did do. He sure fooled Arkan and got rid of the best of his men and killed every one of them. Inevitably he met his fate also and it came from his mentor, Arkan. The men Vojo had killed were with no doubt guilty of spilling the blood of the innocent throughout Bosnia. Vojo did not kill his own compatriots because he felt guilty about what they had done in Bosnia. He killed them so he rise in rank and that is what got himself killed. If there is anything I regret it is meeting Vojo and trying to help him out in crossing over from a boy to a man. I guess he showed me he knew how to be a man but it wasn't the kind of man I hoped for him to be. I had helped him obtain the documents to become a legal citizen in America. I regret that I had had coffee and lunch so many times with him over the few years he was in Las Vegas. I have paid a high price in my heart for every time just thinking that I have known and associated with men like that and even contributed in becoming what they came to be. It was a dark tunnel with no light in sight that I hadn't seen coming. I still hope he did not participate in all of those atrocities in Bosnia. Perhaps I will never know.

Peter and I first became acquainted through our mutual needs and our political ideologies which brought us together yet also set us apart. That was the future of Yugoslavia, whether to be or not to be. We walked down that treacherous road with me trying to assist in the support of Bosnia and him carrying an invisible torch under my feet that he always hoped I couldn't feel. It was as I said however, and at the end of that road I won.

On one of his many visits to Las Vegas from his home in Gold Coast, Australia, Peter made a point that he had to go to Columbia for a business trip, then on to Dallas, Texas, where he had contacts in both intelligence and in the underworld who were close family members of high ranking generals in the Chilean and Argentinean military. He liked bragging about the things that he did. He asked me if I would like to go with him to San Diego and meet some of his friends from the

U.S. intelligence service but he never specified what branch they were from, whether it be the CIA, or Naval Intelligence but I knew who they were already because they were my colleagues. He sure thought that he knew how to get around. As well as working with several of those agencies, we both became involved in the bombing events which led to the breakup of Yugoslavia and the creation of an independent Bosnia. I spoke with my friends on that same day Peter left to go and see them. The agent I spoke with whom I was very close suggested with hope that I hadn't blown my cover.

"Since we are on mission here and bombing Serbia, Kosovo, and all of Montenegro's military bases," I was told, "under no circumstances should Peter know we are on the same team. He is trying to stop the bombing instead of trying to help and we don't consider him to be a team player but we need to know what the other side is thinking in Serbia. Just please be careful."

I always hoped somehow and somewhere Peter would realize his side was the losing side but that didn't even matter to him. We were happy with the information that we got from him and he was happy playing triple agent. I was hoping they would finish him off at the end of the other side of the road but that never happened. Peter enjoyed being 007. How many times in life could have a chance of playing Bond like Peter did? Perhaps he lived through all this because everyone because everyone saw what an idiot that he was. At times his information he gave did serve some useful purpose for us to direct the things we needed to do in the right way and perhaps save a U.S. soldier from being in harm's way. That was enough of a reward for me and after all Peter proved useful. He never had the best interest of the Bosnians at heart. I was hoping that he would show he did have some for some compassion for Bosnia before it was all over but that was not to happen. In his work, he was quite ruthless, but cool. I suppose it might have been because of his father's German blood that he was more detached and efficient than the passionate character of a Balkan man like myself. Though I am a long away from the valley of Gusinje, it is still my nature that I do not feel quite able of trusting anyone who does not become impassioned about what he is doing. A heart without passion is like a hearth without a fire. I find it difficult feeling life without both things together.

One of the finest people I ever had the opportunity to work with was the "Lion Warrior from Utah," and a long time veteran, my great warrior friend Giles Pace. Perhaps he really deserved to be called the American James Bond. Looking back, I am surprised at how little I really knew about who Giles was actually working for, and what his job was. His background was no secret and we had talked about his past many times and his love for the military but I didn't pry into his present activities and he didn't volunteer much information either. The Bosnian crisis had changed everything. We were about to come to know everything there was to know of one another even discovering the coincidence of the day we had both been in Africa and had just missed meeting each other in that tiny emergency room. I always knew he was a true patriot, and a man who seemed to know the influential and powerful everywhere that he went.

It was a good thing that I discovered quickly that when Pace was talking people were listening. From that moment I told myself I shouldn't waste any time when I talk with him and should just get to the point with as much conviction, knowledge and with enough understanding of what subject I wanted to talk with him about. We bonded very well and had some incredible results. His contributions to the war in Bosnia were immeasurable. His actions saved lives and I and the nation are proud of his service and dedication so that we could fly with glory and pride as a freedom fighting people whenever and wherever we are needed. This time it was in Bosnia and we were there with Pace at the helm even though our ambassador in Croatia had threatened to revoke his passport. Pace wasn't going to have any of that. He was going to do what he knew in his heart was right. America is a nation that fights for the rights to freedom and so it should stand.

Pace finally had the chance to meet the infamous Peter, whose name was known for all the wrong reasons. Looking back now I regret ever having Peter as a guest and the dinner when I invited Pace to meet Peter at my home, I was still stung over the events of that night when he and Peter were both at dinner in my home that evening and we discussed one of the many recent times the government of Yugoslavia were using their military power against the Bosnians. What Peter said that Giles later related to me that night in my absence was like a slap in my face . He said to Pace, "The fucking Muslims deserve exactly what they got. They should have figured that out a hundred years ago, when the Ottoman Empire fell. If Alexander or Tito had run them all out then Yugoslavia would be a major European power today."

After Pace related to me after Peter had departed for Zurich, I said, "Well Pace, I'm not really that surprised by what Peter said to you. I know he has no love for my people, perhaps it is for the best that Alexander or Tito couldn't do what Peter said that they should have. If either one succeeded doing what Peter suggested then Yugoslavia would now be a Russian satellite, and a chicken bone in America's political throat today, the same as Cuba is and probably even worse. Peter exposed his true colors to Pace that night shown in that baboon ass face of his. He's still Tito's disillusioned man and no friend of Bosnia's. He never had Bosnia or the Bosnjaks' well being in his heart and clearly had to be motivated by some other factor. I could hardly guess what that might have been, but then I knew that Bosnia was only just a sworn duty and a job to him, and the Bosnians were just another project on Tito's list that he needed to help him dispose of for a bigger Serbia and Croatia.

Pace said it seemed that during his conversation with Peter at my house at the dinner table that it seemed almost as if he were rehearsing what he had already been programmed to do in engineering a cooperate take over with Croatia and Serbia as his clients over Bosnia he had no love for. It is a dangerous precedent to think of nations and people as some profitable commodities to be taken over, even coming from little filthy mouths of people like Peter. In this situation the take over would mean that the name of Bosnia and her people would disappear. It was a low blow to me after I had heard about what Peter had said to Pace. As he told me, it felt like I had been stabbed with the carving knife even though at the time I wasn't present and didn't hear it. Still it is no surprise to hear that coming from Peter and I wanted to keep him on that leash. Again I remembered the advice of Confucius and the consequences later of being rational or irrational. I decided to make sure my leash on Peter was stronger than ever just in case he was capable of causing any damage, he would not be freeing himself from my hold.

I always knew he didn't have any filter for his filthy mouth because he has already been brainwashed and programmed by his mentor Marshall Tito to be like that and so I'm not surprised. Whatever Peter tells you is exactly straight from the horse's mouth but if you question him, he will twist it and deny what you think he means just to save his own horse's ass. Well, he's stupid enough in the way he was talking right at the dining table in the presence of my friends like he thought they approved of his derogatory comments, although I was momentarily busy in the kitchen and might have missed what was said but in hindsight that was probably a good thing.

"Pace, I remember you did seem to be a little upset that night by Peter pushing everyone's envelope. I told Peter after dinner was over that if you defame my people you do a dishonor to me personally. I told him, 'Don't push your luck with Pace, whatever you were saying to him left him looking like he was ready to kick your ass. I hope you will try to choose your words more wisely and there is nothing you could say that I don't already know the way about the way you feel anyway. Pace is a good friend of mine and I didn't appreciate your show of poor manners and disrespect for my hospitality to you.'" Peter always had a way of looking like a poor dog who was used to running loose and free until the owner got fed up with his running and decided to tie him up on a leash. Peter behaved just as that.

Throughout my life, I have always liked to do things for people. All my life, if someone needed something I would walk a mile or longer to get it for them without any personal gain for what I would get from it but just for the small satisfaction that I was able to do something good that day. As for Peter, I had helped him and his family to settle legally in the United States. Yes, I felt completely betrayed by him but again it was no surprise. I swore to him on my mother's grave and on the blood of all my children, that if I ever saw him again, I would cut his balls off his bleeding corpse and stick them right in his rotten mouth. Peter is good at manipulating with his doggie tail between his legs while trying to make you feel like you hurt him more with your words than if you had done something physically to him.

"When I came out from the kitchen, Pace, I sat at the table I could see that you weren't looking too happy. It was obvious there was a clash of personalities and characters between the two of you which I had expected. I figured Peter had been trying to mentor to you. I thought it I should step in and mentor right then and there after hearing him lecturing to you.

"As you remember I said to him, 'Peter, you only come to me when you need something, so all right, what is it?' I was thinking about some advice I'd read from Confucius that when you are about to lose your temper to think of the consequences so you can come out ahead as the winner. So I told him I'd stick around because I wanted him on a leash and that way I could get more use from him then he even knew. He thought I was joking but that was what I wanted him to think. He decided to keep it himself that night about what he had for me."

Now speaking with him on the phone where he was about twelve thousand miles away from me across the Atlantic he still was sounding to me like the same broken record, "Angie, this time I really don't need anything, but I have something that you need very much," he said.

"Peter, that would be the day, when I believe there is nothing in it for you and only for me. No, no, no, no." I laughed wryly, and said, "Peter, remember when you called me the last time I said the only thing that I needed was another couple of hours of sleep. I've been working very hard trying to stop the war in Bosnia, for your information. I just completed what I think was a successful dinner event at the Polo Towers. There were more than eight hundred people, local and state politicians that came and it was sponsored by my good friend Steven Coolbeck and with his help we succeeded to involve the whole community in the state of Nevada in participating in relieving the suffering going on in Bosnia. Steven is not a Christian or Muslim but just a caring man who happens to be of Jewish faith and my good friend. Unlike you Peter with the conditions of a two faced coin. I was so surprised to hear him speak to the audience, expressing his feelings on the war in Bosnia. I can tell you, Peter, I could never thank him enough. I will never forget the help that he gave to us. Our keynote speaker was Bosnian Ambassador Sven Alkalaj, and our lieutenant governor was the guest of honor. What makes you think I need anything from you this time Peter?"

"Listen man, that's all fine what you said," he said rather gruffly. "I'm glad those people are working with you, and you should call all of them right away with what I have to tell you. General Ratko Mladic is attacking Srebrenica and he is going to massacre the people."

I was stopped short. I couldn't even gasp, "What are you talking about?" I could hear the simple truth in his voice since I have known him such a long time and I could tell he was not lying to me. I had of course been following the events in Srebrenica closely, and what he was saying was the fulfillment of my fears. Not even Milosevic, that shifty and treacherous little would-be fascist, would dare to turn the army against the very people it was supposed to protect, and to kill them because they were Bosnians, Muslims. Yet he was clearly telling me that was exactly what was going to happen.

"I'm telling this to you, Angelo, so you don't say that no one tried to save the Bosnian people, at least from the Serbs' side," he said.

That caught me by surprise. "Wait a minute, Peter, what do you mean the Serbs' side? I thought you were German and Croatian."

"My mother is half Serb and half Croatian," he said. "I've been doing some work for Belgrade."

"Well that's great, now I know everything," I said. "You are truly a bastard. What else is new?"

"Just like I said, Mister," Peter replied. "Aren't you listening to what I am saying? It's not about me this time, it's about eight thousand people. General Mladic is rounding up all the men and boys, almost eight thousand of them now, I think, and he's going to kill them all. There is nothing I can do from my position to stop it. You better see if you can do something if you can."

I was astonished he had called me, it was as though he was only trying to make me feel helpless and guilty by telling me what kind of damage was going to be done. "What would you like me to do, Peter, rub the magic lamp and ask for three wishes? If I were that lucky, I would not remember my childhood being hungry and poor. Eight thousand people is a catastrophe for any small country to lose. It's blatant genocide. Nobody would do that, not even the Serbs."

"Well, if you don't call somebody in Washington to tell them to intervene, I'm telling you eight thousand people will be dead, maybe ten."

"When?"

"It could start in hours, maybe a few more days."

"Peter, how do you know this? Who is giving you information?"

"You forgot, Angelo? I'm the Jack of many trades, but none professional."

"Pete, you are not the Jack, you are the joker, always with two faces and both lying. That's why I never trusted you, but this time I think you may be telling the truth."

"General Yankovic is an old man, and it seems he feels some compassion," he said. "Remember the people that you met in Zurich from Badnja Luka, that guy whose brother was killed by Bosnian forces?"

"Sure, but I wouldn't trust that guy with anything," I said. "He's a Serb."

"Hey look, man, he got the call from the General, and I'm

telling you, so don't give me any of that Serb shit," he said. "Now you better quit wasting time if we are going to save these people."

"Okay, Pete," I said. "Okay. You can keep your balls." Apology accepted, but I don't forget that the man can change colors like a lizard, and probably doesn't give a shit about any of them.

I got right on the phone and called the Bosnian embassy in Washington D.C. "This is Angelo in Las Vegas," I told the receptionist, a tight-voiced woman on the other end of the line, who identified herself as Jasmina. "I have met the ambassador and we have a respectful relationship in mutual understanding with one another, and I'm sure he will know who it is. I have some information of international importance to him, and I'd like you to put me through to him, please."

"I'm sorry the ambassador is not in his office, and if you are so close to him you should know his personal number," she said, bored and flat, as though I had called to sell her Girl Scout Cookies.

"In fact I do have all of his numbers but it seems none of them are functional right now, and I thought maybe you would help me. It really is a matter of utmost urgency. I have a very urgent message, a matter of life or death," I told her. "I know you are always able to reach him in an emergency, and this is an emergency. Will you please connect me with the ambassador, as it is very important that I speak with him."

"I'm sorry, I can't do that. You will have to call back another time."

"Wait, you don't understand," I said in frustration. "This is too important for you to make a personal decision and ignore it. Ambassador Alkalaj must hear this. If you will not get me the Ambassador then get me your supervisor."

"I don't have to do anything," she said, "and the ambassador is not available."

Well, there it was, all the mentality of every bureaucratic regime in Yugoslavia or anywhere else, for that matter. Just give a little person a big desk, and they turn into little tyrants. I wanted to tell her, "You make me remember why I am glad I left years ago." Instead, I took a breath, and said, "Ma'am, Jasmina, you don't have to do this for me. This is for eight thousand people in Srebrenica who are all going to be executed by tomorrow morning."

"Yes, and flying saucers will make California fall into the

ocean," she said. "The Ambassador does not have time for cranks with pet theories." She hung up.

I wondered at her smart crack and how she knew where the California coast even was. I turned my computer on and patiently waited for the screen to come up. It seemed to take forever, and every second that passed by, I felt as if I were hearing Peter's voice echoing in my head, "You better do something, mister. I did my part, and you better do something." My first encounter was a failure. I felt like I imagined what a screen writer must feel when he has a great story that is of world significance. To whom do you tell your story, and how do you get through to them, and what do you say to them? My story, upon which hung the fate of thousands of people, had been effectively stopped by the first little petty bureaucrat it reached, like a screenplay rejected by a sophomore reader with a formula checklist making an extra fifty bucks by reading two a day.

It was as though the old order had never left. Innocent people are dying in the streets, people with no clue to why there is a war going on all the time while the same old class of bureaucrats is eating good and drinking good wine out of reach of the hands of these dying people, and the bureaucrats are running the show from both sides of the alley while the little people are dying on both sides of the alley.

I set about to compose an e-mail, directed to the Ambassador, hoping that it was not Jasmina's job to read his online correspondence. "In Yugoslavia, the bureaucracy doesn't have to answer to anyone, at least not to ordinary citizens," I wrote. "Here in America, our leaders are elected officials and feel responsible to answer to their citizens in their community. Everyone is held accountable for their deeds by everyone else. I have a critical message for you regarding the lives of several thousand Bosnians, of the greatest urgency. I have asked your staff in the embassy to relate the urgent message to you, but unfortunately it seems the message was refused by a secretary who introduced herself as Jasmina. I venture to say if the information I possess is genuine, then I should expect you will soon be seeking a new secretary."

It was not until early the next morning that I received a call from the Bosnian embassy from the personal private secretary of the ambassador, named Esmir. He was very professional and very polite. Moments later a soft spoken voice on the other side of the line said, "Mr. Angelo, Ambassador Alkalaj here. What can I do for you, my friend?"

I told him what I had been told by Peter and he was very concerned and of course he took me quite seriously although I could sense the hopelessness in his voice. I debated with him on how he and his government should approach the American government for help and long term relations. "We in America do not waste our time with anyone who is not worthy of our time," I told him. "You, Mr. Ambassador, and your government, better convince American presidents and American people that you are worthy to them in order to help save your country and peoples lives." I reminded him that a few years back the United States declared if the Soviet Union would attack Yugoslavia we would go to nuclear war with them. "Now as we are speaking there are eight thousand people out on the firing lines and many are possibly already dead." I felt a pain of hopelessness throughout my body like I've never felt in my entire life. It's strange how you know when you are not able to do anything and surrender everything to the Almighty and pray and hope that God will only do something about it, and your fear is that it is not going to happen.

The ambassador was persistent in showing his geo-political skill. I was not concerned with his knowledge of communism but in saving lives for the moment in Srebrenica. His concerns with the strategic were past history and there was a new show in town, and if we didn't advertise that we were good performers then we might disappear from the map very fast.

I reminded him that strategy is not only about military affairs but also a nation's reputation. "You must convince President Clinton that the Bosnian people are worth saving, not only for himself, but also in order to save the reputation of the American people."

The ambassador was still grateful and patient with me and my resolve to do something or anything to stop this. I felt he was already resigned to whatever was going to happen and yet he was a man of action and of honor and he did try everything he could, at least that's what he told me but it was immediately clear that there was nothing of any real consequence that he could do.

I was even more convinced that the only thing that might help save all of the Muslim Bosniaks from genocide was to find a way to get more guns to them so they would at least be able to defend themselves from Slobo's goons. So I went to Zurich with Peter again, leaving behind my glamorous life as an insider in Las Vegas as well as the love and security of my happy life with my family. I went with him prepared to meet with a man I hated for the use of the money I was promised would be available for us to buy the guns for Bosnia. I went with Peter prepared to take part in what intelligence informed us of some time ago about a large shipment of guns out of South America headed to Croatia. Half of the shipment came from Peter and my own friends out of Dallas, Texas who were in cahoots with the Chilean and Argentinean military. I was to get seven million dollars in weapons off of that shipment for the Mostar fighters. Alija from Zurich was the one who was to deliver the weapons. I was going to help Peter in return for all of this do some of his dirty work as a team together, arm in arm. I had my own plans for Peter after all was said and done. It was a plan of three powerful men who Peter wanted to whack and cash in on the profits because they were dealing in something I believe nobody should be dealing in at all.

So I found myself once again in a hostile situation where everyone including myself was wearing a mask of some kind, and no one trusted any one else farther than the point of a knife. I truly felt I was at an advantage over all of these low life bigots because I was on the side of the oppressed people.

Our trip to Zurich and our meeting with the generals never materialized for the moment, but all our other blueprints were on the table to be viewed and executed. It looked like the generals had already made a deal, and then the generals did not show up as expected. It seemed Peter got left out of the deal. I was both relieved and disappointed, and I was a little disturbed with myself for both of these reactions. Whoever they were, they had escaped my cleansing sword that night and Pakistan soon afterwards acquired the nuclear technology for the weapons these people were selling.

When Peter introduced me to Alija, I told him my only hope was that he would do the righteous thing by delivering our seven million dollars worth of weapons to the freedom fighters in Bosnia at Mostar. Alija told Peter that if he did that, he would lose all his business and the freedom of traveling through the Serb and Croat territory. He suggested to Peter that we should give him the cash money instead. Perhaps then he could quadruple the money for us and would tell us the details at a later date of how he would do it. He would account for some by investing the money in safe foreign activities, like the very profitable electric power plant in China or in building a road to Budapest with his Italian counterparts from Milano.

I tried to explain to him it seemed obvious to me that if all he did with the country's money was to invest it to make a bigger bank account in the country's name, then the country doesn't get a thing, and might as well never have had the money. The only ones who stand to gain from it are the ones in office who can spend the profits on themselves, for palaces and executive jets. That has been what was wrong with almost every government that was ever in power there. I reminded Alija that my two friends from south America were military people who were willing to give seven million dollars in weapons to Bosnia and the rest of it would go to Croatia.

"I think you guys should just give me the money and I will do what I have said." That was his answer.

"I am not going to invest in the spread of civil war here," he said. "The China project is a good one, but you are right, it does nothing for the people of the Balkan states. I am going to build a highway from Pec to Budapest," he said. "It will do more good than arming the Bosnians for self sacrifice. I appreciate your desire to do something for people in Bosnia, Angelo, and I can put you on the payroll, as an international consultant just as Peter is." He was telling Peter all of this in German which Peter later relayed to me. He had no idea I was Bosnian myself at any time. Perhaps that is the reason he was talking like that.

I was truly floored and felt his attitude was to screw the Bosnians because he felt they were clearly doomed and his interest was only on how to get his hands on the money even if it meant building the Serb Express. Then he had the nerve to try to tell Peter and me and our friends that we should take him up on his offer. I wanted to kill the motherfucker. That is not a metaphorical or hyperbolic statement. I meant to kill the motherfucker dead as dirt. I asked Peter to arrange a meeting with Alija that night, so we could go for a ride.

"Where are we going?" asked Peter.

"In the countryside, just up to those hills," I said. "I want to teach that bastard a lesson so that no money in the world could help him since he doesn't know I'm from the old country and you never told him, right?"

"Yes, your right Angelo, I never told him you are from his people in the old country also." Peter looked in my face, and I think he understood that I was very serious about my intentions. "Okay, Angie," he replied, "I agree he needs a lesson, since he is a punk who thinks he is a hot shot. Alija has some money with him and I think it should be taken away from him since my other plan with the generals looks like won't come true. Whatever it is you want to do with Alija, his money wouldn't be put to good use anyhow, so we can just kick his ass and then let him go."

I could see he was back-pedaling, so I agreed easily. "Okay, you're right. Let's take his money, since it's so important to him, and scare the shit out of him. I think we need some tools from the hardware store. Is there a hardware store here?"

We walked arm in arm, Peter and I, right through the old city of Zurich, down the hill, across the bridge, past the Chinese restaurant, next to the office where Peter had worked at times, meeting with world weapons dealers trading everything from land mines to some Yakolev Yak 36 and Mig 23 fighter jets. He said they had been sold for as little as two thousand five hundred dollars apiece, depending on the quality, from some countries around the Black Sea.

"You know, that Russian General wanted to sell some high grade plutonium," he told me. "You know, you don't even need triggers to make that stuff deadly. It's worse as radioactive dirty bombs than trying to use the stuff for the nukes."

I told him I had some doubt about that. You just don't carry plutonium in your brief case. It's kind of hard to transfer. I told Peter there is an American expression, "hogwash," and I wondered if he knew what it meant. He kind of shrugged and didn't respond. So arm and arm we went.

The hardware store was not very impressive, two stories high, with a balcony on the second floor like some I had visited in the old mining ghost towns of Nevada, nothing like the Home Depot I had come to take for granted in the good old US of A. As we walked around the store, he didn't ask what we were looking for. I picked up a fine strong five-inch ice pick with a big wooden handle, a thin sharp shiny stainless steel spike. I saw the fear in Peter's eyes when he saw what I had picked up. I looked at Peter and before I had a chance to say anything, I read everything in his eyes.

"Angie, I don't think he will show up," he said.

"That will be a big disappointment," I said. "I promise you I won't make a mess and you can take his money. The bastard deserves to die. He has helped Chetniks buy guns to kill my brothers and sisters, and now he wants to rip off the entire Bosnian people. And the son of a bitch is a Bosnian himself, a fucking traitor."

"Angie, he told me he did not like the way your hands look," he said. "He asked me why your hands look so strong like that, and I told him you were a professional martial artist. I can tell you that he did not like what you said to him."

"What was that, Peter, that he did not like?"

"When you told him that Bosnia does not need enemies when it has friends like him," he said. "So I think he's not going to show up. Alija took that to be an unfriendly gesture which was smart of him."

Lucky for him he didn't show up. Looking back on it, I believe Peter probably knew right from the start that I intended to kill Alija, and he had warned him himself.

Alija took treacherous and irresponsible actions with disregard for what his actions would do to our Bosnian people and the consequences, which were with no doubt, grave. Did he know that Peter was no friend of our people, the Bosnian people? I am not sure. I am only telling the truth of what happened. If he had sold guns to the enemy or given them any financial help or cooperated to help with the enemy toward our people or any of those groups, he has committed a crime, at least in my view. No one has the right to play God, especially a little man such as him, with no experience in the political, military or diplomatic field. Whoever had given him authority to run the national Bank of BH and make him the owner of it, they must have known he was expecting material gains for the group of people that he was representing, or that he was supposed to be protecting the people of Bosnia. I believed in protecting the Bosnian people from collaborators like Peter and Alija who were truly not friends of the Bosnians, since now the American Marines are in it, my concern has doubled for their safety as well. The last I heard, Alija is serving a long term sentence for crimes he committed against his people in Bosnia and Herzegovina and Sandjak

As for Srebrenica, the tragedy was inevitable. My people were not given guns, much less the tanks and jets they needed, and they did not survive. General Mladic ordered his troops to execute, to murder, to slaughter the eight thousand men and boys they held in captivity. That is exactly what they did, and they no doubt raped all the women, and their children too. That is the way it has been in Bosnia for a very long time.

So I returned to my home in Las Vegas feeling chastened, humbled by my experience. Everybody had his own agenda, his own racket, his own game, and there was so little I could do. I felt I had failed.

CHAPTER TEN: FORCE OF TRUSTED FRIENDS

With associates like Peter, and friends like Giles Pace, it should have been no surprise to me that I renewed my professional and personal relationships with my old friends I had associated with before in U.S intelligence. I had worked with several agents to keep America and her interests running smoothly around world. Trying to keep Russia on a leash and at the same time defeating her ally Serbia, and ending the Serbian aggression against Bosnia and Croatia, and to bring our troops home safely after our mission was accomplished. That was a pleasant surprise, all in all, as some of my previous experiences with the agents of the world were quite brutal.

One of the ones I couldn't completely trust was my friend and acquaintance Peter from the former Yugoslavia, the one I had to keep on a short leash for so long who was unpredictable and dangerous, capable of hurting anyone without thoughts of the consequences for himself or the ones he hurt. In contrast to him the men and women of the American undercover intelligence operations both in and out of uniform were people that I could look back upon with fondness and respect and left me proud to have had an association with professionals such as they were. It was not like anything I had experienced in the Balkans. There it was an experience of being coerced and used, instead of one of being permitted to assist in a worthwhile cause for freedom. I told myself that this endeavor was not just the sense of the James Bond romanticism about it that excited me, it was something very real, and with a sense of the surreal, yet the people surrounding me were genuine and real. They carry the heavy clouds that can make a nation fall or rise although their agenda is primarily to bring the people out of their despair to see there is hope over the horizon.. I was one of those people who were shown the way to that horizon to experience the kind of freedom I had never known until I was taken under the wings of such people over the years.

During the tragic war raging in Bosnia and Croatia, I was asked if I could lend some assistance or knowledge I may have regarding the former communist Yugoslavian armed forces. I replied without hesitation and with the utmost sincerity, "Our boys are definitely in harm's way. Our Air Force and Navy and Marines are all today fighting the communist army of Yugoslavia, today's Serbia. We do not know just how capable they are or what kind of fight they might put up or how far they are prepared to go to rise up to challenge us. If this war was going on in 1970 or 1980 during Marshall Tito's leadership we would have a hell of a real fight on our hands. In this situation of political turmoil that Yugoslavia is in now my analysis and own personal feelings is that we will kick their butts. They are disorganized and do not believe in what they are fighting for. Most of all they are leaderless.

"I am with you all the way in whatever can be done to keep our soldiers from harm and give them any tools to help them win in the battlefield. I will educate you on the first hand knowledge that I have attained while serving in the Yugoslav armed forces, and I will try to give you all that I acquired during the time I was in service there, in the best way I know how. I will strive to be fully accurate since we can not afford not to be anything but, so that if ever you apply any of the suggestions that I give to you, it will be only be to the benefit of our soldiers and prevent any harm from coming to them. If I can do that I will be more than happy to sit down and talk with you. I instantly realized that I now was being given a once in a lifetime opportunity to really give something back to my country that has given to me everything that I've ever dreamed of wanting."

It was as recently as July 2002 when I had the pleasure to receive a couple of calls, one that came from Long Beach and one from San Diego in California. The first from a lady and the second from a gentleman both whom I have known as selfless and dedicated who made it possible for ordinary people to have their freedom safeguarded without having to wave flags for recognition to themselves. Their work was always done in silence without any fanfare. Everything they were trying to safeguard for us is what most of us take for granted and that is precious freedom. During my conversation on the phone with the agent in San Diego he suggested that there was some important issues that we needed to discuss and it should not be discussed on the phone. We thought it would be a good idea to meet at our favorite place, the Westwind Hotel in the Howard Hughes Plaza.

She, the agent G2, is a lady whom I grew to respect as a capable professional and also a decent human being. She is a person that I wish that I could applaud by her name, but who has to remain as the cryptic Agent G2. The meeting took place at the Howard Hughes plaza on the ninth floor of the hotel. We spent more than six hours exchanging ideas, analyzing the best and worst case scenarios and throwing out our own personal opinions, thoughts about the war, the plight of the people, the political climate, their military targets which needed to be clearly identified and eliminated and many other things as well as their military strategy and readiness of the Yugoslavian army. By this time our U.S. military forces were deeply involved in Bosnia. This was one of many similar very important meetings that we held before and the way things were going it wouldn't be the last. One very important point I stressed to my friends is that we must win this war because if we let Serbia triumph we will then have seven million refugees coming in America of every ethnic and religious background creating a massive threat for our national security absorbing that massive number people in a very short time. We all have agreed that is the most important issue to bring to the attention of Washington. We were all sure that this would carry a lot of weight. And it did.

We discussed the vulnerabilities and capabilities of delivering the punch to the enemy while defending themselves in the meantime from possible attacks. We all finally came to the conclusion that the U.S. Navy would be wise to move the fleet at least twenty five to thirty miles out to sea and the safety of the Adriatic Ocean. We analyzed every scenario possible to protect the navy from any kind of harm from what I call, their dangerous crazy yet outdated torpedoes that Yugoslavia had built and acquired from the help of Russia. I have yet to prove there is any evidence to prove that they may still be in existence and that is what I am afraid of. They are deadly and were used to safeguard the coast on the Adriatic during the Cold War. We had flown many thousands of sorties over Serbia, Kosovo and Bosnia and succeed without losing a single vessel, plane or helicopter from our carriers to the hostile forces except for one stealth fighter that was with no doubt due to the pilot's own cockiness. At the same time we delivered the most awesome military punch of defeat that brought Serbia to their knees. I feel pride that I had a small part in the participation of this especially if I had happened to make any kind of difference in preventing harm from coming to our forces.

I was ecstatic in seeing Serbia brought down to their knees. My father used to tell me an old legend of a story passed down for generations. It said if houses were meant for no one but man, then the wolves should also have them but they wouldn't know how to maintain one so they never wished for one. The Serbs had a beautiful land for a home but did not learn or know how to appreciate it or maintain it. One does not deserve to have a home if he doesn't feel the importance of what it truly means to have a home. I was thrilled to see them get their due, but even with all of my excitement in their being defeated I still felt pity for those innocent and blameless ones who were the ones who lost the most.

My friends wanted to reassure themselves of my happiness and good feelings although we all definitely shared in this emotional moment of victory. I wanted to remind them where I stood for the record, so I told them I'd state that first and foremost I am an American and America's interests come first. Second, I am a Bosnian Bosnjak and do not want to be seen to be anti-anyone, but I am pro American and pro Bosnjak and nothing and no one could ever take that from my heart. The subject was closed forever right there.

Our meetings went very well just like many others we've had in the past. Agent G1 and his partner Agent G2's questions at times seemed to get very aggressive although I didn't mind because we needed to press each other to come out with the blueprint that will possibly help our forces in the battlefields if they are implemented and we knew that whatever we had presented was to be our best we had to offer, and would be well worth taking to Washington D.C. The agents were very straightforward and personal yet I found myself feeling the same way and was very comfortable in answering each question that they threw at me and didn't shy away from asking them challenging questions of my own. The railroad track of challenge was running both ways. After all we were analyzing the military patriotism of Yugoslavia in the 70's during Tito's reign and the Yugoslavia in chaos today under Slobo's reign. Today's Serbian army will not fight because they are only a Serbian army.

Overall I felt like the architect of the plans even if all of my drawings may not be used, I still laid down the designs and my answers were credible and applicable. I wanted every military base in Serbia, Montenegro, and Kosovo wiped off the map. I did my darned best to convince my friends to pass my ideas on to Washington. They did at times and I felt complimented, although each time our blueprints were implemented into action I stressed the importance that we should do everything in our power so no harm will come to the civilian populations and the innocent ones. I knew that this chance and opportunity was once in a lifetime and it would not come around again and perhaps my hard work and that of friends would also free the Serbian and Montenegrin people from their tyrants. I don't hope to claim that trophy but if it did happen that the Serbian and Montenegrin people would be freed from the action the U.S. forces were taking against them, then I would not mind being one of those who accept that trophy for the freedom of all the people. I would not mind accepting a small part of that trophy that would bring the light to all of the people who had only known nothingness. Perhaps this would be a day the sun would shine on them and rightfully for.

As I write this story now on June 4, 2006, Montenegro has become accepted as a sovereign nation as it rightfully deserves. How many of us can claim that life has come full circle? I say the only ones who wait patiently and pave their own way for it will reach that goal. Bosnia is still in a fight for their freedom and to survive as a nation. Perhaps Montenegro will help to heal the wounded knees of Bosnia so she too can stand as a proud nation in the world community.

After all of our hard work that we had done and as much good that happened and as much success we did have, each time I anxiously waited to hear from my friends and about the feedback from Washington. There was never any disappointment, it was always the same, that it was a job well done and a thanks. It was not being told it was a job well done, it was the thanks I never liked. It was my duty and always will be to do whatever I can for my country. I wished to never even hear that word "thanks" again from my colleagues. The expected feedback always came from my friends about how Washington was very satisfied with my proposals and were seriously considering implementing them into action. I have always thought I had no room for failure on this so important once in a lifetime mission. There simply was no room for failure or mistakes.

When I felt the pressure building, I would go home and turn on Pavarotti or Bocelli and turn on the steam room to relax and sing along with them while thinking things through and getting a clear vision of what was going to be at the end of this road. Strangely it worked every time. My imagining was of my wishes of Bosnia to be spared from annihilation by the Serbs, and Serbia being bombed to hell and their military brought down to nothing, with this being the last time they would be a threat to anybody. It looks like all three of the wishes came true. I truly cannot explain how I felt after all of these things came to fruition. I have yet to figure out what the right answer is to that question. If the answer ever comes to me I hope it is truly the right one. That would be that all men on earth can enjoy rightfully what is meant by God. It should be a life free to the pursuit of happiness.

Am I one of those lucky ones who have come full circle? I hope not quite all the way because that could be the end for me and I have much to do yet. I have tried to save lives and make a difference for a better tomorrow always doing so without prejudice. Saving innocent lives is the duty of every human. I hoped I had succeeded on this journey by saving a life without having any bias towards Serbia, Kosovo, Bosnia or Croatia. If I have done than my life's circle may come fully around. It would be the greatest feeling to hold that trophy although I stake no claim on it. I have only tried to save a life but looking through the tragical times of this war, over a million lives were lost with another four six million permanently left without homes. My ultimate wish to be triumphant is perhaps to defeat the villain, yes, but in saving some of the innocent lives I feel I have failed. So the trophy will have to wait for another hero who I hope doesn't find himself in the kind of situation like the one I was in, sometimes feeling mighty and powerful, having the American forces next to my shoulders risking their lives by trying to free the innocent from the oppressors. Each time the Serbs did retreat, they left behind nothing but burning and human corpses. One million were dead and only a few of the villains were brought to justice. Some of them are still free and the world is now still reluctant to apprehend them. We are in a way appeasing these villains and murderers and sending a message for some lunatic leaders around the world that if they try the same thing they perhaps will get away with it too.

I made sure my appearance was professional, sharp and on target to get my point across in the clearest way and that my ideas got across supporting their own ideas and that I was with them one thousand percent and ready to give my life if it need be. That kind of conviction needs to be on display anytime you meet with serious, credible and such fine people as these agents were. After all lives were at stake and our actions could determine whether a nation would fail or rise. This time we were looking for a nation to fall and that was Serbia, the former Yugoslavia. Just as it did happen. A new one was born and that was Croatia and Bosnia.

I know that giving my life or dying for my country is not the thing I want to strive for. I want to strive to live and keep alive to make a difference, because if I am dead I won't be able to accomplish anything for myself and my country.

I have found myself in a group of professionals and diehard Americans, men and women, and have realized that thanks to their service and selfless sacrifices, it has enabled me the chance to enjoy all the beautiful things that I have never had before until I came here to America and also the opportunity of joining with them so that I could help give something back by serving my country. Now it is my chance, and I have been given an opportunity to give something back to society, to fully participate as a fellow American, to serve and keep our country free and safeguard the freedom that even I forget sometimes and take for granted. Thinking about it makes me feel tall, proud, honored, and most fortunate to be one of the few to try and make a difference.

There we were at the Howard Hughes Plaza and my good friend G1 had been waiting for me downstairs in the lobby. We hugged and shook hands firmly the way we always greeted each other as true friends do. I said to G1, "Are you guys comfortable upstairs?"

"Yes, very much. The suite is huge. Angie, I brought a couple more people with me that I'd like you to meet."

I said, "That's great. The more the better."

G1 said, "By the way, Washington wants to thank you for everything that you have done and are doing. Your hard work is being taken very seriously by them."

"I am flattered but I won't accept a thank you for my duty as an American in serving my country. So please forget about the thanks, let's just look at what's on the table and what else we can do." That is what we did.

We walked into the suite where there were three other members of the crew waiting for us. They greeted me and introduced themselves to me. I was ecstatic. What else could I say? But I tried not to let on to them how impressed I was and tried to keep my cool as much as I could. I wanted to hear about what G1 and G2 had come to tell me. Now there were five of us now. The odds between myself and them were four to one although in a professional way and for the good of our country. After long hours of all our debating, planning, map drawings and studying of the Yugoslavian military map, every bridge, factory, road, tunnel, military barrack and airport and navy port we studied, analyzed and carefully considered each and every one of the targets. By the end of the day we finally we found ourselves all on the same page for ensuring that our U.S. forces were going to win.

One of the new members who had come with G1 and G2 asked me how I felt about the chances of the Serbs leaving Kosovo. At the time we were bombing at full scale throughout Kosovo and Serbia specifically targeting their military industry and transport systems by concentrating on the roads and bridges and railroads through northern and central Serbia and Montenegro. "To answer that question for you I need to know what you are thinking," I said. "I already gave you before the numbers of paratroopers and the special police forces that are operating in Kosovo which are about seventy thousand strong but all of you have told me that those are unrealistic numbers and then ask me how it is that I know that. You told me I must be crazy because those numbers must be an exaggeration. Mister, I am surprised they aren't three times as many since there are plenty of volunteers waiting for the Bosnians' and Kosovars' blood. You said those numbers are unrealistic. I had told you that I spoke with Governor Seselj myself and got those numbers straight from the horse's mouth, Seselj himself, and from our buddy Peter as well."

"Sorry Ange. How did you ever manage to do that?" G1 asked.

"Remember I told you I keep Pete on a short leash and when I need him to bark for us he will. The only reward he gets is the acknowledgement and so here it is. Thanks to my and our friend triple agent, Peter."

"Does he work for us too, Ange?" G1 asked. "Is that just a wise crack or an insult to your friend?"

"As for me I don't know, that is something you will have to tell me." We all laughed on that note. "I wanted to bring Peter here with me but you said no, and I can only tell you his feeling were hurt but hopefully there is something you can do to repair that."

"Regarding these Serbian volunteers that we have been talking about, these people are from Montenegro and Serbia, unemployed and hard core extremists. They are on the payroll of President Slobo Milosevic, including the current Governor of Kosovo, Seselj, who is his very close buddy. I mean buddy in the same way as our buddy triple 0 seven Peter is."

G2 piped in, "Please Angie, why can't you leave the poor guy Peter alone? He's been crying a lot lately about you giving him a hard time."

I said, "When he dies I would like to have his body stuffed and placed in one of the national museums of Serbia so they could see just what of kind of people who were carving their futures for them. Then perhaps it would enlighten them as to what kind of people were leading them into regret for everything that happened to themselves and all of the former people of Yugoslavia, but I'd like to get back to the main subject.

"If you'll remember I told you about when Peter was speaking to Seselj in Kosovo from my home here in Las Vegas for over an hour at my expense but it was money well spent. At first Peter was talking with Seselj and during the conversation Peter was telling Seselj to send his best regards to his good friend the notorious Arkan. That made me think for minute. 'Who is this guy here that I'm calling my friend? I hope I won't live to regret it.' Then I thought I can't drop him, he has too much information that could be of value to me."

It wasn't long ago when Peter and Seselj had another long telephone conversation from Seselj's office in Pristina while Peter was again a guest at my house. He told me, "Angie, Seselj says to say hello."

So as not to seem rude I took the phone from him. "Hello, good morning Seselj," and I said it to him in Serbian, "Dobro Jutro."

His reply surprised me. He addressed me by my given birth name saying, "Hello Bajram. When were you baptized with the name Angelo?"

"I am surprised you don't know. Angelo means 'Angel' back in Gusinje and in Serbian Angelo means 'Meljace,' which is very Muslim. I am surprised I thought you were much smarter than that although I am a bit selfish when it comes to others in the world being as smart a I am."

"I hope you are not insulting me." Seselj replied.

"O.K. Seselj if you feel you've been insulted then you are already there and there isn't much I can do to change that but as for myself I know that I am very smart. I'll let you talk to Peter now, I think he's hoping you have good news for him and are going to make him assistant governor." Then I laughed and stepped away from the phone.

Peter looked as if his face was on fire. When he is mad his face looks like the ass of a baboon. He cursed at me, "Fuck you Angelo! I don't know what I ever did to you. Why are you giving me such a hard time lately?"

" Peter it is not me doing it, I think you should look inside of yourself and you'll find out who is doing it."

"I don't know what your saying Angelo."

"Peter it is you who is doing it to yourself. I think Seselj want to make you an offer so you can be a big shot just as you've always wanted. My advice is if he does offer you the position Peter, don't take it because Slobo, Seselj, and all of the rest of them are going to be hanged. Their destinies will be the same as Benito Mussolini's. You better stick close to me if you want to live the rest of your life healthy. Then maybe you will thank me for everything."

I left Peter to his conversation and didn't pay any more attention. G1 told me, "Don't tell me Peter took your advice because if I know him he won't take advice from anyone."

Of course not at first and that is what I was really hoping but later on he did take my advice. When I'd had a conversation on a previous occasion with Seselj when Peter was at my home I gave him my congratulations on his governorship over Kosovo and told him that I hoped he would fulfill the hopes of all the citizens and relieve them from their long and unjust oppression and be confident to put their belief in him. I wasn't shy to mentor to Seselj even though everyone thought he was a tough guy.

He hesitated for a moment. Then he said, "Thank you. I really do appreciate your wise words of advice. I'll try to think of them every time I need to come to a decision."

"Mr. Governor, if I may address you as such," I told him, "just go back in history and as you know no villain has ever enjoyed the glory of ruling expect for the ones who brought justice and prosperity to the people they were overseeing. Perhaps you can bring Kosovo the hope and justice she needs. You are in a position to do some good and this is your moment to triumph or to fail. You have seventy thousand men under your control who could be used for good or to do a lot of damage. Either way whatever the outcome it will be your trophy and I hope the children in Kosovo will glorify you as one who gave them the hope they had never known."

Governor Seselj then said, "Angelo, I wish sometimes that all the decisions were only mine to make. Perhaps then I would be triumphant."

301

I laughed. "Governor I hope the decisions that you make will not come from doctrines like those of King Alexander and Draza Mihailovic."

He addressed me again by my birth name, "Bajram, as I already have said, the seventy thousand volunteer troops are not mine but Slobo's."

"Yes, but you are the one who has control over them. On that note I will leave you with a wish for good health and that's all, so here's Peter."

That was the last time that I ever spoke to Seselj. Some time later he lost his position as governor. Slobo pulled him into Belgrade so he could have more control over him there. Seselj was given a title to be one of Slobo's cronies in Parliament unknowing that he would live to regret it.

The agents and I were talking and debating in the hotel suite on the sixteenth floor of the Howard Hughes Plaza over the best and most effective strategy for defeating the whole mighty Serbian army. Our air force was dominating the skies of Serbia, Kosovo and Montenegro, with the Serbs paying a heavy price. Their industry, military railroads and bridges were being demolished by our U.S. and the allied forces.

The agents G1 and G2 asked me with concern and worry in their voice and showing on their faces about what they could see happening after all the bombing. "We need to punish those seventy thousand volunteers who are nothing more than criminals. These are the thugs who make the honest, decent Serbs and Montenegrins look bad."

"What do you mean by that Angelo?" G1 as well as everyone else started to ask me at once.

"Here we were watching on live television thousands of people being expelled from Kosovo and packed in trains just like Hitler had done during World War II. If I recall correctly, didn't we as freedom loving nations around the world say then that we would never allow anything like this to happen again and let guys like Slobo be able to roam freely around Kosovo packing people in train cars repeating something horrendous that already happened in history that we swore would never be repeated? It doesn't look like we live up to our word. God knows where these people were probably headed and that was to the gas chambers or to a mass execution. This needs drastic action my friends and not just a few little bombs. This calls for some carpet

302

bombing."

G1 looked around to all the people in the room and then looked straight at me with eyes filled with worry. "Angie, you must be out of you mind. Do you know what you are saying? You know that everything that is said here must be reported to Washington D.C. word for word?"

"Well I would certainly hope so." I answered. "No man who wears the uniform of the Serbian Montenegrin volunteer army or the federal army should be allowed to leave Kosovo after all the atrocities they committed there. They should pay with their lives. Perhaps that is the only way that justice can be served for all the deaths they have caused."

One of the agents said, "What you are suggesting would require the involvement of the B-52 bombers."

I said, "Then so be it. If it needs to be done, then so be it. It looks like you find my idea a real possibility, sir."

That agent said, "I'm sorry Angelo. My job is only to be here to listen and observe and report back to Washington. My personal feelings are irrelevant but I do think this could be done."

I said, "Right, are we going to let them go on home singing their victory songs?"

He replied, "We would hope not. I don't think Washington will allow that to happen."

I emphasized that these soldiers are nothing more than thugs, murderers and rapists. There is absolutely no way we that should allow these people, these murderers, leave Kosovo alive. These are the very ones who started the burning, looting and killing from the borders of Austria and Slovenia, through Croatia, Bosnia, and Herzegovina to the banks of the Drina River. Now they put a burning torch on Kosovo and they are doing a hell of a damn job since they've gotten plenty of experience.

I told them, "I want to make it clear to you that I am not here as a talking head for Kosovo or Bosnia. Now I just want to share my knowledge with all of you. We all know the men and women of our armed forces are in harms way. The Serbian thugs will not hesitate for one second if they get an opportunity to harm our forces they will. We will show them through our strength, moral and military might that there is no way in hell they will leave Kosovo expect with their feet forward in exchange for the damage they have done."

G1 injected, "Wait, what do you mean by that? Feet forward?"

I laughed. "Oh, you mean you don't know the meaning of that phrase? It's a one way trip to hell."

He replied, "Thanks for the enlightenment and I think that is just great. I think Washington might think we've all gone crazy by the way we talk today." That was the way G1 analyzed our progress of that day which wasn't that encouraging. I thought I should cool it down a little bit.

Agent G2 asked, "What do you suggest Angelo, how do we stop them? We were told that it is rugged terrain out there, there is no way of stopping them. We received information that they were starting to retreat east to Montenegro through the city of Pec and the mountains of Cakor."

"Whoever you got that information from has no knowledge of that area because they can be stopped dead in there tracks so don't you worry about that," I replied. "I know every single rock of those mountains and hills and roads. I walked them in the hottest days of the summer and the harshest days of winter. I know every single road that there is and there is only one way out of and one way in to that mountain. The Mountain of Cakor is just west of my home town of Gusinje, above the city of Pec and the province of Kosovo, and there is a high straight mountain wall of natural rock formations on both sides with gorges that are miles deep and extremely treacherous. I hope they take that road because it will lead to their graveyard. The road was carved right through the middle of the southern part of the plateau of the mountain and is narrow with treacherous curves that connect Kosovo with Montenegro. Our air force should blast the bridge that is on the west side of that mountain road facing the city of Pec as well as the bridge in Murina over the river Lim. If we allow them to trap themselves in the roads of the mountains we will have them packed in and then we can pick them off anyway we want. There is no way they can make it this way and I don't believe they will even attempt to. If they do take that road I think then their commanders are very stupid. It would be exactly as we just said. I believe they will try to take another route that is easier but longer back to Belgrade."

Agent G2 asked, "If we blow up those bridges then what do you think their reaction will be? Where will they will go?"

"Like I said, to hell. They won't even attempt it. They will all have no choice but to go back first to Pristina, to their stronghold underground Air Force Base. Haven't you heard guys that the Russian military just arrived this morning to protect that base?"

"Yes, I hoped you wouldn't have to bring that up Angelo. It's a disgrace." G1 said. All the others agreed and shook their heads on how likely that might happen. The allied forces in Bosnia where they would have traveled from would have to close their eyes in order for the Russians to travel all the way from western Bosnia unnoticed. They didn't close their eyes but the French and Ukrainians took their positions for them in Bosnia so they won't be missed in Bosnia. These Russian troops were part of the U.N. peace keeping mission in Bosnia. Suddenly two hundred men left their posts in Bosnia to crusade to save the Serbs in Kosovo and no one saw them leave. How could that happen?

G1 and G2 said. "There must be something important inside that base."

"I was thinking the Mig 25s must be inside that underground air base and no one else is there but the Russian pilots and Serbian maintenance crews. They would have no other reason to try to save that base."

G2 said, "I don't know Angelo, I think you are opening a big can of worms."

"I am not opening a can of worms that hasn't already been opened. President Clinton should perhaps we should ask the Ukrainians and Greeks why there are military intelligence people there. Those are the reasons the Russian troops came in to guard the base. There is nothing else of importance for them in it."

G1 looked at me and stood up in front of me putting his hands on my shoulders and his face so close to me I could feel his breath, "I'm sorry, but I can tell you that our government will not take any chances with a confrontation with Russia over this incident, Angelo."

"What, do you take me for a fool? Of course they're not going to, you don't have to waste your energy to tell me that. I have become emotionally involved with this, probably more than any of you are, although if you really wanted to help you may want to pick up the phone and call the base in Aviano Italy and tell them to send a squadron of F-16's to blast that fucking base to kingdom come along with the Russians, Greeks and Ukrainians in it."

There was silence for a moment. "Now your talking stupid for the first time but I know how angry you are. I don't like the Russians any better than you but I'm hoping the retreating Serbian military forces will go on from the base with the Russians included."

"Yes I think that would be great, and then on to Krusevac and I hope that if they do reach it they all drown in the South Morava river. From Krusevac it's a long way to Belgrade."

We said our farewells after the meeting and agreed we would meet again very soon. The bridge at the river Lim had been blown up, just as we had it planned. It was a success with no loss of any civilian lives in Montenegro of our knowledge. That was one of my proud moments for me as a citizen of this nation and being able to participate for a better tomorrow and the freedom of mankind, which after all is what my country stands for, freedom, liberty and justice for all. Just as I have said many times, you have to be alive to make a difference and be patient. Agent G1 and G2 and I had developed a personal bond and understanding with mutual trust and respect for each other. After all I thought, how many times could you convince a squadron of F-15 Eagles and F-16 as well as the newest stealth bombers to fly over your home town to wave in the wind to say hello and good morning bringing well wishes from Las Vegas in America, and to assure Plav and Gusinje that no harm is going to come to them from Kosovo's Serbian militia.

This was a serious business of life and death to us after all. G1 assured the rest of his crew that I had was a patriot and a professional of strictly business and made it clear to them that I was not looking for any kind of a James Bond adventure. I wanted the difference to be made absolutely clear. Saving just one child in that God forsaken war would make me feel rewarded like nothing else. Perhaps I had yet succeeded to do that. Our soldiers lives were in harms way there.

I said, "Anything that I do or suggest that could affect the safety of our troops I will consider carefully." I insisted that they should be developing more contacts from Yugoslavia and especially from Croatia's former ranking navy officers, who are even more knowledgeable than I in the military and intelligence matters about Yugoslavia, and to make better use and strengthen my suggestions for any military actions. I am especially concerned and fearful by the torpedoes they manufactured and acquired with Russia's help. I hoped they had not replaced them with the Chinese Silkworm torpedoes. Looking back now I am happy that I took the interest of learning the body and structures of Yugoslav's overall military. The input I was able to offer from the knowledge I had acquired of Yugoslavia's military during 1969-1970 was put to great use.

Ironically no advanced changes have been made in training, readiness or any other way for over thirty five years. No wonder I was on the target for everything in determining the way that they functioned. Each time some actions were taken against the enemy I was informed of the success and of what I had contributed to prevent the losses of life of our troops and my hopes in always keeping them out of harms way soared. They are the true heroes to me after all.

My friends in intelligence tried to thank me for what I was doing. I found that to be offensive, and I told them if you try to use that word again you will be destroying everything that I have believed in and cherished for the last thirty five years.. "I am first an American. The only thing that connects me across the Atlantic Ocean is my ancestors. Whatever we are doing here together is only my duty as a citizen of this great nation of ours. My desire as I'm sure is also yours is to make sure that our men and women in uniform fulfill their duties and keep that edge in our strategic, political, and economic and of coarse the military around the world. I hope I have been understood. Please quit making me feel as if I don't belong here, as if I were an outsider."

"Oh no, please, that's not what we were thinking at all," Agent G1 assured me. "Washington is grateful and they have considered very seriously every suggestion that you have made."

I said, "Well thanks, but I want them to consider everything we have drawn up together and have this war ended in a matter of days. By the way I am grateful about that bridge on the river Lim that you blew up yesterday and also the lesson we gave to the Serbs that we will get to them anyplace and anywhere they are. It was also great to see that other bridge overlooking the suburbs of the city of Pac."

G1 said, "By the way Angelo, what was the name of that damn bridge over the city of Pec?"

"It was called Sand but some people called it Dry Sand Bridge. Funny name for a bridge, isn't it? The whole area is surrounded by fine sand."

G1 asked, "You heard it shook through the whole valley didn't you?"

I told him, "They probably thought at first it was an earthquake. But on a serious note my friends, this is a direct message delivered to the government of Montenegro that they better not play around with those two fucking losers Milosevic and his assistant Bulatovic from Belgrade. G1 did you realize this guy Bulatovic is from my home town? The second in command to Milosevic and what a loser he is. The day will come for him to regret and be ashamed."

Agent G2 laughed out loud, "It was a spectacular mission and it was just like you said it would be. It was very hard to fly low because of the high slopes of the two mountains and the high horn peak in the middle of the valley facing the town and lake and the very narrow entrance. The pilots said they felt like they were flying through narrow tunnels. The mission was successful just as you predicted and we all had hoped for. Our intelligence reports stated that there were no movements from any Serbian troops toward Montenegro."

I said, "Good news!" I hugged G1 and G2 with both my arms around them and was proud to have been able to have made some kind of a difference in helping to stop possibly seventy thousand murderers that would have come through my hometown by way of Plav and Gusinje and repeated the unthinkable atrocities that had happened just as in Srebrenica and then that would have provoked our air force to defend the Valley of the River Ljuca, Plav and Gusinje and Montenegro would have become something that I and everyone else would have regretted, a demolished state.

Looking back on everything, I would call those agents, "Angles of Hope" and "Preventors of Disasters" for the people of my ancestors land. That was the greatest gift that I could have given in stopping Slobo and Bulatovic's Chetnik volunteer militias from burning the land of my birth like they had done in Vukovar and Sarajevo. While trying to spare Plav and Gusinje from the burning torches of Slobo and Bulatovic at the same time I think Montenegro got spared from being totally bombed by the allied forces.

Everything that has happened so far I think that even whole bottle of extra strength aspirin would have helped. As for myself I can say I was having a major headache from all our efforts of trying to do what was right without having any regrets later. G1 or G2 felt no better and all of our crew was in the same boat and feeling the same way yet feeling proud of our successes so far and knowing what was coming.

G1 said, "Angie maybe we should just finish up for today and start fresh tomorrow."

"Sorry brother, but we ain't gonna quit till I am sure that

everything that we need to do is done. This is the time in my life that I am taking things with the utmost of importance. Our boys are out there. I couldn't bear the thought of making a mistake, and then seeing coffins coming here possibly due to my poor judgment. I absolutely could not accept that in myself."

G2 assured me, "Angelo, we are proud to have you as part of our team."

"Well thanks, I am proud to think that anything that I am doing now might save some innocent lives on both sides of the alley and in my heart at least I know that I did try."

It was late in the evening and we were yet to have left that hotel room in the Howard Hughes Plaza. We thought we would order in some dinner since it looked like we were in for a long night. We ordered pizza for dinner. We were eating our pizza and sliding greasy fingers on the map of Yugoslavia and trying to identify potential targets that needed to be demolished. It was about two in the morning and my mind was drifting to the Adriatic Ocean where our fleet was positioned facing the unpredictable enemy. G2 said, "Angelo, you're daydreaming man, come on."

"No I wasn't daydreaming. I was thinking we need to do something our fleet over in the Adriatic Ocean to keep them safe. Our enemy is an unpredictable one. We can afford no mistakes." We all were down on our knees around that map of Yugoslavia again and mapping out every single island along the coast of Dalmatia without overlooking any harbor or bay as a potential hiding place for enemy torpedoes. We all agreed that our fleet should move deeper into the sea. I reaffirmed what we all thought and agreed was best to do and that was to advise Washington to move the fleet aircraft carriers further back in the Adriatic and also find out the number of Russian scuds being brought from Serbia to the highland plateau of Montenegro overlooking the Adriatic ocean. We need to give stern warnings to the government in Montenegro that if any scud missiles are fired out of their territory against our forces or allies that the repercussions against them will be of horrendous proportion for them. Our advice to them is to stay neutral in this for their own good. As we now know not one single torpedo or scud was ever fired on our navy from them or their territory.

As we were winding down for the evening and the sun was starting to glow over Sunrise Mountain, I reflected back on the time when I was still in the Yugoslavian Army. I had a small part in creating a fleet of tiny torpedo boats that were intended for defense on the coast from ships of war that were now threatening the men and women and their fathers and mothers who had given me a country I could call home. How many of those floating robot torpedoes still existed, I had no idea, but I know now that if they were in the hands of the wrong people they would have tried to harm our fleet. I was hoping that my intelligence agent friends who were with me that night would understand my worries and deliver my and their solutions of how to counter this whole mess of a real yet invisible danger to our men and women in uniform there.

It would be all of our dreams come true if we heard from Washington within the next day that all of our work and effort we put into it were going to be put into action. Mine and all of our suggestion were well received with thumbs up from Washington and our fleet was moved as we had hoped twenty miles out into the Adriatic Ocean and thousands of sorties have been flown over Yugoslavia with only one loss of a stealth aircraft over Belgrade, and one loss of an aircraft flown by Scott O'Brady over Bosnia. I had made suggestions in many of our meetings to convince them that a place that should be blasted was the chief of staff headquarters in the heart of old Belgrade located right behind the Hotel Slavia. But that didn't happen and for whatever reasons we went all the way over to the other side of Belgrade and bombed the Chinese Embassy instead which was located in the new Belgrade. It seemed funny to my friends and me at the time but looking back now we realized it was done for one reason, to remind China that she had been behaving badly in supporting Serbia in their aggression against their neighboring states. After all I would say it had been a success and China had a change of heart by withdrawing their support of Serbia.

After I had first heard the news about the Chinese Embassy bombing I couldn't help but to call up my friend G1 in San Diego and G2 in Long Beach and as they say in California, I was "stoked" and excited to tell them about it but it slipped my mind that they would have known before I did and they did remind me. "I was just getting ready to call you with the exciting news. Thanks for blowing it for me." I told him that it was all great but I was still hoping that we were going to go for our original target at the general headquarters of the military in Belgrade. All of the top ranking generals are in the building

310

at six o'clock every morning. I had always stressed to them that if we chopped off all of the snake's heads then there would be no snakes with fangs to bite us back. To my pleasure we did blow up numbers of many of the important buildings and bridges that we had targeted around Belgrade and our air force tried to kill President Milosevic in his bedroom at the Presidential Palace, but to my disappointment the general headquarters was spared. I considered that to be the prime target I really wanted to be blown up more than anything else. I believed that would have brought an end to the war.

G1 asked me, "Why do you think that would end the war?"

"That building is where the whole brains of the operations for this war is located. Without that the war machine could not function."

G1 said, "Well thanks for clarifying that for me Angelo." How fortunate or unfortunate is it that history always repeats itself?"

I told him, "One historical reminder is when King Nicola of Montenegro sent his army to invade Plav and Gusinje and his General in command, Marko Miljanov didn't obey the orders from the king to conquer the lands and to spare the people. General Marko and his army did the opposite of what the king's orders were and didn't spare the land or the people from their burning torches. At that time there were no outside forces coming to help and save those doomed people. The villains struck again spilling the blood of the innocent, but this time they are being struck back with a power that is unmatchable, from the great American military force, and it looks like that little valley of Plav and Gusinje has been spared from the same dire fate as those who did in 1912 thanks to the flying bald eagle of America."

Agent G1 requested that he, agent G2 and I should arrange to get together as soon as we hear from Washington. I said, "I can't wait my friends. Will you be buying dinner? I would like to have that prime rib they serve at the Circus-Circus Resort Steak House. After all this has been a successful mission so far and we deserve to have a good dinner."

G1 interrupted, "And the government can pick up our tab. I'm just happy for you Angelo for the fact that no lives were lost in the bombing of that bridge At least none that we know of."

I answered, "Yes, do you mean that bridge over the Lim?" And as far as you know there has been no loss of life in Murina, Plav and Gusinje?"

"Yes that is right," G2 replied. "I really do care about all the lives of those who are innocent.."

"Thanks for the great news I hoped to hear. No losses of lives."

To lighten up things a little, G2 laughed and said, "Hey Bajram, Angelo, what is it that you think you are trying to do, read my mind before I have the chance to say anything?"

I said, "No, not at all. I just know that great minds think alike. So I am buying and I'll meet you guys there at six o'clock tonight at the steak house."

I hung up the phone and then I called the Circus-Circus Hotel and Casino and gave my name and asked to be connected to the steak house to make our reservations for dinner. On the line came the voice of my friend Ron who is the maitre'd there. "Angelo, my friend, long time no hear from you! When are you going to come and see me? I miss you, you bum."

"I love you too, Ron," I said. "I will be coming there tonight at six o clock with two of my friends and also my wife and children."

"I haven't seen the children for a long time and I miss them too." Ron said. "I would like to see them. Please make sure that they do come along. Have they grown up?"

"Well let's say every time that I look at them and see how they are growing so fast, it makes me see how I am getting older every day myself but I am enjoying watching them grow. How is your family? Is everybody all right? Is there anything that you need?"

Ron replied, "I have always had respect for you and you have always been a friend to me and that's all that I need is your friendship."

I told my friend Ron, "I've been blessed since coming to this great land and having friends like you who have diverse ethnic backgrounds and yet find we have understanding, respect and a love of life and for our families."

On the other hand I had never looked at Peter in the same way as the kind of friend Ron is to me. Peter was the man whose main interest in me is what he could get out of me and mine was the same in him. He stayed at my home, ate my food, and drank my wine and yet I knew his intentions were not good towards me and he wished nothing good to come to me, in fact he even wished me dead although he never had the balls to make that dream of his come true. For that I punished him by keeping him on leash all the time. Fortunately, people like Peter have helped make me stronger and more determined to finish what I start, and eliminating from my vocabulary the meaning of the word losing.

Agents G1 and G2 arrived and it was great seeing them again. We had dinner at the steak house and as I already had a feeling, I knew I wasn't going to be allowed to have the pleasure of paying because our check was already taken care of, not by our government or taxpayer's money, not by me, but by my respected friend Ron.

My wife had declined to join us and did not come to eat with us but instead took the children to the indoor amusement park located in the Circus Circus, so as to give my friends and me a chance and some space to talk about our next agenda concerning what was happening and the chaos in Yugoslavia. We sat at a far corner table of the room until late that evening drinking just coffee and sodas that night. We compared our notes and discussed the progress of our armed forces. I must admit, it was gratifying looking back on our successes over that period of time and the lives we helped to save and the millions of people we helped keep from harms way so far. We agreed to meet again soon for a discussion on the strength and capabilities of the air force of Yugoslavia. They had not challenged us yet and we needed to analyze why and be prepared against any surprises.

A few days later we met specifically to talk about our concerns and the questions that Washington wanted the answers to on the Yugoslavian Air Force and their ground to air defense. I warned my friends that we should be careful about the way we fly and how low and how fast. We could lose some planes if we were not careful. They will not use any of the Russian made sophisticated radar they have to track us because they know we would knock that out. They will use radios and telephones to let their guys know fifty to a hundred miles away that a plane is coming in and at what certain speed and height. That is where they will get us. It is a very primitive but yet effective way to do it. The next day, Scott O'Brady was shot down, apparently without having been observed by any active radar that would have been detected by his airplane's electronic surveillance equipment and gave him some warning of the danger ahead.

We sat for many hours in our suite the hotel in the Hughes Plaza going over military maps from Yugoslavia, marking them with yellow and black erasable inks. We marked places from Belgrade, Nish to Kragujevac as well as many other places throughout Serbia. How were we going to find a way to figure out how to stop the movements of the army, an army that was unpredictable and scattered all over with scud missiles that we were the most concerned about? Especially right now in Kosovo I thought, if we could just hit those prime targets that would do the trick.

Seselj wouldn't like that. I would have loved to make sure he knew that I had a hand in it. That wouldn't be possible now but one of these days we would make sure to let him know if he lives through it. The intelligence agents wanted some more information about this character Seselj. I told them, "Look guys, there is some things I have heard about him but there is someone else who we all know who knows Seselj like the back of his hand."

G1 asked, "Who is that Angie?"

"That would be Peter."

"Our Peter, our hero?" G1 said.

"No, my little doggie that I keep on a constant leash, remember? But I can give you a little of the history that I know about Seselj and his movements. Maybe if we compare my notes to Peter's notes then we might come to know who the real Seselj is pretty well."

I grilled Peter soon after that on everything about Seselj and he didn't act surprised because someone else from Dallas Texas already recently grilled him on the same character, possibly someone from central intelligence. He had whined and complained to me about it saying they were not very nice either. Peter was curious as to why I wanted to know some information about Seselj too. I tried to throw him off the trail and I asked Peter if it was really true that Seselj was the only member of the Serbian Parliament that wore a holster with a gun when at the Parliament. That was something Peter admired about Seselj. He turned into a talking radio of information after that for me. He started telling me all about Seselj's and the troubled adventures he had had with him all around Europe, Australia and throughout the United States, in Chicago, New York, Los Angeles, and Cleveland.

He told me that a few years back Seselj was decorated and ordained by an organization that carried the late King Alexander's legacy who were the Chetniks and based in Chicago where he was given the title of General Seselj, like one of King Alexander's right hand subjects. Peter said he thought that could never happen, that the Alexander era could ever come back. Undoubtedly Seselj has blood on his hands of many of the migrated workers from Yugoslavia all over the western world and with no doubt he had the help of his friends, like

Peter and Arkan.

I offered Agent G1 a gift. "I have for you the biggest fish that you've been looking for and asking a lot of questions about. I can deliver it to your table on a plate," I said.

"What fish?" he asked.

"The big fish Seselj, my friend, Seselj. Remember the last time we met at the McDonalds at Hughes Plaza and we talked about a man named Seselj?" I asked. "Well I told you that Peter had spoken to him on the phone from my house and also introduced him to me over the phone. Seselj trusts Peter with his life and I think I can deliver him to you on a plate. If you like Peter and I can just make him disappear or if you really want him as you stated at our last meeting then I'm ready to hand him to you at any time without a single hair missing from his head."

She sat back for a moment with a look of surprise in her eyes, as though surprised that I could be telling the truth and not just joking with her. I could clearly see also fear in her eyes of the possible danger. She looked to the others for support before she answered although no one else spoke. She was the one with the authority. I thought that was what she and all of us wanted. "Angelo, we cannot do that," she said patiently. "We are not in the kidnapping business."

"What kidnapping business, who's talking about kidnapping anyone?" I asked. Again she looked for someone else to speak up in support but no one did. I told her "You know the man is a notorious murderer with blood on his hands up to his heart. I have not personally seen him kill anyone but I know that he is commanding the deaths of thousands right now in Kosovo with his and Slobo's militias. I have no idea how many people that he is responsible for killing while he was Tito's agent. If you want Seselj, I'll get him for you. One thing is for certain with the help of Peter I will deliver him to you or if you'd like me to bury him I can do that too. Then again I forgot we are not in that kind of business and have to keep our standards of morality and let him continue his butchering. What a lucky son of a bitch he is."

Agent G2 stepped in because he thought I might be getting out of line, "No, absolutely not. We are not in the kidnapping business and we are not hit men either. Can't you imagine what harm that could do to this country's reputation?"

Agent G1 then said, "G2 that isn't entirely true. We do want to get rid of the thugs like Seselj!"

For a moment in my mind I drifted back into history. I thought about Nicaragua, El Salvador, and Guatemala, Peru, Honduras, Chile, and Argentina from 1970 up to 1984.

"Well," I said, "There are many like Peter and Seselj and I do not think there is anything wrong to recognize and point out exactly what they are and just go ahead and go out and get them. I myself recently went to pay a visit to one of those thugs, Alija Delimustafic in Zurich along with Peter and it was with all your blessings."

"Oh, yes," G2 replied, "Well he is one of the biggest gun runners in Bosnia."

I asked, "Gun runners for whom? Not for the Bosnians."

She then asked , "Angelo, what are you driving at?"

"I just want you to know and understand that I do not flinch away from the idea that sometimes the best way to handle a situation is to dispose of whoever it may be that is doing no good," I told them. "There are some people I think it would be doing a favor to the world and serving justice to get rid of them and if I could be of help in doing that then I will be pleased to."

Agent G1 and Agent G2 made it clear to me that they did appreciate my willingness to swim with the sharks in the deep end of the pool, but those type of activities were just not part of the way we did things. I told them, "Well I am learning and fast. So much for my Agent 007 stuff."

Agent G1 said, "This is off the record and I am talking as a private citizen and not an officer of our forces. If I have to make that decision then I will join you." It occurred to me for a moment that I really was living in a true and healthy democracy where you are free to speak your mind without fear of repercussions.

"Thanks my friend. We must stop these bad guys from doing any more damage than they have already done and don't forget the most important thing is that they are capable and will if they can put our troops in harm's way."

G1 smiled and tapped me softly on the shoulder and said, " I will relate this issue to our superiors. I think that they will be appreciative of the power of the positive energies that we are bringing to the table. These ideas that we have been working on will bear fruit."

I said, "As I've always told you, you have yet to fail in bringing my favorite beautiful music to my ears with your firm conviction for the things that we are doing."

"Don't try flattery Angie, I know you better than that. We talk and think so much alike sometimes I think you must be my twin brother."

Agent G1 requested that I go and meet with an officer who was new to our team, Agent G3, from the naval base in San Diego, California. We were to meet at the usual place and what had become my home away from home, the Howard Hughes Plaza in Las Vegas just off the strip. Before I left to go meet with them I went upstairs to take a shower. As I walked up each step my mind was spinning a million miles per second. What did this new agent want with me? He obviously must want to find out what makes me tick. What will he see in me? Somehow I didn't feel too good about it. They told me he was a nice guy I should enjoy talking to but there was something about the way it had been set up that just didn't feel right but I knew my intuition was right. I knew he couldn't be just another officer. I had the feeling that he was the one who had been reviewing my work and making the decisions on what did and didn't get to Washington. Now we were finally going to meet face to face. It was still just my assumption but one I strongly felt the urge and need to know. It was almost like getting awarded if my assumptions turned out to be correct.

Finally full of all of my thoughts I was in the shower and I started singing not even realizing it, which is unusual for me. I never sing in the shower but here I was singing an Italian opera and to be truthful I think I am probably pretty bad. I thought to myself I hope I am a better convincer than singer but then again there is nothing I would have to convince him of because by now he probably knows me very well already. The only thing that needs to be done is for me to get to know him if he allows me to. I think still that today is going to be the day I will make it or break it. This new guy I think may be thinking that I'm a little too good a maybe a con artist, or I'm not telling everything I should be telling them.

I got out of the shower, dried my hair, splashed on Polo, my favorite cologne, put on my best suit, and I felt like I looked and smelled like a million bucks. I went downstairs and to the garage, started my 944 Porsche, drove to the Howard Hughes Plaza, and by the time I got to the lobby, one of my agent friends was there waiting for me already. I had been asked before to speak with different agents from different branches but I didn't see anything that could be conducive to them and I wouldn't end up looking like a fool so I had always declined before. I was comfortable with the agents I worked with and developed a bond of trust with them. We somehow had a perfect reading of and understanding of each other and I didn't want to change any of that. I didn't see how it would be productive. If any new faces came in, I would have to readjust myself to them and repeat myself all over again and I do not like that. We shook hands and hugged when we met in the lobby as we always do when we meet.

Agent G1 is well built physically and a very sharp guy, always ready for any surprise it seemed. Nothing came as a surprise to him. You'd definitely like to have him on your side if you were facing an enemy. We walked toward the elevators, and during the few moments of riding up to the suite he assured me that the officer I was going to meet was really a nice guy. "Angie, just to let you know, he is my boss and he is really looking forward to meeting you."

I just shrugged my shoulders. "Don't worry , I just hope we will be able to communicate," I said. "Whatever he wants to ask me he can and I will be happy to answer whatever it is I know but I think I may be running out of material. There is hardly anything that you and I have not already talked about. We have gone through military maps and plans, psychological warfare, the warfare planning, the dynamics and structures of all the branches of the Yugoslavian military. We have studied all the bridges, roads, factories, missiles, stockpiles, defense planning of the country, and our capabilities on the Adriatic Coast, even those mysterious torpedoes that I have yet to be able to prove a single one exists but I know they are there. We have examined the southern defense forces of the military in Montenegro, the military housing, the air force bases in Montenegro, Kosovo, and Serbia. I am not sure there is anything we haven't at least touched on."

The door to the room opened like they knew we were standing there without our even knocking and I was greeted by my friend Agent G2. "Hello Angie, it's nice to see you," she said. "You smell delicious."

I laughed. "You know what the smell of Polo reminds me of? When I was a little kid we would cut the grass and then put it in huge cone shaped piles. If the grass was not stacked well the rain and humidity and moisture would make the hay rot and turn into a green mold and the smell of it is just like Polo."

She laughed, "Angie, I always said you were crazy."

I continued, "No, for real. I mean it. I don't really like it but I wear it anyway because I don't want to feel left out since everyone else is wearing it." I wanted to hug her but didn't. I didn't want to embarrass her and thought I better behave professionally. She was in her mid forties and carried herself well and I didn't want to make her uncomfortable, but only feel the respect from me that she deserved.

She took my left hand in both of her hands and looked me in the eyes saying, "Angie, I'd like to introduce you to our commander. Angelo this is the commander. He reached out his hand and gave me his rank and full name. I'll address him now just as Commander G3. His handshake was not as firm as I would expect but rather gentle. I knew in an instant that he was the kind of man who could be capable of a thousand faces and it might take me a lifetime to figure him out. I tried not to let it bother me but after all we weren't talking baseball or football but about matters of national security and perhaps changing the boundaries of the nations.

With my experience in relations with people and the way that I live, hustling and trying to stay alive every day without being hurt or hurting anyone else, I have learned that you must keep your guard up all the time, and size up people before they size you up. This time I knew I was in a circle of truthful friends I could trust with my life and didn't need to look over my shoulder.

I found Agent G3 within a short time of encountering him to be like a chameleon, capable of adapting to whatever environment or circumstances he needed to. Perhaps that was what he needed to be in the position he was in. I doubted he could afford to be anything less.

It was immediately clear to me that this was a part of his professional tactic. These people had become my friends, and they always respected my voluntary participation but I could tell right away that today they were supposed to put a little pressure on me to see if they were any cracks in my knowledge of the Yugoslav armed forces and intelligence. This time it felt like three against one and not like our usual teamwork. I was questioned and they were supposed to see if they could take any of my experience or knowledge apart. That was not going to happen since my memory is photographic of everything. I may not remember what it was I ate for breakfast this morning but I remember every detail that happened forty years ago in sequence of events and forty years from now I'll probably recall that breakfast I had this morning.

We were involved in friendly conversation and started talking about our children and families. I was anxious to get down to business. G1 was of no help for me today. I considered him a deserter for the day. My conversation did not involve baseball. It was a very serious matter. He had been sent on request from Washington D.C. "This time I had better know and be on the ball with everything I have been doing so far," I thought to myself. I know what he was looking for was conformation. "I will do as I always have done and anything that comes out of my mouth should be steady, convincingly confident, strong and clear as always. He should have no doubt of my truthfulness."

After long discussions while looking over the military maps, Agent G3 had been questioning me back and forth not in doubt of my truthfulness, my character was never in question, but only if my memories of the facts remained the same since we were dealing with the seriousness of life and death. I had no doubt of that and if I hadn't been questioned I probably wouldn't have even bothered talking to him. I thought to myself, "Mister, you know I am a professor of psychology only without a diploma hanging on the wall. If you are an enemy, God forbid, I think I could walk you across the water on Lake Mead and leave you thirsting on the other side without your realizing that I had walked you over the water. There is no better way to show your trust in me other than the way you have conducted yourself with me. "

We shook hands and said goodbye. I did not say loudly that I was looking forward to seeing him again nor did he although we both knew we would be meeting again. My thoughts were that this was just the beginning with the way the world is spinning in so much trouble and had no doubt we would be meeting again. I held his hand in a strong grip without letting go and looked straight into his eyes, and said, "Mister, my ancestors' land is on fire right now as we speak and you are here to find out what can be done to put out the fire. I assume you are considering me one of the lead firemen. It's an awesome burden although if that is the way you feel about me I accept it and will do the best I can to lead us all to the where that fire originated from and then we can follow the trail and hopefully extinguish the madness and the dying of these innocent people. If I can help in succeeding with this then our image to the world as a freedom fighting nation will be elevated one step higher, and we need that as a nation. Well, I may not be the best fireman there is but I have tried by shooting off my mouth now for over the last ten hours, and I hope you don't think that I talk that much all the time because I usually would charge a fee for when I talk. In all of this what I just want you to know that I am a die-hard patriot of our country that has given me everything I have dreamed of. Forgive me if you think I've talked too much. I just wanted to make sure that our American troops all come home safely to their loved ones instead of in plastic bags. I doubt if you could ever understand just how much I love this country."

He gave no reply and had his eyes cast to the floor. I let go of his hand and said goodbye to my friends Agent G1 and Agent G2, and stepped into the elevator and rode down to the lobby. Agent G1 put his right arm around me and said, "Angie, I hope I get to see you soon. It was a great meeting. I sure hope it does save some of our boys' lives." That's all I really needed to hear.

I was feeling such great emotion at that moment. I had finally heard what I needed to hear from somebody, especially those magic words, "our boys, our soldiers." I knew the way Agent G1 just spoke to me and by his body language that it came straight from his heart. He was like proof of a picture being worth a thousand words and his few words were like a thousand words to my soul. He had said, "our boys," and I felt deep in my heart that now I truly have a country of my own and I belong here. I am a part of the team that is on a quest that is making history by tearing up another oppressive nation to make out of it a new democratic nation. The only one who could do that is a nation such as ours, the most powerful nation on the planet. What a great time in history it is to be alive and a citizen of just such a nation.

There has been no other nation similar since the times of Rome. People have said that the Roman empire and her citizens were privileged ones. I can only truly say that if anyone has ever dreamed about being alive then and being a Roman citizen, well there is no need to have to dream about it. The greatest days in Rome were only a hint of what was to come here in America. If you are an American citizen and you live in this great nation, your dreams have already come true. I know mine have come true, I can honestly say that life has blossomed full circle and I am not afraid. I know the bloom of this healthy nation will remain for a long time to come.

CHAPTER ELEVEN: DIPLOMACY.

I was trying to accomplish something I thought was really needed by getting guns to the Bosnians, and I finally admitted to myself that by arming them it wouldn't change the fact that they would be persecuted and killed anyway. It would only enable them to fight back some while it took place. The kind of guns my friends and I were able to get in for them wouldn't do justice for them. It would probably lead them to getting killed one day earlier rather than later. That was not I wanted for them. It would have taken the U.S Air Force and an army of the Marines with M1 tanks to save them. That meant that the only way to save them was by getting the U.S to override Butros-Galli and the UN. All of the above has already been done. If becoming a covert operative or a mercenary doesn't work and working with U.S intelligence doesn't make a difference, then what it will take is for masses of the American population to be educated to what is happening across the Atlantic. Then perhaps I as well as others could change the attitudes of people in their hearts and minds and they will want to support us.

I asked my friend Stephen Coolbeck if he could participate by joining me in my fight by facilitating a space in his Polo Towers Resort for us to organize a meeting involving local and state politicians. I believed it could make a difference by bringing people together to hear about what terrible things were happening across the Atlantic.

When I asked my friend to participate he didn't even have a clue where Bosnia was or anything about the war at the time. That convinced me more than ever I needed to get ordinary and business people involved, so I did my best to educate him as fast as I could. I was not that surprised by his ignorance about the war even though he is an extremely intelligent man. It seems that there a lot of Americans who are not geopolitically or geographically inclined, and have very little idea exactly how they as Americans fit into it all. Most think the whole world revolves around America. America is a fasinating and huge nation that sees the world revolving around it and not it revolving around the world. One couldn't really blame them. I pointed out to him that Bosnia wasn't all that far away. I told him it is mirror facing Israel a blink of an eye across the Mediterranian. There was a reason I described Israel using a mirror. Steven is a strong supporter of Israel because of his faith and his roots. I told him help was needed there and fast. To my surprise, he was aware of more than I thought and the importance of putting an end to the tragedies that were taking place there. He clearly understood the importance to not stand by on the sidelines and pretending not to see anything until it is too late like so many people had done during World War II.

With very short time to do it in, Stephen and I had the dinner event organized and set up. We couldn't have done it without the help of his personal secretary, Nina. Invitations were sent out and things were in motion.

On the night it was held Stephen surprised me yet again by pouring out his heart speaking passionately reminding the guests that a house on fire or a country in war is never too far away from your own house or country. "We must extinguish the fire that is raging out of control in Bosnia. I want to help them. My expertise is not in any way shape or form that of a diplomat or a politician, but I can do whatever I can do as a responsible citizen and put to use whatever influence I have."

Afterwords I reminded him that the real influence he certainly had, he should use. "You and President Clinton are pretty good friends. I think your opinion will mattter to him and now it is your chance to see how much of a difference we can make for Bosnia. It seems like your opinions matter a lot to the president and I don't see why he wouldn't take your suggestions seriously. My message could be told to and heard loud and clear through you to the President. You could express what you said to the guests tonight to the president. You said yourself that it is in America's interest first and foremost to save Bosnia. You said that Bosnia could be just as important of an ally as Israel is to the United States. I think the president will at least listen and hear out what you have to tell him."

Stephen said, "When I meet with the president should I tell him he should be looking at this as a long term investment for America?"

"Exactly! You couldn't have said it better my friend." Clearly I could see that he could be a messenger for the good and help to make a difference. I thought to my self, "Stephen is making a small dent in history if he realizes it or not."

Stephen had also spoken that night on the story about the tragedies and triumphs of his people from Palestine and Judea, today's Isreal. It has been passed on to him and over his generations for two thousand years by his father and forefathers. He knew of the lineage of his ancestors from the time they were exiled from Palestine by the Romans after Christ's crucifixion, and then again fifteen hundred years later from Spain by Isabella and Ferninand during the Spanish Inquisition. With sadness he said that after all the time has past his people are still fighting to survive in the new nation of Israel.

Stephen said, "If I am hungry for freedom and crave a nation for my people it's only morally right to give a nation to the freedom-hungry Bosnian people who do rightfully deserve to have one. They don't want to invade anyone else's land. It is their homeland and they have the right to keep it. I want to try help rescue the people who had helped to rescue my forefathers. It is my moral obligation to do everything possible for people not to have to become refugees and wander the world as my people had to do."

I was surprised he could speak so well and he looked pretty good up there. I told him later, "Stephen, you should be running for office."

He answered, "I will if you will be my campaign manager." We laughed and left it at that. Perhaps he was serious and will give me call about it one day. I thought to myself that there is good in the world. When I heard what Stephen had to say and thought of the good hearted people like him it reinforced in me that there is genuine hope for the world.

As much evil as we think there is surrounding us, our resilence and our belief in good for the world will always triumph. I truly believe that there is more good than bad around and inside all of us and that good will always prevail over evil.

Gatherings such as the one that night at the Polo Towers are a testament that when people come together for the good of all, the tree will truly bear fruit and great things can be accomplished.

There is always a purpose for a gathering, holidays, birthdays, or family parties. This time it was something truly different and a matter of saving lives. This gathering's purpose was to save Bosnia so she would not become another tragic statistic somewhere in the pages of history. Those are Stephen's, mine and all the people's who gathered there that evening. Our wishes for that history not to be recorded on bloody scrolls were granted. However the wishes of Milosevic's were different and had almost come true. He wished to make Bosnia history on bloody scrolls. Although she was badly wounded the nation and her people survived.

I can truly attest that good over evil won in this case, yet it is still a continuing bloody drama. The main difference now however is that it is with the power of the pen and paper instead of barrels of the guns. I think I can live with that and so should the rest of the world.

At the nearing of the end of this war in Bosnia the world leaders figured that someone should have to pay and it wouldn't be them. The local leaders that participated in this war were arrested and tried for the atrocities and genocide that were committed against the people. Most of the leaders from the western world could have prevented some of the genocide but chose not to and instead chose to stand on the sidelines and watch it happen. The French president and the head of the U.N. should have shared responsibility for everything that happened to Bosnia. Although I think one shouldbe happy President Milosevic in Serbia never delivered what they thought he was capable of in more atrocities. The world did get tired of waiting on him to finish his dirty work and get rid of Bosnia for good. By the time the war came to an end the west and U.N. cried for the heads of those warlords including Slobo's. They did and most were arrrested with the exception of two of the most notorious who remain free living in a foxhole somewhere in Serbia, Montenegro, or Bosnia. Perhaps have converted fully in their respectful faiths in their Orthodox religions and living lavishly in one of those beautiful monastaries that throughout Serbia and Montenegro. I hope that is not the case, it would be an insult to the others that are faithful in their religion. Some of these leaders were assasinated by their local rivals or some were removed from power and are out of office without the power that they once had to do the same things again and became vulnerable to the very ones they had pushed around before. Obviously they have paid with the ultimate price of their lives.

Many changes were happening in the west. There was new blood elected into leadership with hope on the horizon. John Major of England lost the election, President Bush Sr. lost the election, and Hafiz of Syria had died of old ages. Unfortunately Kadafi managed to survive and is finally enjoying a diplomatic relations with the United States, perhaps he will soon be visiting the White House. The drunk from Russia was also out of office and was replaced with the unpredictable ex KGB director. What a blessing. Tuzman of Croatia never got to live to see the greater expansion of Croatia either.

It seems God did work in a mysterious way. President

Miterrand of France spread his wings to God by dying and even all of his military might couldn't save him. As they say God has his own mysterious ways of doing things. Some of these changes were good and some not but you cannot have everything. The real butcher managed to survive seeming to have nine lives, until his tenth life caught up with him, and he died in his cell in Haag. Two of his lackeys are roaming free through Bosnia somewhere in the caves living as ape men. Slobo, the self proclaimed president of Yugoslavia, died while on trial for his life.

Who is to say that God does not do his job or punish the guilty or reward the innocent of these war crimes? Even though I am not a religious man, I believe that God is around and what form it is that he exists in does not matter too much to me. What does matter is that these people are somehow paying for their henious crimes. No, I am not saying that all of these people actually committed murders but they did allow this mad man free reign and they did carry that destructive ball of fire to commit these crimes for four years without bothering to stop him.

President Clinton and the newly elected Tony Blair of Great Britian finally had enough of it and put a stop to it dead in it's tracks. I cannot help but sometimes think that some of the Western and Arab leaders were sleeping with Slobo in the same bed and were hoping Bosnia was cleared out once and for all as a nation. They didn't realize the one most important thing about Slobo. Through the generations of his family on his mother and father's side the family was nothing but suicidal. After all it's the twenty first century. We should know better than that. We should forget about Richard the Lion, Phillip of France, and Saladin of Syria. This is a new time and age. We have traveled to the moon and the galaxies. We can hear the beat of the hearts of Jupiter, Mars, and Venus. Yet we look so ignorant and pitiful by not being able to look for God with the lights on instead of groping in the darkness with closed eyes and not even realizing that God is within us in our own hearts.

Slobo made a mockerey of the international court of the tribunal in Haag. I don't know who is better off, him behind bars experiencing death in shame, or the men and women that he is responsible for who are dead, raped or buried in unmarked graves in numbering around one half million. At times I wish he could understand the pain and what he himself had lost and was missing as a human. Then I wish he had not been able to feel anything that decent, for the simple reasons that those type of rewards coming from the beauty of nature shouldn't be granted to a beast such as him.

The predecessor of President Clinton, George Bush Sr., is a man that I wouldn't mind to have as my neighbor or friend, someone I could ask for advice. I couldn't choose any better human being. I consider myself privileged to have had him serve as president and the leader of our nation. Yet with his awesome experience in foreign, domestic, international, criminal, senatorial and ambassadorial affairs in his position in the last presidential position he occupied, I cannot help but want to ask him one question myself. Why didn't he lift his hand to call the self installed president in Belgrade, Slobodan Milosevic to tell him to stay put and that people have the right to decide their own destinies without him to decide and do the thinking for them? Yugoslavia was on the road with no stopping to breaking apart. Bush Sr. chose not to do anything at all. He left the burden in the hands of the next incoming president who was President Clinton.

Hopes were high in Bosnia that the new American administraton would take initative. One thing was missing throughout the campaign. That Bosnia was really not an issue in the campaign, and the politicians in Bosnia did not understand what that meant for them, which was life and death. Before Clinton became elected they should have met with all of the major canidates who were running to plead their case to them so that whoever did become president would be familiar and they would already be one step ahead. That was not done.

By the time Clinton's honeymoon was over in the White House, Bosnia was bleeding to death with hardly anything left to be redeemed or saved. I was surprised that Clinton even bothered and finally did decide to do something about it. It would have been easier to just open the doors up to a million immigrants to come in from Bosnia instead of going in and blasting, starting war with Serbia without really knowing what the final consequences would be. The major sticking point was Russia's reaction. Although President Clinton did exactly what I had dreamed for him to do as well every Bosnian and that was giving Bosnia a chance to become a sovereign nation and in good standing as a new member of the world's community.

Every hungry dog on the block was taking a bite out of Bosnia's body. She was bleeding all throughout her boundaries and internally as well. Some of the world tried to rescue her but were not strong enough and it was too late by then anyway. The only surgeon right for Bosnia was America. Without sending the freedom fighting surgeons I would respectfully call them, the Marines, Navy, and Air Force, under the leadership of President Clinton, Bosnia would never have recovered from her wounds in surgery. As of yet I would call it an imcomplete mission. More power to President Clinton. He did what any dignified man should have done. It was long overdue, Mr. President.

By all means and in God's name I truly believe that any disagreement, whether, political, ideological, religious or just a personal difference of opinion between two people or any society should be settled with a pencil and paper and then there will be no losers. No one has the right to take another's life except for the one who granted that life and in this case I believe Mother Earth gave life and will take life.

At the beginning of the conflict in Yugoslavia four nations in the middle east, Syria, Lybia, Israel and Iraq invited the leadership of Serbia to visit their respective capitols to reinforce their full support and to encourage Serbia's aggression against the rest of the former Yugoslavia's republics. It was absolutely uncalled for. Especially when the Isreali leadership invited the Serbian leadership to visit Israel to them encourgement to invade Bosnia instead of doing what should have been expected from them and that was in telling them that the path they were on was the wrong one. But no, they have been at war forty years themselves in a bloody war with the Palestinians. The encouragement of the Israeli leadership was nothing less but a political and strategic mistake that would take time to be corrected. Shame on them. I thought they were more wise and experienced leaders and I have a great personal disappointment in them. But the viligance of the people of Israel about this issue showed that they did not agree with their leadership's actions.

When Itzak Rabin spoke for peace between the Isrealis and Palestinians one of his own decided to kill him. I wrote to him and unfortunately I never knew if my letter reached him or not before his assassination. In the letter I urged him to help me pull my people from the boiling pot of blood in Bosnia. I urged him in my letter to get involved with Bosnia's cause and sooner rather than later. It was the right thing to do.

Two of the bloody criminals responsible, Mladic and his boss

Karadzic, have real blood on their hands and are still free, thanks to indirect French military involvement and some French Canadian general whose name I don't care to mention who stands accused by our people of rape. The French and Russians were playing the part of peace protecters with blue berets on their heads representing the UN. In some instances stories circulated that they too had committed rapes on the Bosnian women themselves. Like they hadn't had enough abuse from the Serbs already.

In this situation the only ones getting protection from the French Legionaires were the two butchers, Mladic and Karadzic. The blue helmets betrayed the trust our people had in them to protect them. Every front page carried headlines saying, "UN tribunal indicts top Bosnian Serbs." The important thing the media failed to mention was that the murderers were still free. They had it all wrong anyway. These bastards were not Bosnian or Bosnian Serbs. They were intruders. One is a Serb from Serbia and one is a Montenegrin.

The born and bred Montenegrin was Karadzic who was a head shrink doctor, no offense to the rest of doctors in the same profession, but this one seemed to be a psychopathic maniac and a mass murderer. I could only compare him to Dr. Mengele or Karadzics' teacher buddy, a lady named Planic. She killed most of the children in her school. Stories were told to the children that she taught days before she helped massacre the boys and girls, and she claims to be a loving mother. However that story is yet to be proven. She is already jailed in Haag for war crimes. I hope she wasn't expecting the Nobel prize for the mother of the year award. I wonder what she gave birth to, a devil with four horns and a long tail?

Maybe her mother and father were such evil people and full of hatred that they taught her nothing better than darkness and destruction. Either way it doesn't mattter. They created a monster that went the way of not having any natural maternal insticts of love as a woman should have. Instead in some ways she discovered that she was capable of being the first woman known in history as a butcher of children. God forbid I hope she's not proud of what she did. She now has plenty of time to reflect on it in jail in Haag.

Such evilness is really is no surprise, as we have all witnessed it in one form or another, knowing that there are people in society such as she. Such examples are only capable of destroying everything good in humanity. Their world is darkness. Most of us were taught to be morally opposite thankfully.

Suddenly Serbia as a nation found herself lying in the bloody wet bed she had made for herself and trying to wash it away. Suddenly every newspaper in the world's headlines seemed to be reporting about the "Butcher of Yugoslavia" being betrayed. That was Milosevic, betrayed by the military, the prime minister, his special police force, and his own citizens. That wasn't a surprise to me. It seems like the media and the rest of the world were missing the point. He wasn't betrayed by his people, he betrayed his people. The media missed the point again.

He should have taken the advice in a letter I once wrote to him. My advice to him was not to crown himself as king and president of Serbia. The ones who had done so before paid dearly with their lives. I wrote him that he was taking his country and his people into a deep hole of Hell and no one would be able to pull them out, not even himself. I advised that it was much easier to get into a war but much harder to get out. His mother Russia would not be there to bail him out because she had her own problems and killing to do in Chechnya. Russia was already hungry and at war with herself and she was destroying her self in Chechnya. Russia was never good at bailing anyone out from their hell of destruction since she is in hell and Serbia was a little too far away from home.

Of course Slobo didn't listen, although he did aknowledge my letter through the embassy in Washington D.C. I received a call from his embassy's military staff attache to complain that my letter was too harsh and unrealistic. After deriding me he asked if I had any family in Yugoslavia. I told him there was no one in my immediate family they could hurt because they had hurt everybody and everything there was that I loved already and there was nothing more they could hurt. I stressed to the colonel that they still had time to redeem themselves from their paths of destruction on themselves and everyone else around them. I repeated that Russia would not come to their aid and the United States would blast them out sooner or later.

It happened just as I said. Aviano Air Force base in northern Italy played a role in that prediction of Serbia getting blasted. Italy was pleased to be a host on this particular occasion, it was her dream come true to tear Yugoslavia apart and thus have no opponents or adversaries on either side of the ocean and at the northern border. That prophecy came true for me.

I have yet to see Serbia show any remorse or offer any apology for what they did. Obviously Serbia found themselves as the losers morally and in battle, angry and disappointed, but unwilling to accept any of the responsibility for it. All the cooking had been done by them and they should eat what they made. They thought they should have won hands down. They should have known better than that. History has taught them nothing in particular. They did as they have always done before, killing innocent people who never did any wrong to them. This generation seems to be even worse than generations before them. My people were hoping the Serbs would learn from their previous mistakes but it seems each time they fail they only become more enraged and still blame others for their own failure as a society.

I'm trying to come to terms about what can possibly be done to feel safe with neighbors like that. Build a wall like the Isrealis did between Palestine and Israel? Definitely not by doing what the Serbs did.

After the election in Serbia, which was nothing more than a sham, Milosevic and his leadership were hoping by the election they were orchrestrating to be seen by the world as a reversal to his new democracy and that the world would forget what happened and the damage they caused just across the border in Bosnia. Contrary to what Milosevic thought would happen, that this election would save his skin, his prime minister instead took over the control of Slobo's internal police and placed Slobo on a one way helicopter flight to Haag. It was a turning point and a death sentance for the prime minister himself. Their ball of rotted yarn was unraveling. The election produced only one good thing. It was the first shovel full of dirt to bury Milosevic.

The prime minister knew that after the election if he hadn't already gotten rid of Slobo then Slobo would get rid of him. Slobo would kill him just like everyone else he had killed. He then possibly had second thoughts about killing him and wanted the cycle of violence to end and thought there must a better way of dealing with Slobo and that was by sending him on the helicopter ride to Haag where he would have plenty of time for reflecting on everything while he badly played his clarinet for the rest of his life. That is what he did to Slobo, but unfortunately by those actions dug his own grave for himself. Days later he was assassinated. A Serb had betrayed another Serb. He was assassinated. The Serbs claim to hate betraying one

331

another but it is in their blood.

It seemed now the whole world wanted Slobo's head on a platter. Slobo was in a place he should have been taken to a long time ago. The world should already have known that he was a psychopath. His mom, dad, and grandfather all committed suicide. They were a family of psychopaths.

Milosevic's hopes to restrain America from getting in the way of his goal to create a greater Serbia with the help of Russia and China were now just an illusion, just as much an illusion as the Bosnian president had that the Muslim world would come to their rescue on a white horse with Saladin at the lead. It never happened. President Izirbegovic's dream was that Saladin would be riding in on an Arabian horse to the rescue which was never to happen. It was the dream of a child not a grown man. The U.S. Cavalry came instead.

Both Slobo's and Alija's dreams were doomed for failure. Alija's dream somehow managed to survive only because of the United States change of heart in siding with the victims and not the villians. That was the moment that he had Serbia beat hands down with the help of the U.S. calvary fair and square. Perhaps that's what Aljia had in mind of the U.S. calvery, thinking of them as Saladin's calvary and whatever his thoughts were, it worked. He watched from his office as the United States Army, Marines, Navy and Air Force did their thing the way they knew how to do it. He didn't even have to get his shoes dirty and watched it all from the window of his presidential office.

There was no more need for the Muslim world to struggle to find a way to help Bosnia survive. The U.S. was already there and doing it for them. This time it was a Christian nation fighting another Christian nation to save the Muslim nation. Bosnia was never a Muslim nation or ever will be. It has always been an ethnically rich and tolerant society for all religions.

The Muslim world was in such a chaotic situation that any help for Bosnia was a hopeless thought. One who cannot help himself cannot help anyone else. Bosnia's only hope was America and in the end the bald eagle did rescue Bosnia.

A few countries were also great participants in saving Bosnia, Malasyia, their neighbor Indonesia, Pakistan, and Turkey. Their participation really made a difference. South American countries, Argentina, Chile, and Brazil were also great supporters for Bosnia to survive as a nation. It really is gratifying that the Christian world rose to the golden occasion of saving Bosnia from sinking into oblivion. Looking back fifteen years later they should be proud of themselves.

All the empty promises from the Russian government never materialized for Serbia from their Russian brothers. How can one who is hopeless be able to relieve the hopelessness of another hopeless nation like Russia? In this case Russia's helping Serbia was absurd and an illusion of Serbia.

Destruction and ruin would follow by way of the West coming from Aviano Air Force base in northern Italy to Serbia. Milosevic's own country and the people of Serbia would think of him in the beginning of the war as a hero. That would fade away. Now he is the number one enemy and hated by the Serbian people for everything he promised and did not deliver for a greater Serbia. Only a lunatic like him could have made a promise like that in this day and age when every household could witness everything happening on their televisions. His idea would not fly and he should have known it. Since all of his promises were washed away in the stream, well, we all know what happens to losers and he will be remembered as a traitor and a failure. The people turned on him and his government like a hungry pack of wolves. They blamed him for everything. This would serve as one more page in history that the Serbs failed themselves just like they had done in the battles in Kosovo and in World War I and World War II. It's was just a repeat of the treacherous ways Serbia has always had of doing things.

The United States and NATO decided to take action and bombed Serbia to kingdom come in hell and rightfully so. They deserved to be plunged into a fire of hell just as they did to their neighbors. They needed to feel what it's like to watch your home being burned by primitive cannon shells like they did day after day blowing up house after house in Bosnia over a span of four years. They were bombarding cannon shells in Sarajevo and every city in Bosnia from the surrounding hills. It must have felt like an eternally long, slow and tourtuous death for the city of Sarajevo and the rest of Bosnia. Serbia's Army were now being burned by the allies, with the American F-15 and F-16's, Royal 9th Squadron Aeroforce Tornadoes, and the brand new stealth fighters which were newly introduced in the American Air Force. Overall the American Air Force did what it was trained to to do and as they always have done. They brought freedom to Bosnia, a freedom that has long been waited for.

The Muslim nations were hopeless to be of any aid to Bosnia and if they could have it would be a war of two great faiths. It was smart for them to try to get more involved than they had. In fact I think they should have been much less involved than they were. Since the war was occuring in the heart of the Christian world in an ancient Roman land it was only morally right for the Christian world to step in. In the perspective of moral issues the ball was in the Christian world's court. They had no choice but to try and rescue Bosnia, after all the Bosnians are their dead decendants. Bosnia waited to receive the Pope's blessing and he finally gave the benediction for a resurrection.

The Muslim world's public relations, I'm sorry to say, did more damage than good. The Muslim world was unorganized and some of their leaders not well respected around the world. I wished in a way that some of them had done nothing except for the nation's help I had mentioned before. We would have been better off and possibly the Western world would have been able to determine what to do to best help Bosnia without so much interferrence that couldn't possibly have done any good and the war may have been cut short saving many more lives.

It seems like they never learn. Out of all the tragedies that happened and the people who died on both sides there is not a family in Serbia, Bosnia, or Croatia, and not to mention Kosovo, that hasn't been touched in some way from the bleeding, pain and the loss of the lives of their loved ones.

It is like a corn field which was hearty and lush one minute and in a matter of seconds a storm came along with hail and winds leveling it and it was gone. All the hard labor and care put into it was washed away. The picture is obvious. There is hardly anything left to harvest. In the case of Bosnia generations were wiped out, never to be. They should have been harvested by God and lived to old age and not murdered by the likes of Planic, Karadzic, and Slobo and Arkan and his White Eagles. The very same things have tragically happened throughout history to the Bosnian people in 1912 and during World War I and World War II and in 1992. This time they wanted to finish the job. The young were killed and they left the old who weren't healthy enough to be able to repair all the damage. Who will plow the field next year or in the years to come? Will there be a future harvest and who will harvest it and for whom?

A very unnatural phenomenon occured during this war. We all,

Christians, Muslims, Jews, Buddhists, or Hindu strongly believe that no parent should ever have to bury their child. The Serbs broke that natural law and made every parents nightmare come true causing tragically unrepairable damage. The Serbs outside of Serbia went out of their way to truly express their feelings and how they felt about the freedom they had never known and that they now had in their new homeland. If one asked everyone of them the question why they had left Serbia their answers would be because of oppression and having no freedom. Yet they forgot all that and dug deep into their pockets for loose change to send so they could buy the military camouflage and bayonets for the murderous bastards to be able to break that natural law and murder those children. The camouflage and boots were paid for by the Serbian immigrants so that these murderers could look more impressive as they killed the innocent. The people who supported them are just as guilty as the ones who pulled the triggers and used the bayonets.

Srebrenica is one sad chapter and just one of the many places throughout Bosnia that will be remembered for the tragedies that occurred there and the two hundred and fifty thousand men, women and children that were selectively taken from their homes by direct orders from General Mladic and his boss Karadzic, the head shrink doctor. These two butchers committed the most heinous crimes against humanity. Their orders were for the innocent people to be taken from the towns and villages that they had lived in for centuries and be executed and then to erase any traces of their dirty work by burying them in mass graves.

These murderers didn't care, for whatever the reasons they came through those beautiful valleys on each and every one of those cursed days of madness. The people had been happy and peaceful since the beginning of time. A beautiful moasic of people and culture that evolved over milliniums. The contributions to the world of these beautiful people were ignored by these two butchers. They couldn't leave them in peace and innocence and simply had to destroy everything that had been built over two thousand years by the systematic destruction of the people and their history. This was not just an ethnic cleansing. It was the total destruction of one civilization and the obliteration of a race of people which happen to be Bosnian Bosjnaks.

While systematically and indiscrimantely executing the people regardless of age or sex, they humiliated many of them in very inhumane ways. Over time we have learned that what we suspected was true and that some of the NATO officers under the cover of their blue helmets who were in Srebrenica didn't lift a finger to stop the Serbs from their rampages of terror on the eight thousand four hundred people. One of these notorious officers was Canadian ranking officer McKenzie who was accused of rape and also collaborating with the enemy but unfortunately he was shielded and protected from prosecution by the U.N. charter.

Every household around the world saw it on television when General Mladic marched into the town of Srebrenica with his mighty army and the blue helmets welcomed him and they convinced the people of Srebrenica to lay down their arms and nothing would happen to them and they would be safe. The mayor of Srebrenica was naive enough to do just that. He welcomed Mladic in their traditonal way with the offering of bread and salt and a with a bottle of plum brandy. Mladic was on a mission and that mission was wiping out Srebrenica for good. I was one who knew what was going to happen but couldn't do anything about it. Every door I knocked on, no one answered. The people were left to the mercy of Mladic and his men. The end result for the Serb general to report to his boss Karadzic was, mission accomplished, but without realizing that this would be the final road to hell for them.

I tried to make some sense out of it all. How can any normal human being not ask himself the question? How could this happen? It has happened before and nobody asked that question so why now? I think if only because now we are more civilized and less barbaric. Secretary General Butros-Galli made sure that the Bosnians would be empty handed and not have anything more to defend themselves with that was more deadly than a plastic fork and knife. By the same token they promised they would defend Bosnia and how they did that was by allowing the Serbs to plunder it.

The Serbs had the green light, to put it bluntly. They quarantined Bosnia with a wall made of their army and cannons placed on every hillside of every town. Their army and cannons could have been made to look like spectators at the Daytona speedway. The cannons could be the racing cars with each gunner was racing to see who could blow up the most houses and do the most destruction and be number one at the end of the day's race. They could think of themselves as formula one drivers with machine guns and a bayonet in each hand so that they could rampage all over the racetrack. That scenario would be for Bosnia a race for death and a great pleasure for the Chetniks. This was not the Daytona racetrack however. That would be an insult to the men and women who participate and fans of the sport.

I hesitate to believe that this was a crusade to wipe out Bosnia once and for all from Europe as a nation of Muslim faith. On the other hand four nations at war with each other supported the aggression on Bosnia. The nations were Libya, Syria, Iraq and also Israel. There is no room for me to argue that the Christian world was on a crusade; it was not, except for Serbia and Montenegro. These four middle eastern nations participated in small ways in that dark chapter in history. Greece had their own political agenda and couldn't keep her hands clean and went all the way and supported Serbia too but stopped short of sending in their army.

I still didn't believe that it was a crusade by the Christians against the people of Bosnia, but only by a few idiots and narrow minded tyrants. There were some Jewish and Christian who participated with me in trying to stop this madness.

We tried to bring awareness by organizing the dinner event. I told my friends that this one sided bloody conflict has already been going on too long. Nine hundred days had already passed. Each day someone had their roots pulled out of mother earth in Bosnia forever from every faith. Families are perishing without a trace.

On September 18th 1995, I made a call to my Irish American friend Kevin. I told him I had thought of an idea and asked if he would please hear me out, since I knew he was well aware of this war across the Atlantic. He had told me he would like to do something and I told him I had idea and I thought it would help expose this terrible war to our citizens who are not much aware of it. Ones who do know what is going on I think feel it is too far from home, and they can't connect with it. Maybe we can help make a connection and help them realize that we all need to get involved.

Kevin is one of those people who is not shy about speaking his beliefs and putting his thoughts into action. He was a three time tour of duty veteran in the special forces in Vietnam and also a man of faith as a Roman Catholic.

"I wanted to come to by your house and see you when you

have some time. I have all my thoughts and plans down on paper. I am hoping you that you will find it interesting.

Without hesitation Kevin said "Angelo, whatever it is, we will do it."

A half an hour later I was at his house. There wasn't any need to knock. He was waiting for me with the door wide open. We shook hands and hugged. I swear each time I see him I feel like I'm seeing Santa Claus because that's the way he looks. He didn't let go of my hand, gently leading me to the dining table. With concern in his voice he said to me, "Angelo, you are worrying me. What's bothering you?" "I cannot sit at home and watch all of this happening. There is something more I can do but I can't do it alone. Everything I have done up to now has hardly made a visible dent. I need to involve more people, people like you. One man can only do so much and sending blankets and canned food is almost an insult. I don't want to fatten my people for a kill, I want the killing stopped. Kevin shook his head and said, "When the killing starts Angelo, it's hard to stop it. I've had that experience in Vietnam. So what can I do?"

"Kevin, I want to invite leaders from around the world to attend a conference for peace in Bosnia." Kevin listened to me with passion and respect as always.

I handed to him what I had written. He was surprised by the first name that was on my list when he saw it, Yitzhak Rabin from Israel. He read it aloud and said that my idea was good and had a lot of potential to be brought to frution.

This is what my letter stated to the prime minister dated January 18 1995,

"Your Excellency, My name is Byram Angelo Kolenovich. I am a Muslim, a Bosnian and a member of Freedom for Bosnia on whose behalf I am writing to you. I hope you'll forgive my taking up some of your valuable time to urge you to involve yourself in the solution to the total raping of Bosnia before it has been completed.

It is with much deliberation that I invite you to involve yourself in this matter. The trouble is in your part of the world and threatens to move closer.

Israel is embarking on what it hopes will be an era of cooperation with it's neighbors and other Muslim states. This is a chance for Israel to strengthen ties with Turkey, Egypt and other area powers that it will be dealing with in times to come. It is also a chance

*to do some good and a chance that should not be passed up.
Perhaps if you and other fair minded world leaders used your good
offices along with the United States and European powers early
enough this tragedy could have been avoided or cut short.*

*As of today Bosnia has suffered destruction like that in the last
war. The only part of the former Yugoslavia that sought to create a
peaceful democracy with a multi-religious state has been attacked,
dismembered and put to the torch by the force of oppression, religious
hatred and division.*

*Our attempts to show that a Muslim state can be open and fair
to others have not been allowed to succeed. Our distinct culture is
being drowned in our own blood. It is not useful at this time to call
attention to our suffering as well as the great contributions to the
European and the rest of world civilizations that we are not being
permitted to continue.*

*At this time it is necessary to convince the west powers who alone have
the ability to force a settlement on the ravenous enemies of Bosnia. It
is in their interests to make such an effort.*

*Appeasing an aggressor does not make him less thirsty for the
conquest it makes his thirst sharper. If Bosnia is lost the conflict will
inevitably expand and escalate.*

*Serbians thirst for territory is old and deep. The next step of conflict
would be the NATO neighbors and members, Turkey and Greece. Then
the fighting would involve well armored and prepared forces that
would be one step closer to Israel.*

*This conflict would split and destroy NATO who has been the
most successful keeper of the peace since the Roman Legion. It would
bring Russian influence into the heart of middle Europe and involve
Russia and the United States in a nuclear armed confrontation. We
thought that we had rid ourselves of that nightmare but inaction now
may bring it back to us.*

*You will shortly receive an invitation to attend a conference in
Las Vegas Nevada about Bosnia. Attached is a list of the other invitees.
The purpose of this conference is to adopt a platform of action and
urge the United States and Europe assuring them simultaneously that
those actions will have the full support of conference members.*

*It is not too late though it is close. The stakes are tremendously high
both for you and the rest of the world. The stakes are limitless for
Bosnians. I urge you to attend. Sincerely yours. Bajram Angelo*

Koljenovic."

My good friend and I put a professional program together and decided to host it in Las Vegas on December 12th thru 17th, 1995. It was to be held at the Riviera Hotel and Casino Resort.

I paid a visit to a friend of mine at the Riviera Hotel, Robert Vannucci, vice president of the hotel. We spoke briefly about the conference and our conversation expanded to the full political ramifications of gathering in this conference.

It was a task that needed planning. Seventy three countries were being invited including prominent senators from the United States like Senator Joseph Biden, Senator Bob Dole, and many others. Of course our president was also invited.

My friend at the Riviera didn't see a problem with what I had been the most concerned about, security for the leaders. He explained that each hotel would accept five to ten dignitaries or heads of states and provide them with necessary security. He told me, "Of course the FBI, state, and local police will participate so security really shouldn't be any problem." I was pleased to hear that security would be well taken care of. We agreed to meet as soon as the invitations were sent out. I would then brief him on the progress of the conference.

The next day I received a letter from Robert and the Riviera Resort stating, "I have reserved the grand ballroom in the convention area for you on December 12 thru the 17th, 1995, for the purpose of the peace conference regarding Bosnia and Herzegovina. Angelo, please if you should need anything call me. Sincerely, Robert Vannucci, Vice President."

We were ecstatic and excited and looked forward to putting the event together. We wanted to make a difference and stop the blood shed. The invitations were sent and I thought the president of France and Chancellor Kohl of Germany should be key note speakers, since they are rivals on this particular agenda. The Chancellor is a supporter of Bosnia, and the president of France on the other hand said he would have liked to see Bosnia sink in the ocean. I thought if I gave him the honor of being a key note speaker in front of seventy three countries and heads of state, maybe he would have a change of heart. Hopefully he would leave his Napoleonic complex at home and come to the conference with a pure heart.

We sent a Fed-Ex special invitation to the president of France, hoping that it would reach him before any other world leader.

Surprisingly we got a response back from Paris in no time at all, stating in a diplomatic fashion that he was grateful and thankful to be invited, recognizing and acknowledging that the conference was much needed. On the other hand it was, "Sorry boys, it's a great idea but I am not coming to Las Vegas."

I thought when I read his letter, "Why should he come to Las Vegas anyway?" There are millions of dollars to be spent and Las Vegas only has gambling. He had Monte Carlo next door. Las Vegas didn't have the status yet such as that in Paris. We do not have the art galleries, museums, opera houses or palaces like King Louis and Napoleon's, but we do have a miniature Eiffel Tower.

The president was not interested in seeing a miniature Eiffel Tower or any of the rest of the replicas of historical monuments at the resorts. He had the real thing all across Europe and besides, he wouldn't be able to show off all his French pride to the world dignitaries.

He wrote politely in the final paragraph of his response letter that he felt the conference should be held in France. That was the last we heard from him.

In one way we did succeed. He accepted our program and used it to hold the same conference of his own in France. I was thrilled that our labors bore some fruit and finally France had had a change of heart deciding to take a lead in this important and historical conference in opening the avenues for peace concerning the war in Bosnia.

One person I was very dissappointed in who didn't send any sort of reply to my invitation, or even send me any opinion on it, was Prime Minister Haris Silajdzic of Bosnia. I was happy to learn however that he had attended the conference held in France. Perhaps he thought we weren't qualified to conduct this conference, but I think the citizens are the ones who make the difference, not the single minded heads of state.

A few weeks later there was an announcement about France holding and hosting the peace conference concerning Bosnia. Every major network in America carried the news announcing the wonderful long awaited and very much needed peace conference that finally was going to take place in Paris.

I admit I was emotional wishing I could be there in body and soul. In a way my friends and I were there. Our ideas of people who truly cared got presented to these world leaders.

The leaders from around the world were to attend. The list of invitee's was the same as ours. I was happy to see the topics of discussion were the same for peace and the security of Bosnia that I had suggested when I sent the invitation to the French president.

One leader who did miss attending was the former prime minister of England, Margaret Thatcher. If she had been there I think the conference would have been more successful. Dignitaries that were to attend were from the far and near East, West and East Indies, North and South continents and of course Europe. It looked to me at first like a genuine gathering. As the upcoming conference drew nearer I developed a different perspective of it.

It looked like most of these leaders were merely coming to show off their fashionable Armani Italian suits. I thought it was as if they may be attending someone's important funeral. I should have known better than that. They were at a funeral but of a different sort not a traditional one. The real funeral was happening about a thousand miles to the south. Mass funerals were occuring every day in Bosnia. I thought these diplomats were heartless people.

Most of these leaders were responsible for what happened, what was happening as well as the half million slaughtered people in Bosnia. They looked like they were coming to count the dead to see how many corpses there were for sure. The corpses were in Sarajevo, not Paris. Again their gathering was another senseless conference and a waste of time.

Bush Sr.'s administration did not warn or tell Milosevic that he would be held accountable for the war, and he saw that as a green light from the American Senate. Senator Bob Dole and many of the other senators did warn him, but he brushed it off since it did not come directly from the president.

Perhaps it was because of the pressure from Evangelistic groups that Bush Sr. had made no effort. He is a seasoned experienced diplomat who was capable of seeing the wrong and doing something about it. He chose not to do anything. The cloud from religious groups is heavy and can cause the outcome of elections for individual candidates. That is one of the reasons that even the president needs to pay attention. Perhaps it leads to them making decisions against their better judgement.

Senator Dole failed to convince our congress, Senate, and the White House to give Bosnia a chance to defend herself. Instead the unwillingness to get firmly involved by the West and ironically some Middle Eastern countries gave Serbia nothing to fear and everything to gain. The dream they have had for forever of a greater Serbia was within the reach of their hands. Their hands were hands of aggression however with no exception given for their Bosnian neighbors. The Bosniaks must disappear from the land forever. That seemed to be their sworn allegiance. Libya, Syria, Iraq and ironically Isreal too supported Serbia's aggression in the beginning of the war.

Isreal as I have mentioned was the fourth country that was supporting Serbia and I think was the icing on the bloody cake. That really hit rock bottom for me. Just yesterday they were fighting for their own surival and they still are. I don't know where they are learning their lessons for being good neighbors and having compassion for ones who suffer as they have.

How could this thing happen? Was it the Israeli government or the Israeli people who decided this? It must be just ignorance of the Israeli government, not the people. I refuse to believe anything else. That any father of the Jewish faith in Israel could sit at home in his living room comfortably watching television and seeing the same kind of people as those that during World War II participated with Hitler in killing Jews, practically almost exterminating them from the face of the earth and that those same Chetniks were now doing that to the Bosnians, is beyond comprehension. The very same bloody thing was occuring in Bosnia with the Croatian Ustashas. Were they in the race in the same game with the Chetniks? Would there be any help on the way? Would history again repeat itself? Is the rescue near?

It did happen. The American G.I.'s did finally come to the rescue.

I think it is worth mentioning that if not for the help of people of Bosnia who had opened their homes to help the Jewish people and the selfless soldiers of America who came to the rescue in World War II that the Jewish people would have had no prayer. They would have only been statistics. They suffered from the first to the very last days of the war. Bosnia and her people were always there trying to save them or any of the Jewish faith people who came seeking help. They were not turned away then or ever.

Who I am to judge the people of Israel, or hopeless Muslim nations such as Libya, Iraq, and Syria? They already have so much trouble and turmoil of their own and no respect from the communities in the world. That would be like hoping for help that would never arrive.

The Jewish people around the world had finally realized that for them to stand by and watch doing nothing would be a mistake. As the war raged on throughout Bosnia, the Jewish faith people around the world and many of their civil leaders spoke against the atrocities that the people of Bosnia were suffering at the hands of the Serbs. As news of the war raging on in Bosnia was reaching all the corners of the world, the Jewish people were finally touched by it and decided to become involved. It looked like the Israeli government was under pressure from the prominent respected Jewish leaders around the world to quit playing with a double headed coin. It would not serve in the best interests for the state of Israel or the Jewish people in general. It seemed like at least this time the Israeli political leadership had come to it's senses. Two wrongs don't make a right. They sent a medical team to Bosnia to try to repair some of the damage that shouldn't have happened in the first place.

Throughout history man has tried to redeem himself from the things he has done that he wished he hadn't done. The new phenomena around the world is to be born again. You are allowed to be a drunk, drug addict, rapist and murderer. You can ask God for forgiveness and tell him you want to be born again, and you can start all over with a clean slate, like not having to pay for your credit cards. Where are we going in the twenty first century with crackpots like this? It doesn't look like the world will be any safer with this fashionable form of redemption.

It is like having a glass of water sitting on the table and it accidentally gets tipped over. The glass shatters and the water spills. We forget someone has to clean up the debris. Who should do it, the one who accidentally knocked it over or the one whose glass it was? I think it should be the one who knocked it over even though it was an accident for a good gesture and also offer to replace their glass of water. Of course good gestures are always welcome and material things are always replaceable. It can heal misunderstandings and build bridges between people or nations.

In this case it's not about the glass of water. War is not the essence of life not to forget but water is. The lives I'm talking about are not in one glass of water and cannot be replaced.

The lives I'm talking about were of real people through the

land of Bosnia. They were Jews, Muslims, Roman Catholics, Gypsies, Hindus, Orthodox Serbs, Protestants, and God knows who else. All of those people are precious.

Perhaps if these people all had voiced their displeasure and demanded the Serbian leadership be held responsible and accountable, they would have saved some lives. In this chaotic situation no one trusts anybody. Everyone is arming themselves with whatever they can because the citizens find themselves with no protection in a land without laws facing armed enemies. The panic is obvious because blood has already been spilled in the streets with too many corpses to be picked up. Every man who is not a familiar face becomes a trespasser or even a familar face is not to be trusted as to be a potential enemy. That had already been proven by every Serb neighbor. Every Serb became a bad omen, neighbor or not, for every Bosnain, with a glass full of poison for certain death. Not to forget the deadly snipers that were terrorizing citizens twenty four hours a day bringing death and destruction with the help of cannons surrounding every city in the state of Bosnia. Chaos reigned from those cannon shells for over four years and the killings went on.

I looked and searched for a reason why for this madness and killing. How can a Serb and Croat nation be filled with so much hatred toward one of their own? Is it just because one is praying to the east to Mecca and one to the west to Rome? Either reasons is not enough in my view of being even close for them to take up arms against and harm one another. On the contrary, they should use their healthy minds and bodies and put that energy to good use to try to rebuild their sick nations which badly need help but not any warlike type help. Instead the deliverence from their leadership was only for more destruction. That was definitely not what most of the people wanted or neeeded.

The leadership of Serbia took the road of destruction instead the road to prosperity. Historically speaking they have not yet learned how to build for themselves or think for themselves. Milosevic was wise enough after he had plundered Croatia to somehow convince Tujman the pizza man to join Serbia and drag Croatia with him as aggressors against Bosnia. Regretably in that he succeeded. Croatian participation against the Bosnian people put Bosnia at a big disadvantage.

During my visit in July of 2005, the scars throughout the nation were obvious and very real and still very fresh. At the Bosnia Resort

Neum by the Sea the Bosnjaks were not welcome. The city of Mostar was still divided. The border is the river of Nrvetva and the old bridge that had been recently opened and hardly anyone used for crossing. The Croatian militia and the Ustasha volunteers still were controlling the southern part of Bosnia. The Serbian Chetniks were granted by the west at the conference in Dayton Ohio a portion of the country in Bosnia to call their own so all the murderers and rapists could now have a safe haven and keep the country split apart for good. I drove from the city of Dubrovnic through the city of Mostar to the city of Serajeveo.

I stayed at a Holiday Inn, the best hotel in the area and the only one. My good friend Majo Dizdar (translator of my books into Bosnian), decided to be my host one night and introduced many of his influential friends to me, generals in the military and some civilians. One of them had an interest in me and wanted to interview me for his television station. I politely declined the interview explaining that I saw no benefit for his station or myself by interviewing me. He persisted saying I was a controversial person in my opinions and views on Bosnia and the war and my own participation in that bloody war. He asked me if I was excited to be in Bosnia and I what I was seeing and how I felt to be there with my people and friends again. It took me a moment to compose myself. I took a deep breath as I was truly drifting back in time during World War II and the struggling and suffering of my father throughout my childhood.

I looked at him and said, "Dear friend, I wish I could say what you would like to hear. I am a man who has always lived by principles and the truth and I wouldn't dare say anything but the truth especially tonight and this is a very special night for me. You asked me and you look for an answer. As I said, I love Bosnia and Bosnian people, but I look around myself and see the land is bleeding, the structures made by you and your forefathers are in ruins and are bleeding. The people as a whole have wounds in their hearts and are bleeding internally. The nation that should be is not. The city of Sarajevo that once was is no more. The city of Mostar that I passed through and once was is no more. I could only compare it to the tragic Indian saga called Wounded Knee. Our people in Bosnia as they are now are living on a reservation. This is comparable to another tragedy that the native man of America experienced from the new European settlers in their land. The native man was pushed out and away by European settlers and in many instances massacred and brutally killed without mercy. This is what the Serbs are doing to our people and much more on a greater scale. Our story in Bosnia is no less different than the one of the native American man. The Serbs make those European settlers look like the good guys. You are very lucky that the Blue Coats are now here to protect our interests on the reservation and I hope they will never lose their interests."

He seemed confused for a moment as if he didn't understand where I was heading with my answers to his questions. He asked me to elaborate more directly and what the point was. I did and made sure he understood every word. He was so excited after he understood exactly what I meant by my answers that he insisted on having the interview with me on his station. My answer was still the same. I told him that he could relate my thoughts to his audience without my being there, and that they should also read my books. It was very emotional and sobering being in Bosnia. On my way back to the United States I found myself again feeling emotional and grateful for my country.

Milosevic was on the path of making sure Bosnia would bleed to death after Bosnia proved she had no desire to support his aggression in the war on Croatia. After he rampaged Croatia he still managed to convince Tujman into joining him to ravage Bosnia together. I always said Tujman should stay what he was and only what he was, a pizza maker and delivery man. Croatia had much brighter and more capable people to lead Croatia to a brighter future as they have now proven under the new leadership of President Masic.

Unfortunately during this aggression led by Tuzman this was one of the many thanks the Bosnian people received from their neighbor, Croatia, and not to exclude tiny Montenegro. Her volunteers finally rose to the occasion and showed their true colors of how noble and what good fathers they were and most importanty what good neighbors. They raged throughout Bosnia looting, burning and raping. I wonder what went through their minds? I recall historically and from my memory a story handed down through the generations by my grandfather to my father to myself. It related that at no time in history had Bosnia ever shown aggression of any kind, either terrritorally or by being unneighborly, toward the people of Montenegro.

The failed society of Serbia and Montenegro and in that matter also Croatia should not in any way try to look for fault under someone else's roof. What they should do is look right under their own roofs and fix the leaks so they would have no reason to blame a third party for their cracks in the roof like in this instance of Bosnia taking the blame for something of their own wrong doing. I don't think there is a word in the dictionary to describe the failure of the three societies, Croats, Serbs and Montenegrian and Bosnjan that were once so closely intergrated with one another. I have no right to judge them but I have a right to express my opinion and outrage on such irresponsible leadership that brought such suffering and pain to millions.

Every honest earthly man should understand that no man is an island by himself. He and all of his neighbors and fellow citizens are parts that make up the land and are the pillars and the foundation for the future of that land or that nation and they must lean on one another. Just like a creation of anything in nature that depends on that stability and strength of all the forces working together and leaning on each other.

In this terrible saga that has unraveled leaving trails of destruction in its wake, these men did not work in harmony as nature had meant. When that happened the men became destructive, harming everyone around them and in the end themselves. How can this unatural behavior of some men who call themselves proud fathers in their homes, happen? How can they come and take up arms and take the law into their own hands feeling at liberty with no accountability to plunder and destroy a nation and everything inside of it, from the people's souls to their hearts and minds and everything in their path? They burn the forests and poison the lakes and rivers and fill up the land with land mines. Destruction of religious and historical monuments, libraries and galleries was everyday, everything the society held dear to their hearts was looted, plundered, and burned. I was told they were not even any birds left anywhere to wake the villages in the early sunrise with their beautiful sounds of song. All the natural things have been wasted by the poison gases that were used during the four years of the war. All of that was not enough for the ruthless blood thirsty murderers. Every day they had to come up with something even more immoral to feed and satisfy their blood lust. They had to deliver their fellow man blows of the lowest points of immorality by breaking into millions of homes and taking the children from their parents, and raping and killing them in front of their parents, an agonizing horror that no parent should ever experience.

They are the men who have done these things during the wars

in Bosnia, Croatia and Kosovo. I can state as a message that justice was not served and I am sad to relate to the reader that these men are living happily around the world without any fear of prosecution, maybe in your neighborhood while trying to pretend that they are good fathers and neighbors just like they were to the Bosnians. I ask myself, "Is the rest of the world just trying to sweep the dirt under the rug? Or is it they just don't want to lift it up since we know what's there and it's likely that they wouldn't be able to handle it?" My suggestion is that we should dig as deep as it takes to find every one of these men and bring them to justice. If they get away with what they did, why should the next generation of their kind not think that they can do the same?

Most of the psychopaths have run away into the world with blood on their hands and escaped justice and are living in Canada, the US, Germany, Belgium, France and my tiny respected Montenegro, that is harboring two of the most notorious cold blooded murderers, finding safe shelter in the houses of God. How can that happen?

I cry for my Montenegro, a proud people yet blind from the hatred of the differences they don't even understand, difference they don't see. Perhaps that is the problem because they don't have any differences with anyone but perhaps their own selves. Each time these monsters made wars on our people our hearts have bled, yet we still have turned the other cheek and always found a place to forgive, hoping that tomorrow would be different. That hope for tomorrow has never come from these monsters. Our willingness to forgive has only brought more suffering and bleeding. We have all bled at the same time and with the same pain and agony and still we are yet to realize that the road for mutual respect and neighborliness is so wide we should be doing everything in our power and by our moral standards of strength and our willingness to stand to defend our families to narrow the road that leads to this madness.

Our enemies should be assured that our strength as a unit, as families and a nation of Bojnaks will never kneel down again and allow our children , which are our futures, to be taken away from us ever again. At the same time our strength should also reach out to our neighbors with an olive branch for peace, security, and mutual respect. We should speak out because we speak the truth and have the strength to defend ourselves. Our neighbors should be kept in check and should know whatever has happened in the past should only be distant memories to them. For us they are painful memories. Nothing with ever happen again to our families simply because we will not allow it.

We will grow and build our cultures and traditions that are not only are similar, but to exist in harmony as one. The family tree that our forefathers sprouted from started as one tree. When that tree became overgrown, the seeds produced new young trees that formed into new generations born into different tribes. Tribes then became respected villages and many of the villages became respected towns and nations. Each village in time developed their own unique way of life that centuries later people identified with themselves by developing their own cultures with a uniqueness and newly evolved mosaics of beauty. Those very identities that evolve everyday unfortunately push people further apart with their desire to identify themselves and belong, yet be different from one another. Perhaps being different from others brings about the conflict.

That is perhaps the beginning and where we find ourselves in conflict and competition. Seeing ourselves as being different from one another is where all conflicts seem to be born. In the world of nature the waves in a turbulent ocean have no boundries or control over their strength, or where they will land against the shores. Man on the other hand was given free will to choose, and has control over his emotions and boundries. I see life as working in the same way as the waves, strong and powerful and yet fragile and vulnerable.

Life is as turbulent as the oceans, and no one promised us anything less before we came to be. We must deal with life and learn. We must be resilient to the obstacles of life just as the sand is resilient to the ocean's waves. We need to learn that our last breath will not be the last day of the sun's shining. It should reassure our offspring that the sun will continue to rise over and over again.

Hope for a better tomorrow for my Bosnia was not a reassuring prospect with the questionable actions by Israel at the beginning of the war and a few rogue nations like Syria, Lybia and Iraq, who supported the villains of Serbia that intruded on the privacy of millions of people in Bosnia in their own homes, violating them and their families. We cannot and should not make the same mistakes to ever again appease an aggressor. Irresponsible actions such as these do nothing to insure our own security and our children's future. What we really do by such actions is unleash every mad man in the world to do as he pleases. We have seen these precise actions of irresponsibilty from world leadership and some of them tried to take advantage of that unleashing and to terrorize the world. Only to mention a few, Saddam Hussein, the new president of Syria, and on the American continent, Hugo Chaves, the president of Venezula, Mogabi of Zambabwe and the newly elected president of Iran. These are people that can put the world in a spin to hell with the help of North Korea. Responsible leadership of the world should never stand for this kind of blackmail. I think the phrase used by George Bush Sr. about world order is the right thing. Anybody who has been leashed should stay leashed. The world be a safer place.

We must plant a seed of commitment and obligation from a moral point of view. The strong nations should not look to be police of the world but instead be protectors of the weak, making sure the leashed bullying neighbors don't break their chains somehow. After all there is a duty of the strong to protect the weak. The strong should walk a thin line between being a bully when needed and an honest broker at the same time. To be a leader of the community and the nations one must earn the respect and trust of the people of the world through their deeds not barrels of guns. If respect is earned through the barrel of a gun I don't see how the world could feel secure or safe no matter who is in charge. One should know that whatever seeds you plant in the ground is the fruit in the end product you will be harvesting so we should be careful what we plant and what we are to reap.

Where does my critism of Israel as a nation apply in this world of ours full of political turmoil? Have I been biased toward Israel? I hope not. We all have the right, including Israel, to that moment of triumph and happiness, but only when it is earned without stepping on others. I have found reason to criticize France, and other nations of Europe, and in some ways even my own country, America. Yet I believe my feelings toward them are not of hatred, but only of disappointment. Perhaps that is where I have a difference with these rogue leaders around the world.

Once again I found myself having tried another way to help my people of Bosnia, and once again I met good people, acting like good and courageous soldiers, and I have had to watch the things we tried to do become footnotes in history. Perhaps there is a lesson there, and I am hoping for too much to happen too fast, and forgetting how this all ties into its historical context.

CHAPTER TWELVE: THE LEGACY OF ABRAHAM

Perhaps there is one historical triumphant event worth mentioning, and that would be Abraham and his thirty thousand people leaving the city of Ur to look for a more prosperous life. Six millennia later Israel finally emerged from her turbulent journey and rightfully so. Now that she is there she should never forget what it took to get there. She couldn't do it by herself. She must have had help to become what she is today.

A man who dreamed of one day reaching this wonderful end of the journey was none other than Abraham himself. With the blessing of Cyrus the Great he moved his tribe from the city of Ur to Palestine. He forgot to ask the Persian king if there were any oil reserves in Sinai or Palestine. How could such a wise man as him forget a most precious commodity that God had buried under his own feet and still chose to leave it behind? He listed all of his riches in order to go into a land that so far had been forsaken by God. He got everything else that he asked for, money, wagons, camels, food, and water. How could he forget that precious commodity that makes the world tick like the clock in Times Square in this twenty first century? He was perhaps too excited with everything he had going on and going to a place such as the Persian king had promised that would have riches beyond his imagination and gaurantee jobs for all the people. So Abraham took the long journey with his people to the coastal nation of ancient Palestine, today called Gaza.

Sadly everything went wrong from the beginning of the trip to the end. Neither Abraham nor any of his people ever saw that beautiful coast off the Medeterrian at Gaza. Some of the survivors from the journey with Abraham settled in the Jordan Valley around the Dead Sea. That was as close as they came to the promised land. It seems that Isreal today should not forget the struggle and long journey for the long awaited recognition and intergration of the communities of the world.

I ask myself the question, "Don't the Isreali leadership and people think that the Palestinians deserve anything less than respect as people and a nation since they were rightfully there before Abraham came?" I believe that if mutual respect had been established between the two ancient peoples that security and trust would have been established and peace would have come naturally by itself and life for their families for long awaited prosperity would come along with it. This also holds true for my ancestorial land of Bosnia as well as the troublesome African continent.

In the nation of Rwanda, the quarrel between two tribes has put them into a spin of killing one another and leading them down the road to hell and so far with no return. Even though we have become more sophisticated in the twenty-first century and perhaps more knowledgable of things and our surroundings, we are still looking for God in the old fashioned way. There is no point looking to the moon, stars, and the galaxies. We should come down from those high and distant places to the real world we live in, and we should not be looking for God in our neighborhoods or next door, but in our own homes and hearts and souls. Trust me, you will find God every time you look right inside of your own self and your life will be fulfilled. The journey from birth until death should be a worthwhile one with many personal accomplishments, no matter how small or large, just as it was meant to be.

I guess we can forgive Abraham for his failed journey. He was probably overwhelmed by the generosity of Cyrus the Great and forgot to ask him for the most precious commodity, oil. The quarrel for the share of the oil between the two stubborn cousins, the Jews and Arabs, has not stopped since the discovery of oil's usefulness. This was a one of the mistakes that Abraham didn't communicate very well on to God, Cyrus the Great, or the king of Persia. It probably still haunts Abraham since he did not understand the need of it in the future for his people. If he had made a fair split on the oil I think this world would have been a much happier place today. There would be no room for complaints from the Israelis or the Arabs. Put perhaps then I wouldn't be writing about this particular drama. I am truly hoping there will a happy ending to it.

Consider that Abraham was better at being a magician than David Copperfield. If I were to meet him in the hereafter I would want to ask a question about why he didn't take the oil, that beloved and cursed black gold, to Israel from his homeland of Mesopotamia over to his new adopted homeland of Palestine. If he had performed that magic successfully, the Israelis and Palestinians would be living in peace today. There would be no war and the rest of the Arabs who are their first cousins would not be objecting to Israel's existence. There would be no reason to object. Everyone would have an equal share and there would be nothing to worry about.

Since Israel became a state in 1948, Israeli education and growth in modern technology has been extraordinary and prosperous, but not without generous help from the the French, England and American taxpayers' money, including my own. That is what helped make Israel become what it is, a little paradise, not a democratic society, but still at times a bullying nation full of arrogance. Yet who wouldn't be, when one has the backing of the bald eagle?

If Abraham had split equally the black gold that we call oil, I think that Mount Sinai and Hadarom could have been turned into an oasis just like Abraham and Moses had wished. Moses wishes for the freedom of his people turned into a magic trick that was doomed to fail. I am not questioning his motives and good intentions for the slaves that the Pharoah made out of the Jewish people, that Moses claimed as his own people. However I don't see how he claimed that title since the Jewish people had been living and working under the Pharaohs for centuries as Egyptians.

One shouldn't forget the Jews weren't the Pharaoh's only slaves, even to the extent that no one has proven that they were slaves. They were the masses of healthy labor that included many other ethnic groups of Egyptian people as well. Forty to fifty thousand Hebrew people couldn't have built the Egyptian nation as it was then. It is only logical to assume there were other ethnic goups and citizens of Egypt who must have participated in building Egypt to be as powerful and mighty as she was. It would serve no justice to only give the credit to one group of people and exclude the rest for building up that powerful nation as she came to be.

Moses' arrival in Egypt was more like a coincidence, or perhaps it was even a planned political manuever made long before he arrived, with the goal of stripping Egypt of it's capable and knowledgable labor force that enabled Egypt to prosper. Perhaps he needed that capable labor for a new nation of Isreal that he could build, just as Eygpt was built to became strong and prosperous. If that was his motive, then with no doubt his magic was performed very well to rob Egypt and the Pharaohs of the most of their able craftsmen and builders. With his final dream on this journey, as we know historically, he had not been very successful, since he had chosen to lead the people through the harshest land there was known at the time, over hundreds of miles of nothing but sand and solid rock. There was no natural resources to use for available food or water at the Sinai peninsula which became tombs of burial for most of the people he led out of Egypt.

Sadly his and the people's dream came to nothing but a failed wish for their long awaited freedom, and became such a nightmare that even when we read about the tragic story today our emotions are stirred and we are affected by this sad chapter of history. Believing that Moses could deliver the promise that he made to his people would be as foolish as believing that David Copperfield can walk through the Great Wall of China today.

A man would have to be happily drunk on a very good wine to believe either of the men's stories. I think Abraham and Moses threw their magic rocks in such deep holes that no one knew how deep the holes were and even if they were able to retrieve them I doubt they could have used the magic rocks with their illusions of granduer in any good way. It looked like the magicians needed much more rehearsal for their agendas. Maluniums liyter in twenty forst cantere flock of ,Rusian hibrus intellectuals answer a chol of,Jerusalem.

There was a conquerer of Babylon, Cyrus the Great, who offered Abraham an opportunity of a lifetime which anyone looks for now and then. It was a chance to show his skill and knowledge in business. Perhaps that is what the Persian king saw in Abraham, a capable businessman. He offered him a job that would be well rewarded and a task that not just anyone could undertake. It was a project of gigantic proportions. To make the project into reality for Cyrus the Great he needed someone with the imagination no less than that of his own who was willing to take on the task. During his search for that type of man, Abraham was a noticeable leader and successful businessman to consider. The contract was granted to him. Abraham was willing to take on the task.

As a leader of his tribe he knew what he had to offer and Cyrus the Great must have believed in what Abraham offered and it was a beginning of journey of history in the making. The plan involved going into the unknown although to a very beautiful strip of land at the coast of the Mediterranean Ocean along with his tribe to what was then called Palestine and Gaza to build a port and trading facility where the merchants could come and trade and where the Persian military ships and vessels could come to be repaired. Cyrus must have been impressed by Abraham's charisma and his ability to understand business from Cyrus' own point of view. After many months of a harsh journey with unforgiving weather, by the time Abraham arrived in Palestine half of his people weren't with him. Some of them were dead from diseases and the hardships of traveling. Some of them found more favorable places to settle before they had reached Palestine.

The fulfillment of Abraham's dream to settle there with his tribe was not meant to be so. Instead the ones who had survived settled on the green and lush banks of the Dead Sea and the valley of the Jordan River where the land was fertile and plentiful. They were happy to settle anywhere where there was enough vegetation to start their lives again. Perhaps Abraham had failed his people in his journey by not being able to keep them all together. With disappointment he left his people in the valley and went to the mountains where he stayed for the rest of his days. He felt sorry for himself for failing in what he had tried succeeding in.

After Abraham went to live in the mountains he did a few things that even today would be considered immoral yet his story has been prophesied as highly moral. Poligamy and having a child out of wedlock was immoral but that didn't interfere with Abraham's road to glory. No one questioned his having a son with an unmarried woman not his wife. He made it in the books of history big time. I doubt that any living man would refuse the glory that Abraham had got. With no doubt he showed he was ahead of his time intellectually and was able to convince masses of the people to believe all that he said and what he thought was righteous. I call that preying on the weak and uneducated. In these times it is a crime that is punishable by the law.

There were many people that came after Abraham with as just as much charisma who were very convincing and compassionate in good ways and some who were convincing in an evil way that people would follow as well without questioning their true motives until it was too late. Even in our century we have leaders who have good and evil leadership qualities. They are very charasmatic and convincing, yet Abraham was at the top of the line beating even that other great magician of all time, Moses who claimed to have single handedly saved hundreds of thousands of people from oppression by the Pharoahs but actually lead them nowhere. Moses failed the people more than the Pharoah did. He practically told them to leave their dishes full of food at home to walk with him a thousand miles away where a promise of plenty of food and homes would be waiting for them, a promise which turned out to be absolute rubbish and untrue. There were no bands of people waiting for the tired and hungry, at least the small number who did make it across that God forsaken desert journey.

If Moses did something like that today in the twenty first century he would be looked at as doing no less than crimes like those committed by the fraudulent preacher Jim Jones of Guyana. The circumstances of the deaths of the many people were different in that one was forceful poisioning deaths and one was from just a tragic journey that was supposed to be for the better of the people and turned diasterous. With no doubt Moses had noble and good intentions and he believed that he could have done it but he was the only one who believed it and unfortunately he wasn't accountable to anyone. He could have been questioned but no one did since he was the almighty Moses. In this situation even the mighty Moses had made a mistake and cost many their lives and shattered dreams for many families. On the other side of the thousand miles of desert there was nothing but more sand and misery, not the promised land of milk and honey he spoke of. In that situation whether intentional or not, a crime was committed against thousands of people.

No poor, hungry and illiterate man would question the authority or the superority of these smart and gifted men in those times just as it is happening in our time. We tend to listen to the ones who speak well and are we are fascinated and mesmerized by their abilities to speak to us in a loud voices and gesturing bodies at the same time to program their messages into us. That is perhaps a weakness of most of us who believe these eloquant and convincing speakers who are able to rapture the imaginations of masses and engrave their thoughts and ideas into them. It was a dangerous precedent then and is a dangerous precedent now.

It was proven again just recently by when the self installed president of Serbia single handedly convinced seven million citizens with his gift of speech that he had perfected and used well, that he was saving the West from Islam. He claimed that the tiny little Bosnia in heart of Eastern Europe, a religiously and ethnically mixed society that has lived in harmony for over a thousand years and developed a mix of cultures that can only be described as a mosaic of beauty was a threat to Serbia and Slobo himself. Slobo with his charismatic speech not only convinced Serbia but the Western world as well. That is when I became really afraid for how vunerable people are.

The only man who saw Slobo as a phony was President Clinton. Almost ninety percent of the American people were still agreeing with Slobo's notion of washing Bosnia into the Adriatic Ocean. Slobo became a champion gladiator at least for the moment. Now it is a sad and shameful chapter in the history of Western Europe. Slobo's message was heard well and accepted. Volunteers from Russia, Bulgaria, and Romania and Greece flocked to win the trophy of Bosnian children's heads and they did. Elementary schools full of hundreds of children inside were mercilessly wiped out killing all the children. The Serbians, Chetniks and the Federal Army in a few of the instances during the invasion of the towns in Bosnia promised people if they would come out of hiding in their homes nothing would happen to them. The people believed them with hope that they would live to see another day and it would be better to be a slave temporarily with the hope that freedom again would soon be near. That was not to be. When the people amassed to the streets out of their hiding places the Serbs opened fire with grenades and machine guns killing twenty five thousand of them. The Christian West and some of the Muslim countries chose to look the other way giving Slobo another day of murderous plundering and burning. Shame on all of these leaders in the world. How could only one man see the injustice? They managed to keep that one man from helping out for quite a long time.

The Serbs rose to the occassion of Slobo's call with wooden pitch forks, sticks, knives, guns, cannons, airplanes and modern navy ships to destroy the mosaic that I mentioned without realizing that they were also destroying a part of themselves. Sadly that was not the first time that had happened. The Serbs became notorious for their brutality. Perhaps Serbia should mourn their lost characters as humans and fly a black flag over the nation's capitol until they find a way to redeem themselves for the wrong done to their fellow man.

As charismatic and capable as speakers such as Abraham and Moses were, in no way, God forbid, am I comparing them in any way to Milosevic. Their intention was to save the people from people like Milosevic. Sadly one can not call a failure a success and the two biblical crusaders for the good of man came to be called prophets. There is nothing there that shows me the success and happiness of all of the people. Instead there was tragedy and the deaths of thousands, intentional or not, a tragic loss of lives. Strangely, they are the ones who survived triumphantly. One can not help but to question what their motives were.

Were they really crusading to help the hopeless and give them hope for a better future? They became the masters instead of saviors. The only good things that happened after the final journeys of Abraham, Moses and all of the prophets is that their teachings made it possible for people to be more conscientous, and charitable to one another. Perhaps they installed the fear of the mighty and untouchable that we call today God and to remind us of our deeds to be judged on judgement day and use as an excuse or reason to kill for.

We as humans wouldn't dare take the chance of standing in front of Him the Almighty on judgment day answering for crimes and sins, but would only hope to answer for the deeds we could brag about and how good and obedient we have been. It shows how unworthy we think of ourselves and that most of us are willing only to follow without ever daring to think of leading. That is where the ambition and drive for power and glory separate masses from the very few who dare to reach out further than their dreams and be a leader of the masses with the conviction in their capability to do so. Sometimes we are lucky to have leaders who do not look down on the masses but reach out a hand to lift the masses from their hopelessness and inspire hope in their hearts.

When leaders forget that they are after all human, then the darkness comes upon us all. The constant battering by the leaders who think of themselves as superior makes us all afraid of our own shadows. We become afraid of what is known and especially the unknown supreme being that most of us rely on for salvation when we are in need. That is the Word of God that we call on quite often. I hope I will not be gnashing my teeth in front of all the honorable prophets, although I have nothing to be afraid of because I am truthful as I hope you as the reader are yourself.

There only a few drama players that star in the time of the Pharaohs, and the time of Biblical recordings. Clearly these players were ahead of their times. For their creativity and imagination that they have left behind, the nations and generations have scrutinized their recordings and beliefs. Perhaps they were thinking of creating new cults and political parties with the dramatic expression in their writings. Since the time that people have chosen to use literature by these great noble men and the knowledge in their writings to guide their lives by, sadly divisions became obvious and the interpretations became varied and blood has been spilled. Nations have been destroyed just for believing one version of the story is genuine and another is perhaps not. I have a hard time believing that that is the word of God when it has led to such massive destruction and pain upon humankind. No generation has escaped from it. I have gone through it, my children are going through it and the next generation has yet to go through it. Now in the twenty first century we are in a major war around the world. One should not lie to himself, we are in a religious war.

Scrunity of these ancient manuscripts by the intellectual elite has preyed on the rest of humanity and the results have been nothing less than diasterous and so painful that one can not help but go back and call on the Almighty and invincible, untouchable body of God. Sadly he has yet to answer the call from the masses who are bleeding and have bled for many millennia. My Bosnia is still awaiting His arrival however it comes, on a white horse or the Pope's limosine, by a powerful voice calling through Muhammed to Saint Gabriel or the arrival of a gentle human being who was cruxified for being good and kind with well meaning for human man. Whoever does come to relieve the pain from the souls who have endured so much, it will be welcome.

Perhaps if Muhammed doesn't arrive with Gabriel maybe he will stop on his way and ask His Holiness on the cross to step down to join them so that the three of them can stop the pain and bleeding of humanity. All of the good that the prophets had meant, we have scrutinized and misunderstood and it has come to haunt human kind and has caused wars and divisions over the tales that were written more more than six millinums ago when the first Buddist manucripts were written, during the turbulent times of Jesus, and Pontius Pilate, and then Muhammed.

The shadows of these noble humans are in our everyday lives and we dare not do anything offensive to their teachings. As history has recorded His Holiness, Christ paid with his life because Pontius Pilate felt threatened and offended from His wisdom and the vision Christ had for the poor and oppressed. Perhaps it was not Pontius but the head of the Jewish synagogue that felt threatened and there was a collaboration between the two producing the results for the prophet to pay with a terrible painful death. The results left a trail of blood after two thousand years, from the unjustified day that the crime of the crucifixion was committed and yet to stop flowing. People are still blamed for what was done just as if it happened yesterday and none of us today really had anything to do with it. Everyone still wants to blame each other like they were the ones who had done it or else trying to protray themselves as the innocent without blame, not being there two millennia ago.

It is obvious everyone is still deaf and blind to that tragic painful day in history that we should not forget wasn't the only one. Crucifixion was a method of punishment in Roman times. It seems in our times we have forgotten that that was Roman law for capital punishment, although with no doubt Jesus Christ was an innocent man who only had the noblest of intentions and we all know what happened to him. Sadly Christ was no match in the body of a human man as the ones who thought that they were so superior and felt as mighty as God. Strangely, His word began to spread like wildfire and the crime against Christ and the way it had been executed, people saw as so unjustified and cruel that masses of people took it very personally and it hit them very close to home. If it could happen to Jesus it could happen to any of them. The people rebelled in a way that none of those in authority ever expected. It was in symbolizing his crucifixion on the cross and their gross sense of injustice that represented for ordinary everyday people a message of hope and it was a cry out for justice to the authorities for the living. No one had thought, the Romans or in the state of Judea, that rebellion in a peaceable way could bring such a powerful blow that would tear apart the Roman Empire. The rest of the story we all know.

Jesus was a passionate believer in his cry for justice. With no doubt he had plenty of material for quarreling about with the authorities, the Romans and the local ones, especially the religious leaders. One could say for either his bad or good luck, he was a student of religious teachings himself although over the years of his learning he saw the injustice and the political powers influence inside government over the peoples affairs. The rich were getting richer while the poor were being forgotten. Most of the elite and wealthy considered themselves not to be ordinary human beings but something superior closer to a supreme power as gods. Obvioiusly Jesus objected to that.

Christianity in my personal view, and Islam, evolved from a neglected, oppressed and forgotten people that were searching for salvation and recognition and for a voice to express they were the same in human shape and form as the elite group who had turned their backs on them. Justice is still as far away as the stars and God that they were looking for.

I think a comparison to this oppressed and disillusioned world could be made by the birth of communism in Russia, with Marx's ideology that started in England in the nineteenth century. The slavery then in the society and in the work place was unbearable with slave labor making up ninety percent of the population. By slave labor I mean they were paid low wages and had no rights or representation. The landlords were merciless to their subjects, the laborers. There was no prejudice for color, race or religion. Prejudice was for all who were working fourteen hours a day and were not in control of their destinies. Capitalism was a symbol of oppression and hated by the hard working men and women.

In this kind of disillusioned and unfair world there is always a seed waiting that was dormant and would soon be ready to sprout. The enviroment was ripe. Russia was the most oppressed society. The phenomena of communism was the recipe for a dream of the masses who had no other hope, and it was carefully studied by intellectuals and peasants alike. It was something out of the ordinary and looked as if it offered hope to the oppressed since the czars had diminished their hopes for better lives. For over a thousand years of their oppression anything new was welcome. So the people embraced the idea of communism and glorified Marx with his pictures on the walls ofnevery street corner.

Another prophet appeared during the revolution, Lenin. He appeared to be a delivery boy to spread the message of Marxist ideology. He was considered at the time as a savior of Russia. One could argue what the comparison is all about. I could only say in my own personal opinion that communism was a form of religion as much as Christianity or Islam although the only fault of it was that man who interperted it to the masses, this new ideology with the name of communism, the man who had spread that message forgot that they were the ones who were oppressed. They became oppressors more brutal than the ones they had fought and defeated. In these

362

circumstances communism was doomed to be bankrupt and default in only a matter of time. Religion or fashion is only good if it makes you look and feel good from inside and out, if not you will wear it uncomfortably until you find the right fit to make you secure and comfortable as well as look good.

One could clearly argue that communism was a great help and a hammer that forced the reshaping of capitalism in the early nineteen hundreds. It helped to unionize and organize labor and to have fair representation and wages for a fair day's labor. Without communism on the other side as an adversary to capitolism, our system in the Western world of justice, perhaps wouldn't have reshuffled their oppressed behavioir toward the labor force and the ones not fortunate enough to feel middle or upper class would remain the same. We have feared communism and have done everything in our power to make sure that the lower classes in society have at least a chance to make a better life for themselves and their famlies.

America is the prime example of it from the time of the very first settlers to the present. Capitalism has proven it is just and offers a chance for prosperity. Communism, we all know what resulted from it, although China is still struggling to prove us wrong with their way of using communism and socialism as a pillar of their state. I hope we can prove them as wrong as we did Russia although that ball of yarn is just beginning to unravel. The defeat of communism in China will only come, and I mean in the only way, with developement of an internally state run economy and just leadership that so far has not shown any fear of expanding and enriching the state with economical growth and at the same time giving the people one step at a time the taste of economical freedom as humans for movement and creativity and the feeling of the right to belong and participate in all of it. That will be the downfall of communism. It seems that China is on the right track. I hope it comes to be beneficial for every one of us.

Competition is healthy when it is sincere and productive for everyone. If this growth in China became an ideological adversary it would be unhealthy for both parts of the world, the East and West. Adversaries usually don't make friends, only mortal enemies. I hope that the interest of the East and West will bring benefits just as the sun does when it rises from the East bringing to life everything that has been dormat throughout the night and when the sun sets in the West giving everything time to rest for another new beginning. Enough of all of this has been said. My Bosnia is still searching for that new beginning and justice for her is far from being accomplished.

Internal and external forces are still in the works. The wounds that have been received during the battles over the four years of the bloody war with all of the bandages that have been put over every wound, it seems that the evil forces from the inside and outside who don't want to see the wounds healing are succeding in ripping off the bandages to rip the wounds open, and the nation of Bosnia is bleeding once again. Again I find the world being insensitive toward Bosnia and her people. I ask myself, "What is it that they cannot see?" or "What is it that they fear?" Bosnia has been there as a state for a thousand years and has never in history oppressed or been aggressive to anyone but on the contrary she has opened her doors to anyone who was oppressed or sought justice for himself and his or her family. That is Bosnia even today, a people with an ancient history and culture and tradition that has been evolving for centuries. It truly is a mosaic of beauty and I consider it a tragedy that even the people from my own country, America, does not give itself a chance to know about Bosnia better.

There is a phrase in America that we say, "It's just like visiting Mecca," but I would recommend leaving Mecca for the next time and go visit Bosnia now and you will fall in love with her and her people.

Bosnia is by no means a perfect society. Bosnia is just like the rest of this beautiful world that we live in. It is still in the making and there are many bricks yet to be placed to become a perfect society. Bosnia is one of the moral pillars of strength to our world. We should not, by any means, try to knock those pillars down. If we do we will find ourselves limping and lame, perhaps in neeed of crutches. It would be sad and tragic for us to allow that to happen.

Perhaps Christ believed the Romans and maybe Bosnia has believed her enemies in that no harm will come to her. Both have suffered the agony and pain of death from a merciless enemy. Perhaps the most powerful of anything is that Christ's enemies never dreamed or expected the result of his punishment which became a dream of hope for all of the unfortunate and poor suffering souls that one can include two millennia later, Bosnia.

From all of this turmoil, one could call political or coincidental, a new ideology and religion was born that came to be called Roman Christianity, that adopted most of the Pagan Roman religion and with no doubt became colorful and beautiful. Some people found no interest in it such as the prophet Muhammed himself. As the story goes he didn't miss out though on Gabriel's message given to him that he should try and spread the message and something good would come from it. People were ready to accept again something new and different and with no doubt it was the right time.

There were many obstacles in the way, the persecution, killing and oppression and many losses of lives. The prophet Muhammed was as persistant as much as Christ had been in his time. He delivered the Koran to the people and the religion of Islam was born. Since the time of the creation of this beautiful respected religion it had spread like a wild fire throughout the masses for the good of mankind at the beginning. The religion flourished for fourteen hundred years until suddenly Islam found herself leaderless.

Tragically the elite of society and these new selfish leaders started to tarnish the teachings of the Koran and saw in the Koran an opportunity for the power to manipulate the masses and control them at the same time and that produced in many instances disasterous results with oppression and loss of progression of the society overall.

Now in the the twentieth and twenty first centuries the teachings in the Koran have been highly scrutinized by everyone and remind me of Christianity in the dark ages when the Bible was used for oppression. The Muslim elite who wanted to control the masses and stay in power did everything to demean the true message of the Koran, so that they could keep the people oppressed and unaware of their rightful freedom and liberty.

The two great religions have crashed again thanks to the radicals in the new evangicalists religions and some of the clerics of Islam. Each group's responsibility was to unite and enlighten their followers about spirituality and love of life for all regardless of their beliefs of their faiths. One could truly say that the laws of nature and the laws of the land had been broken. The laws of nature have been broken since the very first human walked on the earth. Men have lived with death since the beginning of time. The bad outcome of that is that we learned to live with and accept it and the people who were capable of fixing it tried to and paid with their lives. The laws of the land on the other hand have never been perfect because they were written and scrutinized from people who wanted to benefit from them with justification of that being the law for everyone. I think both laws need amendments. The bricks of those laws have been scattered far and wide and only the ones pure in heart will be able to lay the bricks back in the place where they belong and perhaps then the world can be a paradise as mentioned in ancient manuscripts.

The dream for paradise would never happen if we had a repeat of King Richard the Lion, and Phillip of France by his side, squaring off with the mighty Saladin of Syria in a battlefield for the control over the walls of Jerusalem, which wasn't even really about Jerusalem. It was more about the superiority for recognition for the identities of cultures and the nations. Jerusalem then and now was a perfect tool for the few who wished bad for the world. The evangelical Pat Robertson, the late Aytollah Khomeni, ideologist Osama Bin Laden and the Jewish radical from Brooklyn New York, Kahonni who was slain by Arab young men who felt threatened by him, are just a few examples.

The battle for Jerusalem was more for flexing the powers than for liberation of the four walls. What was the crusade for? It was for everything and for nothing and maybe because the economy during Richard's reign was in shambles as it was the same in France. What better reason than to blame people across the ocean? So they thought, let's wage war and divert attention from us and recruit the young and unemployed to be in the crusaders army with hopes to relieve the pressures in the society. The pressure was relieved in one way, most of those men never came home to their loved ones numbering in half a million men. How could one justify another half a million deaths on the other side? The nation of Isreal was only a million people just a few years back and there are many nations today that number no more than a million people. There is no justification, not even for God or anyone for the horrendous number of deaths and with absolutely no justifiable reason.

Each side blamed the other for the blood spilled, that they had everything yet nothing to do with, but perhaps it was only for economical reasons. Perhaps it was hypocrisy, but man has not yet matured enough to be able to reason with himself and have the understanding that each generation is responsible for their own deeds and what bricks they have laid down for the future and not the old bricks laid in the past. No one can change the past, it is only the present and therefore the future we can help shape. Politics then and politics now is still used with perfection as a heartless tool for manipulation of the masses. When religion becomes the tool of politics, or vice versa, the people are most certain to suffer.

Sadly, the religious war in the Middle East, and in Bosnia, is not between three religions, but three branches of the tree which Abraham planted. Until all three recognize that they are exactly that, and that they serve one God, there shall be nothing but war between them.

CHAPTER THIRTEEN: WHAT DOES IT ALL MEAN?

How can one justify thinking that he is killing in the name of his God? The Serb who installed and declared himself as president stated that he was crusading for a greater Serbia, and to save Christianity from the Bosnians. This time it wasn't in Jerusalem, it was right next door in Sarajevo. His message was far from the truth, yet convincing to his vunerable and uneducated masses. The Serbs had fallen victim again to their own ignorance and misunderstanding, just as they had at the battle of Kosovo Polje, in 1389, when they were told the Ottoman army was a Muslim army. That again was far from the truth. The Otttoman army was more Christian than Muslim, and was made up of central European Orthodox, Roman Christians, Greeks, Macedonians, Moldovans, Armenians, Crimeans, Odessians, and Palestinian Jews, as well as many Serb volunteers. That was the Pajzt's invincible volunteer Ottoman army. Serbia was to be apart of the kingdom of the Ottoman empire, after that historical defeat, and had as much rights as any other state of the empire. So Slobo's call for a crusade was unjustified and based on untruths. It was a stupid and ridiculous claim, but the Serbian people fell into his trap and answered his call.

For the Serbian president to declare he was crusading to save Christianity from Islam was absolutly ridiculous, and an insult to any intelligent man, Christian or Muslim. Yet to my amazement the people around the world people believed what came out of the mouth of such a hypocrite as Milosevic who had made that statement.

I always believed that in a decent Christian world the fathers go home every night after a hard day's labor just as my own father had done, looking forward to seeing his children and loving family

I cannot come to grips with where and how President Milosevic had the moral strength to think he was responsible for saving Christianity from Bosnians who have co-existed with the Christian world harmonously since the introduction of Christianity into Europe. The Bosnian people were neither Muslim nor Christian until the thirteenth century when the Balkans were invaded by the Ottomans. It is worth it to mention that Bosnia was the very last group of people and as a nation to finally decide which of the three faiths she wanted to embrace. It happened that she was invaded by the Ottomans and accepted the Islamic faith. Some people say the faith was accepted by bribery from the Ottomans paying off the rich to go along with them and for some it was just easy for them to understand and accept the faith. Before that the Bosnian people without a particular faith were still embracing God and were called Bogomilci, which means, "God loving people." Most of them still call themselves that today.

These two fairly historically new religions, Islam and Christianity, go hand in hand but it is fair to say that man was around long before these respected faiths evolved, and many other religions were around long before Islam and Christianity achieved acclaim as moral foundations for the society of man.

There have been great contributions from Islam and Christianity as well as great misunderstandings, and a great crisis caused by the so-called crusaders of today in the twenty first century. The two religions compliment each other with freedom and respect for human life and they provide plenty of good to man. We should stay on course instead of trying to cheat ourselves from all of the blessings both religions give to us. Bosnian people are living proof of that and over the centuries have taken everything good from both religions and made them compassionate and very special citizens on the planet. On the other side of that double-headed coin unfortunately are the Serbians.

Ones who cannot accept responsibility for their failures always seek to place the blame somewhere else or on someone else. Serbia as a nation has been drowning in mud ever since the very first tribe of Serbs arrived at the Danube and Morova Rivers. Are they cursed because they have no vision, or is it that they just don't they know how to pull themselves out of the mud? It seems like they are always seeking help from the hopeless ones and directions from the blind or complaining to the deaf. With no doubt I can't see any hope by this kind of behavior for Serbia and her people. It seems like the Serbs inherited their habits for immorality and their disrespect for their own lives. Their neighbors have no illusions for expecting anything good from them. There is a clear difference of good and bad, winners and losers. The Serbs have a tendency for imagining how they can commit the worst of horrifying things, when they have the bottle in their hands and are intoxicated on the plum brandy called Sljivovica, a cursed beverage that seems to encourage the best and worst out of the Serbs.

On one of those tragic nights in the hills of Mostar, the man named Arkan and his troops, the White Eagles were drinking all night and singing their ancient war songs, and by early the next morning he had come to a decision. Arkan himself encouraged the men to go down to the outskirts of town and loot and rape. He wished the men happy hunting telling them as he stretched his short body and yawned that he would like to take a nap. They fired their guns in the air to acknowledge the commander's wishes. "All right men, don't come back without trophies. You know what you are supposed to do to those balias' wives, mothers, and sisters. Each one of you must get your bayonets bloody." And so they did, intoxicated out of their minds, and armed with deadly AK-47s.

Then they went down to the outskirts of the town and raped, killed, and robbed the old, weak and innocent ones. They might as well have raped their own mothers as well while they were raping women eighty years old. Maybe they had raped their own daughters as well as the little girls there that were only six years of age. They may have cut their own sons' throats like they did those little Bosnian boys who were eight or ten years of age. How could these evil creatures call themselves loving husbands and fathers? Where did their mothers find the moral strength to call them their sons after knowing what their sons had done? It is beyond me.

Sadly we know that many of those mothers approved of their son's actions just like on that glorious day at Arkan's funeral, after Milosevic's men filled him with hundreds of rounds from their AK-47's. This time Slobo did do something right. The only thing in his life that was an honorable thing that he did, slaying that bastard. But as an old saying around there goes, "The Serbs have killed another Serb, it is nothing new."

During Arkan's funeral his children were dressed in black as was his mother and wife. His mother was crying hysterically over the loss of her son and talking about what a wonderful boy he had been and how God loving he was. Again it seemed only the love of a mother could be blinder than the darkest night because she was the one who had given birth to the miserable bastard with a thousand horns on his head, even when he lay in the grave.

It just so happens I personally knew a boy Arkan had slain with a chain saw, when he no longer had any use for him. The boy's name was Vojo. Don't misunderstand me, he wasn't such an innocent boy either when he got chopped up personally by Arkan, but God knows he looked like an innocent young man at the time when I knew him in Las

Vegas. He used to come in to see me every night at Caesers Palace just to say hello and I would always comp him dinner. I heard Vojo had been killed from a guest in my own home during a conversation over coffee. She was a former newspaper writer for the newpaper Politica and I didn't doubt her story. She was surprised I knew anything about Vojo. Frankly I think she was in shock. The story was that he killed quite a few of Arkan's men. It looked like it was a power struggle for him to grow in rank closer to Arkan and he needed to clear his path and get rid of some of the men and he surely did it. I hope they were the only men he killed. From what I knew of Vojo I think that he was definitely capable of doing something like that, and the men he killed probably deserved it with the blood of Bosnians on their hands. They were the men who were closest to Arkan.

I cannot help but think and hope that he did not kill any of our innocent people throughout Bosnia, and since before the war, when he or any of his friends asked me for help I never turned them down. He sure did need some help, and he and most of his friends weren't too shy to call me up on it either. I will never know if he did or not for sure although I hope his aquaintance with me influenced him not to harm any of my Bosnian brothers or sisters. Perhaps I will never know, but more power to him for Arkan's men that he wiped out in Belgrade with the blood on their hands. As the old maxim goes, "You live by the sword and you will die by it." He took my unanswered questions with him to the grave. In my mind and my heart I will just remember him as I once knew him. I have no evidence against him, but since he became a member of the White Eagles, and walked the treacherous road with Arkan, he could not have been very innocent. I can only hope he hadn't bloodied his hands with innocent blood, and I can only find him guilty by association.

When I met him in1990 in Las Vegas he looked just as innocent as any boy down in the neighborhood, and was young, healthy, and little wild. Horns grow inside of the heart. They don't grow on the head. When they do grow and people aren't paying attention, the horns can become piercing and dangerous just as Vojo's did as he grew into a man. He was rumored to have killed not just once but as many as twenty times, and mostly men who once had called him brother or friend. He only saw them as being obstacles to his goals and his answer was to remove them by executing every one of them. He finally paid with his own life and was killed by his closet friend Arkan, the leader of the clan, who cut him in a thousand pieces with a chain saw. Evil is only exposed by deeds and not by outward appearances. These were the type of young men who were sworn to the ideology of Milosevic and were the recruits becoming the final product for his crusade.

Christianity has flourished over the last few centuries and fought internal wars. Each war brought astonishing changes in the rights for liberty to man and also brought an industrial and economical revolution. The very last major war brought tragedy and despair perhaps like no other. The last war fought, World War II, could perhaps be rightfully called an internal Christian war. As the old saying goes, "After so much bad has been done and all the chips are down, we hope when all the chips have been picked up, then something good will happen." And it did and revolutionized technology science and medicine for the better of the world. At least something good did come out of it.

The Islamic world, however, it seems didn't take a step forward but took two steps back. Degenerate leadership did nothing to bring prosperity like it did in the West. They could consider that progress as being a clash of the cultures. How can economical growth and bettering one's life be a clash of culture or religion? It is only as an excuse to keep the masses poor and in the dark to control them easier. Despair and dissatisfaction of the masses in Islam has reached the pinnacle of despair, and the West is being held as the responsible fall guy. That also is far from being true.

Islam has prospered as a religion for fourteen hundred years. So what is wrong now, and how is it suddenly on a road leading nowhere but to Hell? It's the leadership and it is as simple as that. Islam's plumbing is in need of major repair and without getting rid of the old rusted pipes, I mean the old leadership, there is no hope for it, just as long as they kept the baboon, Milosevic, there was no hope for Serbia. Strangely he had forgotten that he was supposed to be saving Christianity from Islam, and then he went and attacked the Roman Catholic nation of Croatia, plunging it into a fire of Hell. That wasn't enough for him. He may have had a loss of memory about what his reasons for waging war were. He attacked Croatia and burned the city of Vukovar, leaving nothing but ashes. At the same time that he was claiming he was crusading for Christianity he was blasting Croatia, a Roman Catholic nation, to kingdom come.

How could he have made that grave mistake of thinking of Croatia in the same terms as he thought of Bosnia? I am overwhelmed by seeing what I saw or I am fearing for the generations to come from people like Slobo and the world leaders that let him get away with his plundering and murder. It seems like he used his privileged license for doing nothing but harm before it was taken from him.

During the wars in Bosnia, Rawanda, Afghanistan, and Chechnja, I saw only hopelessness and despair with the loss of lives and the loss of hope and silent voices and faces with tears calling for help. Yet it seemed no one cared. It was like the events were just another matinee movie in the living room of everybody around the world who could afford a television set. I found myself sitting hopelessly in my own living room, or at my work place feeling naked in my mind, heart, and my body, and ashamed that I was not able to scream as loud as I could so that I could get the attention of every corner of the world. If that attention could just be there long enough and serious enough for finally getting the recognition of the world to tell it that it is on fire and we need to do something to stop it, then I could feel I had done something.

I thought of myself as being on a stage somehow, feeling as if I were trapped inside a giant bubble of illusion that would burst at any moment. I realized that I wasn't alone in my thoughts. The millions who die around the world in these tragic wars are not participants in stage shows, they are just victims. To the spectators, the world is nothing but a carnival whore house that treats them with everything that God almighty has to offer, the right to life and liberty, prosperity, self-indulgence, and free time, and costs them nothing. It seems nothing has changed since the Colisseum in Rome hosted similar spectacles, where people were entertained by barbaric butcheries in arenas. In these days the stage is in our living rooms. Television allows us to be passively entertained in every way, fantasy or reality. The reality is the world is on fire but people are not differentiating between the fantasy and reality until they see their own roof turning upside down. It seems it only affects the feelings of individuals and not the masses. The show still goes on like nothing is really happening.

This lack of caring or being able to understand what is going on in our world many times brings about tragedy. We are mistaken in thinking that one man's tragedy only belongs to him. That was never meant to be the case. Every man's tragedy is a common thread leading to another man and his tragedy. What happens to one happens to all of us, consequence upon consequence. Depending on how we choose to treat each other, these interlocking threads can either be a rescue net or a snare.

Am I losing hope for mankind? No. I would not be writing this if I had lost hope. Am I disappointed in how men treat each other and are so unaware of their surroundings? Yes. Our understanding for the love of life somehow has never blossomed in full for the majority of us. Until we learn how to nourish life as it is meant to be nourished, the hope for a healthy world that we dream of will never bloom.

Old fashioned slavery has bled out of fashion. There is a new form of that terminology that only is used in business language that the ordinary uneducated do not understand. A blue collar worker is the one that is supposed to be just beneath high society and branded with social security numbers. Is it forced labor? Or just minimum wage workers as we call it? Or organized unions or unorganized labor? Really what is the difference? The gap between the rich and the poor is so tremendous that masses of people don't even dare dream of having any more than they do.

They have been enslaved by the banking and the corporation system. The system does not allow the ordinary laborer to get out of the debt he is in. It is modern slavery that is not based on color, race, or religion but just slavery in general, non-denominational non-discriminatory slavery. Religion is one of the fundamental appeals to most of the poor people around the world. It is really the only thing that they have to turn to since it doesn't talk back, contridict their pain or argue with them. It is a mystical cure for the moment to bring hope to the soul of the faithful, and they pray to ask for help but never get an answer. Perhaps that silence keeps them waiting and hoping. Maybe the Almighty will hear their cry and they will be the ones He will help this time.

What about praying for others who need just as much or much more help than they do? What about the souls of those whose throats have been slit by machetes and bayonets in places that are not too far from our homes? The souls less fortunate in Bosnia, Rwanda, Isreal, Palestine, and many other places around the world, souls who may have no other help may be helped by the prayers, in a mystic yet powerful way.

There is no place to hide from prejudice and dishonesty, and I choose to throw in the white towel. I am not a religious man and I have been left no choice but to surrender, not to the human man, because in man's world the moral weaknesses of the majority determine who has the power to rule, but to that mystical God that I have yet to see. I surrender, but I surrender to the faith I was born into, and that is Islam, not surrending in way some people do, but out of respect for life and the dignity of all humankind. I am truly accountable for every action of mine just as we all are or will be.

How can people like that baboon Milosevic and his cronies manipulate masses of his people? That is another example of the elite going mad and playing God. This time they were not laughing in their private bathrooms looking in the mirror where no one could see them, but showing it by spilling blood and hurting millions of people.

How strangely perverted racism can become is made clear in Rawanda on the contintent of Africa, with two tribes of the same faith and only different tribal names, who took tiny ethnic differences that outsiders couldn't even distinguish so seriously that even though they are the same people, they turned on each other so viciously the killing raged without discrimination for the young, old, men and women. No one was left unscathed. The world stood by and watched the live show with real people and innocent blood being spilled. Not anyone in the world lifted a finger to stop it until finally again President Clinton realized that it was morally wrong to stand by and do nothing. There is after all a natural obligation of the strong to protect the weak and he rose to that occassion with his might and power to stop it in it's tracks.

None of us as humans are more special or better than any other. We are as mother earth has made us in flesh and blood from earth and water and no better than any other creature that stands next to us and lives on this planet. We are all worthy of our lives and have a reason to be here.

No one has the right to take the life of another but the one who has given that life and that is mother earth. Every human should respect the laws of nature and let mother earth deal with it. She knows best as we have witnessed many times when nature turned turbulent and took lives but at the same time gave life. We feel the loss and pain although we do not feel any rage and in a way surrender to it in humbleness. Most strange is that our sense of surrender to nature is not from a feeling of fear, but from having an understanding of the power nature has. I choose to call it nature and some people choose to call it

God, or the mystical power we cannot see, feel or touch. All of the loss and pain is forgotten in the moment when people ask for healing, mercy, and forgiveness. We are all in somehow, somewhere, and in some way believers who more or less are in fear of the judgement day. Religious faith and our surrender to the Almighty must have something to do with it. Otherwise we would be rioting against natural disasters.

The way things are going it seems Hell is on earth and Heaven is waiting someplace else. Just recently Hell on earth was at its best when saw and felt in east Asia on the islands of Indonesia, Sri Lanka, India, and Thailand. God wasn't whispering or trying to warn anyone then but was giving a display of exactly what Hell might look like.

Mount Saint Helens, Manotubo in the Phillipines, Etna in Sicily, the ancient volcano of Pompei, the island of Crete on the coast of Greece, and the hurricanes in China and Bangledesh are all what we call natural disasters that are just taps on the shoulder perhaps to remind us that the Heaven that we live in, we are about to lose it. If we don't take care of mother nature and ourselves she will take care of it for us without asking for permission from anyone. There will be no time for regrets and apologies because mother earth will have none of that. If I had a say in it, I believe we should take care of her and each other and the sooner the better. Pollution, nuclear underground explosions, and particulary France with the nuclear testing in the Pacific Ocean and all the other chemical wastes, it is polluting the only source of life we must have and that is water. How long do we think we can last by behaving the way we are? Not too long. The candle is three quarters burnt. Who is really tough enough to see the last of it burned down? I wouldn't want to be the one to see the earth's very last breath and not because I'm afraid of dying but I wouldn't want to witness such a tragedy. I would consider it the most cursed thing on my soul.

Recently we all witnessed an astronomical tragedy in Indonesia. Some people claimed that their religion was being persecuted by God. I think that is all hogwash and their faith had nothing to do with it. Mother earth again had a little readjusting to do in herself. She did it and those who lived at the core of it are the ones who paid the price for the beauty of the paradise that they had lived in. You might as well say if you live in paradise you can't expect it to last forever. Someone has to pay for it and there are adjustments to make even in paradise. Everything has a price and everyone has a bill to pay that will be due sooner or later.

The island of Indonesia will recover and be just as beautiful as it was before the hurricane. The inhabitants paid a price to live in this paradise and this time it was with the loss of many lives. The cities and towns were wiped from the face of the land. The land resembled perhaps the beginning time of when the earth was created. It was bare and had no life. One man-made structure still stood through all the destruction. It happened to be a house of prayer. Once it was once surrounded by homes of the neighborhoods and people who loved their lives and families. Suddenly all the people and structures were gone except for that one little white building. It could have been a church, synagogue, or a Buddhist temple. In this case there were only Muslims living in that area, so it was a mosque. The building still stood, reaffirming the people's belief in their faith, religion and that their God Allah had not abandoned them. Whatever the reason that building survived, it eased the pain of their horrendous loss and a sense that God had not forsaken them.

Throughout history since the beginning of time, it seems that man has broken nature's laws, or bluntly saying, God's laws. There are quite of few species of men that have disappeared from this paradise of ours on this planet. All of that is man's own doing. Perhaps we should try and save what is left. It would be the right thing to do if not for our own sakes at least for the sake of God whom we worship. Then perhaps we could become as pure and innocent as the earth should want us to be.

In all of the tragedies and loss of life that have occured naturally and through wars, people all over the world have somehow tried to redeem themselves from not caring and shown they care by being truly generous toward their suffering fellow men. From every corner of the globe regardless of their religion they have given generously from their hearts. They have brought hope and spiritual awareness by showing that they cared what was happening on the other side of the globe. God this time was in full force and working through us human beings. We delivered food, clothing, medicine, and precious drinking water, the first and most important source for life.

It seems like the justice from God has been served for some but not everyone. Bosnia had waited four and half years for some justice while they were being slaughtered like lambs. God didn't seem to be anywhere to be found even while they were calling out to him.

President Clinton showed up with the United States Marines. Black Africa and Nelson Mandela waited for more than a century to taste freedom that was meant for them by God and yet the one who delivered it and arrived as God to free them was Nelson Mandela himself after emerging from being imprisoned for over three decades. He not only freed just the black Africans but the white Africanos at the same time from their guilt.

Do not forget, however, that Mandela succeeded only because he was supported by the power of the United States of America. Again the American people were the main force behind it. I am not trying to be offensive to the supreme God of the universe because I think He lives in every one of our hearts and it is all up to us. White Africanos enslaved whole nations of the black African men for centuries. Justice around the world for the ordinary and helpless man is yet to be touched by the hand of God. I am not losing hope yet. In this case faith is a beautiful thing, by having faith we are saved from eternal bleeding and pain so the next day when the sun rises we can carry on and do what nature intended us to do, live and create.

The God that you worship is good and merciful and compassionate regardless of what faith you are. He is the only one who is mighty, and He is my God and everyone's God and we are all His children. For me He is not a God of flesh and blood. He is more than that, the universe, earth and everything else that unifies that body. So I hope you will pray and I will too, and by the end of our personal journeys we might be able to plant the seeds of hope for generations to come, and find the way to respect each other with dignity and without using the sword to avenge our grievances as that butcher Milosevic and the ones before him have done.

We all should be aware and wary of the kind of traumatic speakers and evil dreamers like Milosevic who convinced his people that it was the right thing to do to go and kill innocent people in Bosnia. One can understand, however, that good and evil walk hand in hand. All actions can bear the fruit of good or evil. Every action or inaction does matter and in the end the consequences can be as tragic as they were in Bosnia.

My belief is that Heaven and Hell are right here on earth. Each of us is walking on our own path to the way of Hell or Heaven. We are the map makers of our own paths to the mystic unknown that is at the end of our journey. I wouldn't wish to give anyone the credit until I got there, and then I could congratulate them, or complain to them about what I didn't like that I had left behind me and things that needed fixing or correcting. If we knew for sure that we were going to meet our maker and face a day of judgment, I truly believe that in our current states and minds we would not be capable of handling that kind of pressure. We have not yet learned to become resilient to pressure. We are weak when it comes to the mystical pressure that comes from the unknown more than anything.

Every day every one of us does much that is wrong. Is it just a process of learning or is it just human nature? Perhaps it is both. We have been given the gift of being able to differentiate between good and bad, and yet we prefer to be careless and destructive. Sooner or later when we are standing looking at the gates of Heaven or Hell, we may find that Heaven is a lonely place. Ones who have earned the place in Heaven might refuse it because they don't want to be alone. The other side must be very crowded. Saint Peter perhaps would have a hell of a time trying to convince even the few good souls to take the chance and go into Heaven. I wouldn't blame them if they turned Heaven down because it's a scary thought to think Heaven after life on earth would be a lonely place to be. Truly all of the quarrels between all of us are sad and tragic misunderstandings, perhaps all for nothing.

If Abraham, Christ, and Muhammed were truly messengers of God, and the custodians of Heaven's afterlife, they truly would have to be lonely souls disappointed in everything as far as man reaching the gates of the Heavenly Father. I cannot see how any of us could reach the gates of Heaven and meet these honorable souls with so much sinfulness in the world.

The Hebrew and the Arab are branches of the same ethnic root, and yet they have warred upon each other for five thousand years. The Jew and the Muslim, and the Christian as well, are branches of the same religious root, and yet they stand today each armed with the most hellish weapons ever conceived, ready to exterminate the others as being not God's children, but the enemies of God. In Ireland, the religions in whose names the English and Irish of the same ethnic root are fighting are two figs on the same branch, and yet they kill each other in God's name. In Bosnia, the people have some of their roots in Slavic ground, like the Serbs, and some from the Ottoman. They follow the faith of the Orthodox, or the Catholic Christian way, or the Muslim, or with the involvement of Israel, the Jewish culture. All of these are likewise branches of the same root, in the legacy of Abraham, for better or for worse. Yet the Serbs and the Croats pray to the east or to the west in the same language written in different letters, to the same Father of Jesus, while they kill each other's children. Both of them agree that it is in the best interest of serving God to kill the Bosnjaks' children.

Our religions tell us we are all God's children. Until each of us truly believes that, we shall not be free of the pain of war. Until we forgive the debts owed to our fathers, then we cannot be free of the debts we owe as their sons, and we will condemn our own sons to our fathers' hell. I pray we do better.

Srebrenica is a name that should be spoken with great reverence and anguish, like Auschwitz, with a prayer for the pain of each of the fallen eight thousand, and the tens of thousands of others across Bosnia. Srebrenica, you are a wound on the heart of every man. Until we learn to feel your pain as our own we shall never be free of it.

I pray we do better, for the sake of the lonely and heartbroken woman who was once a mother in Srebrenica, and who now has nothing left but perhaps a little fig tree or a plum once planted by her husband or her son, as the symbol and reminder of her loss. I pray that even in the darkness and tragedy of the hell she lives in today, she still has faith that there is hope for the world. Having suffered so unrightously, if she should lose her faith, then what hope have any of us who have so much, and suffer so little? If we have no hope to give her, then the fate of all our souls is in her hands.

EPILOGUE

By 2000, I had spent almost a decade attempting to use the great advantages I have as a naturalized and patriotic citizen of the United States to help the Bosnians, the Bosnjaks, the people of my own ethnic heritage and my own family. I took part in activities working with international law enforcement and the intelligence community, and I took part in activities that were outside the law of any country. I tried to assist in the movement of intelligence, and in the movement of money, and in the movement of guns. I was prepared to take lives, and I risked my own life. I have spoken to powerful men on both sides of the Atlantic, and I have tried to rally them to use their power to help these oppressed people.

When I think of how many people have been lost, and how many survivors' lives have been destroyed, and how little the world seems to value their loss, I am sometimes disheartened, and I feel there is nothing left I can do. The men and women I have written about in this book are only a handful of the forgotten soldiers trying to do good even in the hell of the many wars like Bosnia, from men like Giles, and Elliot, and Kevin, to the nameless ghost agents of the world of intelligence, and even the callous mercenaries like Peter, who I should always still call my friend, even if we have been on different sides at times.

Quite by accident, that year I met another of those unheralded but gallant warriors who have risen to offer help from the most unexpected places. Like Giles and Kevin, James Post is a highly decorated Vietnam veteran who has devoted years of his life since then trying to accomplish something for the good of mankind, speaking out against the terrible consequences of the absurd things we agree to fight wars about, and punish people for. As a writer, he has lived in quiet anonymity, relentlessly or perhaps just stubbornly trying to put his thoughts and feelings into stories that might move people to rise to higher standards, and to aspire to higher virtues.

James encouraged me to try once again to do something new, something different, that would have a beneficial effect, and to do that by becoming a serious writer, and publishing my feelings and hopes in books. When I showed him that I had been putting all the family stories I could remember onto a tape, and had that transcribed, he agreed it was a story that was important enough to do whatever was necessary to tell it. We began working on "Blood Of Montenegro," an epic historical novel about the influence of three generations of my family upon the history of our homeland, and upon the rise and fall of the nation once called Yugoslavia. James had hardly heard of Montenegro, but as he did as a helicopter gunship pilot in Vietnam, and always has in his life, he put himself fully into the project. What we wrote was so much more than I had hoped or expected that I was and still am very moved that we were able to make it into a reality. He has been like Merlin at my side, and together we have created enchanting things, like spells cast upon the ether. He has given me a renewed sense of purpose, and the belief that even against a whole world of opposition or apathy, I can do something worthwhile.

I do not know what effect I might create by having written this book, but like a prophet, I can only spread these words like seeds, and hope that they will fall upon fertile ground. It is my most fervent dream that one day someone will read these words, and that person will be moved by them to use resources I cannot even imagine, and to do something I might never even have dreamed of great humanitarian importance to help those people I love, and before whom I feel humbled to have been able to do so little.

I believe that will happen. I believe for all the horrors we are inflicting upon ourselves and each other, the good in mankind will surely have the last word.

THE END

Other books by Bajram Angelo Koljenovic:

BLOOD OF MONTENEGRO
  with James Nathan Post

MY HEART AND MY MIND

www.americanhonorbooks.com

www.ingramcontent.com/pod-product-compliance
Lightning Source LLC
Chambersburg PA
CBHW071359050326
40689CB00010B/1701